Manichean Aesthetics

Manichean Aesthetics

The Politics of Literature in Colonial Africa

Abdul R. JanMohamed

The University of Massachusetts Press

Amherst, 1983

A portion of the chapter on Alex La Guma first appeared as "Alex La Guma:
The Literary and Political Function of Marginality in the Colonial Situation," in
boundary 2 11, no. 1 (1983). The chapter on Chinua Achebe originally appeared
as "Chinua Achebe: Colonial Situation and the Generation of Realism," in
Jadavpur Journal of Comparative Literature 18–19 (1980–81).

For Donna

Contents

Acknowledgment

IT IS A great pleasure to acknowledge my debts to the teachers, colleagues, and friends whose direct influence has culminated in the present study. Without the sympathy, encouragement, and tolerance of Daniel Stempel during my undergraduate and graduate studies I would not have been in a position to embark on this or any other critical project. Allen Grossman's unwavering intellectual and emotional support, Philip Fisher's astute criticism, and Edouard Bustin's sympathetic blessing were all essential during the early stages of this study. Michael McKeon's patient and thorough readings of the manuscript in its various stages allowed me to improve it, while his invaluable moral support during a difficult and demoralizing time helped me to complete it. H. Bruce Franklin read a late version of the manuscript and made many useful suggestions, for which I am most grateful. Finally, I would like to thank Fredric Jameson, whose critical theory has inspired a major portion of my analysis, for his encouragement of and incisive comment on my work.

I would also like to thank Leone Stein, whose tireless commitment to this book has made its publication possible, the Wien International Fellowship (Brandeis University), which allowed me to commence this study, and Boston University, which generously financed the last stages of this book. I am grateful to *Boundary 2* and *Jadavpur Journal of Comparative Literature* for permission to include here, in different forms, my articles on Alex La Guma and Chinua Achebe which appeared in these journals.

Finally, I would like to acknowledge my most important debts. My parents' long-term capital investment—moral, intellectual, and financial—made possible my present existence (as a "corporate entity"). To them I offer this study as the first major dividend on their investment. My wife, Donna Przybylowicz, helped at every stage in the production of this book. Without her moral and critical support I would have written a lesser book. My debt to her is incalculable.

Manichean Aesthetics

Introduction

IN THE PAST ten years, colonial and African literatures written in English have begun to attract critical attention. Thus far, however, both general surveys and critical studies of single colonial and African authors have examined such texts in a socio-political vacuum, assuming either that politics are irrelevant to a study of literature or that life in the colonies resembles life elsewhere. Even critical studies, such as *Sociologie du Roman Africain* and *Fiction and the Colonial Experience*, which promise a specific analysis of colonial social experience are in this respect rather disappointing.[1] M. M. Mahood's *The Colonial Encounter: A Reading of Six Novels* aptly illustrates the peculiar hesitancy, if not a veiled refusal, of literary critics to come to terms with the colonial situation. Having chosen six novels "which are concerned with the experience of colonial rule and its aftermath," Ms. Mahood intends to define "ways in which historical thinking on imperialism and on the relinquishing of empire, as distinct from the mere chronicling of imperial rule, might shed light on the traditional and central concern of literary criticism: the work of art as the figment of a particular sensibility." However, this intention is entirely subverted by her selection of three "colonial" writers (Joseph Conrad, E. M. Forster, and Graham Greene) whom she feels "are as innocent of emotional exploitation of the colonial scene as they are critical of its political and economic exploitation." Similarly, the Third World writers she chooses (Chinua Achebe, R. K. Narayan, and V. S. Naipaul) are "quite as distanced from the dominated side in the colonial encounter as the best expatriate writers are distanced from their dominating compatriots."[2] Thus, even though Mahood has thoroughly documented the historical background of the six novels, her assumption of a "distance" between the writers and the colonial ambiance leads to a complete circumvention of the motives, prejudices, conflicts, bitterness, and resentments that define the essential *colonial* relationship between the dominators and the dominated. By thus avoiding the essence of the colonial dilemma, Mahood is able to do ample justice to her other intention—to establish, through an "affectionate scrutiny" of writers she particularly admires, a "parity" between the English and the Third World novels. The successful realization of this intention makes *The Colonial Encounter* a very useful and illuminating comparison. But it is not a study of the colonial *encounter.*

It seems to me that we cannot adequately understand or appreciate the nature of colonial literature and the rise of the African novel until we study them within their generative ambiance. This is so for several specific reasons. Because the colonial writer was often involved in articulating the various theories—the white man's burden, his civilizing mission, and so forth—which sought to rationalize the whole imperial endeavor, his literature tends to be replete with ideological valorizations of his colonial experience. Similarly, because the origin of the African novel lies in the transformation of indigenous oral cultures into literate ones and because this transformation is mediated by colonial occupation, the traumatic experience of that period is naturally reflected in the thematic preoccupations as well as in the styles and structures of the first generation of African novels. Finally, the uniqueness of the colonial situation, due both to the trauma and confusion of its rapid social and cultural transformation and to the richness and complexity of its political and ideological contradictions, provides a fertile field for the study of socio-literary relations. Because an understanding of colonial experience is crucial to a study of its literature, it is best, before defining the scope and nature of this study, to begin with a description of the generic colonial situation, which will be specifically elaborated in the following chapters.

Though it is quite true that social relations are largely determined by economic motives, that the economic imperatives behind imperialism lead to the rise of colonialism, and that the metropole-colony relationship is essentially the same as that between capital and labor, it is the socio-political aspects of the relation between colonizer and colonized that are, from a literary point of view, more significant. Because it is extremely difficult, in a study of this kind, to analyze the entire process whereby economic motives are transformed into social relations which in turn manifest themselves in literature, I shall focus only on the socio-political aspects of colonialism. What needs to be stressed from this point of view is that the drastic measures of imperial domination—population transfers, the policies of "reserve," of gerrymandering, and of forced production, the negation of indigenous legal systems and religions, and, ultimately, the denial of the validity of indigenous cultures—render colonialism at times "an act of social surgery."[3] Furthermore, the changes are so swift that the dominated people "scarcely [have] time in which to devise methods of readjustment or of balancing the various conflicting interests."[4] The social disruption produced by such rapid and drastic changes and the profoundly antagonistic relations between the colonizers and the colonized cause colonial societies to exist in a state of latent crisis: "they are involved to some extent in a kind of social pathology."[5]

The social pathology is produced by the facts of domination and race. The colonizers' efforts toward absolute political, economic, and spiritual domination create in them a feudal spirit, supported by a series of familiar rationalizations: the superiority of white races, their mission to civilize the rest of the world, the inability of natives to govern themselves and to develop their own natural resources, the blacks' tendency toward despotism, their ease in reverting to atavistic barbarism, their lack of intelligence, their hyperemotional and uncontrollable personalities, and so forth. Such claims, designed to rationalize and perpetuate the colonizer's dominant position, are not accurate appraisals of reality but rather projections of the settler's own anxieties and negative self-images: "Whatever a white man experiences as bad in himself . . . whatever is forbidden and horrifying in human nature, may be designated as black and projected onto a man whose dark skin and oppressed past fit him to receive the symbol."[6] These projections are self-contained fantasies that are entirely indifferent to reality; they can be projected on an individual African as well as on the whole African continent—onto the "heart of darkness." Conrad systematically uses this Western notion of Africa as an evil place, bereft of social order, where the darker side of human nature could be played out. But whereas Conrad consciously and ironically uses Africa metaphorically in order to explore the destructive capacity of unchecked libidinal desires, European colonizers, less aware of their own psychic tendencies, see Africa as a literal repository of evil:

> The colonial world is a Manichean world. It is not enough for the settler to delimit physically, that is to say with the help of the army and the police force, the place of the native. As if to show the totalitarian character of colonial exploitation the settler paints the native as a sort of quintessence of evil. . . . The native is declared insensible to ethics; he represents not only the absence of values, but also

the negation of values. He is, let us dare admit, the enemy of values, and in this sense he is the absolute evil.[7]

The absolute negation of the very being of the colonized people breeds a counter negation: "On the logical plane, the Manicheism of the settler produces a Manicheism of the native. To the theory of the 'absolute evil of the native' the theory of the 'absolute evil of the settler' replies."[8] The manichean organization of colonial society has reached its apogee in the "Republic" of South Africa, where the perpetuation and elaboration of "apartheid," the policy of racial segregation and exploitation, have become the major concern of government and where the abusive term for African, "kaffir," literally means infidel. As we shall see in my fourth chapter, "Nadine Gordimer," D. T. Moodie has traced the theological origin of apartheid ideology back to the Calvinistic notions of predestination, original sin, and its highly polarized views of salvation and damnation. Given the theological sources of this ideology, Fanon's definition of colonial society as a manichean organization is by no means exaggerated. In fact, the colonial mentality is dominated by a manichean allegory of white and black, good and evil, salvation and damnation, civilization and savagery, superiority and inferiority, intelligence and emotion, self and other, subject and object.

The colonial society, then, embodies a rejection of the colonizer by the colonized and vice versa. This opposition, however, is accompanied by an equally profound dependency, particularly on the part of the colonialist. For while he sees the native as the quintessence of evil and therefore avoids all contact because he fears contamination, he is at the same time absolutely dependent upon the colonized people not only for his privileged social and material status but also for his sense of moral superiority and, therefore, ultimately for his very identity.[9] Thus, as Sartre says, the colonial system simultaneously wills the annihilation and the multiplication of the natives.[10] On the other hand, the colonized person too is simultaneously attracted and repelled by the colonialist. The ambivalence of the native is the result of his genuine admiration of European technology and his hatred for the system that subjugates and insults him. This major colonial contradiction, caused by rejection and dependency on the part of the colonizer and by attraction and hatred on the part of the colonized, generates a host of secondary contradictions that engulf the colonial society.

For the European settler and administrator, colonial life raises the difficulty of reconciling the notions of political freedom cherished by his home country with the actual political suppression and disfranchisement of the colonized people. He resolves this dilemma by developing a theory of the white man's burden. But this creates another contradiction for him: if he genuinely pursues his manifest destiny and "civilizes" the native, then he undermines his own position of social privilege; if the democracy from his home country is extended to the dominated country, then the colonizer can no longer retain his superior status. These contradictions are an inherent part of the colonial condition and can be eliminated only by an eradication of colonialism itself. For the indigenous person, the colonial situation also creates a dilemma from which he cannot easily disentangle himself. The superiority complex of the European creates a corresponding sense of inferiority in the native, who attempts to overcome this feeling by espousing Western values and social customs only to discover in the end that although the colonial system offers the European as a model for emulation it also effectively blocks the means to education, assimilation, and equality.[11] Even the very option to emulate the European puts the native in a double bind: if he chooses conservatively and remains loyal to his indigenous culture, then he opts to stay in a calcified society whose developmental momentum has been checked by colonization. If, however, the colonized person chooses assimilation, then he is trapped in a form of historical catalepsy because colonial education severs him from his own past and replaces it with the study of the colonizer's past. Thus deprived of his own culture and prevented from participating in that of the colonizer, the native loses his sense of historical direction and soon his initiative as well. The limited choice of either petrification or catalepsy is imposed on the African by the colonial situation; his subjugation and lack of political power prevent him from constructively combining these two cultures and leave him more vulnerable to further subjugation. If he chooses to be faithful to the indigenous values, he remains, from the colonialist's viewpoint, a "savage," and the need to "civilize" him perpetuates colonialism. If, however, he attempts to espouse Western values, then he is seen as a vacant imitator without a culture of his own. Thus colonialist ideology is designed to confine the native in a confused and subservient position. Because these social contradictions and the severance from his own cultural history seriously affect the native intellectual, the development of the African novel cannot be adequately appreciated unless one takes into account the nature of colonial experience.

In this study, then, I shall take up six authors who have substantially experienced the pains and pleasures of colonial society and

whose books are thoroughly influenced by the opportunities and restrictions of their ambiance. I have chosen three Europeans, Joyce
Cary, Isak Dinesen, and Nadine Gordimer, and three Africans,
Chinua Achebe, Ngugi wa Thiong'o (formerly James Ngugi), and
Alex La Guma. Although they have lived in different parts of Africa
and at different times, they have all thoroughly experienced the
generic aspects of colonial society. Where their relations to society
have been specific and unique I have provided the relevant details in
their proper places. However, where the same social background has
informed the works of two authors I have chosen not to repeat the
sociological information. Thus I should stress at this stage that the
description of apartheid society in "Nadine Gordimer" is also applicable to the discussion of Alex La Guma's fiction in the seventh
chapter and that the picture of colonial society in "Ngugi wa
Thiong'o" is equally applicable to Dinesen's context, although she
had left Kenya quite some time before the Mau Mau war.

Throughout this study I shall be concerned with several major
topics, the most important of which is the nature of the influence of
colonial social structure on the literary structures of works produced
within that ambiance. In each of the following chapters I shall begin
by defining the specific colonial situation in which the author finds
himself or herself and how he or she reacts to that environment.
Each writer's experience will be grounded in the structures of colonial society through a scrutiny of the generic rather than the idiosyncratic aspects of his or her biography; that is, I shall be concerned
only with how he or she experiences and internalizes the major features of colonial life; the rest of the author's biography is, from the
viewpoint of this study, irrelevant. I shall thus identify the cognitive
and the emotive aspects of the writers' attitudes and experiences and
then examine how these intellectual and emotive structures are combined in various proportions and repeated, revitalized, transformed,
or rejected in and by their novels and autobiographies. In so doing
my main aim will be to identify and define the ideological structures
that underlie the literary texts and mediate the transformation of
social structures into the thematic preoccupations as well as into the
aesthetic structures and styles of the texts. The theoretical assumption underlying this procedure is that novels and autobiographies are
aesthetic as well as ideological discourses and that ideological discourse is composed of cognitive and emotive components. *Normally,*
the emotive intentionality of the discourse selects and organizes the
various aspects that form the cognitive, that is, the thematic and

formal structures of the text, and *usually,* particularly in realistic fiction, that emotive intentionality is hidden by the cognitive structures.[12] However, sometimes, as in Cary's romances and in Ngugi's first two novels, the former tends to overwhelm the latter. In such cases the subjective, emotive intentionality readily manifests its ideological structure; when this is not the case, each chapter aims to reveal the embedded ideological structure. The last chapter of this study brings together these more or less isolated examinations of socio-literary relations.

I should point out that in grounding the literary structures in social ones I do not identify the former as products of any specific *class* because in the colonial situation the function of class is replaced by race. This is not to say that economic factors are unimportant in determining social and literary relations. On the contrary, as Hammond and Jablow clearly show, economic motives have a crucial function in the formation of colonialist literary images. For instance, before the development of slavery and the triangular trade, Africans "were viewed as real or potential partners in a commercial arrangement in which the British recognized their own dependence upon them. The writers did not engage in polemics or invidious comparisons; even when they indicated distaste at what they saw, it was not made an occasion for moral judgment." However, by the eighteenth century the view had changed dramatically: "African behavior, institutions, and character were not merely disparaged but presented as the negation of all human decencies, African religions were vile superstition; governments but cruel despotism; polygyny was not marriage, but the expression of innate lusts. The shift to such pejorative comment was due in large measure to the effects of the slave trade."[13] Although these kinds of shifts in attitude can be assimilated into a global theory of class conflict, from the viewpoint of the *lived* experience of colonial society the introduction of class relations can be misleading. The major distinction in such a society is *experienced* in terms of race, which, unlike the horizontal division that defines class relations, can function both horizontally and vertically: regardless of the native's relation to modes of production or the amount of wealth he may accumulate, he will always be considered inferior by the colonialist. I am emphasizing race as pivotal to the relations in colonial society in order to provide a phenomenologically accurate description of colonial experience and to avoid two types of distortions. One view misrepresents reality by pretending that racial differences are unimportant in colonial society and thus need not embarrass or concern us; while the other view distorts the world by perceiving everything in terms of class conflict and thus becomes callous to the complexity of lived human experience.

The second major topic of this study, the negative influence of colonialist literature on African fiction, has not received adequate attention thus far because critics have ignored the colonial and racial factors involved in the development of African literature.[14] Although the influence of English literature on African novels is varied and complex, one can distinguish between positive and negative influences. The former implies the decision, conscious or otherwise, by an African writer to use the specific techniques and devices of English fiction. I shall not examine this influence (the presence of which is obvious) because it demands a separate full-length study.[15] But even though an African may adopt the formal characteristics of English fiction, his rendition of colonial experience will vary drastically from that of a European, not only because of the actual differences in experience but also because of his antagonistic attitude toward colonialist literature. The dialectic of negative influence is in fact a literary manifestation of the manichean socio-political relation between the colonizer and the colonized. The black writer finds that colonialist praxis and literature promote a negative, derogatory image of Africa and its inhabitants, and thus he is motivated to attempt a correction of that image through a symbolic, literary re-creation of an alternate, more just picture of indigenous cultures. This study, then, will examine how this dialectic affects the shape and substance of African fiction.

The third major issue that I shall examine is the question of realism because it is important to define the emerging tradition in African fiction. This question is relatively straightforward. In the concluding chapter I shall briefly show that Ian Watt's criteria for the formal aspects of realism are exactly applicable to the African novel. I shall be concise about the formal characteristics of African realism not because they are unimportant but because they are quite self-evident. Much greater time will be spent with Georg Lukács's theory of realism because it seems to me that his insistence on the inclusion in realistic fiction of the representation of totalities and of the conflict between man-as-individual and man-as-social-being is appropriate for the definition of the ideological structures of African novels. Because African writers find themselves caught up in the transition from communal societies to ones based on individualism, their novels naturally reflect a concern with the disintegration of totalized oral cultures and with the subsequent position of the individual. This concern too is a product of colonialism which destroys the older cultures and replaces them with confused hybrids. A related topic, the effects of literacy, I shall take up more tangentially in the concluding chapter. This topic too demands a full-length study, but it is too important to be excluded entirely from the present examination. Literacy is important not simply from a mechanical viewpoint or because it opens up a new world for members of an oral culture but because, as Jack Goody and Ian Watt have shown,[16] it destroys the important function of "structural amnesia" in oral cultures and makes available, through documentation, a specifically defined and limited past. Thus literacy displaces "mythic" mentality and leads to the development of a historical consciousness which in turn is very important, as we know, for the development of the novel in Europe and in Africa.

These and various other minor topics are examined in the novels and autobiographies of the six writers. My choice of the authors is schematically and dialectically determined. In order to make this study geographically comprehensive, I have chosen two writers from each of three different regions: Cary and Achebe from Nigeria, Dinesen and Ngugi from Kenya, and Gordimer and La Guma from South Africa. Similarly, I have chosen these authors because of the variety of themes, topics, and formal and ideological characteristics manifested in their literature so that I may cover the gamut of colonial and African writing and ensure the greatest possible comprehensiveness of the conclusions I draw from this study. Thus I have selected Joyce Cary because he was a part of the colonial government in Nigeria and because he brings to Africa and develops in his fiction the theory of the white man's burden and the rhetoric of savagery and the need to civilize. I have chosen Isak Dinesen because her attitude is dialectically opposed to that of Cary: she is a farmer who imports and elaborates in her autobiographies the theory of the noble savage and the decay of industrial civilization as well as the rhetoric of paradise and innocence. Finally, I have picked Nadine Gordimer because she was born in Africa and because she attempts in her fiction to demythologize the European experience of Africa and explores the dilemma of the liberal consciousness that is trapped between its own humanistic values and the highly antagonistic manicheanism of apartheid. In contrast to colonial literature, the novels of the three African writers typify different aspects of the realist tradition that attempts to balance the European denigration and romanticization of Africa and to depict the problems inherited from colonialism. I have chosen Chinua Achebe because his fiction best illustrates the dialectic of negative influence, and because it documents the disintegration of the totality of a past oral culture and reveals the present dilemma of individuals caught between historical catalepsy and petrification. I have included Ngugi wa Thiong'o because his future-oriented novels reveal the problems caused by the peripeteia of values and grapple with difficulties of cultural reintegration and regeneration in the wake of an anticolonial war. Finally, I have selected Alex La Guma because the substance and style of his fiction reflect the drastic attenuation of black life in the apartheid society of contemporary South Africa and because he depicts the drastic transformation of depressed individuals who manage to develop an awareness of their political conditions. This study also implicitly compares three pairs of writers in order to trace the various aesthetic, ideological, experiential, and political oppositions between the white and black authors. Because the relation between colonial and African literatures is dialectical, the work of a given author can be adequately understood only in terms of its opposite. Thus Cary's "racial romances" must be read in contrast to Achebe's realistic novels; Dinesen's idyllic utopia in Kenya must be understood in juxtaposition with Ngugi's portrayal of the havoc caused by the Mau Mau war; and Gordimer's depiction of the effects of apartheid on the conscience of liberal white South Africans must be read in conjunction with La Guma's representation of the more drastic consequences of apartheid for the blacks (as well as "Coloureds" and Indians).

Through these dialectics and triangulations, this study attempts to define the major landmarks in the range of colonial and African responses to their social predicament. Because my choice of authors is schematic, I feel that the conclusions I reach are generally applicable to the work of many other writers who are not included in this study, though, of course, specific modifications would have to be made in the general conclusion if other authors were to be included by an extension of the triangulation process. By comparing the writings of these six authors, I have tried to bridge the gap between the broad general surveys of African fiction and the quite specific examinations of individual authors. In so doing my aim has been to define the outlines of the emerging *tradition* of African fiction. However, because I do not trace this tradition by using the coherent narrative of conventional literary history but on the contrary by analyzing a series of paradigms chosen for their dialectical opposition to each other, it might be useful to present at this stage a brief historical overview that will allow us to locate the six specific studies in a larger historical scheme.

Joyce Cary served as a colonial officer in Nigeria from 1913 to 1920, at which point he retired due to ill health. All four of his African novels were published in the 1930s (*Aissa Saved*, 1932; *An American Visitor*, 1933; *The African Witch*, 1936; and *Mister Johnson*, 1939). Because the Depression provoked the British government to raise tariff barriers around its empire and to exploit the colonial economies in such a way as to mitigate as much as possible the economic pressures at home,[17] this was a period in which the status quo had to be maintained at all costs. Cary's fiction must thus be read within a context that demanded an ideological justification of the status quo. Isak Dinesen, who lived on a coffee farm in Kenya from 1914 to 1931, published her first autobiographical work, *Out of Africa*, in 1938 and the second one, *Shadows on the Grass*, in 1960. As the structures of these works and the hiatus between their publication show, Dinesen essentially inhabited an atemporal world. Nevertheless, the larger influx of British officers and N.C.O.'s into Kenya after the 1914–18 war did influence her increasing antipathy toward bourgeois society which she had sought to escape by coming to Kenya. Finally, Nadine Gordimer, born in South Africa in 1932, published her first novel, *The Lying Days*, in 1953. Thus she has published most of her work during a period marked by a drastic contradiction: as most of the African colonies were gaining their independence in the late 1950s and 1960s, the Afrikaners had achieved control of the government and were ruthlessly systematizing the subjugation of the black South Africans through an elaboration of the apartheid doctrine.

Publication of the vast bulk of modern African literature coincides with the dissolution of the British Empire in Africa. While Chinua Achebe and Ngugi wa Thiong'o were publishing the novels that we will be examining—Achebe's *Things Fall Apart* was published in 1958, *No Longer at Ease*, in 1960, and *Arrow of God*, in 1964; Ngugi's *Weep Not, Child*, in 1964, *The River Between*, in 1965, and *A Grain of Wheat*, in 1967—Africa was being politically transformed.[18] Nigeria achieved independence in 1960 and Kenya in 1963, but the enormity of this change is best reflected by the fact that between 1960 and 1966 thirty African colonies became politically independent. For various reasons the movement toward national liberation gained momentum after the Second World War.[19] The Atlantic Charter and the independence of India fed, in their different abstract ways, the African desire for emancipation, which received a more concrete impetus from African soldiers returning from foreign military service. Greater British reinvestment in the infrastructure of colonial economies and the expansion of education, particularly in West Africa, both contributed to actualizing the African desire for self-rule. Finally, pressure produced by migration to urban areas and the increasing militancy of trade unions led to heightened expectations and ferment. The decade of the 1950s, which was formative for writers of Achebe's and Ngugi's generation, became the period of campaigns for regaining independence.

However, as Basil Davidson remarks, these campaigns were "movements with mass support" but without "mass participation."[20] That is, an educated political elite used popular support against the British government, but it had little desire to reform the fundamental social and economic structure of the colonial period or, indeed, to share any power with the people whom it exploited. This group was primarily interested in transferring political power from the colonial bureaucracy into its own hands. The gap between the elite and the people meant the lack of any significant social and economic change that would benefit the general public. African writers and artists, however, are major exceptions to the callousness of the elite: they provide one of the few links between educated Africans and the rest of the people. Achebe has thoroughly criticized, in various discursive essays and in his acerbic satire, *A Man of the People*, the corruption and hypocrisy of modern African politicians (and, as we shall see, he has also astutely analyzed their causes), while Ngugi has earned a term in prison for doing the same in his *Petals of Blood* and other recent writings. Thus in addition to articulating the desire for political freedom and restoring some of the dignity to African cultures, these writers have kept alive the more worthy aspirations that motivated the anticolonial movement. South African writers like Alex La Guma, most of whom are in exile or in prison, similarly constitute a part of the vanguard that is still battling what is in effect a colonial government. But unlike Achebe and Ngugi, they are not obliged to step into a gap between a black political elite and the people whom it is exploiting. As all La Guma's novels (published mainly in the 1960s)—and particularly his depiction of urban guerrilla warfare in *In the Fog of the Seasons' End*—illustrate, such a gap does not exist in South Africa because the systematic, indiscriminate repression of *all* Africans by the apartheid government ensures a profound integration of the political/literary leaders and the average African.

We shall be examining the six writers in this context of rapidly changing social and political reality. In doing so we shall discover and analyze some themes that these writers have in common. However, the reader should be warned that this is not a study of any specific literary themes: rather, it is a study of contradictions and relationships. In the following pages I shall be examining how socio-economic contradictions influence the writers and how they are taken up and transformed by their novels and autobiographies, and I shall be defining the antagonistic relationship between colonial and African, a hegemonic and a nonhegemonic, literature.

Joyce Cary

The Generation of Racial Romance

It has been universally assumed that in his African novels Joyce Cary was writing realistic fiction. Though critics have questioned the mimetic adequacy of the novels, they have insisted that Cary's portrayal of Africans is "authentic," and consequently they have tended either to apologize for Cary's colonialist viewpoint or to reproach him for it.[1] Most of this criticism is substantial and useful in its own way, but I believe we can better appreciate these novels if we treat them as romances rather than as realistic fiction. Such a treatment would seem to make the whole mimetic question relatively unimportant, but ironically we can appreciate the novels as romances only if we examine them within the rich socio-historical background of African colonialism which was the source of Cary's experience and which is the ambiance of the action within the novels.

An understanding of the background is also important in differentiating between the "authenticity" of the attitudinal structure behind characterization and the "inauthenticity" of some of the characterization in the novels. The critical failure to make these distinctions leads not to fruitful discussions of characterization per se but only to an amplification of the formulaic devices that are traditionally used to represent Africans in colonialist literature.

Thus, for instance, Harry Barba feels that the tragedy of Aladai in *The African Witch* "represents a triumph for the primordial, retrogressive urge that dominates the Nigerian: for totem and taboo, for ju-ju, and for the more advanced but equally destructive stages of primitive ju-ju Christianity."[2] The retrogressive urge, then, is common to all Nigerians regardless of cultural or individual differences. The argument becomes more explicit in Barba's discussion of Johnson's death: "Yet even when he is put to death, we sense that he lives on. For Mister Johnson is Africa, contemporary Africa if you wish, the Africa which can sing about itself even as it is caught up in the crocodile jaws of transition. . . ." Individual faults or merits are here ascribed not to individual personality or even to the sociology of a particular culture but to all Nigerians and eventually to all Africans. This is the formulaic device that we might call the "racial pathetic fallacy," for it attributes human characteristics, through race, to genetic nature; if these primordial urges are innate, then nurture has very little chance of checking them. Harry Barba once again obliges us with his amplifications: "Like Uli, Aladai shows a response to the call of blood which is stronger than the influence of his contact with civilization."[3] Golden L. Larsen succinctly describes another "basic assumption of Cary's about primitive psychology": "The instability of native personality, which on a social level shows itself as an oscillation between ecstatic laughter and fear or terror, under extreme pressure breaks down into wild eroticism and phallic worship on the one hand and self-mutilation and human sacrifice on the other." And again: "Johnson's own elation and despair are but less than dangerous manifestations of a capacity in the lower pagan for orgiastic rituals, self-mutilation, and human sacrifice."[4] As he amplifies this assumption, Larsen attributes the behavior of two dissimilar characters, Aissa and Johnson, to the governing forces that underlie ecstatic laughter and terror: both states of mind are characterized by highly charged emotions and by an abandonment of rational control. This generalization claims that all "native" behavior is irrational and emotional.

Characterization in Cary's African fiction is based on such formulas (and their function will be discussed later), but most critics accept and amplify them because they do not consider it important to examine Cary's novels within their generative ambiance—the political, social, and psychological imperatives and contradictions of the colonial society. Though Cary's African novels, as a part of his whole oeuvre, can be examined legitimately and fruitfully without specific references to colonial society,[5] it is equally important to consider them within their colonial ambiance.

The relationship between Cary's novels and the colonial situation has been rather sketchily discussed by some critics.[6] M. M. Mahood, however, has devoted the first half of her book, Joyce Cary's Africa, to a discussion of Cary's experience while he was in the Nigerian Colonial Service from 1913 to 1919.[7] The rest of the book renders an astute analysis of Cary's African fiction. Unfortunately, the "fact" and the "fiction" of Cary's Africa remain separate in Mahood's analysis, probably because she feels that the artist's imaginative universe deals only with eternal themes and is not to be sullied with mimetic references. As she puts it: "It is, however, important to realize at the outset that Cary did not at any time write a novel 'about' Nigeria. In *Aissa Saved* he uses Borgu and Kontangora as satisfyingly distanced settings for a book about the fundamental mysteries of the world and the varying faiths by which individuals come to their own terms with this injustice." She insists further that Cary's Nigeria is neither that of another expatriate nor that of another Nigerian because Cary possesses an "imagination which 'dissolves, diffuses, dissipates, in order to recreate': and the world of his recreation has a poetic intensity which makes it most unrealistically real." Now just as it would be futile to attempt a direct, concrete, and simplistic correlation between Cary's novels and Nigeria, so it would be critically unsound to insist that there are *no* relationships between them. Cary's views on Africa were not static; he kept reflecting on his experience and changing his views, and as Mahood informs us *much of this reflection took the form of writing novels about Africa.*[8] If the novels are reflections of Cary's actual experience in Nigeria, then an examination of how colonial society is transmuted into the symbolic reality of his novels is clearly pertinent.

It is not necessary, in examining the transmutation of Cary's life experiences into the symbolic structures of his novels, to scrutinize all the biographical details of his stay in Nigeria. My concern is not so much with the relation between biography and literature as it is with the effect that the social experience in a colonial situation has on the literature that grows out of that context. Because it is clear that the final form of Cary's attitude to the colonial experience was not substantially different from that of his fellow district officers in the African Colonial Service,[9] we shall be concerned with the *generic* rather than with the personal aspects of that social experience.

When Joyce Cary embarked for Nigeria, he had virtually no training for his job. He had attended a few lectures on medicine and on Nigerian customs, and had been introduced to surveying methods. Malcolm Foster tells us that the Colonial Service, more for economic reasons than for any other, "had given the new recruits no substantial training at all."[10] Yet, although Cary had no other training or profession, Foster feels that "he was almost ideally suited for the job" because an "Assistant District Officer in the Nigerian Service *had* to be jack-of-all-trades: Joyce may not have been much else, but he was that." Thus Cary, armed with absolute ignorance, set off to administer vast territories in Nigeria. These young assistant district officers

> were like recruits out of basic training who are put in charge of whole regiments or divisions and shipped off to fronts where scarcely anything is known of the terrain or the enemy. Joyce, when he sailed for Lagos, probably was better equipped than any of the rest.
>   Which isn't saying much.[11]

Foster's simile describes the situation accurately except that the soldiers of the regiments or divisions that Cary was to command were in fact the hostile Africans.

Ignorance, however, did not produce reluctance or anxiety, for the recruits were also armed with the romance of exploring Mungo Park's Niger and its wide tributaries and of liberating and civilizing the enslaved Africans. "The bush officer's text was Kipling's 'clear the land of evil, drive the road and bridge the ford.' " According to Lord Lugard, the governor of Nigeria at that time, the task was far more varied and grand. In addition to his "normal work," the assistant district officer had to discharge the functions of the postal, custom, police, and engineering departments, and he had to coordinate the military service and the activity of the native chiefs and labor. "To him alike the missionary, the trader and the miner would look for assistance and advice. The leper and the slave would find him a protector."[12] Cary moved into this atmosphere of idealistic, paternalistic despotism and soon began to speak of himself as "Lord of some 10,000 sq. miles."[13] En route to his first post in the Bauchi Division he was asked to deal with a boundary problem:

> They gave me the authority to change the boundary if I liked, and since it appeared to be the best thing, I did change it over a ten mile line. More than a hundred farms were affected, and I don't know whether my report will be well received—but I am protected from revision by my authority which I took care to get in writing and as explicit as possible.[14]

This letter, though still containing some of the romanticism associated with the job, marks the beginning of Cary's realization of the awesome nature of his task and of some of the problems inherent in it. On the one hand, the letter shows Cary's anxiety, caused by the necessity of protecting himself from the arbitrary reactions of the colonial government, and, on the other hand, it shows Cary's absolute authority over the natives and his casualness in the exercise of that power.

Cary's letters show his rapid disenchantment with the colonial government. At times his criticism of the authoritarian and self-serving system is objective and uncommitted: "This country out here is run, as far as officials are concerned, on purely Russian lines—with an iron clad censorship. . . . It's Hush-Hush when things go wrong, and blunders are made and some wretched A.D.O. gets chewed up, Mesopotamia on a small scale all over the Coast, and all through India too." Similarly, his criticism of the aimlessness of colonial policy and of the fiscal stringency of the government is detached and even amused: "It's a comical country, and the truth of all the shilly shallying is that the Governor is past his day, a shilly shallier, and very penny wise and pound foolish in all his short sighted policies." However, when Cary is personally affected by the financial stringency and authoritarianism of the government, he becomes angry and committed. When the full pay of a district officer, which Cary (then an assistant district officer) had been receiving for doing the work of a D.O., is reduced to that of an A.D.O., and when his mail service in the bush is cut back to two deliveries a month, Cary becomes vitriolic. For the junior officer in the service, Cary says,

> there is no redress, no Trade Union, no one to ask questions in Parliament. Any official who ever objected would be a marked man. Two men were hounded out of the country by the Government only a year or two ago, for trying to get better conditions for junior officials.
> . . . Lugard is a mean man, and a spiteful man. He will take a great deal of trouble to put an enemy or a critic out of the way.[15]

Cary's romantic feelings about working in Nigeria give way to bitterness toward the government that was exploiting him; instead of being a "Lord of 10,000 sq. miles," Cary now saw himself as an exploited worker. When in 1919 a Civil Service Association was finally formed, he was elated and expressed strong hopes for improved conditions, better pay, and better retirement pensions. However, his grievance with the colonial administration was based not only on self-interest but also on the inefficiency of the government:

> I really believe that there is no government in the world so mean as the British—so mean, so time serving, so shortsighted, so hypocritical. Do you know for instance what is the basis of government in Southern Nigeria, what pays the tax, what is the basis of trade, it's gin, gin by the millions pound worth. . . . And Southern Nigeria is enormously rich—one of the richest palm oil countries in the world—but 75 percent of the oil nuts rot every year for the lack of picking. The Government prefers to carry on on gin, rather than develop it.[16]

After Cary had retired from the Nigerian Civil Service he was still critical of the fact that the Africans only received shoddy material goods, the rejects of Western technology, and that they did not get "our magnificent art or science or literature or philosophy."[17]

Yet while Cary was growing bitter about being exploited by a system that was not seriously concerned with promoting the welfare of the Nigerians, he was also developing a strong antipathy toward the same Africans for whose well-being he seemed so concerned. His dislike for blacks was partially based on the paternalism and the European sense of superiority that characterized colonial relations at that time, but it was further strengthened by Cary's feeling of isolation within a hostile population. Initially, when Cary was in Nafada with other white officials, he did not feel particularly isolated because he was part of a *group* surrounded by a foreign culture; he could turn to other Englishmen for companionship and amusement. However, when he was sent to the bush, away from the English officials, his insularity became complete. He could not communicate with the blacks who surrounded him: though he had written and passed his first Hausa language examination in February 1917, he could hardly speak Hausa and had to rely on the limited Coast pidgin-English. And, of course, the Nigerian who attempted to speak English was at a disadvantage because his limited knowledge of it made him sound like a child or a fool; he was therefore treated by the unthinking English listener as just that.

The linguistic barrier was reinforced by colonial assumptions of European superiority, which subverted the normal social dynamics between the stranger, Cary, and the Africans, that is, the group with which he sought to interact. Now, the ideas about the cultural patterns and values of a foreign society which the stranger brings with him from the interpretive scheme of his own culture have their origins in the vague, often defensive generalizations about the otherness of the foreigners. These ideas serve merely as a handy scheme for understanding the foreign group as an object; they do not furnish a reliable guide for personal interaction between members of the two societies. Thus if a stranger seeks to enter a foreign culture, he has to transform himself from a detached, unconcerned observer into an individual who actively participates in the alien culture and thus begins to understand it through personal involvement and experience.[18] Of course, such a transformation is predicated on a certain open-mindedness and respect for the values and behavior of the foreigners. European colonialism, however, created a peculiar society in which the colonial administrator, such as Cary, dominated the alien culture but never sought to establish direct social relations with individual members. The interaction between the white man and the African, based on the notion of white superiority, was strictly limited to that between the ruler and the ruled, between the master and the slave. Social intimacy between the two was strongly discouraged; white supremacy, it was felt, could be maintained only "by upholding the standards of European life and the prescribed social distance from the Africans."[19] Under these circumstances the stranger did not transform himself. Instead, he remained more or less an outsider, and the Africans continued to be the objects of his interpretation rather than individuals with whom he was involved and upon whom he depended for his self-identity. The result of such aloofness was that the stranger's knowledge of the alien society remained insulated; responses of the foreigners were not allowed to alter significantly the preconceptions of the stranger.

As a member of the colonial administration, Cary could not help being caught up in the dichotomies of the colonial society. He was isolated not only by his inability to communicate but also by the absence of a desire to understand. During his rule in Borgu, Cary seemed to accept the fact that Africans were different, but he made no effort to understand the differences. Furthermore, his linguistic and social isolation was compounded by the unwillingness of the Africans to tell him the truth. In any official inquiry Cary was frustrated because he was told whatever the Africans thought would appease or gratify him. An article he wrote after retirement from the service articulates the reasons for this: the natives' view of him as a mysterious dictator prevented them from telling him the truth because they never knew how he would interpret or use it and because "a still more subtle cause of treachery infecting every relation in absolute government is the irresistible desire, even among its loyal supporters, to keep things sweet."[20]

Cary's isolation was so complete that it led to a virtual nervous breakdown and paranoia. In a letter to his wife he complains that "I was reduced to making faces at myself in my lamp-shade tonight, which acts as a distorting mirror, for a little human companionship and amusement."[21] However, he did not admit until much later that he had felt paranoid:

> No one not placed in such a position can fully realize the sense of blindness and distrust which took possession of me in those first months of solitude in Borgu. I say "took possession" because it was at once like a foreign invader seizing on my mind, and a sort of demon. I would wake up at night and feel as if the dark itself were

an immense black brain, meditating, behind its thick featureless coun-
tenance, some deep plan for a new and still more surprising outbreak.[22]

This paranoia is caused by his isolation and his inability to know
what went on around him in Borgu, but, in the absence of any definite knowledge of African motives or behavior and in keeping with
the generalized European notions of native savagery, Cary chooses
to ascribe the worst possible intentions to them. At times this fear is
expressed in direct tirades:

> But no black man on God's earth is reliable. Let those blasted "my
> brother the poor black" put that in his pipe [sic]. No black man is
> morally, or mentally, or even physically reliable. Not one can you
> trust. They are charming fellows plenty of them (not my foul cook;
> who has the face of a devil and is morally and mentally a debased
> scoundrel) but you cannot trust 'em. I don't know about Indians and
> Aryans generally. They aren't black, strictly speaking, I suppose, and
> I don't know 'em. But your black, your Negroid, and his near relative
> is a broken reed. . . .[23]

In this repeated correlation between certain psychological attributes
and the color black, there is no reference to individuals or even to
cultural characteristics; Indians and Aryans are excluded from consideration as much for the fact that they are not black as for Cary's
ignorance about them. The same vagueness and generality characterize his happier and more tolerant statements about Africans:

> I find as much virtue in these savages, who worship something not
> very much different from the Devil—and pretty much the same duti-
> ful ideals—as in England. They respect and care for the old, they
> feed the sick and the poor—there are no cases of people starved to
> death—they pet and spoil their children. What would be wrong with
> us is wrong with them. It is true that many things which are wrong
> to us are not wrong to them, but it is a question whether they are
> essential.[24]

Cary's perception of the Africans, then, remains that of a stranger:
when the judgment is negative, color is correlated to undesirable
psychological attributes; when the judgment is positive, the foreign
society is vaguely compared to the home group. In both cases the real
cultural differences are dismissed as unimportant. Because a whole
group, the colonial administrators, subscribes to this racial dichotomy, Cary does not have an opportunity to see that his appraisal of
the Africans might be mistaken. And so Cary accepts the myths and

attitudes prevalent in his time: he sees Christianized, educated Africans as natives who have too often all the European vices and none of the virtues, and he also agrees with the corollary idea that Africans who retain their traditional cultures are preferable to those educated in the Western style.[25] He tells his wife that the only way to make men do their work is to give them responsibility and "that is exactly our whole plan out here. To teach these people to rule, by letting them practice the art."[26] Caught up within the contradictions and the singular logic of colonial society, Cary is not troubled by the double-think evident in the notion of ruling somebody in order to teach him how to rule; he does not see that colonialism in fact prevents Africans from governing themselves.

This, then, is Cary's social experience in the colonial situation. In the bush he is cut off from his fellow Englishmen and surrounded by natives with whom he cannot communicate even if he wished to do so. As a colonial employee, he feels exploited and, as an administrator, a developer, and a civilizer of Africa, he feels betrayed by the bureaucratic inefficiency, the authoritarianism, and the hypocrisy of the colonial government. In his relationship with the Nigerians he functions as a dictator whose inability to understand his subjects translates itself into a paranoid fear of their unpredictability (which in turn translates itself into the notion of the emotional and intellectual instability of the "African personality"). Cary's experience is centered on his sense of alienation and is flanked by his attitudes toward the colonial government and the Nigerians. This, therefore, is the structure of feelings: isolation, flanked by bitterness and betrayal on the one hand, and paranoia, distrust, and the consequent assumption of savagery on the other. This structure, it must be emphasized, is not idiosyncratic to Cary's psychology, but rather it arises out of the sociological predicament of the colonial situation.[27]

After retiring from the Nigerian Civil Service, Cary began his career as a writer. His first four novels, *Aissa Saved* (1932), *An American Visitor* (1933), *The African Witch* (1936), and *Mister Johnson* (1939), are all set in Nigeria and deal with his African experience. In each book the basic structure of feelings manifests itself in different dramatic incarnations; the characters, settings, plots, and so on, vary, but the central structure repeats his social experience in Nigeria. We can best appreciate the manner in which this affective structure determines the shape of Cary's fiction by first examining the manifestations and functions of isolation, of his criticism of colonial administration, and of his antipathy toward the Africans in all four novels taken as a whole, and then by analyzing how each novel varies from the others in accordance with the alterations in Cary's affective attitude.

The experience of isolation runs throughout Cary's four novels and is often pivotal to their plots. At a basic level it is caused by linguistic ignorance: a young, inexperienced A.D.O. in *An American Visitor* is faced with an angry crowd yelling "Go away white men— we don't want you" and "Death to the strangers—death to the whites." Ignorant of the native language, and therefore of his danger, he answers the shouts with a polite "Good evening and good health."[28] The results of isolation, however, are rarely comic. Usually, the language barrier is overcome only to be succeeded by a more profound cultural one. The district officer's customary reliance on his political agent for all information concerning the natives leaves him at the mercy of that agent. Thus, when the Resident in *The African Witch*, in the process of investigating a charge of witchcraft, demands to see the priestess of a "ju-ju" cult, he is told by his political agent that she has been out of town for a month in spite of the fact that she is actually standing forty yards away in full view of both men (*AW*, 140). Such isolation renders the colonial administrators helpless, and their ignorance often becomes pivotal for the novels' plots: in *Aissa Saved*, the D.O., while trying to build bridges, is totally unaware of the battle that is taking place between Christians and pagans, and the missionaries are oblivious to the real intentions of their converts; Rudbeck, preoccupied by the road construction, is unaware that the revenue for it comes from illegal road taxes imposed by his assistant, Mister Johnson. In *The African Witch*, the Resident and his colonial officers are playing bagatelle while the Rimi people are preparing for a war. Not satisfied with this juxtaposition, Cary indulges in extremely heavy irony by having the Resident remark "I suppose the soldiers were playing bagatelle in India on the day the Mutiny broke out" (*AW*, 279).

Ignorance, however, is not the only source of misunderstanding. Accurate information about native intention is often misinterpreted either because of wishful thinking or because of tenacious preconceptions about native behavior: informed that witchcraft and torture, banned under the British rule, are still taking place in his town, Burwash responds with a polite letter denying the possibility (*AW*, 130); in *An American Visitor*, Bewsher, when informed about a Birri attack, chides his native servant for seeing things that aren't there, for being ill with "yellow fever" (*AV*, 212). Isolation caused by ignorance and misinterpretation is augmented by the astute manipulation of D.O.'s by native administrations. As Cary puts it: "Native states in Nigeria are accustomed to sudden changes of power and tempo. Each new district officer is likely to have his own tastes and his own policy. The important thing for the native ministers is to know beforehand what his tastes are and to cater for them" (*MJ*, 145–46). To this end the waziri (i.e., the chief minister) blackmails Johnson to reveal secret reports (*MJ*, 68); the waziri in *Aissa Saved* successfully manipulates Bradgate in order to produce the desired results in a criminal trial (*AS*, 113–16); and his counterpart in *The African Witch*, through deception and murder, puts his candidate on the throne and presents his choice to the Resident as a legitimate fait accompli.

The problems caused by the linguistic gap, the factual ignorance, the misinterpretations, and the subsequent shrewd manipulations of the D.O.'s are compounded in Cary's novels by cultural friction, that is, by the conflicting purposes of the African and European cultures. The officer's attempts to change native social institutions and to make technological improvements are usually met with traditional resistance and sometimes with sabotage: in *An American Visitor* Bewsher's attempt to form a federation of the Birri tribes never succeeds; the road in *Mister Johnson* is built in spite of the strong opposition from the emir; and in *Aissa Saved* the pagan leaders have already burnt one bridge and promise to do so again should Bradgate succeed in building another one. One result of this friction is that Cary's African novels are marked by confrontations that stress the mutual ignorance and violence of the opposed forces. Because such isolation, friction, and confrontations are an inherent part of the colonial mission, the district officers and the author tend to tolerate such problems; the frustration is accepted with good humor because it is a part of the white man's burden, a part of his moral duty to civilize the African.

However, Cary is more indignant and critical about the harassment of his Nigerian officers by the colonial government. The composite view in his novels shows clearly, although never explicitly, that the avowed purpose of the imperial mission to develop and civilize Africa is disregarded in practice. The colonial government is depicted as a self-serving bureaucracy whose prime concerns are to save money and to preserve its false image as a peacemaker in Africa. The well-intentioned colonial officials and Africans are consistently hampered, used, and discarded by the government.

The construction of roads and bridges is made virtually impossible by unnecessary financial stringency. In *Aissa Saved* Bradgate wants to build a bridge (over the Akoko River) that would "double the trade and wealth of the country." The Treasury's denial of a thousand pounds for a permanent bridge elicits the narrator's bitter disapproval:

> In this the Treasury did its duty, which is not to produce wealth or advance the welfare of the people but to scrape and hoard; and to invent new obstacles in the way of officials who desire to spend everything.
>
> For the Treasury, roads, bridges, hospitals have nothing to do with trade or humanity, but are counters in a game.

When Bradgate, taking advantage of a drought, attempts to erect a temporary bridge costing thirty pounds, the Treasury again refuses "on the grounds that the Public Works department did not approve of temporary bridges." The P.W.D.'s objection is based on a jealous possessiveness of its prerogative. Bradgate, then, is rendered virtually helpless by this bureaucratic tangle: "In this warfare which breeds a race of the hardiest letter writers and most brilliant obstructionists in the world, a bush officer like Bradgate, enthusiastic about his schemes, sentimental about his pagans, had no more chance than a curate among the city sharks. He was diddled all around and made to look like a fool." Frustration leads Bradgate to embezzle money from the allocation for uniforms and extra services and, with additional money from his own pocket, to undertake the building of a temporary bridge (AS, 70–71).

In Mister Johnson, the district officer, Rudbeck, is faced with similar objections to his road construction projects, and he too uses the same form of embezzlement, which, we are told, is common throughout the colonial service (MJ, 79–80). Before he is sent on leave, Rudbeck does manage to build a thirty-mile road which does not connect with any others. The increase in trade produced by this road to nowhere astounds his superior, Bulteel, who has in the past forwarded Rudbeck's request for road money to the Treasury with an evasive bureaucratic comment: "Mr. Rudbeck's views deserve serious consideration when finances allow of further road expansion" (MJ, 142). Even though he now realizes the beneficial effects of the road (because the increased revenue from the trade has been helpful to his career), he refuses to request road money from the Treasury. Instead, he encourages Rudbeck to embezzle more money and at the same time implies that the risk is entirely Rudbeck's and not his (MJ, 144–45).

The implications are clear: the Treasury is primarily concerned with making profits that it does not wish to reinvest. This kind of contradiction of the avowed policies of development is exemplified perfectly in Cary's treatment of education in *The African Witch*. Aladai, a pretender to the Rimi throne, has cut short his own education at Oxford in order to return and claim the emirate. To his numerous requests for educational development in Rimi, the Resident replies that no one can exaggerate the importance of education, but that Rimi is poor and that progress toward this goal has to be "slow, no doubt, but sure" (*AW*, 69). This refusal to establish even an elementary school is symbolized by the fact that the "education bungalow" has never been occupied by a teacher and that Rackham, the commanding officer of the police, has converted it into a gym where he "[teaches] his men gymnastics, boxing, singlestick, and [amuses] himself by the hour" (*AW*, 123). Cary makes it clear, through a discussion of education among the white residents in Rimi, that the implicit policy is not to build any schools at all (*AW*, 301).[29]

Along with his criticism of the contradictions between the avowed colonial policy and the actual practice, Cary also includes an indictment of bureaucratic whitewash—of the bureaucracy as a source of "white magic." The magical power to alter undesirable aspects of reality resides in the literary skills of the administrators. As the narrator of *The African Witch* puts it:

> Experience, therefore, had convinced the Resident that, in a world where it is impossible for the rulers to have personal contact with the ruled, and government must willy-nilly depend chiefly for its data on reports and discussions by letter, the wording of the reports and letters is an important matter. Real things—the lives, happiness, destinies of living people—depend quite as much on literary skill as upon the political ability of an official. (*AW*, 184)

Yet this principle, it turns out, is a euphemism for a habit of mind that seeks to "combine the minimum of information with the appearance of complete openness" (*AW*, 216). Thus the sentence "I can't find the old letters about Joseph Makurdi's claim to this site, as the files have been eaten by ants" is changed by Burwash to " 'The present situation in regard to Joseph Makurdi's claim is complicated by a gap in the correspondence relating to the original application'—or hiatus—yes, 'hiatus in the correspondence. This has produced an impasse which may prove difficult to surmount' " (*AW*, 185). In a society where reports are more important than reality, the lack of information about native actions proves to be a blessing in disguise, for it allows the bureaucrat "a free hand in the composition of [reports]" (*AW*, 239). However, the distortion of reality in this bureaucratic universe clarifies the real preoccupation of the colonial administration. When Burwash is simultaneously faced with three problems—a request to investigate the murder of the aging Emir, which Cary has depicted graphically, a letter from Aladai threatening war, and a query from the Treasury asking from what source "the sum of nineteen shillings and 4 3/10 pence has been credited to court receipts miscellaneous in April ult."—he first attends to the financial problem, which he considers most important (*AW*, 255).

Burwash's preoccupation with reports and letters is a clear tribute to the power of bureaucracy in an autocratic colonial society. Thus, when Rudbeck's embezzlement is discovered, the consequences are mitigated by Bulteel's bureaucratic influence. He causes the report to be delayed and rewritten in a precis form so that when it reaches the colonial secretary the words " 'embezzlement' and 'forgery' are translated into overspending votes and unorthodox accounting for expenditure" (*MJ*, 115). Cary insists on indicting administrative whitewash by contrasting gruesome violence in the novels with the inconsequential mildness of the Official Court of Enquiry reports: in *Aissa Saved*, the judge investigating the several riots, the sacking of villages, and the numerous murders exonerates the officials in spite of their direct and indirect responsibility (*AS*, 158–59); in *The African Witch*, the "Resident's action in preventing further bloodshed by his prompt warning to the rioters that violence would not be tolerated [is] strongly commended by the Enquiry," whereas the events in the novel make it quite clear that his inaction and prejudice are ultimately responsible for the riots (*AW*, 301). Elizabeth, the African witch, who organizes the riots, is praised for her "moderating control" over the rioters (*AW*, 277). Thus, in an autocratic colonial society "white magic" is powerful; undesirable aspects of reality can be altered easily on paper in order to create an idyllic image of society. Bureaucrats like Lord Lugard develop the idealistic vision of white man's burden and by the use of "white magic" they perpetuate the illusion of a good society and successful fulfillment of noble intentions.

Although Cary is severely critical of bureaucratic authoritarianism, inefficiency, and obfuscation, he generally avoids questioning the aims and nature of the colonial mission itself. On the few occasions that such problems arise, Cary's narrators hastily retreat from substantial consideration of the issue. For instance, the heroine of *An American Visitor*, Marie, does perceive accurately the nature of imperialism: "it was because she liked [the Birri people] so much that she hated to see them fixed in a position of domination and cruelty, in an artificial structure where even kind little Jukes and good-natured Frank were obliged to play the part of exploiters; and Mr. Gore, who looked like St. Francis, to be a tyrant over the conquered" (*AV*, 16). However, Marie and Mrs. Vowls, who voices similar sentiments in *The African Witch*, are never allowed to develop their insights. Cary negates their view by making the other characters and the narrators dissociate themselves from the two women; Marie is dismissed because she is an American idealist and anarchist and Mrs. Vowls because she is a senile crank as well as a sentimental anarchist.

Cottee, a miner in *An American Visitor*, momentarily focuses sharply on the contradiction between the avowed colonial policy of "civilizing" the natives and the actual practice:

> it does seem rather strange that we won't let these poor devils have any of the comforts and conveniences that we couldn't do without ourselves. I think sometimes it's due to a kind of prejudice—like that of the old squires who tried to keep their laborers in smock frocks and wouldn't let them learn to read and write. . . . Why, we don't even teach them English. We behave exactly as if English books and English ideas would poison them. (*AV*, 97)

However, the moment passes, the implications of this accurate insight remain unexplored, and Cottee reverts back to his usual explanation of colonial problems: "We haven't got a system at all—no sort of principles. None of the people we send out have the faintest idea of what they are for" (*AV*, 98). Most of Cary's characters and all of his narrators subscribe to Cottee's latter opinion and see all colonial problems as products of a *confused* and *incoherent* policy; Cary systematically dissociates himself from the fleeting insight that the problems are the result of a policy that has a duplicitous structure with a rigorous subconscious logic.

Whereas Cary succeeds in avoiding an explicit consideration of the duplicitous structure, his novels cannot altogether ignore the practical effects of the hypocrisy; the real heroes of the white/good society, the district officers, are caught firmly within the contradictions. Their beliefs in the overt imperialist ideals and their attempts to realize their goals are genuine; in their paternalistic concerns for the natives' welfare and in their attempts to protect the rights of blacks against commercial encroachment, the D.O.'s motives are pure and noble. But, as we have seen, they are constantly frustrated by bureaucratic reluctance and red tape. Thus trapped between the supposed aims and the real intentions of colonialism, the district officers begin to question their actions and the goals of colonial policy. For instance, Bradgate, piqued by a clergyman's accusation that he is serving commercial and selfish interests, begins to question his own role and even suspects that the administration's studied neglect of religious and secular education for natives is somehow immoral. However, he dismisses these thoughts as soon as they have occurred, for he does not wish to face their implications (*AS*, 112–13). At times such conflict results in despair. When Rudbeck is not only blamed for the rise in crime, a result of increased trade on the road that he and Mister Johnson have built, but also ordered to hang Johnson, he succumbs to depression: Rudbeck "feels more and more disgusted and oppressed, like a man who finds himself walking down a narrow, dark channel in an unknown country, which goes on getting darker and narrower; while he cannot decide whether he is on the right road or not" (*MJ*, 224). More often, however, the officers take refuge in traditional English stoicism and devotion. When Rudbeck asks questions similar to those of Bradgate, he is silenced by a warning from his superior that he will be labeled a Bolshevik if he persists in such speculations. Rudbeck responds by paraphrasing Tennyson ("ours not to reason why") and dutifully continues to do his share in the apparently aimless, blundering imperial mission. These besieged district officers are the only characters from the white/good society that receive Cary's uncritical sympathy.

If we treat characterization in romance as a feature of its mental landscape, then the above patterns of criticism and sympathy can be seen as the novelistic manifestation of the affective structure of Cary's attitude toward colonial government. His sense of betrayal manifests itself as empathy for the heroic district officers who are admired and pitied, like Tennyson's cavalrymen, for their foolish courage and devotion to a rather hopeless fight. On the other hand, his bitterness toward the colonial government is expressed in the overt criticism of bureaucratic whitewash, authoritarianism, and inefficiency. His fundamental agreement with the civilizing mission of imperialism leads him to negate his insights into the deeper logic of colonialism by associating them with idealism and anarchism. Thus Cary creates a white/good society whose motives and purposes are benevolent and morally just, but whose administration is confused and inefficient. The real heroes of this society, then, are the D.O.'s and A.D.O.'s who are in perfect accord with the high moral purpose of the colonial endeavor, but who are frustrated and hampered by bureaucratic obfuscation and native intransigence. Cary's treatment of the white/good society obviously deviates somewhat from the idealization typical of traditional romance, and we shall see later the ideological reasons for this bifurcated and realist-satiric presentation.

Cary's treatment of black/evil society conforms more readily to some of the classic features of romance. Characterization of blacks is based on a traditional series of similaic and metaphoric formulas prevalent in colonial societies and literature as well as on rhetorical devices unique to Cary's fiction. The formulas are an organic part of the narrative perception and language and are so intertwined and symbiotically related that the following brief categorization, by isolating them, reduces the power derived from their accumulation and pervasiveness.

The most popular formula equates Africans to children.[30] In the preface to *The African Witch*, Cary claims that an "overcrowded raft manned by children who had never seen the sea would have a better chance [of survival] in a typhoon" than would the Africans in controlling their own destiny in a modern world (*AW*, 12). Because this formula is not only a literary device but has become an integral part of colonialist ideology, it is used without due consideration and produces absurd results. Cary gives us the sociological reasons for the seriousness and responsibility of Tanawe, a child of twelve or so: "Kolu children of old-fashioned families like Makunde's were remarkable for their gravity and decorum; . . . they were strictly brought up and made to behave themselves as far as possible like grown-ups" (*AS*, 33). Cary's judgment is later verified by Tanawe's actions. However, adults from the same tribe who have converted to Christianity are described and depicted as naughty, irresponsible children.

A close variation of this formula is found in the depiction of Africans as emotional and irrational creatures: "Akande Tom's reasoning was not logical or definitive. It was a part of his feelings. The whole process was one of thought-feelings carried by every part of his nervous system, from the ends of his crinkled hair to the tips of his long, thick-jointed toes" (*AW*, 149). The deficiency of reason and abundance of emotion are, of course, magnified when the Nigerians gather in a group. The individuals then are no longer human: "They were simply nerve centers, intoxicated by noise, and the stimulation of various glands by hatred, fear, rage, and excitement, to make more noise and to produce more hatred and blood lust, not consciously directed at any special object. They would have murdered anybody at the slightest direction from outside. They only wanted cruelty, blood, more stimulation—the only way to release" (*AW*, 214). The African, then, is not only constantly on the verge of hysteria and devoid of any reason but also lacks will power.[31] This notion of the native as an irrational, hyperemotional being is so thoroughly a part of the colonialist ideology that it becomes the structural principle for the characterization of Mister Johnson. He is presented as a clown/buffoon whose wild, imaginative personality condemns him to grandiose fantasy; he perceives himself as an English gentleman yet cannot avoid breaking into wild, improvised song and dance at the slightest provocation. Because no self-respecting English gentleman would behave as Johnson does, he becomes an easy target for Cary's ridicule. Cary is not concerned in this novel with an exploration of the causes and nature of the peculiar combinations in Johnson's personality but only with using him as an object of derision.[32]

Another formula, the equation of the African to various animals, is used to reduce him further to a nonhuman category. When Judy Coote, in *The African Witch*, tries to make a *positive* generalization about African affectionateness, Rackham answers that "this [is] characteristic of animals, too" (*AW*, 96). Similarly, the narrator informs us that Aissa's maternal instincts are very strong but adds: "That kind of love is a natural thing, as cheap as air or water, and common to cats, bitches and hyenas" (*AS*, 46). The final step in this formulaic reduction is the ascription of the natives' characteristics to his race and, thus, to genetic nature. In *The African Witch* the formula that African "blood" is emotional and irrational, yet cunning, is repeated like a mantra designed to induce a mesmerized state of belief. This "racial pathetic fallacy" attempts to place the native in a subhuman category somewhere between Europeans and wild animals. For the colonialist mode of perception, blacks are evil primarily because of their otherness, because of their difference from Europeans. The formulaic devices are designed to reinforce the otherness; constant reiteration of the native's subhuman image facilitates the maintenance or increase of the distance between the white colonialist and the black other. Characterization based on these formulas originates in colonialist ideology but results in a feature typical of racial romance: the black characters are simultaneously archetypes and stereotypes.

Cary's use of a specific variant of the animal metaphor, the black as monkey or ape, clarifies both the romance and ideological function of black characterization. This metaphor is applied only to "accultured" blacks, that is, to those natives who superficially or substantially emulate white culture, but not to "pagan" blacks who have no

desire to copy the Europeans. Cary's treatment of both types of natives conforms to the traditional colonialist habit of despising the
former and patronizing the latter.[33] His sympathy for the "pagans"
causes him to represent them in terms of normative psychology, sociology, and politics, whereas characterization of "accultured" blacks
is determined by racial myths. We have already seen the contrast in
narrative attitudes toward Tanawe and the Christian converts in
Aissa Saved. Other critics have noted similar differences in *Mister
Johnson* and *The African Witch*.[34] The most telling example of the
narrative distortion necessitated by the attempt to satisfy this affective bias can be found in the depiction of Elizabeth and Coker in
The African Witch. The "witch" Elizabeth, who is indifferent to and
even contemptuous of white civilization, is shown to proceed in her
search for other witches like "a police detective" attempting to solve
a crime (*AW*, 33). Her deductive methods contrast rather incongruously with the mental functions of Coker who aspires to white
values by claiming to be a Christian minister: "Blood-love, blood
hatred, were the ethics of Coker's religion; its theology was the
geyser [in the lower part of his brain], the hot fountain shot out of
primeval mud" (*AW*, 50). Whereas the former description provides
the reader with useful information for understanding Elizabeth, the
latter example only vents the narrator's hatred of Coker and attempts
to channel forcefully the reader's affective response.

The major contrast, however, between the representation of
"pagan" and "accultured" Africans is to be found in a comparison of
An American Visitor to *Aissa Saved*, *The African Witch*, and *Mister
Johnson*. In the former novel the Birri form a traditional society relatively untainted by Western values, and the consequent absence of
affective violence allows the narrator to do some justice to the Birri
as a distinct society and to the African characters as individuals. For
instance, the narrator's lengthy description of the beauty and tran-
quility of Nok village (*AV*, 53) contrasts sharply with the vehement
repugnance in the description of Fada (*MJ*, 99). Similarly, the coherent and orderly dancing of the Birri is dramatically different from
the dancing in *Aissa Saved*, which is presented as spontaneous mass
hysteria (*AV*, 82; *AS*, 54–55, 152).

Birri society is coherent because it is an organic entity with its own
moral order. Uli's delight in this congruity and his peace of mind are
shattered when he breaks the sexual taboos of society (*AV*, 53–59).
Although no one accuses him of any crime, his conscience punishes
him: "This was the punishment that had fallen on him. The punishment of those that broke the law of things—this confusion in his

head, worse than pain. He was going mad. And he had no friends"
(*AV*, 81). His conscience, however, is appeased as soon as he is able
to reintegrate himself into the rituals of Birri life (*AV*, 83–84, 203–5).
The plausibility of these explanations of the changes in Uli's character is a product of the narrator's empathy, which also extends itself
to the marginal Birri, such as Henry. Although the latter is alienated
from Birri society, he does not aspire to become a white man: rather
he only seeks to use the commercial opportunities of colonial society
in order to make money. This aspiration, it would seem, does not
arouse the colonialist's anger, and thus Henry too is depicted in a
normative manner (*AV*, 25, 157).

On the other hand, "apes" like Coker earn the hatred of white
characters and eventually of Cary's omniscient narrators as well
primarily because they "imitate" white people. The presumption of
espousing European values marks out such characters for violent
punishment. In *The African Witch*, the white residents of Rimi re-
sent Aladai and Coker's invasion of the exclusive white paddock at
the racecourse not simply because the rules of segregation have been
violated but mainly because the blacks are dressed in European
clothes, which become a symbol of African presumption. The emotional reaction of the Europeans is quite violent: Mrs. Pratt, "gentle
and timid by nature," wanted to "strike the smiling faces—beat them
down," and Rackham "too, wanted to do something violent—to inflict public humiliation on the pair" (*AW*, 15–17). Now just as Rackham does humiliate Aladai by a public beating, the narrator too
relishes the whipping of Akande Tom who has also dared to wear a
suit. When Tom returns to his mistress, Elizabeth, the narrative
presents him as a proud, confident man who through fear turns into
"a baboon, shuffling to and fro," then into "a lizard," then a "frog,"
then a "snake," and, finally, into "a flattened, boneless mass—a black
jelly, protoplasm" (*AW*, 306–9). The whole process, of course, is
witnessed by a crowd that "delighted in Tom's misery and terror."
The narrator too seems to take pleasure in this orgy of hyperbolic
linguistic reduction of a man to nonhuman status.

Such antipathy toward the "apes," who, in the terms of romance,
are demonic parodies of Europeans, is pervasive and responsible for
the gruesome mutilations and decapitations of the "accultured"
blacks. Jack Wolkenfeld has rightly pointed out that these "accultured" blacks are scapegoats and that violence toward them is cathar-
tic for the narrators of Cary's novels,[35] but he is unable to account
for the selectiveness of the violence. The rigorous subconscious logic
of the actual colonialist ideology can, however, explain the use of

pharmakos. Because the perpetuation of the colonialist's privileged position is directly dependent upon the "uncivilized" state of the native, any African who assimilates Western culture threatens the privileged status of the European. Thus the imperatives of colonialist ideology demand that the otherness of blacks, their subhumanness, be preserved at all costs: emulation cannot be allowed to succeed. The strong influence of this ideology on Cary's fiction accounts for the systematic humiliation and, more often, for the violent death of virtually all "accultured" Africans. Their elimination allows native political power to remain in the hands of unpresumptuous "pagans" and safeguards the socio-political privileges of the colonialists. Cary's romances closely parallel colonialist ideology. Blacks are treated as the "shadows" of whites—the "uncivilized pagans" are diametrically opposed to the civilized whites, and the upstart "accultured" blacks are bad imitations of Englishmen. The systematic elimination of the "apes" is designed to separate permanently the good and evil societies; it is the very presumption of the "apes" to possible mobility toward goodness and equality that arouses the narrator's violent antipathy—their removal restores the society to its "pure" state of manichean opposition and equilibrium between good and evil.

Moral and social distance between good/white and evil/black societies is further reinforced by the use of several rhetorical strategies unique to Cary's romances. His use of landscape to re-emphasize the evilness of Africans, which becomes essentially a variation of the "racial pathetic fallacy," is best exemplified in *The African Witch*. Aladai and Dryas witness a sunset and a boatman's campfire. The flames from the fire "made a little dome of light in which [the boatmen] sat, like a private congregation over the mouth of hell." The nearby trees "twisted and dwarfed by the fire, caught the flickering light which made them seem like burnt skeletons of the damned thrown out on the rubbish heap of the earth's surface." Because the sunset throws up a similar dome of red light, the narrative equates the hell of the campfire to the hell of Africa: "It was as though two camp-fires burnt in the same African desolation, above and below—not a grand, but a mean, desolation; raw, senseless nature" (*AW*, 167). This hellish landscape, with the Africans as devils, naturally troubles Dryas, but for Aladai "the scene was beautiful, because he felt its savage desolation, which was at the same time a challenge and a delight" (*AW*, 170). The savagery of the continent is seen as having such strong affinities with the savagery of its inhabitants that the former can eventually be seen as being the source of the latter: "The black stream [of natives] trickled out of the black wound of the path, and slowly spread upon the bare trodden ground of the ju-ju place" (*AW*, 257). Africa, then, oozes the qualities that are inherited by its inhabitants: evil, savagery, and blood lust. What were previously similitudes finally become metamorphosed into an organic unity between Africans and Africa. A night scene full of drumming, laughter, and distant animal noises is described as a "heart beating through the murmur of blood; the workings of a body; the amusement and sharp, unexpected pain of a living creature; and now it seemed to be frightened. It was a stupid savage heart, like that of a beast" (*AW*, 252). Similitude thus gives way to metonymic displacement that is symbiotic: the "savagery" of a black individual can be used to characterize Africa as "evil"; negative associations of Africa (Africa as hell, as white man's grave, as the heart of darkness, and so on) can be used to deprive him of his humanity. In a Christian universe, where man has dominion over nature and where he is in constant combat with the devil, any man who is associated with primitive nature or hell is automatically inferior or evil. (The extent to which Cary imposes a notion of evil on Africa is evident from a comparison of his attitude to drumming in the above quotation with that of Conrad in *Heart of Darkness* where Marlow rightly speculates that the sound of drums has probably as "profound a meaning as the sound of bells in a Christian country.")[36]

The second strategy of estrangement is furnished by the repeated shifts in the roles and attitudes of the narrators who always speak from an unlimited editorial-omniscient point of view. However, they often slip from this role, occasionally becoming members of the white society and at times addressing the reader as if he belonged to the same colonialist community and had knowledge of specific unstated events in the novel. These slippages, occurring at crucial points for the reader's understanding of Cary's black protagonists, provide only distanced and superficial views of the characters. For instance, in *The African Witch*, Aladai, without having received an invitation, visits the "Scotch Club," a regular evening gathering usually attended only by whites. When the outraged white residents leave the club and retire to their bungalows from which they can easily observe the rest of the outdoor meeting, the narrator too moves with them in order to describe the painful interactions between Aladai and the few residents who have stayed out of politeness. From this perspective, the narrator is able to present the proceedings of the club as those of a comic circus (*AW*, 121). Similar increases in the distance between the narrator and Aissa completely rob the latter's religious experience of authenticity. In *Mister Johnson* the predominance of this remote point of view allows Cary to portray the protagonist as a ridiculous buffoon. The repeated use of this distancing maneuver relieves the narrator of the burden of seriously describing the pain and frustration that his central African characters might experience because of their colonial predicament.

The narrator's change of roles is facilitated by his aloofness from the black protagonists and his subsequent close proximity to some of his white characters. While speculating on the motives behind Coker's messianic religion and his hatred for whites, the omniscient narrator actually becomes a member of the white community: "It seemed odd to suggest that Coker's real motive in murdering several white people was to provoke reprisals, and so bring the necessary suffering upon Africa. This theory could not be proved, of course, because Coker's motives were unknown to himself; but it was suggested by a man who knew something about morbid psychology and primitive religion—which are nearly the same thing" (*AW*, 209). The implication is that the narrator is privy to the analysis of the anonymous "authority" and that both of them are discussing Coker's motives. Furthermore, the tone of the whole statement is that of gossip; it recalls the absurd generalizations that are used by the white protagonists in their Scotch Club meetings (see e.g., *AW*, 197). This collusion between the narrator and his white characters is reinforced by the former's occasional assumption that his reader is an ex-colonial officer. Thus, while discussing the bagatelle games played by the white residents of Rimi, the narrator comments that bagatelle on "Rubin's board was a special game. Those who have played it at all will remember some of the shots, such as . . ." (*AW*, 281). The different shots that he then discusses make it clear that he is not referring generically to bagatelle but specifically to Rubin's board. Similarly, in *An American Visitor*, the narrator becomes a confidant to the Dobsons and addresses his gossip to Bewsher's acquaintances in England (*AV*, 132).

These shifts in the narrators' roles would not be particularly important were it not for the fact that they are frequently accompanied by a change in attitude toward the "accultured" blacks; from a relatively neutral stance the narrators gradually move to a more antagonistic, racist attitude similar to that of some white protagonists in the novels. The coincidence between the narrator's and characters' attitudes is particularly evident in *The African Witch*. Rackham is the first white man to express his distaste of Aladai's acculturation: "It's a regular old chestnut isn't it?—the cannibal chief in the Balliol blazer" (*AW*, 19). The joke clearly implies that for Rackham the

merger of the "African personality" with the notion of English education and civilization is ridiculously incongruous. This denial of the
possibility of cultural synthesis is soon taken up by the narrator,
who in asserting his opinion reflects a traditional colonialist axiom.[37]
While describing Aladai's elated mood, he comments that only "the
consciousness of Miss Coote's nearness, which was like that of a
tutor, and of his English clothes, prevented him from laughing, crack-
ing his fingers, singing" (AW, 67). "Acculturation," then, is not even
skin-deep; it is as superficial and as easily discarded as clothes. According to the logic of this argument, Aladai would soon revert to
his original savage state if he were deprived of the trappings of
European civilization and companionship. Because the European
characters in the novel shun him, this is precisely what happens: "He
[Aladai] was dressed in the famous coat, put on over a blue kilt.
His legs were bare, and there was a small white skullcap on his
shaved head. He looked like the cannibal chief in the comic papers,
in his old school blazer. The white patch sewn around the spear-hole
in the pocket made a good imitation of a school shield" (AW, 263).
The narrator, then, has completely taken over Rackham's rhetoric
and attitude, along with their implication that the African cannot be
civilized. Similarly, Aissa is portrayed initially as a hyperemotional
religious mystic, yet at the most crucial moment the narrator dis-
tances himself from her in order to present an external comic view;
the central part of her religiosity is initially presented in great detail
as an authentic mystical experience, yet the narrator later reduces it
to a hysterical fit (AS, 153–57). She is thus doubly damned for being
emotional and ridiculous.

   The overall effect of such shifts and changes in attitude is twofold.
They result in the final depiction of some "accultured" natives as
schizophrenics. But more obviously, the increased distance serves
to simplify the black character's response to his predicament, and it
limits the reader's sympathy. The resultant simplification of moral
issues involved in racial relations in colonial societies is one of the
central characteristics of romance: "Romance avoids the ambiguities
of ordinary life where everything is a mixture of good and bad, and
where it is difficult to take sides or believe that people are consistent
patterns of virtue or vice."[38] A corollary effect of the simplification
and the coincidence between the narrators' and white characters' attitudes toward blacks severely curtails the multiplicity of viewpoints
necessary for a more thorough representation of reality.[39] The absence of perceptual complexity and the denial, through association
with idealism and anarchism, of other possible interpretations of

African characters and reality result in another typical feature of romance: the domination of the text by a single, highly subjective and monolithic viewpoint.[40] The affective intensity of this subjective antipathy is manifested in the gratuitous violence toward "accultured" blacks that is relished by the narrators of *Aissa Saved* and *The African Witch*.

The violence, however, is not a product of subjectivity per se but of a series of schizophrenic double binds and contradictions that are an inherent part of colonial societies. The influence of these binds on a writer like Cary, who was intimately involved with colonial policy and practice, eventually surfaces in his political writings, in the basic structures of his fiction, and in the characterizations of his "accultured" blacks. It is best, however, to examine first the concrete manifestations of these contradictions in Cary's novels and then trace them back to their ideological roots.

Toward the end of *The African Witch*, Aladai is presented as a schizophrenic. The English part of his personality resides in his upper brain—" 'it's very odd, all this,' said the brain, in a European voice. 'But what nonsense,' said the brain briskly, like a tutor, but less polite." Whereas the savage part of Aladai, located in the lower reaches of the brain, is swayed easily by the "reasoning of blood soaked for a million years in the agony of beasts." The English veneer of Aladai's mind is objecting in vain to his natural, inevitable reversion to savagery and witchcraft (*AW*, 291–94). It must be emphasized that Aladai's schizophrenia is not the result of any *individual* psychological malfunction (for the novel provides no such evidence), but it is caused by his "Africanness." His schizophrenic portrayal is a logical extension of Cary's assumption that there are two constitutionally incompatible states of being: a man can be either savage or civilized, but neither can he move from the former state to the latter nor can he combine the two. Similarly, the belief that Africans are irrational, naive, and incapable of political self-government results in Cary's presentation of Aladai as a political agitator who has no practical political sense whatsoever. Aissa is also a product of similar contradictory assumptions. Her view of the Christian God as a provider of earthly rather than heavenly pleasures is contradicted by her desire to sacrifice herself; she is simultaneously presented as a pagan who is only interested in sensual pleasure and a Christian who interprets the notion of self-sacrifice literally. Thus, she too is depicted finally as a schizophrenic violently torn between two voices, one that "moved inside her like a small animal waking from sleep and shaking itself" and urging her toward a physical self-

sacrifice, and another voice urging self-preservation and sensual glut-
tony (*AS*, 200–202). However, the most glaring contradiction in all
of Cary's African fiction is found in the very intention behind *Aissa
Saved*. The preface to the novel claims that "faith in ju-ju stands
badly, a few dry years, a very little 'contamination' from a government instructor destroys faith in the lingam" (*AS*, 8). Yet the action
of the novel shows that this primitive faith is anything but shallow
and ephemeral; the attempt to convert Aissa only results in the same
old "ju-ju" practices in the name of Christ. The schizophrenia of
Aissa is a result of the colonialist's contradictory desire to show, on
the one hand, that African cultures are superficial, that they have no
substance or depth, and, on the other hand, to demonstrate that the
savagery of the natives is so deeply and profoundly rooted that they
can never be civilized. Mister Johnson too is caught between similar,
but much better sublimated, binds. His characterization is based
equally on his "innate" predisposition to be a hand-clapping, singing,
childlike buffoon (an elaboration of the African-as-emotional-child
formula) and his adamant desire to become an English gentleman
(which makes him the object of satire). However, because he can
only rise in the esteem of his English masters by obediently fulfilling
their desire, which is to build a road to nowhere without adequate
funding, Johnson raises the money by levying illegal taxes on those
who use the road. When the corruption is discovered Johnson is dismissed. Now, whereas Cary is clearly indicting bureaucratic idiocy,
he is also satisfying the colonialist prejudice that would like to see
Africans simultaneously as naive children and as very cunning and
corrupt savages.

Thus Cary's romances impose on the African a double bind from
which he cannot escape. If the colonized native consents to remain
"savage," then he is relegated to a petrified society, because the momentum of indigenous social development has been checked by
colonization. (For instance, the power and position of native rulers
in Cary's novels, as well as in actual colonial societies, are dependent
entirely upon British support and no longer upon relations between
the rulers and their subjects.) If the African tries to assimilate
Western values, then he chooses a form of historical catalepsy, for
colonial education severs him from his own past and replaces it with
the study of European history. Furthermore, his attempt to emulate
the colonizers is resented; he is ridiculed and characterized as an
"ape."

The binds of the African, however, are really projected versions
of the contradictions that engulf the colonizer. The pervasiveness of

such transference is verified by Hammond and Jablow: "Throughout [colonialist] literature the image of Africa and the British image of themselves are intimately related: one is the obverse of the other, Africa *is* whatever the British *are not.*"[41] The double bind that colonialists project arises from the contradiction between colonial policy and practice. The policy aims "to develop" Africa: to educate the African, to teach him to rule himself, to instill Christian virtue in him, and so forth. Cary himself urged "total development"—social, political, and economic.[42] However, the philanthropic aspect of the policy is accompanied by highly profitable commercial exploitation and by the creation of privileged status for the colonizer. The wealth and particularly the privileges produce a sense of superiority that becomes fundamentally important to the identity of the colonizer. Thus if he vigorously pursues the overt policy, he undermines his own pleasures derived from wealth and superiority. If he ignores the policy, then he feels guilty because he subconsciously realizes that he is transgressing against his own moral ideals or, at least, against those of his culture. The ideological roots of the conflict between desire and guilt can be traced back to the larger contradiction between the democratic/egalitarian imperatives of the English society and the imperialistic/autocratic imperatives of colonialist theory and practice.

The colonialist's inability to resolve these contradictions produces subsequent ones which befuddle an otherwise logical mind. Thus Cary is able to criticize the government for not educating the Africans while arguing that "[education] would bring in more violence, more barbarities; it would break up what is left of tribal order, and open the whole country to the agitator" (*AW*, 12–13); he is able to claim that the British are ruling Africans in order to teach them how to govern.[43] He is able to recognize that guilt caused by these contradictions finds easiest release in violence toward the African who emulates the colonizers. In *The African Witch*, Mrs. Vowls explains to Aladai that the colonialists are the worst enemies of Africans, that their philanthropy and friendship are a shallow cover for the guilt they experience for having stolen Africa and enslaved her people, and that the British hate the Africans *because* they have stolen the country from the natives: " 'They will hate you more than the rest,' she continued, 'because you are as good as they are—in education. I mean—you are better in every other way—' " (*AW*, 71–72). In spite of these insights Cary dismisses Mrs. Vowls as a senile crank and violently punishes all the "accultured" African characters at the end of the novel.

In attempting to define the precise nature of Cary's racial romances and in tracing their ideological sources, we have to consider both the general opposition between white/good and black/evil poles of his fictive societies as well as the contradictions that influence characterization and organization in his works. Northrop Frye's general definition of romance is applicable on the whole to Cary's African fiction:

> The essential difference between novel and romance lies in the conception of characterization. The romancer does not attempt to create "real people" so much as stylized figures which expand into psychological archetypes. It is in romance that we find Jung's libido, anima, and shadow reflected in the hero, the heroine, and villain respectively. That is why the romance so often radiates a glow of subjective intensity that the novel lacks, and why a suggestion of allegory is constantly creeping in around its fringes.
>
> . . . [Where the novelist deals with *personae* and stable society the] romancer deals with individuality, with characters *in vacuo* idealized by revery, and, however conservative he may be, something nihilistic and untamable is likely to keep breaking out of his pages.[44]

As we have already seen, Cary's romances conform to these criteria. Only a few of Cary's "pagan" Africans, in *An American Visitor*, are portrayed as individuals against specific social backgrounds of the tribe. The vast majority of his Africans, particularly the "accultured" blacks, exist in a social vacuum—in their attempt to emulate European culture they reject native societies but are themselves ignored or rejected by white colonialists. The characterization of these blacks is based on stylized elaboration of similes such as the African as a child, as a savage, and as an emotional, irrational dependent being, and so on; they are at once archetypes and stereotypes. They are also shadows or demonic parodies of civilized whites—the pagans are uncivilized and the accultured are "bad copies of English gentlemen." The subjectivity of the romances manifests itself in the narrators' opinionated assertiveness about questions of racial characteristics, in their tendency to drop their objectivity and become protagonist-reporters, and in the coincidence of the white characters' and narrators' attitude toward blacks. The intensity of the subjective antipathy results in gratuitous violence toward blacks that recalls the nihilistic tone of Kurtz's hatred in *Heart of Darkness:* "Exterminate all the brutes." However, Cary's racial romances vary from the traditional pattern in the presentation of both blacks and whites.

Cary's Africans are generally characterized through similaic association with children and animals and by metonymic reduction. However, the narrators' very conception of black characters is determined to some extent by metaphoric transference. For instance, because both Ali (in *Aissa Saved*) and Johnson are teenagers and because Aladai is about twenty, they cannot help behaving immaturely. Yet the narrators expect them to behave like adults and mock them when they fail to do so. To the extent that characterization is determined by the absorption of metaphors into the structure of ideological perception and conception, Cary is much closer to myth, albeit racial myth, than to the central tradition of romance.[45] Similarly, the contradictions in the colonialist attitude to Africans result in the presentation of "accultured" blacks as schizophrenics, which becomes another departure from traditional romance patterns.

The most significant variation, though, is that the white/good society is depicted in a realist-satiric manner. The refusal to idealize the English administration can be traced back to Cary's bitterness toward colonial government and to his belief in the democratic/egalitarian imperative of English society which allows and even obliges him to criticize his own culture, whereas his negative idealization of Africans can be traced back to his dislike of and paranoid feeling toward the blacks in Nigeria and to the imperialist/autocratic imperative which demands that Africans be seen as a subhuman group. However, Cary's criticism of the white/good society does not alter significantly the good-evil polarity of romance, for in contrast to his condemnation of the African savagery and evil, the white colonial society, with all its faults, and the heroic D.O.'s, who are blameless, virtuous, good samaritans, seem pure and enlightened.

Even if we take these variations into account, it is clear that Cary's African fiction is still essentially a version of romance. His novels do not fit into the mainstream of English romance but are part of a subgenre, the "racial romance" that flourished in the English empire. We can understand their nature as romances better if we take into account what Frantz Fanon has called the manichean structure of colonial society. Only then can we see that the allegory that lurks behind Cary's romances is essentially the same as the one that defines such a society: it is the allegory of white and black, of civilization and savagery, of superiority and inferiority, of good and evil, of the elect and the damned, of the self and the other.

That such a society should facilitate, and (as we shall see later) even demand, the writing of "racial romance" is not surprising. For if the "social affinities of the romance, with its grave idealizing of heroism and purity, are with the aristocracy,"[46] then the feudalistic colonial society, with its Europeans as aristocrats and its blacks as serfs, provides the ideal conditions. If the essential raw materials for romance are magic and otherness, then the "ju-ju" in Africa provides the former and the savagery and blackness of Africans provide the latter. If romance flourishes in transitional periods when society is torn, when alternatives are grasped as hostile but unrelated worlds, and when social order is in the process of being undermined and destroyed by other nascent movements,[47] then again colonial society fulfills all these conditions. In the 1930s, when Cary was writing his racial romances, the social order imposed by colonialism was beginning to be challenged by nascent nationalistic movements, and European society too was beginning to experience the conflict between democratic and fascist forces. Given these social conditions and the subsequent necessity for "racial romance," the socio-political function of Cary's African fiction was not to demonstrate a genuine purification of black/evil society, not to show the complete triumph of colonialist order over African anarchy, but precisely to maintain the colonial status quo by achieving a compromise between the two forces. The elimination of "accultured" Africans at the end of all his romances leaves only the "pagans," who still need to be "civilized," thus insuring the perpetuation of colonialism. Cary's criticism of the colonial government does not affect the maintenance of the status quo, for, as we have seen, he never questions the fundamental purpose of colonialism but only satirizes bureaucratic inefficiency. What Frye calls "kidnapped romance," that is, the absorption of romance into the ideology of an ascendant class, attempts to justify the social function of that class and to idealize its acts of protection and responsibility.[48] Cary's "racial romances" do in fact justify the perpetuation of colonialism even if they do not wholeheartedly idealize the ruling bureaucracy.

Cary himself was troubled by a vague awareness that colonialist ideology, or, as he viewed it, the African setting itself, compelled him to write a certain kind of fiction. On the one hand, he found the African setting very useful because it permitted a certain kind of simplification: "The attraction of Africa is that it shows these wars of belief, and the powerful often subconscious motives which underlie them, in the greatest variety and also in very simple forms. Basic obsessions, which in Europe hide themselves under all sorts of decorous scientific or theological or political uniforms, are there seen naked in bold and dramatic action" (*AW*, 10). Although this setting is attractive, Cary tells us in the same preface to *The African Witch* that after he had completed *An American Visitor* he did not want to write any more fiction about Africa and that he particularly wished "to avoid the African setting which, just because it is *dramatic, demands* a certain kind of story, a certain violence and coarseness of detail, almost a *fabulous* treatment, to keep it in its place . . ." (*AW*, 11, italics mine).

Obviously the "simplicity" is not endemic to African societies but is an inherent component of colonialist perspective and ideology. Therefore, slight and temporary changes in Cary's perspective of and attitude toward the colonial endeavor produce significant variations in the configuration of his novels; they do not all uniformly fit the above definition of "racial romance." The configurational variations clarify the extent to which these romances are determined by certain ideological components and by Cary's affective attitudes. As we have seen, Cary's sympathy for traditional "pagans" and his antipathy for "accultured" Africans respectively lead to the normative presentation of individuals and society in *An American Visitor* and to a stylized presentation of stereotypically reduced characters and social institutions in the other three novels. The bifurcation of sympathy and antipathy, which correlates quite systematically with the need to perpetuate colonialism by suppressing the "accultured" Africans, leads to the major variations: those novels dominated by pure antipathy tend to be closer to the ideal racial romance, while those dominated by sympathy tend to be removed from the ideal.

Thus Cary's first novel, *Aissa Saved*, which is marked by the narrator's antipathy toward the religious aspirations of Aissa and other Christian converts, shows signs of the simplification that is so necessary for romance. Even when Cary's thematic concern is focused on religious consciousness and even though he had researched the "watch-tower movement" in West Africa, he is unable to interpret adequately the complexity of his material. In this novel he presents the material as the "commandments" of a native revivalist, messianic movement. The "orders of the Kingdom of Heaven, by Ojo, servant of God" run as follows:

No one is to have or keep any property which is abolished.
No one is to use money which is abolished.
No one is allowed to marry as fornication is forbidden.
It is forbidden to drink beer, gin, whiskey.
All judges are abolished including the white judge. Only God is judge.
    All laws are abolished except the law of God written in His book.
All books are to be destroyed except God's book.
Those who do not become Christians are to be killed, and the white
    men who are not Christians shall be driven away. (*AS*, 182)

Now, in a colonial society where channels of political protest or action are completely blocked for the natives, the transference of political reactions to religious activity is common; religions become to some extent smoke screens for politics. Such revivalist movements express opposition to racial discrimination by exaltation of African values and a corresponding rejection of European values; their resort to the Bible allows them utopian visions which alleviate their present misery; and their direct appeal to God allows them to bypass colonial and church authorities and even to justify rebellion against them. Thus their prime function is to overcome the insecurity created by economic, political, and cultural domination of the colonizers.[49] Clearly the above "orders" mentioned by Cary are designed to fulfill some of the same political-religious functions. Yet Cary is not at all interested in the complexity of this combination of religion and politics. He only interrupts the narrative in order to cite these "orders" as a "curiosity" that was later sent to the governor. Even though Cary convincingly shows that Marie (the American visitor in his second novel) turns to religion out of social and personal insecurity, he is unable to apply the same insight to African religious movements. The process of simplification is of course accompanied by the portrayal of accultured natives as wild, hyperemotional, uncontrolled, bloodthirsty, cruel savages. Thus by rendering them as directly antithetical to the civilized Europeans, Cary produces an almost perfect racial romance in *Aissa Saved*.

However, Cary's next novel, *An American Visitor*, which does not contain any threats to colonial stability from aspiring blacks, is least like a romance. As we have seen, the natives in this novel are quite content to exist within their traditional culture and the D.O. is anxious to protect them from external encroachment. Thus the absence of *political* antagonism between the Africans and the colonial administration leads to a corresponding lack of aesthetic stylization and opposition between the white/good and the black/evil worlds. The harmony of purpose allows Cary to present the two worlds in a more realistic manner. In comparison to *Aissa Saved*, *An American Visitor* is essentially a benign novel full of authorial guilt about the whole colonial endeavor. However, the very accurate criticism of the duplicitous structure of colonialism is diffused and masked by its relegation to outsiders like the American Marie and "exploiters" like Cottee, while the guilt is expressed indirectly through Bewsher's attempt to protect Birri territory from the English mining interest that represents the commercial arm of colonial enterprise.

But in his next novel, *The African Witch*, Cary reverts to the romance structure of *Aissa Saved*. Once again the colonial administration is criticized for its inefficiency, confusion, and ignorance, while the Africans who emulate Europeans are portrayed as apes, and the traditional natives are presented normatively and realistically. Aladai, who wishes to establish a school for native children, reverts to savagery as soon as he comes into contact with his own people, and Cocker, who aspires to become a Christian minister, reverts to ju-ju and human sacrifice. Cary's antipathy for these accultured natives is best exemplified by his description of Cocker's "natural or primitive religion" which is nothing more than

> herd communism, herd fear, herd love, blood ties and race hatreds.
>   Such a religion is pre-human, even in its ritual of blood. Beasts fear blood, and drink blood. It has a special significance for them. (*AW*, 209)

This description, which shows neither objective accuracy nor intellectual rigor, is remarkable for its violent negative emotions. Cary's antipathy, which forms the basis of his racial romances, finally manifests itself through the fact that he subjects such characters to the same degree and kind of violence that they themselves are supposed to embody. The configuration of the racial romances is produced by the projection of Cary's hostility.

Mister Johnson is also defined partly by such projection, but it is a rather ambivalent novel that combines antipathy and guilt. Johnson too attempts to emulate the Europeans, and consequently he becomes the recipient of his share of physical punishment: he is beaten by various Africans and, finally, apparently mercifully shot by Rudbeck. However, instead of using violence, Cary manifests his antipathy toward Johnson's imitation of Englishmen by ridiculing his attempts. In order to succeed in presenting Johnson as a buffoon who incongruously and absurdly "apes" English values and tastes, Cary has to withhold his own sympathy and intellectual understanding from his protagonist's aspirations. By thus distancing himself from his character, Cary is able to portray the hysterical, hyperemotional, and absurd Johnson as the complete antithesis of the typically controlled, calm, and dignified Englishman; the ridiculousness of Johnson's behavior is directly dependent upon the tacit agreement between author and reader that civilized people conduct themselves in a manner diametrically opposed to that of Johnson. Although the opposition and distance between the "evilness" of Johnson and the "goodness" of the civilized person is not, strictly speaking, a *moral* one, the sense of superiority that Johnson's antics afford the reader is, in its psychological payoff, really no different. However, Cary's antipathy is accompanied by a powerful guilt that is particularly evident at the end of the novel. When Johnson has been condemned to death for stealing from and murdering Gollop, Rudbeck, who is entrusted with his execution, repeatedly asks Johnson to absolve him from his possible indirect responsibility for the clerk's predicament. Rudbeck is afraid that his denial of a salary advance and his negative recommendation of Johnson may have respectively led to theft and the harsh sentence. Such a sense of accountability is understandable to some extent, but when Rudbeck asks for complete acquittal, when Johnson repeatedly insists that the blame is entirely his own, when the hero all too willingly absolves his master and then asks, as a personal favor, to be executed by Rudbeck himself, and, finally, when the latter willingly does so and is later proud of it, one begins to suspect the *function* of Rudbeck's powerful desire for absolution and Johnson's abject but apparently genuine humility. This ending clearly identifies Cary's own sense of guilt and his desire to be forgiven some unnamed trespass, but nevertheless he still portrays Johnson as a buffoon and eventually kills him. The same ambivalence is revealed by the dedication of the novel to Musa, Cary's assistant in Nigeria, which is followed by the motto "Remembered goodness is a benediction." But if Johnson represents Musa, then clearly the remembrance of the latter's moral "goodness" through the representation of him as a buffoon, a thief, and a murderer, that is, as the antithesis of civilized human behavior, defines Cary's deep ambivalence about his African experience which, in combination with the moral judgment that underlies the manichean structure of colonial society, produces the bifurcated structures of Cary's racial romances.

The point that I wish to stress here is not that Cary should be faulted for inadequately representing African reality, but that his belief in the nexus of values and ideas that comprise the colonialist ideology limits his perception and determines the shape of his fiction. The power of this influence is demonstrated by the simple fact that when Cary turned his attention to British settings he stopped writing romances and began producing realistic novels. His English novels, which take up some of the same themes as his African romances, do much greater justice to the intricacies of character and theme; they contain neither the narrative shifts nor the contradictions of the romances. Yet, whereas his realistic British novels represent some of the complexities of English society, his African romances reveal not the complexities of *African* cultures but rather the "worldness" of the colonialist world; the "racial romances" reveal the "horizons" of colonialist ideology—they are an indirect manifestation of the shape and strength of that ideology.

Isak Dinesen

The Generation of Mythic Consciousness

DINESEN'S RE-CREATION OF her experiences in Kenya, overtly structured by a metaphor equating Kenya with Paradise, falls within the mainstream of an established tradition that depicts eastern and southern Africa as secular utopias. "The Africa of this [tradition] is beautiful, open, sun-drenched—a golden land that preserves ways of life now but a memory in Britain—a nostalgic fantasy that, born of a distaste for the present, glorifies the past."[1] Yet there is a religious aspect of Dinesen's experience and metaphor that transcends the secular implications and that constitutes, as we shall see later, the truly mythic character of her autobiographical works. The religious facet, however, derives from the secular one, and therefore cannot be appreciated without an elaboration of the latter.

Dinesen inherited her attitude to Africans from her father's pre-occupation with the Rousseauesque tradition of the noble savage. As Parmenia Migel tells us, Dinesen's father, who had spent some time with the American Indians, never tired of reminding the young Karen that the "Indians are better than our civilized people of Europe, [that they are] closer to nature, more honest. Their eyes see more than ours, and they are wiser. We should learn more from them."[2] Influenced by this tradition and the prevailing view of Kenya as a secular paradise, Dinesen transposes this image of the noble savage onto the Masai warriors: they are "unswervingly true to their own nature, and to an immanent ideal." Even "their weapons and finery are as much part of their being as are a stag's antlers."[3] The self-sufficiency, the unity, and the naturalness of the Masai are admired in contrast to the mechanized, urbanized, and contrived life of contemporary Europeans.

Because Europe before the First World War had become mechanized and gloomy, Africa provided the needed liberation from the confinement of the bourgeois industrial society: "Here at last one was in a position not to give a damn for all conventions, here was a new kind of freedom which until then one had only found in dreams. It was like beginning to swim where one could stretch out in all directions, it was like beginning to fly where one seemed to have left the law of gravity behind . . . it was glorious, intoxicating."[4] Kenya confers upon its privileged immigrants a sense of vitality and grandeur which they could not find in Europe. Within this liberating and intoxicating atmosphere, the immigrants act out their antique fantasies by behaving like knights errant.

Out of Africa presents us with a series of these aristocratic misfits who are able to create a nostalgic idyll in Kenya. Dinesen's two closest friends, Berkeley Cole and Denys Finch-Hatton, are characterized as atavistic outcasts, exiled by an uncongenial industrial civilization. Berkeley Cole, Dinesen feels, would have been more at home in the court of King Charles II, or he "might have sat, a nimble youth from England, at the feet of the aged d'Artagnan, the d'Artagnan of *Vingt Ans Après*, have listened to his wisdom, and kept the sayings in his heart." His wit is likened to that of Congreve and Wycherly, but he has the added virtues of "a glow, grandezza, [and] the wild hope." Denys, however, is more flexible and "could indeed have been placed harmoniously in any period of our civilization, *tout comme chez soi*, all up till the opening of the nineteenth century." And Dinesen places him in an "English landscape, in the days of Queen Elizabeth. He could have walked arm in arm, there, with Sir Philip, or Francis Drake." It is the very atavism manifested by Dinesen and the two aristocrats that apparently allows them to be comfortable in Africa and that, in their view, permits the natives to develop an "instinctive attachment" for them (*OA*, 213–16).

Dissociating themselves from the debasing commercial and mechanistic values of the twentieth century by coming to Kenya, these aristocrats proceed to set up an idyllic pantisocracy in the "white Highlands." Berkeley and Denys treat Dinesen's house as a "communist establishment": "Everything in it was theirs, and they took a pride in it, and brought home the things they felt to be lacking" (*OA*, 212). To this "Silvan Retreat" come other friends who, being tired of agricultural and commercial topics, want to discuss "love, communism, prostitution, Hamsun, the Bible," and so forth. This oasis in the intellectual desert, however, is not confined to the aristocrats only; Dinesen regularly plays the Adagio of Beethoven's Piano Concerto in G-minor for her cook, Kamente (*OA*, 227), and another servant, Abdulahi, a ten-year-old genius, is periodically allowed to beat Berkeley and Denys at chess.

Yet the paradise would be incomplete were these intellectual pursuits not accompanied by manifestations of virility and sportsmanship. Hunting provides this balance. Characteristically, Dinesen raises this activity to a high emotional, sexual, and religious level: hunting in general is "ever a love-affair," but lion hunting is "an affair of perfect harmony, of deep, burning, mutual desire and reverence . . ." (*SG*, 53, 57). Both the hunter and the lion are pictured as singing a Te Deum before the battle (*SG*, 57). Dinesen eventually prefers hunting with a camera which she compares to a "platonic affair." Yet these glorious emotions clash with the studied rituals of polite society that also attend the hunting expeditions. Thus, for instance, after having shot a lion at dawn, Dinesen and Denys sit down to a breakfast of claret, raisins, and almonds while the servants skin the lion (*OA*, 231). On other similar occasions Berkeley would insist on transporting Dinesen's best champagne glasses into the forest so as not to mar the event with vulgar utensils. The incongruities of these hunts are clearly similar to those of the fox hunt in England: the point is that the models used to structure this secular utopia are not indigenous to Kenya but are brought from aristocratic Europe. These knights errant attempt in vain to isolate and preserve some of the European social models while leaving behind those they consider odious; however, the commercial, mechanistic civilization that they sought to abandon eventually follows them to Kenya. As Dinesen puts it, up until the death of Berkeley, who was the entire colony's standard of wit and humanity, "the country had been the Happy Hunting Grounds, now it was slowly changing and turning into a business proposition" (*OA*, 223).

In her own way, Dinesen attempts to fight the coming changes (see *SG*, 16). But, unable to alter single-handedly the British colonial policy, she resorts to criticizing the new middle-class settlers by dividing both animals and humans into two categories: the "respectable" who, like domestic animals, derive their "existence and prestige" from "their relations to the community" and the "decent" who, like wild animals, obtain their authority and validity directly from God. Naturally, Dinesen and her aristocratic friends are "decent," while the rest of the settlers, the merchants, and the noncommissioned officers are "respectable." Of course, under this rubric it is Victorian respectability, with its commercial and religious implications, that is under attack: the Protestant Missions are ridiculed for the amount of time, energy, and money they spend in order "to make the Natives put on trousers—in which they looked like giraffes in harness"; the businessmen are criticized because "under the motto of 'Teach the Native to Want,' they encourage the African to evaluate himself by his possessions and to keep up respectably with his neighbors"; and the government is chastised for "turning the great wild plains into game reserves" (*SG*, 17–20). In this light-hearted mockery of respectability, Dinesen is also criticizing in a substantial manner the economic, religious, and ethnocentric motives at the heart of the colonial endeavor. In contrast to the colonialist's urge to subdue and reshape the native and the African environment, Dinesen exalts the freedom of the untamed: "We registered ourselves with the wild animals, sadly admitting the inadequacy of our returns to the community— and to our mortgages—but realizing that we could not possibly, not even in order to obtain the highest approval of our surroundings, give up that direct contact with God which we shared with the hippo and the flamingo" (*SG*, 18). Although the respectable world lent itself to easy mockery, it was a powerful force that finally destroyed Dinesen's secular utopia. Ironically, precisely because she could not keep up the mortgage, she was forced to sell the farm to urban developers who subdivided and turned it into a suburb of Nairobi.

These, then, are the politics behind the drama of the secular utopia. From the point of view of the *African* context of Dinesen's experiences, the politics are superficial; Kenya and its indigenous people provide the stage and the props used to enact the drama conceived in Europe. The desires to preserve certain romantic values and to flee or fight the values of industrial civilization are acted out in a conveniently idyllic setting in Kenya. However, Dinesen's more substantial interactions with the Africans gradually, but profoundly, alter some aspects of her personality and values and eventually influence her art. Her assimilation of various elements of the indigenous cultures has a significant effect on the religious component of her Edenic metaphor and on the structure of her autobiographic works. Yet the intellectual and aesthetic changes are to a great extent determined by the nature of the social, political, and economic interaction between Dinesen and the Africans. Thus we must first examine the ecology of Dinesen's colonial predicament before defining the aesthetic nature of her autobiographies.

Like Joyce Cary, Isak Dinesen was affected by the social experience of the stranger, and by the racial division, the privileges, and the psychological parasitism of the colonial situation. However, whereas Cary reacted to the social isolation within a foreign group by becoming paranoid, by rejecting any real contact with the Africans, and by withdrawing further into the protective distance provided by the notions of racial superiority, Dinesen went in the opposite direction: her greater strength of character and keener insights allowed her to remain open-minded and therefore to analyze and understand the disintegration of her social self. With characteristic openness Dinesen wholeheartedly embraced the new society around her, abandoned social interaction based on insecurity in favor of a community based on dependency,[5] and made a transition from the scientific-empirical to the mythic mode of consciousness.[6] None of these shifts were absolute, but they were all substantial and genuine. An examination of the structures of her experience and the nature and effect of her social, psychological, and epistemological shifts, then, has to begin with the sociology of the stranger.

Out of Africa, in accordance with its tendency to exclude all painful or unseemly experiences, only gives us hints of her life as a stranger. The descriptions collectively produce a social context similar to Cary's, wherein the initial problem is the absence of adequate communication. "It was not easy to get to know the Natives. They were quick of hearing, and evanescent; if you frightened them they would withdraw into a world of their own, in a second like wild animals which at an abrupt movement from you are gone—simply are not there. Until you knew a native well, it was almost impossible to get a straight answer from him" (*OA*, 18). The obvious effects of such isolation are quite predictable: "At times, life on the farm was very lonely, and in the stillness of the evenings when the minutes dripped from the clock, life seemed to be dripping out of you with them, just for want of white people to talk to. But all the time I felt the silent over-shadowed existence of the Natives running parallel with my own, on a different plane. Echoes went from the one to the other" (*OA*, 20–21). The tenuous relationship, indicated by the parallelism and the "echoes," is worsened by the apparent indifference of the natives to the emotions of the colonialists. For Dinesen the apparent absence of gratitude in the natives seems to "annul your existence as an individual human being, and to inflict upon you a role not of your choosing, as if you were a phenomenon in Nature, as if you were the weather" (*OA*, 127). In such circumstances the news brought by a white visitor becomes "bread to the hungry minds in lonely places. A real friend who comes to the house is a heavenly messenger, who brings the *panis angelorum*" (*OA*, 17). In addition, she also has to resort to such strategies as growing European flowers and keeping European pets in order to maintain contact with her original society.

However, these are only hints of the loneliness and isolation that Dinesen had to suffer. On the whole the autobiographies are filled with pleasant social experiences; Dinesen never openly discusses the profound effects of these experiences, but they are fortunately preserved in the notes she made for a lecture delivered at Lund University. The thoroughness and lucidity of her analysis of the stranger's predicament merits lengthy quotation: as a result of this isolation, she says,

> You will find that not only will your surroundings change and be strange and unknown wherever you turn, but that you yourselves will eventually ask the question, "Who am I? What do I look like?"
>
> As long as you are a child at home, this question does not arise, all your surroundings can answer it; they are in agreement and their common judgment usually affords the basis of the evaluation we make of ourselves. . . .
>
> But one day you come to a people who see us with different eyes. Even if you learn their language, they won't have the same kind of ears you are used to addressing. . . . If you tell them that your father is a managing director or a bishop or a general, it won't mean anything to them because they don't know what a director or a bishop or a general is. . . . They won't even know that you are polite when you raise your hat, and well-dressed when you are in tails.
>
> And while you are divesting yourselves, in a way, of your social and intellectual attitudes one by one, it will slowly dawn upon you that, after all, these may not have constituted your true being, and that something remains behind when they disappear. Who am I then, since I am no longer the same person I have previously been taken for? Then the truest answer must be: a human being. Simply and solely as a human being you meet the black, primitive people.
>
> This experience was for me a kind of revelation, not only of the world, but also of myself. And I say that it was a great and unexpected happiness, a liberation . . . one more step in this direction, I thought, and then I will be face to face with God.[7]

For Dinesen the disintegration becomes the basis for a reconstruction of a more complex personality and a more profound social relationship with the natives. In fact, the possibility of such a reformulation itself seems to hasten the shedding of former social and intellectual attitudes. Speaking of the Scandinavians' tolerance for the social differences between the Africans and themselves, she comments that their "sense of individuality itself was lost in the *sense of the possibilities* that lie in interaction between those who can be made one by reason of their incongruity" (*OA*, 17, italics mine).

The greater complexity of this reconstructed personality arises from the fact that the unity encompasses two elements that were previously incongruous. Dinesen is insistent on this point: "In order to form and make up a Unity, in particular a creative Unity, the individual components must needs be of different nature, they should even be in a sense contrasts. Two homogeneous units will never be capable of forming a whole, or their whole at its best will remain barren" (*SG*, 4). Like this frequently repeated sexual metaphor, Dinesen's other imagery used to characterize this relationship stresses the idea of completion and fulfillment. Thus, the disintegration of the self leads to a more complex and enlarged universe: "the discovery of the dark races was to me a magnificent enlargement of all my world." She compares her discovery to that of "some one with an ear for music [who] had happened to hear music for the first time when he was already grown up; [his case] might have been similar to mine. After I had met with the Natives, I set out the routine of my daily life to the Orchestra" (*OA*, 17–18; see also *SG*, 5).

Dinesen's experience as a stranger is a genuinely liberating one that profoundly augments the superficial license provided by the privileges of the colonial society: the freedom not to give a damn for conventions pales in contrast to the freedom from a prefabricated self. The disintegration of the self also allows her to experience the transcendent qualities of that self which lay buried under the encrustations of the social personality. In the final analysis, then, the exfoliation of the social persona, the sacredness of the experience, and the reconstruction of the self account for the religious aspect of the Edenic metaphor. Yet, because the privileges of the colonial society play a substantial part in the restructuring of the self, it is necessary, before exploring the religious aspects of the Edenic experience and metaphor, to examine first the colonial situation of the Kenya settlers per se, which will allow us to distinguish and appreciate the differences between the prevailing black-white relations and those between Dinesen and the Africans, and then to analyze the latter relationship itself in order to gauge the extent to which her liberated self is influenced in its reconstruction by the natural and social environments in Kenya.

Unlike the colonial economic policy in Nigeria and other West African colonies, where the primary thrust was on mining and trading, the British policy in Kenya was focused on the attempt to settle the best farming lands with English and European migrants. The subsequent attempt to develop a capital-centered mode of agricultural production in an area where agriculture was essentially precapitalistic (in the sense that the bulk of the production was for subsistence rather than for the market, and the means of production, namely land and labor, were not exchanged on the market for money) created a systematic conflict: "Independent peasant production and capitalistic settler production therefore existed as sharply antagonistic modes, and any effective development of the one precluded an equivalent development of the other in the same social universe." In order for the settlers to gain control over the means of production, they had "not only to establish some kind of monopoly over the infrastructure created by the colonial system, but also to be in a position to undermine the control which the African system had had over their own productive capacity."[8] Hence, the colonial government, constantly pressured by the settlers, embarked on a policy that alienated the African's land, taxed him in order to finance white agriculture, and coerced him into the labor market.

Large areas of the best agricultural land were expropriated from the Gikuyu (who were crowded into reserves) and then given, at very little or no cost, to English syndicates, investors, and farmers. The Crown Land Ordinance of 1902, which empowered the governor to parcel out land as he saw fit, was followed by extensive land alienation, as was the court decision in 1921 which ruled that regardless of the native land-tenure systems, all land—even that which had been put aside for African "reserves"—was Crown land.[9] Such systematic alienation of land put tremendous pressure on the Gikuyu in the reserves and finally led to the Mau Mau rebellion. Although the alienation of land made it plentifully available for the settlers, the money raised from the hut and poll taxes was invested, both before and after the 1914–18 war, in settler agriculture: the Africans got no returns on their taxes.[10] If the Africans resisted the alienation or the tax ordinances, they provoked punitive raids from the government forces, which resulted in the forces' seizing their livestock and auctioning it to the settlers at low prices.[11] Because the natives could only obtain cash by working for the white farmers, the taxes, which had to be paid in cash, were not only designed to raise revenues, but also to coerce the Africans to work for the Europeans. But, because taxation did not produce a sufficiently large or consistently available labor force, the settlers argued that the quantity of land designated to the Africans be further limited so that it would be more difficult for them to exist by subsistence farming. Finally, these colonists were even able to persuade the government to prohibit the natives from growing cash crops such as coffee, tobacco, and cotton because this measure too would increase the labor supply, keep its price down, and eliminate native competition.[12]

The pressure caused by scarcity of land, by the problems of taxation on the native land, and by the settlers' demands for cheap labor led to the compromise form of tenancy known as "squatting," which allowed the Africans "to settle" on their own land, now *owned* by the European farmers. In return for cultivating such "unused" land, the native had to provide the settler with 180 days of labor per annum at minimal wages. The African had to accept such an agreement because the overcrowding, the subsequent overcultivation and overgrazing, and the demands of taxation left him without an alternative. For the colonial farmer this system was attractive because the subsistence farming mitigated the upward pressure of wages, because the squatters provided a ready source of permanently available labor, and because the farmer could thus control the native's crops and livestock.[13] For both the moderate-size farmer, such as Dinesen (6,000 acres), and the large farmer, such as Lord Delamare (1 million acres), this meant the creation of a new feudal culture. The owner became the new Lord of the Manor and an agent of the colonial government: he collected the taxes on his farm, controlled police access to his property at will, and so forth; he could choose to look after the welfare of his serfs or ignore it if he wished (as was the case most often). A testament to the callous abuse of the colonialist privileges is the fact that due to the absence of proper sanitation, housing facilities, and adequate nutrition, plus the effect of the 1914–18 war, when the natives were drafted into the carrier corps, the African population declined from 4 million in 1902 to 2.5 million in 1921.[14] Mannoni's judgment that the relationship between the French colonialist and the native produced in the former only a feeling of superiority without a corresponding sense of duty is perfectly applicable to colonial development in Kenya.[15]

Dinesen is a major exception to the above pattern of conquest and irresponsible exploitation. Her strong sense of obligation and her genuine affection for the Africans are overwhelmingly evident in her sentiments and actions. Possessing an unusual understanding of their colonial problems, she is sympathetic with her squatters' bitterness at having to pay 50 percent of their paltry wages for taxes; she equates their hatred of the *Kipandi* (a passbook similar to the one still used in South Africa) with her loathing of the identification card she had to carry during the Nazi occupation of Denmark; and she appreciates their view of her as a colonialist landlord: "They very likely regarded me as a sort of superior squatter on their estate" (*OA*, 9). Finally, when her farm is sold, she goes through a great deal of trouble and red tape in order to procure for her squatters a single large piece of land in the reserve so that their community would not disintegrate. Her success in this venture is "a great appeasement. . . . I have not often felt so contented" (*OA*, 378).

Dinesen's sense of responsibility for her squatters also manifests itself in her medical practice. On most days she would devote an hour to treating the minor ailments of these natives, but when she could not cure a patient she would have him treated at the nearby Mission Hospital at her own expense. For example, in this manner she saves Kamente's life. Although her medical practice clearly exposes her to various tropical diseases, she minimizes the real danger as well as her genuine concern for the welfare of the Africans with her characteristic bravado: "I was not afraid of plague, since I had been told that one would either die from the disease or rise from it as fit as ever, besides I felt that it would be a noble thing to die from an illness to which popes and queens had succumbed" (*SG*, 78). The grandiloquence of this gesture is in fact a self-mocking disguise for her real dedication which manifests itself in her desire to return to Africa and set up a native hospital funded by the money she had made from the sales of *Seven Gothic Tales*. That such dedication was atypical in the colonial situation is ironically highlighted by the inclusion of a story in *Out of Africa* of a neighboring doctor who refuses to treat Dinesen's squatters during medical emergencies because he was used to catering to the "Elite of Bournemouth."

Equally atypical is her decision to establish and support an evening school on her farm. In a colony with only a few religious schools, which were concerned more with proselytizing than with any practical education, Dinesen's educational endeavor becomes a great source of pride for her and the squatters—it is the "favourite place on the farm, the center of our spiritual life" (*OA*, 32). Toward the end of her stay in Kenya, when she is burdened with financial problems, she manages to scrape enough money together to send one of her young servants to a Moslem high school in Mombasa. Dinesen's anomalous concern for African education is dramatized by her narration of an incidental anecdote, ironically entitled "Fellow-Travellers," about a Belgian who is enamoured with "*Notre grande mission dans le Congo: Il faut enseigner aux nègres à être honnêtes et à travailler. Rien de plus. Rien. Rien. Rien*" (*OA*, 305). She similarly contrasts her humane treatment of the natives with the story of Kitosch who was beaten to death by his English employer because he rode one of the horses without permission (*OA*, 278–83).

Yet Dinesen's largess toward her squatters is not consciously or deliberately humane; it is based rather on implicit trust and affection.

She has genuine respect for all her servants, particularly for their pride. Farah, her "major-domo," is portrayed as a "Gentleman," who is sufficiently different from Dinesen in terms of "race, sex, religion, milieu and experience" so that together they form a "Unity" (*SG*, 12). In any of the Somali clan feuds Dinesen always sides with the Habr Yunis because Farah belongs to that clan. Farah and Kamante manage her house and farm: "Farah was my cashier, he had charge of all money I took home from the bank and of all my keys. He never drew up any accounts for me and would hardly have been able to do so, nor would it have occurred to me to demand it from him" (*SG*, 23). Not only is Farah the cashier, but at times he even controls the priorities of expenditure: such trust and loyalty for a servant are unique in any colonial situation.

These attitudes and actions earned Dinesen the rare respect from later African nationalist leaders,[16] and the displeasure of her colonial contemporaries—she was labeled "pro-native" (i.e., nigger-lover) by the settlers.[17] Because her squatters and servants were not involved in colonial politics, they provide a more unbiased gauge of the effect of Dinesen's attitudes and actions. Their opinions are also important because her relationship with them creates the atmosphere that in turn generates the Edenic metaphor. The effects of Dinesen's concern for the natives are summed up by Kamante's reminiscences, wherein he characterizes their relationship as that between "black and white keys of a piano, how they are played and produce melodious verses. . . ."[18] Dinesen's largess too is verified by Kamante:

> That means if somebody was chased away by his master she would employ him in her garden and give him places to build his house, together with a piece of land where he could grow some crops.
>
> Many people proceeded from Majeng, Ruira, Thika, Nairobi, even Uganda and Mombasa to stay. She would not expel those who were staying in her farm without working. She only liked them. In actual fact she employed a lot of Moslems.

If they were ever short of food, Dinesen would make up the deficiency. The squatters' life was so good that "nobody took the *shamba* to be of Europeans. We took it to be ours. We found this garden belonging to all of us. Therefore we had no idea of leaving the garden. . . ." Kamante's final compliment reveals that for the natives Dinesen was no longer a "stranger"—"Even people coming to the *shamba* could not say that they were going to the farm of a European. She was of such good nature."[19]

Thus Dinesen becomes an active member of the squatter community and participates in their daily personal and cultural life. For instance, she is present at the birth of Farah's son and at his sister's wedding. Because of Dinesen's active concern with and interest in the differences between herself and the native cultures surrounding her and because of her particular experience as a stranger, she does not distance herself through the notions of racial superiority. The Africans, aware and appreciative of this fact, consider it significant that unlike other whites she does not get angry at them, but rather she laughs at the cultural differences that produce incongruities and misunderstandings. The strength of her empathy can be measured by the fact that when she is preoccupied and inattentive to her squatters, they view the withdrawal as her retreat into white society (*OA*, 137). The relationship is not just one of tolerance but has strong emotional bonds: as Dinesen says, the "understanding between us lay deeper than all reason" (*OA*, 332).

This deeply emotional relationship is symbiotic. Just as Dinesen's empathy and interest modify the African view of her potential usurpation of their lands and of her potentially haughty and complacent colonialist personality, so their function as her serfs and the effects of their "primitive" mentality respectively influence her self-perception and alter her "advanced" mentality. In other words, the colonial situation creates her position as a "superior squatter" and, through the experience of the stranger, enables her to "divest" her intellectual attitudes, thereby rendering her receptive to the mythic consciousness that surrounds her. Dinesen is perfectly aware that her self-image as an omnipotent master and philanthropist is a reciprocal function of the Africans' willingness to act as her servants and of their receptivity to her benefaction: her role as Lord of the Manor is entirely *dependent* upon their role as serfs. This dependency-support system is as responsible for the Edenic metaphor as is Dinesen's transference from the scientific-empiric consciousness to the mythic.

Dinesen's concern for the welfare of her African squatters, her respect for their dignity, and her general, but genuine interest in their cultures lead the Africans to accept, respect, and even venerate her. The effect of this adulation, which significantly affects her personality and art, is indicated in her mistaken generalization about the African view of Europeans: "In some respects, although not all, the white men fill in the mind of the Natives the place that is, in the mind of the white men, filled by the idea of God" (*OA*, 374). Grandiose and improbable as this may sound, Dinesen herself believes and even experiences it as a fact. In order to understand her feelings of omnipotence we must first define the nature of the psychological satisfaction that she derives from her role as judge, doctor, and Lord of the Manor.

As the judge at the Kyama, a Gikuyu court of justice, and at similar courts for the Somalis, Dinesen's curiosity leads her to distinguish and analyze the difference between the European and Gikuyu notions of justice and even to embark upon a study of the Koran and the Minhaj et Talibin (the manual of Islamic law). In spite of her genuine knowledge and interest, she is quite aware that her presence at these courts is ritualistic: "As I knew nothing of their laws the figure that I cut at these courts of justice would often be that of a Prima Donna who does not remember a word of her part and has to be prompted through it by the rest of the cast. This task my old men took upon themselves with tact and patience" (*OA*, 100). Her awareness of the possible superficiality of her role and of the Gikuyu's use of her concurrence with their judgment to protect themselves from the interference of the district commissioner's English law, however, does not prevent Dinesen from being seduced by the apparent power of her role. She attributes their anxiety to win her agreement to the "fact" that "I [was] indeed magnetic, a law of Nature" (*OA*, 103). The power that her situation confers on her becomes irresistible: "my position as a judge to the [G]ikuyu held a profusion of potentialities, and was dear to me" (*OA*, 104). What may appear as a contradiction in Dinesen's perception of herself as a "Prima Donna" and as "a law of Nature" is in fact an oxymoronic strategy: the narcissistic pleasure she derives from her own importance is mitigated by her realization that she is deliberately being indulged by the natives. This combination disarms the reader's potential criticism of her colonialist narcissism.

The strategy is more clearly evident in her role as doctor, which she seems to have cherished more than any other and, as we have seen, to which she devoted a great deal of energy, time, and money. Toward the end of her stay in Kenya when she was about to lose her farm, Dinesen describes herself as obtaining particular gratification from treating the burns on the legs of Wawerru. Aware of the pleasure Dinesen finds in treating her squatters, Kamante tries to ensure the boy's regular attendance at her clinic. Thus, like the elders who instructed the prima donna at the trials, Kamante too is indulging Dinesen's desire to perform the role of a doctor. His calculated indulgence is loudly echoed by the whole squatter community. One day while riding, Dinesen spots Wawerru (who has stopped coming for treatment, although his wounds have not yet healed) and rides after him while he scurries off to his parents' hut. Dinesen, angered by his ingratitude, follows him into the hut and only then realizes that "I had not, until now, in my mind associated my success or failure in curing Wawerru's legs with my own fate, or with the fact of the financially troubled farm" (SG, 97). Suddenly facing the failure of her farm, she breaks down and weeps in the hut. The next morning when she wakes up and goes out, she finds a large group of squatters awaiting her. After some moments of tense silence, an old woman asks Dinesen to treat a burn on her arm, and then gradually similar demands for medical advice are made by the rest. Slowly Dinesen realizes that the natives

> in a common resolution had agreed to bring me what, against all reason and against all inclination of their own hearts, I had wanted from them. They must have been grappling with, imparting to one another and discussing between them the fact: "We have been trying her too hard. She clearly is unable to bear any more. The time has come to indulge her."
>
> It could not be explained away that I was being made a fool of. But I was being made so with much generosity. (SG, 101–2)

Again there is the realization that she is being deliberately humored, but there is no hint of duplicity or ulterior motives behind the indulgence. The absence of bad faith makes the charade, the repeated, ritualized enactment of the dependency-support system all the more powerful and binding. As with the judicial situation, here too Dinesen's successful enactment of her role is centripetally structured and dependent upon African support.

Both the centripetal qualities of Dinesen's universe and the crucial function of the dependency-support system reach their purest form in the master-servant relationship between Dinesen and Farah. The latter becomes her alter ego, for when she is sailing away from Kenya she describes her sense of loss as she sees Farah's form diminishing on the dock: "I felt as if I were losing a part of myself, as if I were having my right hand set off, and from now on would never again ride a horse or shoot with a rifle, not be able to write otherwise than with my left hand. Neither have I since then ridden or shot" (SG, 4). She remembers her African servants as "part of *my existence* there" (SG, 7, italics mine). The self thus includes the servants and depends upon their support for completion: Dinesen and Farah make a "unity," and her introduction to the Africans becomes an expansion of "*my* world." When Dinesen is about to leave Kenya, Farah, wearing his splendid Somali robes and sword and looking like "Caliph

Harun-al-Rashid's own bodyguard," escorts Dinesen on her errands. When visitors come to the empty farmhouse,

> [he stands] forth, holding open the doors to the empty rooms as if he [were] doorkeeper to an imperial palace.
>
> No friend, brother or lover, no nabob suddenly presenting me with the money needed to keep the farm, could have done for me what my servant Farah then did. (*SG*, 47–48)

Even in defeat, the alter ego helps the ego to maintain the dignity that is crucial to a nostalgic re-creation of the African paradise, and enables the focus of the centripetal world to retain the power that keeps its universe together. Dinesen's dependency upon the individuals and the atmosphere is so strong that not even death can separate her from Farah. The news of his death is initially bewildering for Dinesen, but after a while she recognizes a pattern that allows her to retain her claim on him: "more than once before now I had sent him ahead to some unknown place, to pitch a camp for me there" (*SG*, 135–36).

However, as we have seen, Dinesen's world is not exclusively centripetal; her largess and genuine concern for and interest in the natives also invoke their respect, loyalty, and adulation. The social universe, then, is simultaneously centripetal and centrifugal: it is characterized by a dynamic balance. Its structure is based on mutual respect and dependency. Dinesen articulates her awareness of this dependency in a theoretical, schematic manner in the section entitled "Of the Two Races" (*OA*, 264–65). She feels that if Europeans

> had been told that they played no more important part in the lives of the Natives than the Natives played in their own lives, they would have been highly indignant and ill at ease.
>
> If you had told the Natives that they played no greater part in the lives of the white people than the white people played in their lives, they would never have believed you, but would have laughed at you.

Although this notion of mutual dependency is an accurate representation of Dinesen's personal experience, her schematization of it has several problems. It is improbable that most whites in Kenya, or in any other colony, saw themselves as being dependent on the Africans. In fact, Mannoni's generalization points in the opposite direction:

> The colonial's personality is wholly unaffected by that of the native . . . ; it does not adapt itself, but develops solely in accordance with its own structure. It is inevitable, therefore, that misunderstandings should arise, for there can be no harmony between monads. . . .

What the colonial in common with Prospero lacks, is awareness of
the world of Others, in which Others have to be respected.[20]

Dinesen, then, is clearly an exception to the general unwillingness of
the colonialist to recognize the otherness of the native (we have
already seen the effects of racial solipsism in the analysis of Joyce
Cary's fiction). Dinesen's schematization also erroneously implies
that the dependency and reciprocations are equal: in fact, Dinesen
is the leader and the natives are the followers, for she equates their
relationship to that between Napoleon and his troops. Her central
position as the leader provides an organizational basis for her world
without disturbing its dynamic balance; the egocentric organization
produces a world that is simultaneously subjective, that is, defined
by Dinesen's idiosyncratic perceptions, and objective, that is, non-
egotistic and full of empathy.

The egocentricity of Dinesen's experience allows her to play her
ultimate role—that of God. Although her autobiographies do not
furnish an evolutionary view of this role, there is no doubt that the
egocentricity, the omnipotence, and the omnipresence conferred by
her various roles, as well as the Africans' use of her as a symbol of
Christianity, lead to her final role. Dinesen's function as the symbol
of Christianity is crystallized in her relationship with Kamante and
Kitau. When the former converts to Christianity, Dinesen, being
curious about the "idea he attached to the name of Christianity,"
tries to catechize him. However, she only receives from him the
answer that "he believed what I believed, and that, since I myself
must know what I believed, there was no sense in me questioning
him" (*OA*, 51). Dinesen does not interpret this answer as an evasion,
but prefers to see it as "his positive programme, or confession of
faith." Thus, Kamante's belief is directly dependent on Dinesen's:
it is a belief based on absolute faith in her. Similarly, Kitau, having
decided to become either a Christian or a Moslem, wants to work for
Dinesen so that he can make a more informed choice after observing
her behavior as a Christian.

Dinesen, therefore, becomes a minister of Christianity: she ad-
ministers faith and becomes a model of the Christian universe. This
"alarming experience" of being a symbol is substantially reinforced
by her actual ability to administer faith and to witness its magical
effects. The whole section entitled *"Barua a Soldani"* (*SG*, 51–74)
is a testament to faith. In this episode she is able to alleviate the
pain of a squatter, whose legs have been crushed by a falling tree,
by holding to his stomach a letter from the King of Denmark. How-

ever, it is not the magical quality of the letter that is solely responsible for the miracle, but Dinesen's presence as well, for the squatter insists that she herself should hold the letter to his stomach, otherwise the pain would return. After this incident the letter becomes a celebrated source of anesthesia, and the natives develop a code for its use: "It would do away with pain, in this capacity it was infallible, and no ache or pang could hold out against it. But it must be made use of solely in uttermost need" (*SG*, 68). Later Dinesen characterizes this blood-stained letter as a "covenant" between her and the Africans.

Her ability to administer faith becomes the main phenomenological step toward her experience of herself as a creator: the minister of faith easily becomes the creator of life. Since she saved Kamante's life by nursing him, she looks at him with "something of a creator's eye" (*OA*, 31). The most explicit statement of her experience of the divine role is made when she transcribes one of her squatters' names in a document. The native, upon hearing his name put into writing for the first time, gives Dinesen a "great fierce flaming glance, so exuberant with laughter that it changed the old man into a boy, into the very symbol of youth." Dinesen interprets this experience from her divine position: "Such a glance did Adam give the Lord when He formed him out of the dust, and breathed into his nostrils the breath of life, and man became a living soul. I had created him and shown him himself: Jogona Kanyagga of life everlasting" (*OA*, 120–21). Jogona guards this document with great care: "He could not afford to lose it, for his soul was in it, and it was the proof of his existence. . . . the flesh was made word and dwelt among us full of grace and truth" (*OA*, 121). For the Africans, the introduction to written language is a profound experience. Dinesen characterizes their attitude to the written word as that to "gospel truth" and to "the scriptural word" (they would not doubt the most fanciful statement so long as it was in writing), and their experience of written language is represented by her as a "deep religious triumph." To the extent that Dinesen is the source of this religious feeling and to the extent that she ministers the transformation, her representation of herself as a creator is not just fancifully hyperbolic; rather it is a statement of her genuine experience as the source of a universe that is being transformed by her initiative. The centripetal quality of her position and the generative nature of her experience, then, lead her to feel that for the natives the white man *is* God (*OA*, 374).

Dinesen's sense of omnipotence, her view of herself as a god, and her transformation from empiric to mythic consciousness (which we shall examine shortly) together constitute the substantial, religious component of her metaphor of Kenya as a paradise. Whereas the secular aspect of the latter is based upon the social freedom that the feudal structure of the colony affords its aristocratic immigrants, the religious element derives from the transfiguration of Dinesen's consciousness through her interaction with the natives. The cultural differences between the Africans and Dinesen as well as the specifically modified feudal relationship between them permitted her a series of religious experiences that establish the basis of the metaphor. Her acceptance and use of mythic consciousness constitute the practical formalization of the religious experience.

Having shed her indigenous social and intellectual attitudes, Dinesen is entirely open to the African cultures and, at times, actively seeks to understand the native psyche. She has frequent and involved discussions about African, Islamic, and Christian theologies with her Somali and Gikuyu servants. However, because she is not interested in the African consciousness in the quasi-objective manner of an anthropologist, her appreciation of it tends not to be analytic or definitive. She is, nevertheless, aware of the primary difference between the European and African mental orientation and indicates this fact while describing her function as a judge. The natives' desire to have her in this position she ascribes to "their mythological or theological mentality. The Europeans have lost the faculty for building up myths or dogma; and for what we want of these we are dependent upon the supplies of our past. But the mind of the African moves naturally and easily upon such deep and shadowy paths" (OA, 104). Yet nowhere in her autobiographies does Dinesen provide us with a workable definition of this "mythological mentality." In order to gauge more accurately the impact of the latter upon Dinesen's mind and upon the structures of her autobiographies, we have to turn to Ernst Cassirer's definition which (though superseded by Levi-Strauss's more "objective" analysis of the "primitive mind") is singularly applicable to the cultures described by Dinesen.

Cassirer's definition of mythic consciousness is too complex and extensive to be summed up successfully. It is sufficient to indicate here the most crucial differences between mythic and scientific-empirical orientations and to utilize specific aspects of the definitions as they become germane to the analysis of the organizing consciousness in Dinesen's autobiographical works. The definition centers on what Cassirer calls the *concept of the object* and the *concept of causality*. In the operations of the scientific-empirical consciousness "the general concept of objectivity as well as its concrete realizations rest on a progressive *analysis* of the elements of experience, on a critical operation of the intellect in which the 'accidental' is progressively differentiated from the 'essential,' the variable from the constant. [The object from its 'ground,' the cause from its effect, etc.]"[21] Of great importance within this operation is the fact that the *synthesis* toward which empirical thought strives always presupposes a corresponding *analysis*. In this sense all empirical thought is dialectical and achieves its characteristic form through this reciprocal, binary operation of analysis and synthesis.

In contrast to the operation of empiric consciousness, in the function of mythic mentality

> the nuances of significance and value which [empirical] knowledge creates in its concept of the object, which enables it to distinguish different spheres of objects and to draw a line between the world of truth and the world of appearance, are utterly lacking. . . . Instead of the dialectical movement of thought, in which every given particular is linked with other particulars in a series and thus ultimately subordinated to a general *law* and process, we have here a mere subjection to the impression itself and its momentary "presence."

The relative absence of the analytic element and the abundance of the synthetic component distinguish the mythical consciousness from the empirical one. The result is that for the mythical mind "every simultaneity, every spatial coexistence and contact, provide a real causal sequence." The principles, such as *post hoc, ergo propter hoc,* which are logical fallacies for empirical knowledge, are for the mythic mind viable modes of causality. Cassirer characterizes the mythical imagination as a "polysynthetic" one:

> Whereas empirical thinking is essentially directed towards establishing an unequivocal relation between *specific* "causes" and *specific* "effects," mythical thinking, even where it raises the question of origins as such, has a free selection of causes at its disposal. Anything can *come from* anything, because anything can stand in temporal or spatial contact with anything.

These two concepts, of object and causality, are central to Cassirer's definition of both the empirical and the mythic orientation. From these concepts are derived all the particular configurations of the mythical mentality which we shall take up as we need.

Dinesen herself is aware of these central differences in the two mentalities, but her representation of them is typically suggestive and evocative rather than precise and analytic:

We Nations of Europe, I thought, who do not fear to floodlight our own inmost mechanisms, are here turning the blazing lights of our civilization into dark eyes . . . essentially different from ours. If for a long enough time we continue in this way to dazzle and blind the Africans, we may in the end bring upon them a longing for darkness, which will drive them into the gorges of their own, unknown mountains and their own, unknown minds. (*SG*, 92)

Dinesen points to the same distinctions that Cassirer makes. The European tendency to "floodlight" the "inmost mechanism" of the mind is clearly a figurative reference to the analytic emphasis of the scientific-empirical consciousness, whereas the "dark eyes" and "unknown minds" refer to the mysteriousness of the universe preferred by the mentality that stresses the synthetic function. Dinesen's awareness of the fundamental difference is accompanied and augmented by her constant exposure to some of the specific manifestations of the mythic consciousness. An examination of these particular instances will permit us to comprehend better the manner in which Dinesen assimilates parts of that mentality.

For instance, Cassirer tells us that for the mythic mind a name "expresses what is innermost and essential in the man, and it positively 'is' this innermost essence. Name and personality merge."[22] For Dinesen the mythological mentality is illustrated by the animal appellations that the Africans assign to the Europeans. The natives come to think of the persons endowed with these names "as both men and beasts." And Dinesen feels that, since there is a magic in these designations, eventually the recipient himself recognizes the signification of his name as representative of his own essence. For evidence she cites the case of a colonial government official called "Bwana Tembu" (Mr. Elephant) whom she meets later in a London zoo while he is contemplating the elephants. Such incidents of mythical mentality abound in her autobiographies, and, although they have a substantial effect on her, they cannot all be considered here. It is sufficient to examine some of the salient examples of "mythical causality" of which Dinesen in time becomes the object. She is surrounded by natives whose minds function in this "shadowy" manner, and the best example of this is Kamante. He has mastered the most subtle cuisine of Europe, but, Dinesen tells us, he remembers the recipes in a peculiar manner: "He had named the dishes after some event which had taken place on the day [the recipes] had been shown to him, and he spoke of the sauce of the lightning that struck the tree, and of the sauce of the grey horse that died. But he did not confound any of these two things" (*OA*, 38). In Kamante's method the absence of an analysis of the food, which would enable him to subordinate the various recipes to some inherent order, leads to these random connections: the sauce is not *caused* by the lightning, but neither does it seem to have been caused by any factor inherent in the ingredients. Thus, any extraordinary association will suffice to identify a recipe.

It is the randomness of causal connection that Dinesen says accounts for her popularity as judge and doctor. Her lack of adequate knowledge of the Gikuyu judicial system and the consequent element of chance in her decisions seem perfectly consonant with the Gikuyu system which, unconcerned with the specific causes (such as motives or mitigating circumstances) of a given crime, focuses on establishing the fact that a crime *was* committed and then spends most of its time on the fine details of recompensation (*OA*, 115). In other words, the Gikuyu judicial system is only concerned with the beginning and the end of the process. Similarly, Dinesen feels that her reputation as a doctor is heightened because she makes many mistakes, whereas professional doctors, who succeed more often, are not esteemed as much (*OA*, 25). She attributes her reputation directly to her fallibility (*SG*, 77). Here again the natives seem to find the randomness of her cures more attractive because it makes her decisions and actions more magical. That is, the haphazard success or validity of her deeds inspire wonder analogous to that inspired by God's acts (*OA*, 25). The awe, which springs from the inability to understand the specific causality of an event or conversely from the infinite causal possibilities posited by the "polysynthetic" imagination, Cassirer characterizes as the "relatively solid core of the idea of *mana*," which is "simply the impression of the extraordinary, the unusual, the uncommon."[23]

In addition to being surrounded by the mythic consciousness, Dinesen is also turned into its source. To the extent that she is able to conjure up magical cures, such as the *Barua a Soldani*, she becomes simultaneously the source and the object of *mana*. Dinesen is well aware of the effects of this phenomenon; she dreads it, but also finds pleasure in it:

> Because of their gift for myths, the Natives can also do things to you against which you cannot guard yourself and from which you cannot escape. They can turn you into a symbol. I was well aware of the process, and for my own use I had a word for it—in my mind I called it that they were brass-serpenting me. . . .

. . . In regard to our misfortunes they looked upon me as the congregation looks upon the priest, who empties the cup alone, but on
their behalf.

There is this about witchcraft, that when it has once been practiced on you, you will never completely rid yourself of it. I thought
it painful, a very painful process to be hung upon the pole, I wish
that I could have escaped it. Still, many years after, there will be
reasons when you find yourself thinking: "Am I to be treated in such
a way?—I, who have been a brass-serpent!" (*OA*, 106–8)

Dinesen is influenced by her environment and her role to the extent
that she admits to a tacit belief in witchcraft (*OA*, 139–40).

Dinesen, then, becomes a pivotal part of the social, cultural, and
spiritual community that surrounds her. Her relationship with the
natives is itself characteristic of the bonds between the self and community when the mythical consciousness predominates: in such a
situation, "subjectivity has as its correlate not some outward thing
but rather a 'thou' or 'he,' from which on the one hand it distinguishes itself, but with which on the other hand it groups itself.
This thou or he forms the true antithesis which the I requires in
order to find and define itself."[24] As we have already seen, Dinesen's
notions of her relations with the natives, of the opposition in unity,
conform to the pattern that Cassirer describes. It is the same dynamic
relationship that we have called centripetal and centrifugal, and for
which Donald Hannah quotes one of Dinesen's mottoes:

> The great Emperor Otto
> Could never decide on a motto
> He hovered between
> '*L'Etat c'est moi*' and '*Ich dien*'[25]

Dinesen's relation with the community is characterized by this dual-
ity: on the one hand, it consists of the imperial self with its virtually
divine right to possess everything, and, on the other hand, it involves
a "stupendous obligation"—she would die for her serfs if necessary.
The coexistence of the power of absolute ownership and the obligation of absolute responsibility allows Dinesen to talk in a detached
manner about the mythic consciousness of the natives and to espouse
simultaneously some of the same attitudes.

Thus, she is able to describe accurately the mythic nature of the
African notion of God: "they had preserved a knowledge that was
lost to us by our first parents. Africa, amongst the continents will
teach it to you: that God and the Devil are one, the majesty coeter-
nal, not two uncreated but one uncreated, and the Natives neither

confounded the persons nor divided the substance" (*OA*, 20). This is a significant feature of mythical theology in that the monotheism of such a religion is "only a *relative* monotheism: the God who is here postulated is *one* only in the abstract sense that he is yet undifferentiated, that there is still nothing with which he can be compared or to which he can be opposed."[26] There are two important consequences, from our point of view, of this definition of God. First, the most obvious point is that Dinesen identifies this attitude to God as being prelapsarian, and it therefore becomes an important element in structuring the religious aspect of the Edenic metaphor. The second substantial factor is that, given the *undifferentiated* notion of God, that is, the absence of a dialectical opposition of good and evil, man can expect *anything* from this "primitive" monotheistic God. Man cannot expect such a God to be *reasonable;* He can be capricious and benevolent at will, or He can be both simultaneously. The point, then, is that such a definition is again magical because it posits infinite possibilities in the divinity and because such an attitude can only lead to the awe of *mana,* which includes both the sacred and the profane elements.

Dinesen appropriates this definition for her own purposes and links it to similar aspects of the Islamic and Judaic ideas of God: "When the Africans speak of the personality of God they speak like the Arabian Nights or like the last chapter of the book of Job; it is the same quality, the infinite power of imagination, with which they are impressed" (*OA*, 23). In this definition the infinity of God-as-imagination is clearly beyond human reason: "What is completely unforeseeable, and not consonant with rule or reason, that is an act of God" (*OA*, 374). Although it cannot be definitely demonstrated here (given the scant biographical information on the writer's life and work)[27] that Dinesen absorbed this notion of God's infinite imagination directly from the natives, there can be little doubt that she was strongly influenced by the mythical mentality of the Africans. That this imagination comes to play a crucial role in her fiction is indubitable, and its important function has been thoroughly stressed by Donald Hannah. His whole argument cannot be recapitulated here, but it is important to emphasize his conclusion that in the process of reading her fiction the answer that Job gave to God is the same one "we are made to give; we become as Job. For Isak Dinesen, only by the exercise of the imagination, in life, as well as in art, can we comprehend the design, understand the purpose of our existence—and be reconciled to our lot. This is the full extent of the function and the importance of imagination for her."[28] For both

Dinesen and Job, an important ingredient of imagination is the sense of awe that permits empathy to exercise itself. As David Daiches points out, Job's problem with God disappears in "a note of wonder— wonder at the grandeur and immensity of creation."[29] For both of them, awe and imagination are more important than rational under- standing.

The importance of imagination for Dinesen's personality and work is also illustrated by its role in her dreams, where she forsakes her allegiance to "the organizing, controlling and rectifying forces of the world, the Universal Conscience," and instead pledges it to "the wild, incalculable, creative forces, the Imagination of the Universe." The forces in these dreams "have set us free as mountain winds, have liberated us from initiative and determination, as from responsibility. . . . each of their boons is a gift, baksheesh, and their highest gift is inspiration. A gift may be named after both the giver and the re- ceiver, and in this way my inspiration is my own, more even than anything else I possess, and is still the gift of God" (*SG*, 110–11). There are several significant factors that must be noted in Dinesen's views of dreams and reality. First, it is quite obvious that God as infinite imagination is also the source of Dinesen's human imagina- tion. Of greater importance is Cassirer's warning that the characteris- tic structures of mythical consciousness can only be appreciated if we remember that "for mythical thinking and mythical 'experience' there is always a hovering between the world of dreams and the world of objective reality."[30] It is significant, then, that when Dinesen moves into the realm of "Universal Imagination," she forsakes the "organizing, controlling and rectifying forces," that is, she abandons the organizing structures of the scientific-empiric consciousness and moves into the "polysynthetic" realm of the mythical consciousness. Her characterization of the movement from the empiric to the mythi- cal realm as a liberation is identical to her definition of the move- ment from Europe to Africa. She finds in Africa a "new kind of free- dom which until then one had only found in dreams" (*OA*, 135). The imagery she then uses to describe this freedom is similar to that used in representing the freedom confirmed by the dream-universe of Imagination. Mythic consciousness, then, is identified with Africa.

It thus becomes clear that Dinesen's sojourn in Kenya had a pro- found influence on her. The development of her sensibility, her movement from a scientific-empiric mode of thought to a predomi- nantly mythic mode, can be seen as a product of her experience as a stranger and of the particular relationship between her and the na- tives. To be sure, the inherent factors of her personality are also responsible for the transformation: the role of her open-mindedness and her thirst for new experiences cannot be overlooked. It is impossible to work out a specific calculus for the interaction of the various factors: nevertheless, one can indicate the salient features of the phenomenology that are responsible for structuring Dinesen's autobiographies and ultimately her fictional work.

The structure of her attitude is determined by three closely related phenomenological imperatives. She derives the first one from her interpretations of Islamic and Judaic theologies. In contrast to Christian theology, which is concerned with justifying the ways of God to man, Islam is more interested in saying yes in a "universal and unconditional" manner. Both Moslems and Jews "are a communion of yes-sayers, they are in love with danger, with death and with God" (SG, 29–34). The second imperative (really an extension of the first) is what she calls the capacity for "Unconditional Surrender" to experience. She speaks of the Gikuyu funeral custom, where one is put out on the plains to be eaten by various animals and thus reabsorbed by the Universe (a custom she prefers to Christian burial) as an indication of their "silent, all-embracing genius of consent" (SG, 89). Aesthetically, Dinesen considers the success of a perfect dancer not as *his* achievement, but rather as "the supreme triumph of [his] Unconditional Surrender" to the music. Once again, she valorizes abandonment over control. She derives this notion as much from the Islamic-Judaic tradition as she does from the Gikuyu, whose ability to survive slavery she attributes to their genius for surrender to destiny. In their acceptance of fate "they differ from the white men, of whom the majority strive to insure themselves against the unknown and the assaults of fate. The Negro is on friendly terms with destiny" (OA, 23). Analogous to her qualified rejection of the analytic, organizational aspect of empirical consciousness is her rejection of the doubt that also characterizes the Western scientific tradition. This allows her to replace skepticism with an unqualified affirmation of *all* experience. The third imperative, really a deepening of unconditional acceptance, she defines as her abhorrence of coitus interruptus. Not only does she accept and affirm all experiences, including the droughts that were partially responsible for the failure of her farm, but she also clings to them until they are consummated.

Along with wonder, these three imperatives determine the nature of Isak Dinesen's autobiographies. Both the mythical and the empiric consciousnesses are evident in her work; although Dinesen seems able to move comfortably from one to the other, the vision that creates her autobiographies is fundamentally mythic. Similarly, the thematic preoccupations and structures of her tales are also informed by this vision and by her African experience, although systematic and detailed correlations are beyond the scope of this chapter. However, one can indicate the basis of these connections. For instance, the affirmation of all experience by her characters can be correlated to her "yes-saying"; the prevalence of disguised identities and the repeated hints of the absence of a "true" or "permanent" self can be linked directly to her experience as a stranger; the subservience of character to plot can be related to her admiration for the African's "friendliness" with destiny; and so forth. In addition to these experiential correlations, one must also note the effect of Dinesen's exposure to the formal aspects of oral narrative while she is in Kenya: during her transition from empirical to mythic mode of thought, she is also reading the *Arabian Nights* and composing tales that both Denys and her servants are always anxious to hear. Her exposure to an oral tradition and the ready audience for her oral narratives are clearly significant factors in the shaping of her imagination, voice, and her choice of the "tale" as the major vehicle of her art.

Her vision and imagination are best exemplified in the cock and chameleon incident that occurs when Dinesen finally accepts the inevitable—that she will have to sell her farm and leave Kenya. The imminent loss of her farm depresses her because she has no future plans or prospects, and because the pattern of her life has no coherence or meaning. Her life, she feels, cannot be completely chaotic, "but there must be some central principle within it. If I could find it, it would save me. If I looked in the right place, I reflected, the coherence of things might become clear to me. I must, I thought, get up and look for a sign" (*OA*, 368). In this mood she goes out to look for a sign and stumbles upon a cock that is about to pounce on a chameleon; but the latter, though frightened, sticks out its tongue as if in defiance, and the fowl, momentarily taken aback, strikes swiftly and plucks out the lizard's tongue. Since the chamelon, unable to gather food because of this loss, would die slowly and painfully, Dinesen mercifully kills it with a stone. A few days later she realizes that this incident had been the "most spiritual answer possible" to her call for an explanation. The powers "had stood on my dignity more than I had done myself, and what other answer could they then give? This was clearly not the hour for coddling, and they had chosen to connive at my invocation of it. Great powers had laughed to me, with an echo from the hills to follow the laughter, they had said among the trumpets, among the cocks and the chameleons, Ha, ha!" (*OA*, 370). The incident illustrates the fertility of her "polysynthetic" imagination and vision. Great significance and meaning are attached to an incident that would normally have been viewed as a common occurrence on a farm. The apparent randomness of the association of significance to the sign may be mitigated by Dinesen's awareness of the traditional function of the chameleon as the messenger of God in African and Gikuyu mythology.[31] An acute tendency to see correspondences everywhere would create a universe of prolific significations, which would be chaotic unless it were subordinated to some organizing structure. This chameleon-cock incident, then, reveals not only a superabundance of the polysynthetic imagination but also the acute desire for an organizing "central principle" that could save it from chaos.

The central organizing structure of her vision and her work is clearly stated in the opening pages of *Out of Africa:* "The Natives were Africa in flesh and blood. The tall extinct volcano of Langonot that rises above the Rift Valley, the broad Mimosa trees along rivers, the Elephant and Giraffe, were not more truly Africa than the Natives were. . . . All were different expressions of one idea, variations upon the same theme. It was not a congenial upheaping of heterogeneous atoms, but a heterogeneous upheaping of congenial atoms" (*OA*, 21). What constitutes the congeniality of the atoms, the unifying factor that underlies all this diversity, is never stated by Dinesen. But the substance is clearly magical: "When you have caught the rhythm of Africa," she says, "you find that it is the same in all her music. What I learned from the game of the country was useful to me in my dealings with the Native people" (*OA*, 16). That is, once you have found the secret of the congeniality of atoms, you can understand everything about Africa.

The central structure of the vision, then, is the radical metonymy which is subsumed under the characteristic "law of the *concrescence or coincidence of the members of a relation in mythical thinking* which can be followed through all its categories."[32] Under this general law, the postulated relations "are such that the elements which enter into them not only enter into a reciprocal ideal relationship, but become positively identical with one another, become one and the same *thing*." Thus in the category of quantity, "the part not only *stands for* the whole but positively *is* the whole." Similarly, in terms of quality there is "the same characteristic coincidence of the members of the relation: for mythical thinking the attribute is not one defining the aspect of the thing; rather, it expresses and contains within it the whole of the thing, seen from a different angle."[33] The *radical* nature of these mythical relations cannot be overstressed. Whereas in metonymy of conventional literary rhetoric the displacement takes place in the realm of the sign and the signified but not actually in the realm of the referent, in mythical thinking the displacement is real in all three realms.[34] Thus, for Dinesen the natives *are literally Africa in flesh and blood.* That Dinesen understands and is influenced by Gikuyu mythical thought is aptly illustrated by an incident where nine Gikuyu shift their allegiance from Protestantism to Catholicism. All the settlers explain this conversion by the theory that the natives had seen better prospects of making money by adherence to Catholicism, whereas Dinesen insists on the genuineness of the reason given by the Gikuyu. They had converted, she tells us, because they preferred the doctrine of transubstantiation to that of consubstantiation. In other words, they chose the theory of the Eucharist that reflected the law of concrescence or coincidence of the members of a relation.

The radical metonymy, then, is the primary structure of Dinesen's vision that provides organization and coherence to her autobiographies, for the overall "organization" of the two books is characterized by the pervasive mythical vision which is bound by mere facticity. Mythical consciousness "lacks" the ability to escape the power of phenomenal objectivity "by *measuring* it against something not given, something past or future."

> And if this mediate criterion is absent, all "truth" and reality dissolve into the mere presence of the content, all phenomena are situated on a single plane. Here there are no different *degrees* of reality, no contrasting degrees of objective certainty. The resultant picture of reality lacks the dimension of depth—the differentiation of foreground and background, so characteristically effected in the scientific concept with its distinction between "the ground" and that which is founded on it.[35]

Dinesen's autobiographies are situated on a single plane—they do not have "depth." The chronology of her two books is extremely vague, for events are recorded as they come to mind: the essential principle that constitutes the relation of events is contiguity. Similarly, there is no spatial depth: Dinesen does not distinguish between foreground and background. Nor is there any historical or personal teleology inherent in the organization of events. The books do not possess coherent *formal* structures. The only design that can be defined is constituted by the psychological and mythic structure of the consciousness.

As we have seen, this structure is characterized by the dynamic balance between the centripetal and the centrifugal tendencies of the relationship between Dinesen and the natives. This balance is a product of the interaction between the colonial situation and the openness of Dinesen's personality. If colonialism had not created a feudal society, the centripetal forces would not have been brought into play. Similarly, without Dinesen's strength of character and responsiveness, the centrifugal tendency would not have materialized (as is the case in most colonial relationships).

Just as the locus of the two tendencies is clearly Dinesen herself, so the source of the radical metonymy that constitutes the mythic structure is also her consciousness. The mythic mode is used to organize Dinesen's *experiences* of a diverse Africa in a metonymic manner. She excludes from her autobiographies all mention of unseemly or painful experience, such as her husband's desertion or her serious illness. She only includes those events that exude or are surrounded by blissful, uncomplicated, though at times, ironic emotions of an innocence regained. In this sense the events that comprise the autobiographies are not "a congenial upheaping of heterogeneous atoms, but a heterogeneous upheaping of congenial atoms." The experiences congeal in that blissful affective quality which is never stated but which is perhaps indicated by African laughter: "There are few things in life as sweet as this suddenly rising, clear tide of African laughter surrounding one" (*SG*, 102). Dinesen pays tribute to this emotional attribute, affirms the profundity of her African experience, and confirms her belief in name-magic by choosing "Isak" (meaning "laughter") as the first part of her pseudonym. The radical metonymy, therefore, provides the deep, mythic, as well as phenomenological, structure of Dinesen's autobiographies, while the more mundane literary metaphor of paradise furnishes the surface structure. The metonymic structure is the foundation upon which the various experiences and events of Dinesen's African life as well as her literary metaphors are scattered like so many heterogeneous atoms.

Nadine Gordimer

The Degeneration
of the Great South African Lie

ALTHOUGH THE "Republic" of South Africa is technically an independent country, it is, for all practical purposes, a European colony to the extent that its fundamental socio-political-economic structure is still the same as was that of other colonies: a large indigenous population is dominated, in the final analysis through military force, by a small number of European immigrants. In many respects, South Africa is the epitome of the worst aspects of colonialism: it has rigorously systematized and codified the inequality, oppression, and deprivation of the subjugated people in ways that are fairly well known. However, for readers who may be unfamiliar with the situation in that country, I shall provide a brief survey.

Apartheid (separateness), a socio-religious philosophy that furnishes tremendous economic benefits for its advocates, seeks to segregate the white community from the Africans, "Coloureds," and Indians in every aspect of life, to deprive the nonwhites of all legal, political, and economic power, and to keep them subjugated as long as possible. Coercive apartheid laws date as far back as 1856 when the Master and Servant laws made the breach of contract by or the "insubordination" of a nonwhite servant or laborer a *criminal* offense. Similarly, the infringement of the Pass laws, which control the African's mobility and residence, and the nature of his work, became a *criminal* rather than a *civil* violation.[1] Ludicrous as these laws may seem, they are rigorously enforced: for instance, in 1968–69 an average of 1,735 Africans were prosecuted *each day* for violating the Pass Laws.[2] The steady attack on the few legal rights of blacks culminated in the abolition of habeas corpus in 1976. The absolute authoritarian rigidity of the legal system and the paranoia of the white government are reflected in its decision to include "tampering with property" within the definition of sabotage (1962), which in turn is later subsumed under the definition of terrorism (1966).[3] Thus what would be petty theft in most countries could be interpreted as an act of terrorism in South Africa.

The denial of legal rights is, of course, matched by the deprivation of political freedom. In the first year of its accession to power in 1948, the Afrikaner Nationalist Government disfranchised Indian representation in Parliament and the Natal Provincial Council, and after a prolonged fight removed the "Coloured" voters from the Cape Province ballot in 1956.[4] Henceforth, the vote—and therefore the legal control of the nation—was the exclusive privilege of the white South African population which amounted to a mere 16.7 percent of the total in 1974.[5] The black Africans, of course, never had the vote, but all their efforts to organize themselves in order to press for some change have been systematically and ruthlessly thwarted. The attempt by the African National Congress (ANC) to voice its grievances through civil-rights campaigns led to the enactment of the Suppression of Communism Act (1950) and the Criminal Law Amendment Act (1953). The former outlaws, along with communism, any action that "aims at bringing about political, industrial, social or economic change within the Republic by the promotion of disturbance or disorder, by unlawful acts or omissions," whereas the latter act makes it an offense to violate any law "by way of protest or in support of any campaign against any law or in support of any campaign for the repeal or modification of any law."[6] In other words, any political action by the disfranchised nonwhites constitutes a criminal offense; even a protest against their political disfranchisement is a crime. Like the Pass laws, these political restrictions are systematically enforced by bannings (i.e., confining a person to particular areas), house arrests, imprisonments, torture, and death of the leaders of any resistance movement.

The social effect of such repression can be illustrated for our purposes by two brief examples. Various Pass laws, designed simultaneously to ensure the supply of black labor in urban and industrial areas and to prevent the migration and settlement of blacks in the cities, result in the disintegration of black families: for instance, the husband is forced to live in men's "hostels" in or near white residential areas while the wife and children are banished to the poverty-striken "Homelands." Another gauge of the social predicament of blacks is the deliberate restriction of their education by the government. The Nationalist education policy was unambiguously articulated in 1953 by Dr. Verwoerd, then Minister of Native Affairs:

When I have control of native education I will reform it so that natives will be taught from childhood that equality with Europeans is not for them. . . . People who believe in equality are not desirable teachers. . . .

There is no place for him (the Bantu) in the European community above the level of certain forms of labour. . . . For that reason it is of no avail for him to receive a training which has as its aim absorption into the European community.[7]

The implication of this policy is fairly clear: the African is not allowed to participate in "civilized" white society because he is considered an inferior savage, and his education is designed by his civilized superiors to ensure that he will continue to remain an inferior. In order to guarantee the mediocrity of African education Verwoerd threatened to cut the salaries of black teachers and in fact decreased the expenditure for black education from £8.54 per student in 1953 (compared to £63.18 per white student) to £6.15 by 1962. Verwoerd further disrupted African schools by making them use vernacular languages rather than English as mediums of instruction; because there were almost no text books in the seven vernacular languages, the effect on education was drastic. In 1947, before the Nationalist accession to power, 54.8 percent of the black students passed their matriculation exams, but that figure had dropped to 17.2 percent by 1960, after which point it began to rise again.[8]

As one might expect, these socio-political inequalities are determined and motivated by the desire of white South Africans to retain the vast bulk of the national wealth for themselves. According to the 1969 estimates blacks (68 percent of the population) received 18.8 percent of the personal cash income while whites (19.2 percent of the population) received 74 percent.[9] Contrary to one's expectations, this disparity is increasing rather than shrinking: whereas the difference between the average black and white wage was 2,435 rands per annum in 1969, by 1972 it had increased to 3,824 rands per annum.[10] This kind of economic gap is maintained by the Afrikaner's *political* control of socio-economic power. For instance, various forms of legally enforced racial job discrimination ensure that nonwhites are not allowed to practice certain professions, trade in white areas, or hold most skilled jobs.[11] Whites and nonwhites doing identical work are paid disproportionately according to their race and, of course, until recently nonwhites have not been allowed to form trade unions. The human effect of the resultant poverty and squalor is indicated by the black infant mortality rate for one to four year olds which is twenty-two times higher than the rate for whites, by the death of 50 percent of the children before the age of five in some African "Homelands," and by the fact that the income of 70 percent of the Africans in Johannesburg falls below the subsistence level for healthy living.[12]

The contemporary economic exploitation of nonwhites in South Africa has its ultimate roots in slavery and indentured servitude. As George Fredrickson has shown, preindustrial exploitation, based on a rather flexible and arbitrary racial discrimination, was skillfully adapted to the more systematic needs of gold mining in the 1880s and 1890s, which became the basis of industrialization in South Africa.[13] Because profitable exploitation of the low-grade gold ore would have been impossible without the coercive use of ultra-cheap Africa labor, modern industrial South Africa has been built up by a drastic syphoning of surplus value. The systemization of economic exploitation was paralleled by political consolidation of white power: "The emergence of segregationism as a deliberate public policy coincided quite closely with the establishment of a self-governing union in 1910."[14] And the triumph of the Nationalist Party in 1948 brought these economic and political tendencies to their logical conclusion. As Fredrickson notes, a majority of white South Africans persist in denying the principle of economic and political equality and in fact derive their sense of identity and security from an ideology of white supremacy.

This ideology justifying racism, which inevitably affects the fiction of Nadine Gordimer and Alex La Guma, has been termed the "Afrikaner Civil Religion" by T. D. Moodie. Derived from Calvinism, this "religion" claims that its adherents (mostly white South Africans of Dutch and Huguenot stock) are people elected by a sovereign and intensely active God who guides their destiny by shaping the mundane affairs of men.[15] Their election is defined against and tested by the threat of contamination from the English and the Africans. D. F. Malan, the first prime minister of the Afrikaner Nationalist Government, clearly characterizes the African threat: "God also willed that the Afrikaner People would be continually threatened by other Peoples. There was the ferocious barbarian who resisted the intruding Christian civilization and caused the Afrikaner's blood to flow in streams. There were times when as a result of this the Afrikaner was deeply despairing, but God at the same time prevented the swamping of the young Afrikaner People in the sea of barbarism."[16] The Afrikaner saw the Boer War as an attempt to destroy the elect society. Any suffering to which he is subjected is simultaneously considered a divine test and an assurance of God's favor; just as Christ's passion is followed by the resurrection, so the Great Trek was followed by the establishment of the Afrikaner Republics. This cycle of suffering and reward is infinite, so that any threat to his power now or in the future will be seen as another divine test. The Afrikaner is thus imbued with a resilient and self-perpetuating sense of superiority.

A series of English and African threats led to the systematic isolation and jealous protection of the purity of Afrikaner consciousness and culture. In time the uniqueness of their culture acquired a religious significance, and its separation from possibly contaminating agents became a sacred duty: anyone who tried to overcome their separation was considered demonic. Thus apartheid, the *civil* side of their religion, has become not just a metaphorical but a *literal* manichean doctrine which uses biblical notions about the tribe of Ham to support its view of the black man as an agent of evil: the terms used to describe Africans, "kaffir" and "bliksem," literally mean "infidel," or "evil other." Because racial differences are grounded in the divine act of creation, racial integration is not only foolish, it is sinful. Segregation is therefore justified because it is the corporeal manifestation of the divine will: apartheid as a social program, it would seem, is the implementation of God's plan. The sacred origin of apartheid also firmly insulates the doctrine from all human reason because the sufficient reasons for the election of the Afrikaner, and the subsequent damnation of the evil African, are not comprehensible to man, but only to God. Thus however arbitrary, cruel, and irrational the apartheid system may seem, it has its own divine meaning which is enacted by the elect.

Only if we thoroughly comprehend the "divine" nature of this "Civil Religion" can we appreciate the extremely close affinity between the apartheid system and German fascism, which influenced it during its codification in the 1930s,[17] as well as its rabid fear of integration and miscegenation which supposedly weaken the white race. Only with an understanding of apartheid's *quasi-metaphysical* (rather than the merely social or political) sense of superiority can we appreciate the power of the desire for separation expressed in the following *Die Transvaler* editorial:

> It is not so much the overwhelming number of non-Europeans but the destruction of the feeling of *difference* and *otherness* which is the great danger for the preservation of the European and his civilization in this multiracial land. As long as liberalistic bishops and canons,

professors, students, and politicians can freely attend church and hold meetings and socials together [with blacks], apartheid will be infringed in its marrow. (Italics mine)[18]

It would seem that in order to maintain this feeling of *difference* and *otherness,* which constantly reinforces the Afrikaner's sense of moral and metaphysical superiority and goodness, he is willing to suppress and exploit the black man as ruthlessly as necessary. The sense of superiority gained from this manichean polarization allows him to live happily amongst a host of moral and social contradictions: while claiming privileged access to Christian compassion, he denies humanity to the blacks; while worshiping justice, he practices racial discrimination; while claiming to be civilized, he tortures people who attempt to exercise their political rights; while arguing that he is developing Africa, he systematically retards African development, and exiles, tortures, and murders African intellectuals and artists; while pretending to be independent from the blacks and promoting "disinterested" theories of "separate development," he depends entirely on the exploitation of cheap African labor for his comfort and wealth; and while zealously fighting godless communist totalitarianism, he has in fact created the most ruthless, authoritarian, and systematically inhuman society in the contemporary world. It is within the context of this violent, antagonistic, and manichean society that we have to examine the fiction of Nadine Gordimer and Alex La Guma.

Unlike Cary and Dinesen who spent their formative years in Europe, Nadine Gordimer was born in 1923 in Springs, a small mining town near Johannesburg, and grew up in this stratified, bigoted, and manichean atmosphere of South Africa. Although her childhood was quite normal, she was caught in the contradictions of South African society from the beginning; despite being Jewish she was obliged to obtain her primary education in a convent. According to Gordimer, one of the immutable childhood experiences, which conditioned her perception and interpretation of the world and which later came to occupy the central position in her fiction, was the problem of racial difference: "To be born a South African is to be presented with *given* facts of race on the same level of reality as the *absolute* facts of birth and death." Yet she did not inherit the otherness of blacks as a *neutral* ontological fact, rather it was valorized for her in a manner that became profoundly problematic: "If you are [born] white, *you begin from the premise of being white.* Are they different because they are black? Or are they black because they are different?"[19] The experience was disturbing because it included the

implication that blackness was the external sign of a moral difference, a sign of punishment, an emblem of evil.

Unlike most white South Africans who adhere to this childlike
view of black alterity as a moral and metaphysical fact, Nadine
Gordimer was able to break away from the poverty of such an
ideology at a fairly early age. Even as a young student she was a
rebel. She repeatedly ran away from school because she disliked the
pressure of uniformity and the tyranny of regulation; her "bolting"
was a "dream-defense" which later "became the practical, sub-con-
scious cunning that enabled me to survive and grow in secret while
projecting a totally different camouflage image of my life." In the
course of her secret life, synonymous with her initial literary endeavor (she began writing fiction at the age of nine and published
her first story at sixteen), she educated herself about the real nature
of her society:

> I was looking for what people meant but did not say, not only about
> sex, but also about politics and their relationship with the black peo-
> ple among whom we lived as people live in a forest among trees. So
> it was that I didn't wake up to Africans and the shameful enormity
> of the colour bar through a youthful spell in the Communist Party,
> as did most of my contemporaries with whom I share the rejection of
> white supremacy, but through the apparently esoteric speleology of
> doubt, led by Kafka rather than Marx. And the "problems" of my
> country did not set me writing; on the contrary it was learning to
> write that sent me falling, falling through the surface of the South
> African way of life.[20]

While writing and educating herself, Nadine Gordimer experienced a radical psychological rupture which she calls a "second
birth"—she discovered the "great South African lie." The realization
that white society was trying to conceal the simple fact that blacks
were people led her to understand that her identity as a South
African had to be formed through a resolution of the black/white
dichotomy, that the two races had to be unified under a central,
definitive experience of black-and-white as people with undifferentiated claims to life, whatever else—skin, language, culture—might
distinguish them from one another. The actual revelation may have
been an epiphanic one, although Gordimer does not provide a specific
location for it in her autobiographical statements, but the consolidation of her new identity became a prolonged process of fictive and
discursive analysis of ideological and political motives of apartheid,
which has preoccupied her ever since. Her personal contacts with
blacks afforded her emotional comprehension of the effects on them

of the fears and hatred projected by whites and of the mutual dependencies and demands of the two races. She also learned a great deal from her white liberal and radical friends in the antiapartheid struggle. She singles out in particular an Afrikaner woman, an organizer of racially mixed trade unions (who seems to be the model for Anna Loew in *A World of Strangers*), from whom Gordimer learned that "we [South African] whites are not Europeans and that in order to be *anything* we must change profoundly." In her novels, Gordimer reflects her agreement with this observation by subjecting the white South African consciousness to a prolonged analysis, with a weary eye on the privileges and ease which "subconsciously hamper the will to change."[21]

The analysis of South African ideology and the tracing of its connection with European liberalism as well as the attempts to change white consciousness and define a new identity have been aired by Gordimer in a few discursive, analytic articles and interviews,[22] but the preoccupation with these issues has predominantly manifested itself in her imaginative work. The eight novels and some of the short stories she has written thus far constitute a map of the frontier area of black/white relations in South Africa. Her fiction is a direct response to the moral dilemma created for her by the manichean bifurcation of apartheid society which has refined the essential characteristics of colonialism to their pure fascistic embodiment. The more she writes the more radical her analysis becomes. This unflinching and deepening commitment in her fiction is paralleled by an explicit refusal to divorce politics from literature. When asked in an interview by Andrew Salkey whether or not she is offended by the intrusion of politics in her ("protest") fiction, Gordimer replied that the effects of politics permeate even the most private sector of people's lives and that because her writing draws from the substance of society around her, the fiction naturally includes South African politics.[23] She goes on to imply that her opposition to apartheid sustains her as a South African writer, that she could never manage to commit herself to the same degree in another country if she moved, and finally she acknowledges that she uses her fiction as a weapon against apartheid. Her books, however, are not polemical or propagandistic; on the contrary, the more radical her critique, the better her writing becomes.

Yet her clear-sighted and realistic commitment and attempt to arrive at an "honest answer, without self-pity for the whites or sentiment about the blacks," involve her in a series of personal contradictions which are refractions of the larger contradictions of South

African society: she finds that her skin color implies that she is an oppressor of blacks, yet her liberal, at times radical, views make the whites see her as a traitor; she is caught between a desire to leave South Africa, thereby avoiding the whole dilemma of racism, and a terrible, obstinate, and fearful desire to stay—"I feel the one desire with my head the other with my guts";[24] finally, she finds that the black militants' increasing rejection of liberal or radical white cooperation is a phenomenon that she understands rationally and even accepts as necessary, but that she is hurt emotionally by this racial rejection. Like her search for a new white South African identity, these contradictions are also responsible for the substance and shape of her novels; her white protagonists' repeated departures for Europe at the end of many of her novels reflect the tensions of her conflicting desires. Nadine Gordimer's fiction, as we shall see, is fraught with the moral problems and anxieties of an intelligent and enlightened white consciousness which has severed its ties with what it considers to be a bankrupt European liberalism and which, in spite of itself, is committed to endure a hideously bifurcated and explosive South African society.

One of Gordimer's first short stories defines in bold outline the fundamental problem that the rest of her fiction elaborates. In "Is There Nowhere Else Where We Can Meet?" she presents us with a young white woman walking through the countryside in the morning. Through the girl's fine, intellectual, moral, and aesthetic sensibility Gordimer depicts her idyllic and sensual communion with nature. Suddenly disturbed by an encounter with a desperate, hungry, and tired black man dressed in tatters, her initial reaction to this antithesis of herself is a guilty recognition of how material deprivation has rendered him dull, which contrasts with her own alertness. However, when he chases and menacingly confronts her, she is gripped by an abject fear: "For a moment it was Fear itself that had her by the arms, the legs, the throat; not fear of the man, of any single menace he might present, but Fear, absolute, abstract. If the earth had opened up in fire at her feet, if a wild beast had opened its terrible mouth to receive her, she could not have been reduced to less than she was now." This fear of the other—of an alterity that, Gordimer insists through the imagery of Hell and wild animals, is not sociological but rather ontological—robs the articulate, sensitive protagonist of her reason: she makes animal sounds, gibbers, and is unable to scream. However, she is soon relieved when, in a brief tussle, she realizes that the threat is not sexual or even personal, that the man only wishes to possess her money and a small parcel that

she is carrying. She escapes, leaving the man with her material possessions, and briefly contemplates calling the police as soon as she
reaches some houses. But upon rational reconsideration she changes
her mind: "Why did I fight, she thought suddenly. What did I fight
for? Why didn't I give him the money and let him go?"[25]

In this short allegorical story Nadine Gordimer opposes the wealth
and education of the whites to the poverty and subsequent intellectual and spiritual deprivation of the blacks, and, by centering that
opposition on the manichean fears, she emphasizes the precarious
balance of the antagonistic forces. Yet by endowing her protagonist
with an intelligent sympathy for the socio-economic condition of the
blacks and by stressing her refusal to call the police, Gordimer indicates her commitment to a search for that other moral and socio-
economic location where the whites and blacks can meet as dignified
equals. The girl's final refusal to call the police, her decision not to
hide behind the legal and military barrier that apartheid uses to separate whites from blacks, the self from the other, and her willingness
to relinquish some of her material possessions represent her lack of
prejudice and her reflexive open-mindedness, which become the basis
of Gordimer's search. Similarly, the contrast between the pathos and
regret of the titular question and the actual violence and fear in the
story briefly defines the essence of Gordimer's attitude toward the
harsh antagonisms of South African society. The allegorical story
traces the territory that is subsequently explored and charted in detail
by her eight novels.

The development of Gordimer's fiction is divisible into three
stages: the bourgeois phase, which includes *The Lying Days* (1953),
A World of Strangers (1958), and *Occasion for Loving* (1960); the
postbourgeois phase, comprised of *The Late Bourgeois World* (1966),
A Guest of Honour (1970), and *The Conservationist* (1972); and the
revolutionary phase, consisting of her two latest novels *Burger's
Daughter* (1979) and *July's People* (1981). The three novels in the
first group examine different facets of a struggle between liberal
bourgeois values inherited by the characters and the horrors of apartheid. Whereas all these novels end with the protagonists recoiling in
shock from the fascism of South African society, the novels in the
second group conclude similar struggles with a more definite, if at
times implicit rather than explicit, rejection of bourgeois values, and
the characters commit themselves more openly to forces opposed to
apartheid. Finally, in *Burger's Daughter* and *July's People*, both set

in imagined political and military revolutions in South Africa itself, the characters are faced with the dilemma of choosing sides in the revolutions and redefining their identities in nonbourgeois terms. The slow political evolution implied in the development of these phases— the repeated examination of the same problems and values from different angles and the hesitancy in accepting the logically inevitable new positions and values—constitutes one of the strengths of Gordimer's fiction. Her reluctance to abandon easily the values that have been so useful in the European liberal tradition allows her to examine in a painstakingly thorough manner their efficacy for the present and future. Thus her final rejection of the liberal creed is all the more convincing.

Gordimer's first novel, *The Lying Days*,[26] an experiential, though not factual, autobiographical *bildungsroman*, focuses on the sexual, political, imaginative, and, most importantly, the moral growth of its heroine, Helen Shaw, in the South African society before and after the Afrikaner Nationalist Government came to power (1949). Gordimer, however, does not examine her character's development in isolation: just as society provides the context for Helen's growth, so the heroine's problems and struggles are a comment on the social malaise of the country. In fact, in all of Gordimer's novels the relation between individual and society is symbiotic; the repeated demonstration that one cannot isolate the private from the public, as well as an examination of the problems caused by the manichean racial bifurcation, forms the chief common denominators of her fiction. The successful symbiosis between the personal and the political prevents her writing from deteriorating into propaganda and, in fact, constitutes its major strength. In *The Lying Days* the deliberate variety and the careful selection of individuals who mediate Helen's development ensure the irrevocable infusion of political concern in her moral growth. Yet, as we shall see, Gordimer's experiment leads to the ironic conclusion that in South Africa, moral growth can be attained only at the cost of radical alienation from self and society.

Gordimer begins the first section of the novel, "The Mine," with a terse demonstration of a child's ability to accept alterity and to mythologize it easily into polar opposites of black/evil and white/good. The latter tendency is thoroughly reinforced by Helen's white bourgeois environment. Oblivious to sharp contrasts between black poverty and white wealth, Helen passes her teen-age years in a state of physical well-being and an atmosphere of moral and intellectual sloth. This section ends with a brilliant image of Helen's and the community's superficial lives being reflected by the surface of a pool of water, while the linked questions of sex and race are successfully relegated to Helen's subconscious as represented by the mine. These two images become an analogue of Helen's psyche: substantial feelings and desires are located in the subterranean darkness, while life on the surface continues its shallow and uninformed ritual. Gordimer succinctly and clearly shows how the petit-bourgeois world of fixed values and daily routine dulls Helen's mind and renders moral growth impossible.

In the second section of the novel, "The Sea," which continues the elaborate water/mirror imagery of birth, fecundity, and exposure, Gordimer presents us with the evolution of Helen's internal life. In perfect consonance with the paucity of life in the mining town, Helen's growth is predicated on her discovery of the nature of lack. Her affair with Ludi, who rejects both apartheid and bourgeois values, arouses her dormant consciousness into intelligent self-awareness. Trying to recall every detail of their first kiss, Helen begins to understand that her sexual desire (and desire in general) is based on a lack that will never be absolutely satisfied. This recognition quickly leads to a broader realization that life in the mining community had been "conducted on a surface of polite triviality that was insensitive to the real flow of life that was being experienced underneath, all the time, by everybody" (*TLD*, 62). Having loved the man, she accepts what she initially perceives as his abhorrent political views. Thus love, sex, and politics, the most private and the most public, are inextricably combined in the inception of Helen's moral development. After Helen's return to the mine, Ludi's absence initiates the most significant period of her growth. Now unhappy with the social life of the town, she increasingly withdraws into her imagination in order to be with him, and thus, in time, she discovers her own abstract potentiality. In the infinitely rich world of her imagination her attention gradually shifts from Ludi to a larger arena: in order to fight the intellectual sloth and boredom of the mine she voraciously reads European and American writers and thereby discovers a more profound lack—the poverty of the white South African culture. In this initial definition of colonialist society, a phenomenon that Gordimer will examine repeatedly, she stresses its suppression of African culture and its inability to sustain the richness of European art and values (*TLD*, 82). Having allegorized the African and European worlds into stylized, abstract opposites of the evil and good societies, the colonial culture deprives itself of any possible synthesis and condemns itself to a paltry reality that can be no more than a shallow, calcified version of Europe, for its attempt to imitate European values and culture quickly turns into empty snobbery and pretension. Helen's experience of this cultural poverty propels her to the university in Johannesburg in order to discover a more substantial world and self.

With Helen's search for her identity begins the ironic pattern of her growth. As she progressively defines the correct behavior for self and society, as she attempts to live according to these beliefs, and as her moral consciousness develops, she becomes further alienated from herself and her community. The gap between inner and outer, between moral awareness and social actuality, which had fascinated her, continues to grow. After Helen's brief and fruitless encounter with some liberal students, Gordimer mediates her heroine's growth and alienation through three distinct individuals so that Helen is exposed to and enriched by the diversity of possibilities.

Although she does not fully realize it until the end of the novel, Helen is in love with Joel, an astute, self-confident young Jew. Gordimer uses him as a critical mirror for Helen: "I had the curious feeling that he saw me as nobody else had ever seen me" (TLD, 127). At every turn in her life Joel advises and supports Helen; he bolsters her sagging self-confidence, makes her aware of her potential, and persuades her to have faith in her search. In spite of a strong mutual attraction, their relationship is never consummated because they are unable to overcome their own internalization of ethnic barriers that will not tolerate the union of a Jew and a gentile.

The second mediator is a more explicit inverted mirror image of Helen. She first sees Mary Seswayo, one of the few black women at the university, in a mirror, and as their glances meet, Helen for the first time recognizes—in the other woman's face—her own idealistic anticipation of boundless intellectual stimulation and infinite justice that she expects the university to offer. This friendship allows Gordimer to explore the intellectual and personal dilemma of morally sensitive white South Africans. Helen easily concludes that apartheid has denied blacks not only decent wages and social freedom but even love, jealousy, concern, friendship, and personal pride, in short, "everything that made us human" (TLD, 144). However, unsatisfied with this accurate but easy insight, Gordimer goes on to depict brilliantly the moral conflict between selfishness and altruism. Having given Mary a ride to her shack in a shantytown, Helen imaginatively projects herself into Mary's life. The resultant emotional and existential comprehension of the black predicament provokes an apparently perverse reaction: immediately after dropping Mary, Helen deliberately relishes a sumptuous meal and makes love in a cold, casual, and impersonal manner to her male companion whom she does not find particularly attractive. Guilt and fear of her own implication in the exploitation of blacks cause Helen to take refuge in self-indulgence: it is easier to be selfish than to be altruistic. Whereas Gordimer implies that most white South Africans would permanently resolve such a conflict, as Helen initially does, by becoming callous and egotistic, she allows Helen neither to escape into a world of personal desires nor to rush into an equally self-indulgent rebellion. On the contrary, she continues to confine Helen within the bounds of this moral dilemma in order to explore unflinchingly the alienation that moral growth necessarily implies in a society built on the great lie of racial superiority and inferiority, of opulence and abject poverty. Helen's sustained quandary results in her more deliberate, explicit awareness of alienation of self and society. Later, while meditating about Mary's social situation, Helen comprehends her alienation in a strong epiphanic experience: "I had an almost physical sensation of being a stranger in what I had always taken unthinkingly as the familiarity of home. I felt myself among strangers; I had grown up, all my life among strangers: the Africans, whose language in my ears had been like the barking of dogs or the cries of birds" (*TLD*, 167–68).

Thus for Gordimer (and Helen), as for Cary and Dinesen, the central social experience of colonial society is that of the "stranger" (her second novel, *A World of Strangers*, is a more systematic exploration of this phenomenon). Like Dinesen, Gordimer too realizes that the "home" culture, in this case the white South African society, will never lead you to question the fundamental assumptions on which it is based. Like Dinesen's experience, Gordimer's, as we shall see, also leads to a dissolution of the self and to a second birth; that is, it leads to the beginning of a new identity and the rejection of the racist notion that the inferiority of Africans is quasi-ontological. Gordimer, however, does not pursue this experience to its mystical, quasi-divine climax, as Dinesen does. Rather, in deference to the political realities of South Africa, she admirably confines her protagonists, and therefore herself, to the difficult and painful space between their own commitment to the eradication of the distance between self and other and their realistic awareness that the antagonism between self and other *is* the entrenched foundation of apartheid ideology.

Because in all her novels Gordimer is more interested in *existential* moral awareness rather than in mere *intellectual* understanding, she makes sure that her characters thoroughly experience their predica-

ments. Consequently, Helen is forced to experience even more profound alienation before her education is considered complete. She is
shocked once again when her parents are outraged by her proposal
that Mary be allowed to stay with them during the exams. In deference to their racism she even suggests that Mary could sleep in a
lean-to, a space "for things that [have] no place." Their intransigence
drives her to leave home, and the effects of apartheid are thus seen
to penetrate gradually into the personal realm. Just as Helen had
wanted to bring Mary into a no-man's land—neither in black nor in
white society—so she too now moves out toward the same frontier.
Both of them converge as moral orphans of apartheid: Helen becomes
an orphan because she rejects her racist parents and Mary because
apartheid laws will not allow her parents to live with her in Johannesburg. But in spite of Helen's obvious attraction toward her inverted image, the practical problems created by apartheid laws prevent her from continuing her friendship with Mary. The political
superficiality of a liberal group of students, with whom Helen
fraternizes after she can no longer see Mary, convinces her that she
has to reject "the nurturing of sterile gentility" and the bourgeois
habit of making the necessities of life the whole business of living
(*TLD*, 216, 187).

This insight is followed by an even more profound personal experience of apartheid made possible through the mediation of Paul,
a noble (bright, handsome, charming) young white man from Rho-
desia whose fluent mastery of Zulu and Sesuto and whose job as welfare officer for Africans make him less of a "stranger" in South
Africa than the rest of the liberals. Helen falls madly in love with
him, and they happily live together for some time. Her love for Paul,
like her attraction toward Ludi, is based on a combination of personal and political appeal. However, Gordimer ominously surrounds
the blissful, bursting happiness of Helen and Paul with the increasing
oppression of blacks under the first Afrikaner Nationalist government led by Malan (1949). Through Paul's work, Gordimer depicts
and allows Helen to experience the graphic details of African hard-
ships under a fascist government (see the description in *TLD*, 233,
235, 241, 244). Given the sympathetic personalities of Paul and
Helen, the political oppressiveness of South Africa soon impinges on
their personal relationship. Gordimer focuses on the most symbolically significant infringement of the private realm by public events
through the effects of the Mixed Marriage Act on Helen and Paul.
This act, passed by the Nationalists soon after their accession to
power, prohibits interracial marriage or cohabitation and gives the

police complete freedom to invade homes in order to enforce the law. Paul relates to Helen the humiliating details of police entering the bedrooms of various "Coloured" people with whom he has been working as a welfare officer. Paul and Helen's horror of such invasion demoralizes them and even interferes with their lovemaking. Gordimer's insistence that private and public realms of life are, in the final analysis, inseparable, goes beyond the actual physical relationship of the two lovers. While Helen is falling asleep after making love to Paul, car headlights that flash through their window remind her of the search lights of police enforcing the Mixed Marriage Act. In the subsequent semiconscious dream, her mind associates the present disgust with a previous incident when Joel had to scrape off a condom from the heel of her shoe. Her recall of this incident fills her with shame, as it had not done at the time.[27] This association represents Gordimer's firm conviction that in a police state such as South Africa even the purest, most platonic relationship is not exempt from moral contamination.

In the long run, the practical disruption of the lovers' relationship by fascist politics is more significant than the symbolic violation of Helen's sexual and emotional privacy. Both Paul and Helen know that his work as a welfare officer, while alleviating the miseries of a small number of black individuals, is in fact implicitly supporting the continuation of apartheid by reconciling Africans to their political disfranchisement. In order to continue his work Paul has to pretend that it has some meaning, although he knows that it will not give Africans an education, skilled jobs, political self-determination, or even the right to build their own houses. While Paul cannot extricate himself from this double bind, Helen begins to understand that their lives, based on the incorrect assumption that they will soon win the *temporary* war against apartheid, cannot tolerate indefinitely the contradiction of fighting a massive, permanent war with Paul's faith in meliorism. Their problems are further complicated by the government's threat to dismiss Paul if he continues to consort with "radical" Africans. The contradiction between Paul's desire to continue working for the government *and* to help the radicals renders him increasingly irritable and irrational, and eventually leads to the destruction of the relationship with Helen. She finds that she can live with him only if she avoids their irrational predicament. The disintegration of their affair marks the climax of Gordimer's demonstration that in a fascist state not a single facet of the private life of a morally aware person is immune from political contamination. The highly charged manichean paranoia of the apartheid government is responsible for Paul's inability to combine meliorism with a more fundamental struggle for African rights, which in turn is what causes Helen to stifle herself in order to save their relationship. In this ironic twist Gordimer is able to show convincingly that apartheid can even turn love into a prison.

The dramatic climax of the novel, marked by the coincidence of a series of events—Helen's resignation from her meaningless secretarial job at the welfare office, the general strike against apartheid, the riot, the death of her black friend, and the imminent break between Helen and Paul—is closely followed by the climax of Helen's moral development. Gordimer's irony is strongest at this point, for the culmination of Helen's "education," her realization of the pernicious and persistent power of apartheid and the complete divestiture of her idealistic naiveté and faith, coincides with the nadir of her demoralization, with the utter dejection and alienation that are mirrored by a whole month of aimless, confused inertia in Paul's apartment. Gordimer uses the convergence of enlightenment and demoralization to show that apartheid causes most significant damage not by its violent physical oppression but through the spiritual and psychological depression it produces in sensitive individuals.

The climax and nadir are followed by a brief period of consolidation and resolution before the end of the novel. Choosing the only apparent way out of the morass, a break with Paul and departure from South Africa, Helen decides to leave for England. Although she feels that she can overcome self-alienation, she knows that she cannot reconcile herself to apartheid: "It's like—like having a picnic in a beautiful graveyard where people are buried alive under your feet. I always think locations [African townships] are like that: dreary, smoking hells out of Dante, peopled with live men and women. —I can't stand any more of it. If I can't be in it, I want to be free of it. Let it be enough for me to contend with myself" (*TLD*, 331). However, her struggle with herself and society is once more mediated by the black other. On the night before her departure she sees through her window a group of young black minstrels playing an "infinitely mournful, infinitely longing" popular song which suddenly calms her agitation. Through this symbol of hope and joy, of *art*, in the midst of human suffering and misery, her attitude and decision are changed:

My mind was working with great practicalness, and I thought to myself: Now it's all right. I'm not practicing any sort of self-deception any longer. And I'm not running away. Whatever it was I was running away from—the risk of love? the guilt of being white? the danger of

putting ideals into practice?—I'm not running away from now because I know I'm coming back here.

I was twenty-four and my hands were trembling with the strong
satisfaction of having accepted disillusion as a beginning rather than
an end: the last and the most enduring illusion; the phoenix illusion
that makes life always possible. (*TLD*, 340)

Having resisted the temptation of an exclusively personal salvation,
Gordimer ends the novel with a deliberately anti-Joycean refusal of
permanent exile and political disengagement.

The rest of Gordimer's six novels can be seen as various avatars
of the phoenix—as repeated attempts to elucidate and define the
liberal white South African consciousness that is trying to overcome
the manichean bifurcation of society. Almost all her novels end in
various forms of disillusion, but she always returns to the same concerns. Helen's refusal to abandon South Africa is another facet of
Gordimer's refusal to disregard the injustice and the human misery
caused by apartheid; Helen's conflict between the desire to leave
South Africa and the desire to stay is a reflection of Gordimer's similar conflict. The power and the persistence of these antithetical feelings, that is, her obligation to fight apartheid and her wish to avoid
the whole problem, the heroic struggle of her conscience, can be
measured by the fact that all of her novels close with progressively
profounder analyses of these contradictory desires.

Gordimer's next novel, *A World of Strangers*,[28] returns to the
same themes: the political and moral growth of a liberal protagonist
and the social effects of apartheid. However, this novel contains two
major departures from the previous one. Whereas Helen's moral
growth and alienation are slow, complex, and deliberate processes
dominated by Gordimer's irony, *A World of Strangers* presents us
with relatively dramatic changes in the consciousness of an already
mature, sophisticated, detached, and *formed* Englishman. The result
is a clearer and sharper statement about individualism and social responsibility in South Africa. Second, whereas *The Lying Days* is a
fairly straightforward *bildungsroman*, the second novel contains a
more intricate structure of relationships. Gordimer uses a "stranger,"
Toby Hood, a young Englishman without racial prejudice, as the
central character of the novel in order to explore in a more dramatic,
stylized, and symmetrical manner the effects of manichean antagonism on the liberal sensibility of an emancipated European.

With the exception of Toby, the stylized characters in the novel
stand for various principles or attitudes. This, however, does not
mean that they are poorly or imperfectly drawn characters as Robert

F. Haugh has suggested.[29] On the contrary, the limited representation, verging at times on caricature, is perfectly consonant with the central meaning of the novel: in a world of strangers, in an apartheid society predicated on stereotypes, one is only able to glimpse a restricted, incomplete view of others. Furthermore, Gordimer's use of two major characters, Steven and Cecil, as leitmotifs of Toby, that is, as characters who reenact his preoccupations in substantially different contexts, results in an expressionist presentation of characters.

The four major characters with whom Toby becomes involved are arranged symmetrically around him: the characters are divided in two politically opposed groups—Steven and Cecil are self-indulgent and apolitical whereas Sam and Anna are self-sacrificing and politically committed; Toby is caught in his shifting sexual attraction for two white women, Cecil and Anna; and the two white women racially balance Toby's affection for the two black men, Steven and Sam. Because Toby narrates the events of the novel from a limited first-person viewpoint and because all the characters are connected with each other through his experience and judgment of them, the symmetries are converted into a series of triangular relationships with Toby always at the center. As the events of the novel shift and change so do the triangular relations, with the result that the novel becomes a kaleidoscope reflecting different patterns of socio-political attitudes and stances: the readjustment of a few basic elements—in this case the socio-political attitudes being examined—creates a series of complex configurations that reveal the range of possible permutations. The character stylization is enhanced by a symmetrical arrangement of cityscapes and social life. Gordimer deliberately and systematically contrasts white suburbs with African "locations," the sumptuous meals, the material luxury, and the ease of European life in South Africa with the poverty, squalor, and harshness of life in black ghettos (compare, for instance, the party at the "High House," p. 133, with the one in an African "location," p. 123). In this novel Gordimer has found a structure that is perfectly suited for showing how the limited range of political and racial attitudes in a manichean society affects an intelligent, self-aware stranger.

Gordimer centers this shifting world on Toby, who represents the best aspects of the liberal, humanistic Anglo-Saxon culture. His native intelligence, self-awareness, and innate sense of decency are augmented by his inheritance of the empirical tradition: he is cynical but thoroughly open-minded and devoutly committed to judgment based on personal experience. His open-mindedness, particularly the lack of racial prejudice, makes him a "stranger" in the context of

South African bigotry: he does not espouse the manichean valorizations of apartheid. But he does share with the white South Africans
one of the basic tenets of Western liberalism: the right of the individual to pursue his happiness, to fulfill his desires, and to realize his
potential. The irony, of course, is that whereas in England no one is
barred *categorically* from the pursuit of these humanist ideals, in
South Africa over three-quarters of the population is systematically
prevented from pursuing *any* goals or desires. Once more Gordimer
creates a context in which she can examine the contradictions between the ideals of Western humanism and its complicity in the
development of a fascist state.

The genesis of Toby's dedication to liberal individualism and to
self-fulfillment symbolically identifies the source of this cultural
contradiction, particularly as it is developed in the context of European colonization. Toby grows up in an English household obses-
sively committed to defending the rights of all oppressed people—
from German refugees in the first war, through the Spanish Civil
War (his father fought for the Republicans), to the various independence struggles in India and Africa. Young Toby's impressionistic
world is full of mountains of political pamphlets, innumerable radical
visitors, endless committees, letters to newspapers, and political
rallies which have no bearing on his personal life. So in reaction to
what he perceives as an abstract and stultifying preoccupation with
political ideology, he dedicates his life to the enjoyment of personal
experience and the satisfaction of his desires.

In this rather brief presentation of Toby's background, Gordimer
implies that Western democracies have forgotten the origins of their
freedom. Once political and personal freedoms have been consolidated (in written or unwritten constitutions) after prolonged and
bitter historical struggles, they are so taken for granted that one becomes oblivious of the interdependence of personal and political liberty and consequently callous to other people's fights for political
freedom. Thus the just pride of European countries in their democratic governments did not prevent them from imposing autocratic
rule on their colonies. Yet Gordimer's treatment of this contradiction
contains a delicate and optimistic ambivalence. On the one hand, she
implies that the disjunction between personal and political freedom
is a product of historical amnesia, yet on the other hand she shows
that Toby's familial, "ideological" heritage, along with his experience
in South Africa, eventually allows him to understand the personal
value of political freedom. In other words, a proper appreciation of
history will liberate the European from this contradiction. (Gordi-

mer's next novel, *Occasion for Loving*, is a more systematic exploration of this problem.)

The mirror imagery of *The Lying Days* becomes the structural principle of *A World of Strangers*. Toby discovers the limitations of his self-indulgence by watching its reflection in Cecil and Steven who in their own ways are consummate narcissists. Constantly emanating "the incense of the rites of female self-worship," Cecil has become an object of her own desires. Her narcissism symbolizes the white South Africans' valorization of themselves as the only politically and morally sound culture and their complete disregard for the welfare of other races. Like Cecil's superfluous celebration of self, which eschews all contact with the external world, the white South Africans too worship their election to salvation. Gordimer shows that the fate of unrestrained self-indulgence and narcissism in Cecil's white world is complete alienation from reality. Similarly, she uses Steven to demonstrate the results of the same pursuit in a black world that is drastically limited and impoverished by apartheid. He refuses to be involved in antiapartheid organizations or even to imitate the bourgeois culture, as his black friends do by acquiring small shacks in the ghetto, because the material deprivation imposed by apartheid exacts too high an emotional cost for such investments. Instead, he successfully dedicates his life to creating an image of himself as a carefree, sophisticated dandy, and cultivates a romantic image of himself as a black man who has mastered the poise and self-confidence that white South Africans have developed because of their personal and political freedom. Because Steven is unable to fulfill his desires due to the restrictions imposed on him by apartheid, he is forced to fashion himself into a mask of his own desires. But his pretensions, like Cecil's, do not provide substantial satisfaction, and he loses himself in pursuit of a carefree, indulgent individualism: he is killed while escaping from a police raid on an illegal Indian drinking club. In the final analysis, he throws away his life in pursuit of an illusory self-image. The shock of his friend's death forces Toby to recognize himself in Steven and leads to a crystallization of his relationships with Anna, an ostracized lawyer working for the civil rights of blacks, and Sam, who is always sacrificing his personal comfort and ambitions for the welfare of his extended family. Both are diametrically opposed to Cecil and Steven, and Toby finds himself increasingly attracted by their altruism. While mourning Steven's death at Sam's house, he suddenly becomes aware that his commitment to these two people may be the destiny that he knew would someday claim him. He has thus come a full circle to realize the value of his historical and familial heritage: "I felt myself suddenly within the world of dispossession, where the prison record is a mark of honour, exile is home, and family a committee of protest— that world I had watched, from afar, a foreign country, since childhood" (*AWOS*, 253).

Yet unlike *The Lying Days*, this novel is not content with merely showing the moral development of its protagonist. Gordimer insists that the lesson learnt from the symmetry of opposites be committed to memory. At the end of the novel Toby temporarily leaves Johannesburg with two newspaper cuttings in "polarity" in his wallet. One is an account of Anna's arrest on a charge of treason (in fact she is arrested for giving legal advice to an organization of African women), and the other is a story about a charity cabaret arranged by Cecil and her husband after their wedding. Toby's commitment to Anna's cause, it seems, will remain stronger if he keeps in mind the experience and the image of the abandoned narcissism. His allegiance is also reinforced by his promise to Sam that he will return in time to become the godfather of his friend's child. The symbolism of the final scene underscores the future realization of that promise. Once more Gordimer ends her novel with the tension between the desire to leave and the desire to stay, though clearly the latter commitment is far stronger in this book than in the previous one: unlike Helen, whose promise to return is rather vague, Toby is dedicated to specific people, and his promise to Sam is made under the watchful eyes of an Afrikaner policeman.

A World of Strangers thus defines Toby's experience in political and historical rather than in general cultural or racial terms. Although the whole South African culture is a strange world for Toby, he specifically identifies three people as "strangers": Steven, Cecil, and himself. Anna and Sam are never classified as such even though their philosophy and commitments are initially alien for Toby. The novel therefore emphasizes the fact that black and white individuals who ignore the *political* aspects of the world are the real strangers in South Africa (and perhaps elsewhere too). Toby's experience of alienation is a rite of political passage that allows him to become a more complex and complete person. Thus for Gordimer, as for Dinesen, this experience is liberating: it is positive and opens up new horizons and provides an entrance to a world richer and more complex than the one that preceded the "second birth." However, whereas Dinesen's experience results in an abstract, mystical unity in a mythical world, Gordimer's results in an increasingly complex awareness of the historical realm. In her world the new identity can only be consolidated through a systematic analysis and understanding of one's cultural and personal history, in this case of the bourgeois liberal heritage.

Gordimer's next novel, *Occasion for Loving*,[30] focuses on the problems of historical responsibility and amnesia. In fact, this ambitious novel sets out to examine the nature of the *occasion* for loving as it is defined by contradictions between two fundamental matrices of human endeavor: the diachronic and the synchronic. Gordimer's novel scrutinizes the relevance, importance, and culpability of the Western development of these two matrices for the specific problems and conditions of South Africa; she analyzes the causes and effects of apartheid in terms of an awareness and acceptance of historical heritage and in terms of a more detached, atemporal, structuralist-scientific approach to society. Through a juxtaposition of these two major components of Western culture she is able to show that the particular configuration of apartheid and other colonial societies is produced by a studied negation of the democratic tendencies inherent in the development of Western countries and valorized by their histories.

Nadine Gordimer is able to ensure the success of this highly abstract undertaking by presenting her characters as specific, concrete human beings as well as analogues of larger cultural forces. Her characteristic ability to depict people and places, the psychological and social aspects of reality, with great clarity and precision prevents both the concrete and the analogic levels of meaning from overwhelming each other. The consequent balance and tension result in a brilliant novel that can be read simultaneously as a tragic love story and as an analysis of the effects of the contradiction between the diachronic and the synchronic on the South African "occasion," that is, on the possibilities of love and compassion in a manichean society.

Once again Gordimer's characterization is stylized, though not as dramatically as in the previous novel. Tom Stilwell, a historian, and his wife, Jessie, are analogues of the historic, communally oriented, diachronic tendencies, whereas Boaz Davis, a musicologist studying primitive African music, and his wife, Ann, are analogues of scientific, individually oriented, synchronic tendencies; the Stilwells have been born and bred in South Africa and are committed to staying there, whereas the Davises (who are living with the Stilwells while in South Africa), though born in southern Africa, have been living in Europe and plan to return as soon as Boaz's research is completed. The stylization is further enhanced by differences in the male/female functions within the analogic representations. Tom and Boaz respectively embody the objective, theoretical concerns of the diachronic and synchronic tendencies, whereas Jessie and Ann manifest them through their subjective, internalized, and personal actions and preoccupations. The major cast of analogic characters is completed by the introduction of Gideon Shibalo, a black painter, who represents the black South African conflict between historic and ahistoric tendencies, and who activates the plot of the novel by falling in love with Ann.

The theoretical side of the diachronic tendencies is represented by Tom's current project—a history of the European invasion of Africa that will neither valorize European superiority nor romanticize precolonial African cultures. On the practical and political level, Tom's commitment to a complex diachronic world is reflected by his fight against the government's ultimately successful attempts to bar Africans from the university where he happens to be teaching. The denial of advanced education, which is a cumulative product and an embodiment of Western history, would in effect isolate the black African from the material and intellectual products of Western culture as well as from its history. Thus Tom's commitment to history is theoretical, practical, and political.

Jessie's relation to the past is far more personal and affective. It manifests itself incidentally in her views of Christmas and the African miners' dance, both of which have been deprived of their traditional significance. Although she does not wish for a resurrection of the African past, she is horrified by the strangulation, the sudden end, of that culture; its past is destroyed, its present abominable, and its future ambiguous and problematic. However, Jessie's main historical concern is personal; throughout the novel she is engaged in an extended meditation focused on how her given "occasion"—that is, her personal and social relationships with her parents and with Morgan, her son from a previous marriage—affects the nature and strength of her love. Just as Tom, in his commitment to historical accuracy and continuity, fights the attempt to withhold Western education from blacks, so does Jessie, in her efforts to love in spite of her parents' selfishness, refuse to accept the diachronic disorientation produced by the absence of love and compassion. Through her analysis and subsequent transcendence of past handicaps she is able to love her current husband, Tom, and their children, and throughout the novel she makes a strenuous and finally successful effort to love Morgan. She overcomes the lack of adequate verbal communication between her son and herself by personally retracing his escapades in bars and bordellos. Her attempt to put herself in Morgan's place by experiencing his alterity and her commitment to live according to a code of "decency" by treating others as subjects become the sole means of solving the problems of her personal heritage.

Thus Jessie's heritage reflects certain aspects of the moral and political morass created by apartheid, and she shows a way out of those dilemmas by successfully liberating herself from that heritage. The selfishness and avarice that define her personal "occasion" imply, on the analogic level, the exclusionist and materialist tendencies of white South Africa; the absence of love indicates the lack of compassion in South African society; and the personal discontinuities she experiences correspond to the disjunction between European values and colonialist practice. By rejecting democracy, that is, by treating blacks as the *objects* of their self-centered desires, the white South Africans have radically disconnected themselves from the political development so central to the Western history and theory of progress and meliorism. Jessie's transcendence of diachronic and synchronic interpersonal distance implies that Europeans in South Africa can similarly overcome racial antipathy by individually subjecting themselves to a thorough and open-minded experience of black alterity.

The synchronic representation of Western culture is manifested in Boaz's "scientific" musicological studies which allow and in fact oblige him to examine selected parts of South African reality with "impartial" and "disinterested" eyes. He is only interested in the atemporal structure of African music and instruments, and not in their historic development. Although he is personally emancipated from racism, he insists that he intends to shun "politics" and to avoid the whole question of apartheid and moral responsibility because it has no bearing on his work. Yet Jessie prophetically warns him that it will not be easy to do so in South Africa where apartheid has contaminated all modes of human relations.

The disregard for historical context and development, deliberately espoused by Boaz as a professional necessity, is an intrinsic and natural essence of Ann's personality. She confines herself to a radically synchronic view of life: "The present was the only dimension of time she knew; she woke every day to her freedom of it" (*OFL*, 93). Her egotism and self-absorption exclude not only the past and the future but also intellectual abstraction; she is incapable of being moved by general notions of injustice and only responds to concrete suffering that she can witness. And Gideon falls in love precisely with her aura of concrete freedom, which she generates with her spontaneity, enthusiasm, and innocence, and which includes her childlike ignorance of race as an explosive issue in personal and socal relations in South Africa.

In contrast to her, Gideon is a frustrated man, bitterly aware of his bondage. He is a talented painter who has been forced to relinquish a scholarship to Italy by the government's refusal to issue him a passport because of his political activity. His subsequent decision to refuse an exit permit, which would allow his departure but prevent his return to South Africa, has turned him into an aimless, brooding character who can no longer paint. Thus apartheid, by isolating him from the larger, diachronic movement of Western and world art, deprives him of a personal, synchronic outlet for his creative energies. This severe limitation propels him, like other black individuals, into renouncing personal desires and committing himself further to a communal fight against apartheid. He knows that only through this collective effort can he achieve an identity and a sense of historical direction.

Yet the social situation creates contradictions of which Gideon is unaware and which he cannot overcome easily. In spite of his support of a collective diachronic movement he, unlike Jessie and Tom, is intellectually unaware of the importance of history. During a discussion of African history at the Stilwells, Gideon insists that the African must forget his past, for when he accepts what Western civilization has to offer at present, he also accepts the future that it implies, and because the African past is irrelevant to that future he must not cling to it. Yet as Jessie clearly realizes, Gideon's past, his life in the brutal, squalid locations to which apartheid has condemned him, is an experience that permeates his life and actions. Gideon's personal connection with the African past, Jessie feels, gives him a continuity which is magical in its power to attract others. According to her, Gideon possesses an innocent, unconscious awareness of history which, unlike the Stilwells' deliberate, conscious analysis and understanding of the past, is not weighed down by inherited burdens and responsibilities. It is this historic innocence of Gideon, as well as his bondage and frustration, that makes him very susceptible to the synchronic vitality of Ann. She models for him, inspires him to recommence his painting, and rekindles his desire for personal freedom. The affair between Gideon and Ann is strong enough to flourish in a benign environment, but too weak to withstand the frustrations created by racial segregation. Unable to cope rationally with the pressures of a manichean society, Ann suddenly returns to Europe with her husband, once again shattering Gideon's hopes for freedom.

At the analogic level of meaning, Gordimer's treatment of the Davises and the affair between Gideon and Ann implies a powerful criticism of the cultural forces, whether scientific and technological or personal and avaricious, that are historically irresponsible. Gordimer demonstrates that even if one deliberately or spontaneously ignores one's involvement in the general, inclusive process of culture and history one will not be left untouched by them: Boaz's attempts to eschew the politics of race are utterly futile. Through Ann's fantasy about Gideon's death, Gordimer condemns the colonialist's typical need to resolve his own conflict between his desire to dominate the native and his consequent guilt by wishing, and sometimes practicing, the annihilation of the colonized subject. Finally, through the sudden departure of the Davises, Gordimer also indicts those who, at the first sign of "trouble," abandon the problems they have created in the colonies in order to return to their home country, which they believe to be the only repository of "civilization." What Gordimer clearly identifies and criticizes is the ahistorical, exclusionist mentality of the colonialist who either wishes to dominate the native or chooses to ignore his existence.[31]

With the departure of Ann and Boaz, Tom, Jessie, and Gideon are left to suffer the consequences of their encounter with the Davises. For Gideon the repercussions are drastic: he drinks himself into a stupor much as he had done when the passport and, therefore, the scholarship had been withheld from him. Ann's abandonment of Gideon implies that apartheid and those Europeans who tacitly support its existence have once more denied him the chance to live freely and to realize his individual artistic potential. If we treat Gideon as a tragic hero, then the flaw in his character has to be his attempt to strive for self-fulfillment and his hubris has to be his belief that his personal desires can be, or have a right to be, satisfied in a society deformed by apartheid. Thus by writing a quasi-tragic novel Gordimer poignantly shows that the kinds of personal freedom that most of us take for granted are extremely risky luxuries for those condemned to live in the fascist society created by apartheid. But Gordimer's novel is not tragic; that is, it is not concerned exclusively with the fate of a heroic individual; rather it focuses on the *occasion*, the social circumstances that produce freedom and bondage. Therefore, through Jessie's and Callie's constant reminders to Gideon, Gordimer insists that the latter's and his compatriots' only freedom lies in committing themselves to the political and historical necessity of overthrowing apartheid. For Jessie and Tom, two historically aware people, there is a modicum of redemption; Jessie and Morgan are

reconciled at the end of the novel by having witnessed and experienced together the anguish, humiliation, and absurdity of the story of
Ann and Gideon. Reconciliation between mother and son is made
possible not through discursive dialogue but through a common experience of Gideon's history. However, there are negative repercussions for them too. Their belief in "the integrity of personal relations
against the distortions of laws and society," a belief that is a part of
their Western historical inheritance, is badly shaken.

Yet the gloomy ending of the novel, which implies an unavoidable
racial conflict, is belied to some extent by the existence and nature of
the novel itself. *Occasion for Loving* is a product of a project similar
to the one to which Tom and Jessie have committed themselves: a
clear-headed analysis of South African history designed to culminate
in an unsentimental definition of its present condition. The end of the
novel, then, warns us to remember its contents. It implies that the
manichean racial tension and opposition in South Africa can still be
resolved if those who have produced and supported apartheid are
willing to recognize their responsibility through a thorough analysis
and understanding of the South African *occasion*. The absence of
compassion in the South African political system can only be reme-
died through a clear awareness of the history that produced it—
through a comprehension of how democratic Europe was able to
create a perfectly fascist regime in South Africa in the name of civilization.

The conclusion of the novel also clarifies the ever-present contradiction between the desire to stay and the desire to leave. The need
to depart, now clearly associated with the Davises, implies historical
irresponsibility whereas "staying," associated with the Stilwells'
commitment, indicates an acceptance of the culpability for the problems created by colonialism and a dedication to resolve them no
matter how much personal suffering and danger this may entail.
With this clarification and commitment Nadine Gordimer ceases
being a "colonial" writer to the extent that the colonialist mentality
is marked by its belief that "home" and "civilization" are located
back in Europe, that life in the colonies is a temporary exile in an
outpost surrounded by savagery and barbarism.

These three books form a coherent group to the extent that they
are all novels of recognition. All of them culminate with the shocking
realization that apartheid is indeed appalling and that the liberal
creed is useless in this setting. Yet this knowledge is followed by a
relative stasis. There is no action in any of the novels to change
society; rather they end with a desire to leave that is eventually

conquered and with expressions of intentions, of promises to continue the struggle. However, the narrative repetition is balanced by a progressively deeper understanding of the historical causes of apartheid. In fact, the problem of historical determination itself increasingly becomes one of the central issues. And one would suspect that a historical understanding of one's present "occasion" would eventually result in imperatives for future action. Indeed the second group of novels is distinguished from the first by its greater commitment, no matter how vague at times, to the forces opposed to apartheid.

Gordimer's next work, *The Late Bourgeois World,*[32] a short but important novella, focuses on the decisions to accept the responsibilities for colonial society and to embark on a course of action that will morally and practically support those who are oppressed by apartheid. If this novella's heavy reliance on Gordimer's previous depiction and analysis of the South African socio-political-moral situation were considered a fault, then *The Late Bourgeois World,* out of its context in her oeuvre, can be considered a weak novel. However, if, as Gordimer herself insists, any given novel must be understood as a part of the totality of an author's work, then her novella can be seen as an important transition in her moral and stylistic development.

The substance of the novella is itself the definition of a transitional moment in the life of the heroine, Elizabeth; the work compresses her entire past, present, and potential future into a single day during which she rejects the major portion of her personal and political bourgeois past and decides instead to support the radical "underground" which is attempting to overthrow the apartheid government by force. The day begins with the news of the death of her ex-husband, Max Van Dan Sandt, and ends with her joining forces with the guerrillas. Most of the time between these crucial events is filled with bitter recollections that reveal the history of Max and Elizabeth—their short-lived marriage, his relation with his parents, Max and Elizabeth's participation in protests against apartheid, Max's sabotaging of a post office, and his subsequent imprisonment, betrayal of his compatriots, and suicide. During the course of this retrospective day, Elizabeth decides that her previous attempts to refashion and revitalize her bourgeois heritage have been fruitless and that her new life, though more dangerous and insecure, will be more substantial and rewarding. This moral and political transition, decisive for Elizabeth as well as for Gordimer, is perfectly mirrored by

the style and structure of the novella. However, the death of bourgeois culture, though acceptable as the given premise for Elizabeth's
transformation, is not convincingly conveyed as a felt experience.

The decay of European middle-class culture is represented primarily through Elizabeth's attack on the avaricious and racist fixa-
tions of Max's parents, the Van Dan Sandts, whose mixed genealogy,
that is, their Flemish and English blood, implicates both the Afrikaner and English sections of white South Africa. The desire of this
rich, established, and powerful family (Max's father, a member of
Parliament, was on the verge of becoming a cabinet minister before
the collapse of the Smuts government) to accumulate more wealth
and power, simply for its own sake rather than to promote a vision
of a better society, is considered by Elizabeth to be an indication of
its demise; the absence of any goal or direction, other than living
comfortably and even luxuriously, is the measure of bourgeois society's moral collapse. Within the South African context the bourgeois obsession with personal material comfort manifests itself in
the denial of any civil-rights to the nonwhites who would otherwise be competing for the same resources. Elizabeth feels that the
material greed which motivates apartheid and which is justified by
the "great lie" of racial superiority soon leads to a contagious blindness that eventually destroys the class itself. She thus rejects the
"code of decent family life, kindness to dogs and neighbors, handouts
to grateful servants, [which] have [not] brought us much more than
bewilderment" (*TLBW*, 11–12). Elizabeth finds an alternative to such
a life in the request of Luke Fokase—a member of the "underground"
conduit that smuggles Africans out for guerrilla training—that she
allow them to use her bank account to channel money into the
country. In spite of obvious danger she agrees.

The symbolism of Elizabeth's semiwakeful thoughts reveals the
values that form the basis of her choice. The semidream juxtaposes
the suicide of Max, who has drowned himself in the sea, and the first
spacewalk of American astronauts, both of which have shared the
newspaper headlines that day. Max's suicide, with its regressive association of returning to the sea, is rejected as an emblem of life dedicated to its own prolongation and comfort, which Gordimer characterizes as a larger, cultural manifestation of individual narcissism
that she has already renounced in her previous novels. On the other
hand, the astronauts' attempt to master "something *outside* our
physical environment," associated with movement away from the
earth and, therefore, with an expansion of the human horizons, be-

comes a transcendence of human limits—the "limits of life: our death." The endeavor to conquer human finitude by projecting one-self into inhospitable space is considered closer to God than is the self-serving bourgeois culture. The logic of this association may be weak, but the significance of this dreamlike symbolism is clear: the astronauts represent for Elizabeth a courageous attempt to go beyond the narcissism of bourgeois life and to transcend action based on the fear of death. Elizabeth is valorizing the submission of self to and the consequent understanding and acceptance of an alien alterity—space, death, or the "kaffir." She is opposing self-transcendence to individual and cultural narcissism.

The manner of her decision to help Luke stresses its moral, cate-gorical nature as well as its potential for personal liberation. Like a child, she can only find one "reason" to justify her new commit-ment—it is simply summed up by the word "because." Her decision is based on an emotional, personal renaissance—a bursting forth of a new life that cannot be evaluated or judged in terms of the now irrelevant "rationality" of self-interest. Along with this danger, she is willing to accept, as a further definition of her new life, the prob-ability of a sexual affair with Luke. The conjunction of the political and the personal in Elizabeth's "love" for Luke marks a new depar-ture for her. Her rejection of the bourgeois culture and her rebirth into a new world are indicated by her ironic use of the Orpheus-Eurydice myth. Her equation of herself to "pale Eurydice" being left behind in "her musty secrets, her life-insured Shades" by Luke, the departing Orpheus, implies a fundamental reversal of the traditional manichean allegory; in Elizabeth's use of the myth, the political "underground," the black world of Luke, is the substantial, real, *hu-man* world, and the "pure," "civilized," white bourgeois culture of South Africa becomes the repository of evil—the actual hell.

The structure of *The Late Bourgeois World* is perfectly suited to the drastic nature of Elizabeth's metamorphosis (the past culminates at the commencement of the narrative and the present ends with a decision which has significant implications for the future). The struc-ture of the novel reveals the pivotal nature of her choice. However, one can argue that the style of the novella, its presentation of her past through a series of retrospections, is unable to communicate the emotional experience that leads Elizabeth to the radical rejection of her culture. The main problem is that the reader is never able to see and experience for himself the values, lives, and preoccupations of Max and his parents, and yet these characteristics are made to bear the burden of demonstrating the disintegration of bourgeois culture. All the past is presented primarily through Elizabeth's analysis of it rather than as action the reader can witness. Because the narrative is mediated through her terse condensation it remains flat—the element of time is absent from the novella. Max's death precipitates a recapitulation designed not to enlighten the reader, but to benefit the narrator herself: it seems that Elizabeth reviews the past primarily in order to reinforce her decision to break away from bourgeois society.

The Late Bourgeois World is a far more subjective work than Gordimer's previous novels. *Occasion for Loving* is an excellent blend of the subjective and objective elements; the reader is able to experience thoroughly the anguish of Jessie, the frustration of Gideon, and the pleasures of Ann's unreflective innocence, as well as to see and understand the complex problems caused by apartheid laws that keep Gideon and Ann apart. This kind of judicious combination of the personal and the social, the subjective and the objective, which is one of the major strengths of Gordimer's style and vision, is lacking in her novella. Yet the predominance of the subjective in *The Late Bourgeois World* is not really a weakness if one reads this novella as a culmination of the movement begun in *The Lying Days:* a thorough analysis of the predicament of the white liberal South African. After having examined in an objective, thorough, and lucid manner the concrete social contradictions and moral dilemmas that beset previous avatars of the liberal consciousness, in *The Late Bourgeois World* Nadine Gordimer presents in a subjective manner the subjective decision of the protagonist to abandon bourgeois values.

This novella thus marks a political and a stylistic transition in Gordimer's work. The abandonment of bourgeois institutions and beliefs that define, stabilize, and "objectify" the self leaves the protagonist and the author with nothing but their subjectivity and their moral imperatives. This liberating yet dangerous juncture is perfectly reflected in the style, which presents the entire dilemma from a subjective viewpoint, and in the structure, which captures the drastic transition in one crucial day. The liberating rupture between Gordimer and the bourgeois culture, rather reminiscent of Isak Dinesen's similar experience upon meeting the black people in Kenya, is in fact an important part of what she describes as her "second birth," which is more a process of constant reassessment and gradual detachment from the bourgeois culture that has turned fascist than it is an epiphanic moment of total liberation. Because in this slow development the fascist society does not disappear when it is rejected by the protagonist or the author, Gordimer is repeatedly forced to encounter its objective presence. Thus the problems of subjectivity and objectivity are never resolved entirely. Gordimer's next two novels, *A Guest of Honour* and *The Conservationist*, try rather unsuccessfully to solve the problematic relation of self to society and the stylistic question of subjective-objective balance; she is only able to find a perfect solution to these problems in her best novel, *Burger's Daughter*.

The Late Bourgeois World, however, does continue to clarify one of the major contradictions running through Gordimer's work. The tension between the desire to leave South Africa and the wish to stay is transformed in this novella into a more radical opposition: leaving is now associated with Max's betrayal of his comrades and his desertion through suicide, both of which are considered particular forms of narcissistic self-indulgence; staying is now represented by Elizabeth's decision to risk her life and freedom, to abandon a narrow notion of self-interest, by actively supporting the guerrillas. With this clarification, with the unambiguous shift from liberal equivocation to a radical commitment, it would seem that the contradiction has been sufficiently resolved for it not to occur again. While it is true that the desire to leave is never very strong in the novels that follow, it nevertheless recurs in more subtle and nostalgic ways.

Because neither the bourgeois nor the fascist world will disappear and because one cannot easily extricate oneself from the deep roots of a bourgeois humanist ideology, Gordimer bases her next novel, *A Guest of Honour*,[33] in a fictitious, unnamed central African country that has just won its independence from Britain. The freedom that this setting affords from the moral strictures and odiousness of apartheid allows Gordimer a more leisurely exploration of the nature, function, and strength of the liberal ideology manifested in the character, beliefs, and actions of Colonel Bray, as well as in the socio-political-economic structure that the country has inherited from colonial rule.

Gordimer's examination proceeds through a relatively simple plot. Colonel Bray, who was a district commissioner in the country while it was still a colony, had nurtured the People's Independence Party (PIP) from its inception to its final success in winning national independence from Britain. However, his efforts had so incensed the white settlers and the colonial government that he had been deported ten years before the country achieved independence. The novel begins with his return, as the guest of honor, to the independence celebrations. However, Bray's intentions of returning to his retirement and academic work in England (he is writing a history of this country's colonial administration) are soon pushed aside by his concern over the growing rift between Adamson Mweta and Edward Shinza, his friends and, in a sense, his protégés, who had been the original coleaders of PIP. Mweta, who is now president of the country, does not wish to alter the economic structure of the nation which is dominated by a large European mining company; he plans a rapid economic development of the country through large investments of foreign capital. The rest of the novel demonstrates unequivocally that Mweta's "policy" in fact means a complete abrogation of national control of economic and, later, political and military policies: the country ends up being managed by and for the benefit of the mine. Edward Shinza, whom Mweta has managed to exclude from the government, wants to organize the economy of the country along socialist lines and to subordinate the interests of foreign capital to those of his own countrymen's welfare. The struggle between him and Mweta, which focuses on the control of the Trade Union Congress (TUC), becomes increasingly acerbic and violent. It begins with union strikes, intimidation of organizers, and a fight to control the TUC, and rapidly progresses to riots, attempted coups, attacks by white mercenaries from the Congo, and the eventual invasion by British troops to restore calm and order. Bray makes a heroic but unsuccessful effort to mediate between his two friends who are both trying to claim his exclusive support and sympathy. Finally recognizing the futility of mediation and reluctantly acknowledging Mweta's corruption, Bray decides to support Shinza, but before he is able to undertake any substantial effort on his friend's behalf the novel comes to its effective conclusion with Bray's assassination.

Gordimer's depiction of the colonial government and its legacy reveals some of the contradictions that we have already encountered. Through Bray's experience the reader is able to see that whereas colonialism was supposed to promote education it in fact had done abysmally little to train teachers; whereas the empire was supposedly teaching the colonized how to govern themselves, it in fact had suppressed all forms of political thought. The final paradox, according to Bray, is that the alien, autocratic rule of colonial government has destroyed all sense of communal obligation in the colonized subjects and has predisposed them toward the acceptance of autocratic leadership after independence. The English culture that cherished the values of liberalism and democracy, embodied in Bray, had produced in its colonial government social structures that were antithetical to its own avowed values. The current British interests in this African country, represented by the gold mine which produces 40 percent of the national income and thereby effectively controls the economy, clarify the reasons behind this contradiction. The overriding motive of the mining company is maximization of profits; the welfare of its employees or of the country is irrelevant. In order to ensure its profits the company bribes and eventually controls Mweta. In return for his power he ruthlessly exploits his people and thereby ignites a rebellion, which the British troops are invited to crush. Gordimer implies that freedom from colonial domination is illusory unless the economic motives for domination are eradicated first.

However, Gordimer is less interested in exploring the contradictions of colonialism per se than in examining those of the liberal ideology as they are manifested in the personality of Bray and in his attitude toward the problems of this country. The contradictions between the overt and covert aims of colonialism that had so plagued Joyce Cary are easily transcended by Bray because he realizes that "the future of colonialism *was* its own overthrow and the emergence of Africans into their own responsibility" (*AGOH*, 246–47). Thus, although Bray as an individual can transcend the paradoxes of colonialism by helping Shinza and Mweta to organize PIP and by deliberately rejecting the covert aims of colonialism, the actual contradictions of the system still persist for ten years after his return to England and even after independence, in the form of neocolonialism. In pitting Bray against this awesome institutionalization of selfish interests, Nadine Gordimer makes certain that he is an individual who is thoroughly capable of taking up the challenge. She portrays him as a heroic embodiment of the best aspects of English liberalism. The foundation of his personality is a profound unselfishness: "a code so deeply accepted that it had never been discussed—one was available wherever one was of use" (*AGOH*, 6). His "decency" is manifested in various ways: in his valorization of individual interests and welfare above those of institutions, in his compassion for the poor, in his abhorrence of violence and desire for civil order, in his unusual physical bravery, in his traditional insistence that justice must be *seen* to be done, and, most importantly, in his unimpeachable honor.

By endowing Bray with an impeccable character and a profound moral commitment, Gordimer has designed the novel not to test his *personal* stature so much as the validity and efficacy of the beliefs that he represents. She is interested in exploring the vitality, durability, and depth of liberalism in a hostile environment diametrically opposed to the now relatively stable and placid English culture from which his liberal code originates.[34] The disruption of African traditions by colonialism, the conflict between various political ideologies and between various personal ambitions, the heightened sense of expectation, and various other factors that attend the emergence of a new nation all lead to a volatile atmosphere in which the values of liberalism can be examined under stress. Within this setting Gordimer astutely utilizes the similarities and differences between Bray and Shinza in order to expose the limitations of the liberal ideology. Both men are equally dedicated to communal rather than personal welfare. Shinza's ideological commitment is clear and unwavering from the beginning; in his readiness to use violence he is unconcerned with the traditional liberal dilemma about the contradiction between means and ends. As the situation deteriorates, he is able to use without any qualms whatever means are necessary to gain his ends. By contrast, Bray seems blind and paralyzed. For instance, he is extremely slow in realizing that Mweta is corrupt or that Shinza is silently planning the overthrow of his rival. In his attempt to reconcile the two men, he keeps insisting to Mweta that Shinza is neither jealous nor ambitious and that he only desires to become the theoretician of the party, a sort of elder statesman, and to Shinza he explains Mweta's economic policies as slow but steady realism. In both instances Bray is in fact projecting his own attributes and desires onto his friends: "He defined it precisely as that to himself, to hold his ground that what he believed was flatly reasonable" (*AGOH*, 291). Gordimer repeatedly provides both the reader and Bray sufficient information to interpret and predict events, but Bray refuses to accept the evidence while the reader cannot help doing so.[35]

This repeated conflict between Bray and the reality of events makes one exasperated with his willful blindness even though one continues to admire his courage and integrity. When he eventually recognizes that Shinza is ideologically right and Mweta wrong and that Shinza has no choice but to attempt a coup, he is very reluctant to act according to his *intellectual* insights because he cannot overcome his liberal habits and assumptions. Bray's earlier characterization of his function within the colonial context provides us with an insight into his liberal inertia. He feels that under the colonial government he was a symbol of the "voluntary relinquishment" of racial intransigence and hostility. This vision of himself, along with his Gandhian creed of *satyagraha*, is essentially based on good faith. But in the tumult, ambition, greed, and idealism of a country in the midst of a revolution, a philosophy of action based on good faith becomes entirely redundant.

Whereas the persistent naiveté engendered by his code makes Bray rather insufferable, the self-awareness encouraged by the same code redeems him and re-establishes his heroic status. For instance, in the various riots and fighting in the country, Bray finds himself instinctively siding with the forces of "law and order," but upon reflection he realizes that his concern for "common humanity" and "keeping the peace" makes him act in favor of the "legal" forces that are repressive and highly unjust. His self-awareness reaches its climax when he claims that his physical myopia is symbolic of his ideological nearsightedness (*AGOH*, 431). However, Bray's predicament becomes truly touching when he realizes that his practically firm, but morally ambivalent decision to help Shinza overthrow Mweta by force enmeshes him in contradictions that he may never be able to resolve. By violating his belief that the lives of individuals should never be sacrificed for the abstract principles of civilization, he feels that he is transgressing the "instinct in himself that he had unconsciously regarded as the most civilized," and he remains unsure whether this infraction of his "own nature" is "a tragic mistake or his salvation" (*AGOH*, 465). This ambivalence defines, from Gordimer's viewpoint, both the essence and the limitation of liberalism. Bray is never able to demonstrate a practical resolution of his dilemma because, on his way out of the country in order to raise funds for Shinza, he is assassinated either by Mweta's thugs or by the mine workers who mistake him for a white mercenary.

Yet Gordimer not only refuses to iron out the ambiguity but in fact reinforces it. After dismissing a racist and self-righteous explanation of Bray's death, she deliberately juxtaposes a conservative and a liberal evaluation of his life. The conservatives see him as a liberal meddler who got what he deserved, whereas an English monthly examining "The Decline of Liberalism" sees Bray as a man who had "passed over from the scepticism and resignation of empirical liberalism to become one of those who are so haunted by the stupidities and evils of human affairs that they are prepared to accept apocalyptic solutions, wade through blood if need be, to bring real change" (*AGOH*, 503). Gordimer's insistence on this ambiguity leads one to feel that Bray's dilemma and indecision are a refracted version of an authorial ambivalence. On the one hand, she criticizes the quixotic luxury of liberal beliefs and assumptions; one of the mottoes of *A Guest of Honour*, from Turgenev, claims that "an honourable man will end up by not knowing where to live." But on the other hand, she seems to admire Bray's *commitment* to his ideals: the other motto, from Che Guevara, implies that Bray is another heroic Guevara willing to risk his life for his beliefs. This authorial ambivalence seems to be a product of a valorization of self and a criticism of the inherited social values, and as such it continues the trend begun in her novella. Having rejected bourgeois society and liberalism, Gordimer scrutinizes the individual's entrapment by the deeply internalized ideology; having shown how "liberal" society is capable of stifling the growth of love, compassion, justice, equality, and other values that it claims to cherish, she turns inward to a speleology of the self that is confronted with a drastic social and moral crisis for which society has no answers. Gordimer is primarily concerned with the predicament of her white protagonist who is trying to transcend some of the limitations of his inherited culture.

Gordimer's understandable preoccupation with these aspects of subjectivity takes its toll on the novel. Judging by the amount of space and energy devoted to the description of social, economic, and political structures and dynamics of this hypothetical country, it is clearly evident that *A Guest of Honour* intends to do justice to the objective conditions within which Bray's heroism and limitations are to be enacted and evaluated. But her attempts to depict a specific and concrete society in turmoil are not entirely successful. Specific aspects of mundane reality are all aptly conveyed through Bray's personal experience; the concrete uniqueness of the hypothetical country is fully realized in the novel. However, the novel is unable to convey adequately the connection between the concrete reality and the social process because political events are reported through gossip among various characters. The problem with this indirect representation of the economic and political disputes is not that Bray's summaries are unreliable but that the overwhelming dependence on such condensation tends to make the political process entirely hypothetical and unreal, particularly when the summaries are invariably coupled with implausible ideological debates between various politicians. Gordimer's almost exclusive reliance on this combination of gossipy summaries and academic debates tends to reduce the political upheaval in the country to a theoretical, academic problem.[36] The contrast provided by the graphic descriptions of riots and violence further emphasizes the abstractness of the political process. A similar contrast is produced by the existence of a single instance—Bray's persuasion of Semstu and his supporters to vote for Shinza (*AGOH*, 246–49)—that gives us an insight into the fears, resentments, hopes, confusions, misunderstandings, selfishness, and various other contradictory, emotional, and circumstantial factors that are inevitably involved in the transformation of subjective experience into objective socio-political processes and institutions. Thus while various intellectual opinions about the political processes are available to us through the debates, we can appreciate the human complexities of these processes only through Bray's personal experience of them, and because he is preoccupied with the problematics of his own values, our objective understanding of the country's politics is severely limited.

It is possible to argue, quite accurately, that this limitation is not really an inadequacy of the novel, but that it is a stylistic correlative of Bray's moral myopia. The fact that the narrative viewpoint coincides with that of Bray until his death (when it shifts into alignment with that of his mistress, Rebecca) would further support this argument. Yet whether the absence of the objective depiction of socio-political processes is seen as an intended correlative of Bray's subjective preoccupation or whether it is viewed as an unintended stylistic shortcoming, the point remains that this novel continues the trend begun in *The Late Bourgeois World:* Gordimer focuses on the subjectivity of her liberal-cum-radical protagonist at the expense of an adequate portrayal of social conditions and processes. In *A Guest of Honour* the focus shifts from resolution of specific objective problems of the country to the subjective question of how Bray will overcome the contradiction between the pull of his inherited values and his desire to transcend their limitations.

Although the novel does not provide a synthesis that would transcend the terms of the subjective contradiction, it does confirm, without ambiguity or hesitation, Bray's commitment to the search for a solution. Once again this is done through the conflict between the desire to stay in Africa and the desire to leave. In fact this novel begins with a version of this opposition: Bray's return to Africa after his deportation already prefigures his strong commitment. Although he had planned to stay only for the duration of the independence ceremonies, his intentions are soon subverted by his rekindled affection for Africa and by his desire to participate in the social transformation of this country. Subsequently, the conflict between staying and leaving becomes transformed into an opposition between Europe and Africa that is formulated in dramatic and significant ways through the polarization between Bray's home and wife in Wiltshire and his house and mistress (Rebecca) in the Gala district: "The house in Wiltshire with all its comfortable beauty and order, its incenses of fresh flowers and good cooking, its libations of carefully discussed and chosen wine came to Bray in all the calm detail of an interesting death cult; to wake up there again would be to find oneself acquiescently buried alive. At the same time, he felt a stony sense of betrayal" (*AGOH*, 130). Clearly Nadine Gordimer is rejecting once more the moribund comforts and values of bourgeois culture. The repudiation is reinforced by Rebecca's visit to Europe after Bray's death. Gordimer opposes this liberal European culture to the material sparseness, the political challenge and excitement, and the vitality and rejuvenation of Bray's life in Africa. The strength of Gordimer's commitment to remaining in Africa is finally confirmed by Bray's death in Africa and by Rebecca's discovery of a decadent culture in Europe.

However, the progressively clearer definitions of these conflicting desires do not ease the predicament of Gordimer's liberal-cum-radical protagonists; on the contrary, their situation becomes increasingly precarious. They are caught between Helen Shaw's definition of South Africa as a graveyard where people are buried alive (*TLD*, 331) and Bray's similar view of Europe; emigration to Europe is now as repugnant as acceptance of the repressive apartheid society. At home neither in the facism of South Africa nor in the self-indulgent liberalism of Europe, Gordimer's protagonists have no choice but to continue their struggle in that narrow black-and-white frontier society until, like Bray, they die. The precariousness and stress of this confinement account for the increasing subjectivity of her novels that reaches its climax in her next novel, *The Conservationist*.

The Conservationist,[37] a lyrical, mystical, and symbolic novel, marks the climax not only of Gordimer's subjective explorations but also of her use of death as a means of conveying commitment to South Africa and overcoming the racial contradictions created by apartheid. In fact the whole meaning of the novel is represented through Mehring's yearning and anticipation of his own death which becomes the culmination of his mystical desire to transcend the boundaries of the individual self and to merge with the constant flux and continuity of African society and nature. Yet despite its mysticism, the novel is not apolitical: as we shall see, it manages to combine spiritual transcendence with political salvation by skillfully juxtaposing and then intermingling the black and white societies of South Africa.

The novel depicts two worlds that are superficially coterminous but stylistically and substantively disjunct. The omniscient narrator presents the world of Africans and Indians, which forms the background to the main movement of the novel (there is no conventional plot), through a simple description of the social surface, of the immediately and objectively observable and verifiable facts of mundane life. The narrator's consistent refusal to penetrate very much below the surface in order to show us the inner lives of the Africans further emphasizes the distance and objectivity of this style, typically illustrated by the following passage: "The man who was looking for work shook his head slowly before them all. The black and white checked cap defined young Izak's head clearly, but his head was still dusty from the morning's work, it had a mothy dimness, half-effacing itself into the perimeter of the firelight. The fowls settled again; the children coughed in their sleep; a woman brought around the last of the beer" (*TC*, 61). The narrative only qualifies and elaborates physical details; the events in the lives of the blacks are presented as discrete entities that are linked by narrative association or temporal sequence but not by an analysis of causality. Yet as the paratactic sentence at the end of the passage implies, the black culture has its own rhythm and meaning, the mystery of which the narrator does not wish to violate.

This society parallels Mehring's entirely subjective world, which the narrator renders almost exclusively through his increasingly intricate dramatic monologues that allow us to see society and nature through his discriminating and sensitive eyes. His dramatic monologues—mostly one sided, angry rebuttals of the liberal criticisms of his former mistress, Antonia, and his son, Terry, who have both deserted him—are usually rhetorical stances designed to justify his own opinions and attitudes. Mehring's progressive isolation from his other friends and the increasing vehemence of his monologues become a direct measure of his alienation from white South African society. His acute and sensitive awareness of nature increases along with his distance from family and friends. The following passage illustrates both the communion with nature and the hostility toward his white friends:

> The howls have throbbed themselves out and sunk away into the peace. This place absorbs everything, takes everything to itself and loses everything in itself. It's innocent. The pulse, the rhythm now is a coming and going of flights of birds just after sunset. The oceanic swaying of layers of boughs and swathes has stopped; the force of gravity sinks everything that is of the earth to the earth, chained to a ball of molten ore that has rolled over the dark side. All the weight of his life is taken by the tree at his back. Swallows are a flick of dark flying droplets. From the far curve of the sky, finches: they spring up

and down in and out of the line of their formation as they go. Darts of doves aim at some objective of their own. Like showers of sparks, birds explode into the sky, and—a change of focus—close to his eyes gnats are raised and lowered, stately, as they hover in their swarm on strings of air. He feels (see him in her crystal ball and have a good laugh if she likes) almost some kind of companionship in the atmosphere. You predicted it—right—you are so clever, your kind, you always know the phrase:— The famous indifference of nature really sends people like you, doesn't it—it's the romanticism of your *realpolitik*, the sentimentalism of cut-throat competitors—(TC, 189–90)

The smooth progression from a disturbance to an intense, lyric appreciation of nature, to a physical awareness of himself, then to an intimation of the dead African's presence, and, finally, to one of his internalized quarrels defines the rhythm of the subjective world of *The Conservationist*. Mehring's communions with nature increase in intensity until his death unites him permanently and completely with the dead man and nature.

The objective and subjective worlds run parallel to each other and even coincide considerably, but they never intermingle in a *socially* significant manner. Mehring's relationship with the blacks on the farm, consisting of exchanges between a kind, indulgent master and his servants, is confined to the necessary mundane farming chores. The result is a lack of any social depth: the significant meaning of the novel is conveyed through a mystical union between Mehring and a dead African, which begins for Mehring as another bothersome farm problem. An unidentified black man is found dead by the stream on his farm, and when the police unceremoniously bury him on the spot, Mehring is outraged. But because he is unable to remedy the situation, the dead man begins to haunt his conscience and to exert a powerful subconscious pull on his mind until the two become united with each other at Mehring's death. Thus Mehring is finally identified, through the dead man, with all the black ancestors who in turn are equated by the novel with nature.

In order to understand the significance of these transferences we have to begin with an appreciation of the perseverance, resilience, and permanence of the black society on the farm. Although Mehring owns the *deed* to the farm, which passes to another white man at his death, the novel clearly demonstrates that the Africans not only manage the farm, but that, as a result of their work on it over several generations, they have de facto tenure of it. It also becomes evident that, in addition to the actual prolonged possession of the farm, the Africans have a coherent tradition and a cultural continuity that

Mehring lacks: the blacks have their own morality and extended family structure that, because of its clearly defined set of relationships, allows them to protect and support each other. The objective narrative systematically substantiates Mehring's observation about African resilience: the community on the farm remains virtually unchanged through the tribulations of a bush fire, a drought, and a flood. The novel equates the blacks' ability to survive with nature's similar capacity for regeneration (e.g., *TC*, 231, 234) and hence implies that, like nature, they are the real conservationists. The last of the many quotations in the novel from Reverend Henry Callaway's *The Religious System of the Amazulu* shows that the cyclical, repetitive nature of Zulu notions of ancestry already encompasses a perfect understanding of conservation as an essential ingredient of their religious and cultural heritage.

Mehring's world, unlike that of his servants, is devoid of continuity. He is a business tycoon whose complete isolation from ancestors as well as descendants makes a mockery of his rather trendy notions of conservation: he inherits nothing from anyone and he has no one to whom he can bequeath his carefully "conserved" possessions. Conservation without community, the novel implies, is at best a contradiction in terms. His progressive isolation from family and friends culminates in an emblematic scene where he listens with disinterested, aesthetic curiosity to the messages that have been left on his telephone answering device: like the machine, Mehring hears the messages but does not reply. His total isolation from the white community becomes a social correlative of his belief that "[to] keep anything the way you like it for yourself you have to have the stomach to ignore—dead and hidden—whatever intrudes" (*TC*, 73).

Yet ironically, Mehring's conscious and deliberate attempt to isolate himself from his white friends is paralleled by his increasingly powerful attraction toward the dead African—buried and hidden on his farm. The latter movement is comprised of three interdependent components: Mehring's progressively intense and prolonged communions with nature, the gradual dissolution of the social and psychological boundaries of his personality, and his increasing preoccupation with the fate of the dead man which eventually turns into an identification with him. Gordimer does not present this movement as a logically coherent narrative, but rather she evokes it through a lyric description of Mehring's consciousness that, taken as the whole subjective narrative, resembles an uncontrolled dream that is constantly fluctuating between the primary visual experience of the deep dream state and the more coherent narrative elaborations of the shallower, secondary state. Through the use of lyric description and compacted metaphors Gordimer allows us to witness the former state as eruptions of arbitrary, disconnected images in Mehring's consciousness, and through his associative meditations about more conscious experiences she depicts his somewhat more coherent organization of these images.

The whole subconscious movement begins and develops through an initial juxtaposition between Mehring's concern with the possible destruction of fowl eggs and his annoyance with the bureaucratic problems caused by the discovery of the dead man on his farm. Thereafter the combination of potential birth and actual death is developed through the dead man's pull on Mehring, which manifests itself in his repeated withdrawal to meditate by the stream where the dead man was found and buried. He frequently falls asleep at the stream and wakes up to find himself lying there in a position identical to that of the dead man—with mud in his mouth and flies and midges in his eyes and nose as if he "were a corpse" (e.g., *TC*, 37, 87). Such images of physical resemblance are repeated till the "presence" of the dead man begins to pervade Mehring's subconscious and conscious thoughts and the two men begin to merge:

> Tracing his consciousness as an ant's progress is alive from point to point where it is clambering over the hairs of his forearms, he knows he is not the only one down at the reeds. He does not think of *him*, one of them lying somewhere here, any more than one thinks consciously of anyone who is always in one's presence about the house, breathing in the same rooms. Sometimes there arises the need to speak; sometimes there are long silences. He feels at this particular moment a kind of curiosity that is in itself a question: from one who has nothing to say to one to whom there is nothing to say. Falling asleep there he was not alone face-down in the grass. There are kinds of companionships unsought. With nature. Nature accepts everything. Bones, hair, teeth, fingernails and the beaks of birds—the ants carry away the last fragments of flesh, small as a fibre of meat stuck in a back tooth, nothing is wasted. (*TC*, 190)

Just as ants are agents of a cyclical ecological process, the most fundamental form of "conservation," so Mehring's consciousness becomes an agent that absorbs the presence of the dead man into himself and gradually but inexorably allows him to merge, through the dead man, with nature and Africa.

Gordimer balances the metaphoric elaborations of the secondary dream state, like the ant in the above example, with the primary images of the deep state in order to suggest the metamorphosis of

Mehring's mind from that of a businessman to that of a mystic. The most crucial instance of such images is Mehring's solitary celebration of a New Year's Eve under a polarized sky. He begins the evening by witnessing, with an intense self-awareness, a sky that is perfectly divided between the turbulence of a magnificent, dark thunderstorm and the clarity of a cold, luminous full moon, and he spends the rest of the night watching the thunderstorm gradually converging on and eclipsing the moon. Only after experiencing this symbolic ascendancy of the subconscious over the conscious mind and of blackness over whiteness does Mehring finally accept the presence of the dead man on his farm.

The actual physical resurfacing of the dead man during the flood marks the final stage of Mehring's descent toward his meeting-in-death with his other. His mind, increasingly invaded by images of birth and death, growth and decay in the stream valley, begins to disintegrate: the mundane psychological and social codes that he has internalized begin to loose their meaning. Finally, even the boundaries of Mehring's identity burst open in a sensual transcendence of self (*TC*, 245). This is followed by his rapid movement toward his death which, though problematic on the objective narrative level, has quite a definite and clear symbolic meaning. The repetition of various phrases and images which have been used to describe the death of the black man are used by Mehring to describe his own death, which, on the factual level, is highly and, one supposes, deliberately ambiguous. He has picked up a prostitute who apparently lures him to a disused mine dump where he is to be killed and robbed. At least, that is his fantasy. In a very subjective and hallucinatory passage Mehring describes his own death in such ambiguous terms that it becomes impossible to determine whether he has really been murdered or whether he has gone mad. Gordimer offers no objective verification.

The final chapter of the novel describes, through the objective narrative, the blacks on the farm building a coffin and burying an unidentified man. Even at this stage it is unclear whether they are interring Mehring or reburying the body of the black man that had been uncovered by the flood. The circumstantial description of the funeral—the absence of any friends, family, or descendants to mourn him—is equally applicable to Mehring and the black man. This deliberate ambiguity seems to have been designed to dismiss the factual, mundane level of understanding and interpretation as unnecessary and irrelevant; instead our attention is guided to the symbolic and mythic meaning of the novel.

At the figurative level of meaning it becomes perfectly clear that the identities of Mehring and the dead African have merged. The symbolic meaning is corroborated by Antonia's prediction that Mehring would develop a mystical attraction for the blacks, that he would wish to be buried on the farm, and that no one (that is, none of his white friends) would know where he was interred (*TC*, 168, 167, 184). Mehring's salvation, it would seem, lies in his apparently inevitable desire to unite with the black man, for by merging with the dead man Mehring has become one of the ancestors of Africa and through them he has blended with nature. Only by thus transcending the racial barriers of apartheid does he become an inhabitant of Africa: in his death he "took possession of this earth, theirs; one of them" (*TC*, 252).

The egg symbolism that applies to the younger generation of all three races in the novel further corroborates the above interpretation of conservation and inheritance. The African children are able to consume or conserve real fowl eggs, whereas Jalal, an Indian boy completely hemmed in and frustrated by the restrictions of apartheid, is reduced to painting a huge peace sign in the shape of an egg, and Terry, Mehring's son, who simply leaves South Africa in order to get away from apartheid, takes, as a present for his mother, an alabaster egg—a petrified image that mockingly negates the potential for life of its original. The living heritage of South Africa, Gordimer implies, can only belong to the blacks. The Europeans and Indians have only two choices: either they must abandon Africa, as Terry does, or they must become "African," as Mehring does. Unless, like the latter, they "merge" with Africa, unless they accept and incorporate into themselves the otherness of Africans, which apartheid seeks to keep at a distance, they will be confined to a frustrated and empty symbolic expression of coexistence (Jalal's peace sign) or they will be obliged to dissociate themselves from the development and continuity of the *African* culture (Terry's alabaster egg). Thus this becomes another version of the dialectic of leaving and staying. The desire to leave, represented by Terry's commencement of a new life in the United States, implies not only a rejection of apartheid but also an abandonment of the black component of South African life. But for those who are too attached to the *Africanness* of the country's culture, staying means becoming African in a rather vague, mystical sense.

The mythical transformation in *The Conservationist*, based on a mystical-symbolic union of a black and a white man, is reminiscent of Isak Dinesen's use of mythic consciousness to transcend the opposition between self and other, and Mehring's merging-in-death with nature is another version of Dinesen's desire for a Gikuyu funeral—where the body is left on the plains to be reabsorbed into nature through animals and insects that thrive on carrion. Yet whereas Dinesen's *Out of Africa* and *Shadows on the Grass* are characterized by a transcendent calm that is produced by her dominant position in an apparently harmonious centripetal feudalistic society, *The Conservationist* is pervaded by a rather shrill and, at times, almost hysterical tone that is a result of Gordimer's internalization and sublimation of the bitter racial antagonism and general precariousness of South African life under apartheid rule. Whereas the purpose and organization of Dinesen's autobiographies are straightforward—she unhesitatingly creates blissful utopias—the configuration of Gordimer's novel remains problematic and vague.

In spite of the intricacy, charm, and evocative power of Gordimer's lyric prose, the overall structure of *The Conservationist* and the nature and implication of Mehring's transformation are too ambiguous and his mysticism is, at times, uncomfortably close to a pathological state. The weakness of the novel lies in the imbalance between the subjective and objective narratives: the former overwhelms the latter. The predominance of an ambiguous subjectivity in the novel seems to be a stylistic correlative of Gordimer's practical dilemma as a white South African writer. The bifurcation inculcated by apartheid has so antagonized the population of South Africa along purely *racial* lines that a radical white person, sympathetic to the black plight, is faced with the quandary of how to define herself as an "African." Because blanket repression has oversimplified the political situation in South Africa—in a *racial* war people will be killed because of their *skin color*, not because of their political and social beliefs or practice—it becomes difficult for anyone to imagine the detailed social and cultural ramifications of the "Africanization" of a white person. Because a practical synthesis between black and white cultures is rendered actually and even potentially impossible by the decades of apartheid segregation, Gordimer resorts to a rather vague mystical-symbolic merger in *The Conservationist*. The strain produced by the manichean society and the attempt to transform the liberal consciousness are revealed in the pattern traced by the three novels in the postbourgeois phase. A remarkable parallelism between the first and second group of novels shows how powerful historical determinism can be. *The Late Bourgeois World* is similar to *The Lying Days* in that it represents the coming-to-consciousness of a young South African woman dissatisfied with her environment. *A*

Guest of Honour parallels *A World of Strangers* in that both novels explore from a European perspective the problem defined by the previous novels: both examine the European roots of a South African dilemma. Finally, *The Conservationist* and *Occasion for Loving* both analyze the more ephermeral aspects of a manichean society. Whereas the latter novel investigates the possibilities of love under fascism, the former considers the possibilities of a more general humanism: both novels ask how a decent life is possible in a racially divided culture. The tenacity of the liberal heritage evidenced by the parallelism is also responsible for a certain repetition within the second group of novels. Although *The Late Bourgeois World* attempts an emphatic rejection of bourgeois liberalism, the hold of the liberal past cannot in fact be dismissed in a summary fashion. Thus Gordimer is forced to re-examine in a more thorough way the historical roots of that ideology in *A Guest of Honour*. Yet even after this historical examination, the transition to the revolutionary phase has to be mediated by a novel, *The Conservationist*, that eschews history and resorts to a mystical connection in order to unite European and African consciousnesses. This attempt to escape history, as we have seen, results in a highly subjective and ambiguous novel. Only when Gordimer sets out to find a more practical *political* and *historical* solution for the problems of racial division does her style regain a more optimal balance between subjectivity and objectivity.

   The excellence of *Burger's Daughter*[38] is due to a judicious combination of the relative simplicity of its plot, the elegance and appropriateness of its style, and the integrity, acuteness, and courage of Rosa Burger's attempt to define her "self." The novel is primarily concerned with Rosa's examination of the priority of her own values, desires, and needs against a nexus of values furnished by the apartheid society in South Africa, by the bourgeois culture in Europe, and by the discipline, compassion, and political ideas inherited from her communist father. Given the simplicity of the plot, the major movement of the novel—Rosa's exploration of her cultural inheritance—is a subjective journey that is perfectly rendered through the bifurcation of the narrative, as in *The Conservationist*, into objective and subjective components.

   The skeletal plot of the novel is barely sufficient for a short story. Because the death of her parents (her father's in a South African prison) has released Rosa from the burdens of the struggle against apartheid, she finds herself free to reconsider her life. Upon the encouragement of her lover she begins to examine the conflict between the self-sacrificial creed of her communist inheritance and her desire for self-fulfillment which stems partly from her own human needs but which is strongly advocated by her lover, Conrad, a champion of bourgeois values. After some soul-searching she decides that she can no longer sustain the self-sacrifice and anguish entailed by her predicament in South Africa and leaves to join her father's former wife, who has also deserted the self-imposed rigors of the Communist party in order to live a blissful life on the Mediterranean coast of France. There Rosa falls in love, is blissfully, obliviously happy, but upon meeting her "brother" Baasie, a young black man who had grown up with her in the Burger household, she decides that the pursuit of self-satisfaction is an illusory charade and that because one is never free from human suffering, it would be more meaningful for her to suffer on behalf of a self-transcendent cause in South Africa than for selfish reasons in Europe. She returns to Africa, becomes involved in the fight against apartheid, and ends up in prison.

This simple plot is rescued from banality by the narrative style and structure and by the rigor and delicacy of Rosa's self-scrutiny. Unlike the disjunctive relation of the objective and subjective narratives in *The Conservationist*, the two narratives in *Burger's Daughter* are complementary: the objective representation provides a fuller context which perfectly clarifies the subjective story. The proportional relationship between the two also accurately reflects Rosa's mood and preoccupation: the subjective narrative predominates in the first part of the novel which contains the bulk of her self-analysis, whereas the objective narrative overwhelms the subjective one in the second part when Rosa is less preoccupied with herself because she is in love, and the two narratives are more balanced in the third part when she has resolved her conflict.[39]

Within the objective narrative the omniscient powers of the narrator are carefully limited. In addition to confining itself to fairly factual information about the motives, desires, and mental processes of the various characters, the objective narrative adopts a calm, sober, neutral, and unobtrusive tone that, by contrast, highlights the lyric intensity of the subjective narrative. The former further enhances this effect by including within itself the mechanistic perspectives of the Communist party and the South African Bureau of State Security (BOSS), both of which treat Rosa as an object in a large impersonal game, as well as various "factual" documentary material such as newspaper reports and a pamphlet from the "Soweto Students Representative Council." In contrast to the blandness of the objective narrative, the subjective one has a powerful and controlled lyric intensity that is able to win the reader's complete sympathy. This is primarily due to a major change in the dramatic monologues, for unlike Mehring's, which are antagonistic, rambling, and subconscious, those of Rosa are carefully modulated conscious confessions to specific absent individuals. All the monologues in part one of the novel are addressed to Rosa's lover, those in the second part to her father's former wife, Katya, and those in the third part to her father, Lionel. Because all three individuals form a very sympathetic audience for Rosa, her monologues are never forced to become defensive, belligerent, or sentimental—thus she constantly strives for accuracy, intricacy, and honesty. The tone of her confessions varies in keeping with their content: at times it is objective, intelligent, and analytic, at times vulnerable and demanding genuine sympathy, at times angry and hurt, but never self-indulgent, self-righteous, or moralistic. As she is careful to point out, her monologues are neither apologias nor accusations. This strategy that combines the assumption of the audience's, and therefore the reader's, sympathies with the systematic variation of the tone produces a candor in her confessions that becomes absolutely irresistible: no matter how indifferent or hostile the reader may be, he cannot help being won over by Rosa's predicament and her attempt to find a way out of it. Thus seduced into entering the labyrinth of Rosa's life, the reader is able to experience almost at firsthand her hopes, frustrations, desires, and resentments, as well as her intellectual analyses of self and society.

Gordimer renders the stylistic bifurcation of the novel even more complex by making the subjective narrative, which contains Rosa's entire self-examination, in turn oscillate between a subjective and an objective pole and by endowing her heroine with an intricate and ironic awareness of this fluctuation. Rosa's attempt to avoid self-delusion is emphasized by the fact that the first subjective chapter of the novel consists entirely of a single sentence stressing the objective imperative of her self-analysis: "When they saw me outside the prison, what did they see?" (BD, 13). Her endeavor to see herself through the eyes of others is balanced by her narcissistic gaze at herself in a mirror. In fact she realizes that an original (subjective) and a mediated (quasi-objective) version of herself has been internalized in the very manner of her perception: "it is impossible to filter free of what I have learnt, felt, thought, the subjective presence of the schoolgirl. She's a stranger about whom some intimate facts are known to me, that's all" (BD, 14). That the tension between the presence and absence of self and her awareness of the polarity are products of her mode of existence is revealed during her recollection of the day when, at the age of fourteen, her first menstrual cycle began while she was waiting outside the prison in order to visit her mother: "But outside the prison the internal landscape of my mysterious body turns me inside out, so that in that public place on that public occasion . . . I am within that monthly crisis of destruction, the purging, tearing, draining of my own structure. I am my womb, and a year ago I wasn't aware—physically—I had one" (*BD*, 15–16). On this day too begins the lifelong surveillance of Rosa by BOSS. Thus her simultaneous yet unconnected existence as an object of public scrutiny and as a locus of private experience reflects her predicament as a bifurcated social being.

The very existence of the subjective and objective narratives in Gordimer's fiction reflects the burden of contradictions generated by the manichean South African environment. In a society replete with contradictions the Gordimerian self, hating apartheid culture, living in the sparce black-and-white society, yet unable to change social institutions to suit its own values and beliefs, is repeatedly forced to retreat from the divisive society in order to examine its own consciousness, values, and priorities. In this process the self is obliged to consider the socially enforced bifurcation between the subjective and objective as a fundamental ontological condition that permeates the very process of perception and conception. The complementarity of the two narratives in *Burger's Daughter* is a stylistic improvement compared to the previous novel, but the technique and its implication remain the same. Thus in this novel Rosa's awareness of the division and oscillation of self between the subjective and objective poles of existence and the anguish and frustration of her attempt to define herself are mirrored by the tension, the electrically charged gap, of the stylistic bifurcation. Yet in a sense she is able to transcend the disjunctive polarity because she realizes that both the private and public versions of herself are equally concocted, that no one perspective or set of signifiers can represent her completely.

Rosa's self-analysis is inspired by her lover, Conrad, whose self-centered bourgeois values and experiences provoke her to examine her own communist heritage, which in its suppression of personal desires in favor of altruism is profoundly other-oriented. However, the most fundamental stimulus for Rosa's self-analysis is not Conrad but the mystery of death. Her ambivalence about Lionel Burger's death ("to exult and to sorrow were the same thing for me" [*BD*, 63]), which frees her yet leaves her with a moral burden, is supplanted by her encounter with the death of an alcoholic, who quietly expires on a park bench while Rosa is having lunch there. Unlike the death of her brother and parents, the meaning of which is obscured by personal emotions and circumstances, the stranger's demise provokes her to contemplate the ontological nature and meaning of death, and, therefore, of life, which no political or social ideological inheritance is capable of explaining. This ontological mystery forces Rosa to examine and reconstruct her life. Her exploration of the labyrinth of "self" thus centers around two major propositions: the often repeated "now you are free," and the fundamental question that pervades the novel, "What else was I?" (*BD*, 40, 65). Gordimer focuses these two related questions about the nature of freedom and being through Rosa's analysis of her communist inheritance and the "good life" of bourgeois society. It is the *manner* in which she inherits her father's ethos, rather than the communist theory or praxis per se, which becomes the main cause of her anguish. Her parents' concern for others is experienced by Rosa as an extension of their love for her; the needs of Baasie, or of other unknown black children, or of oppressed people in general are as important as those of Rosa. Although their compassion and love is deep and boundless, Rosa does not occupy a privileged position in their affection. Thus because she has not learned the distinction between privileged love and a general sense of affection, her own feeling of moral obligation is not an abstract idea that she can easily discard whenever she wishes: rejection of the generalized obligation would necessarily entail an equivalent rejection of her parents' love for her as an individual. After her father's death she is theoretically free to abandon the burden of her concern for others, but it is so deeply ingrained in her emotions that she cannot do so without tearing apart her own personality.

The anguish caused by Rosa's attempt to renounce her sense of obligation and to overcome the habit of suppressing her own desires permeates the first part of the novel. It is brilliantly epitomized by her recollection of Noel De Witt, a young communist who has been imprisoned. Because he has no family and because it is vital for the Communist party network that someone communicate with him, Rosa's parents encourage her to visit him as his fiancée. Rosa, however, really is in love with Noel, but because she is afraid to jeopardize any aspect of the party's cause she refuses to admit this to her parents or to Noel while she continues to visit him for years. Thus she stoically plays this charade, pretending to be something that she would in fact like to be but afraid that expression of the real desire would be detrimental to the functional value of the role. Her recollection of this episode is full of pathos and irony. In her bitterness she accuses herself of having prostituted herself to political necessity, but she soon realizes that in the Burger house prostitutes, considered to be products of economic necessity, are not despised. Thus her father's ethos even deprives her of self-contempt. The major drawback of such a life is that it has robbed her of personally valid experiences and a distinct identity.

Rosa's attempt to renounce her heritage and define her identity through her own choices produces the novel's climactic moral and psychological paradox which is specifically Rosa's but which, in its general validity, also demonstrates the ontological depth of her self-analysis: "To be free is to become a stranger to oneself" (*BD*, 81). She would like to use her new found freedom to become herself, that is, to gratify her most intimate repressed desires. Yet in order to do so she would have to discard her past, her parents, and her values; that is, she would have to reject herself as she is. Rosa's analysis even leads her to consider how the nature of perception itself may affect her self-definition. Proceeding once more through a dialectic of subjectivity and objectivity, she opposes secrecy, the exclusively personal perception of self, to the mediated, public view of her being. Because she has been brought up in a communist household, constantly watched and harassed by the police, secrecy has become second nature for Rosa, but she realizes that this deeply ingrained habit eventually makes it impossible for her to acknowledge or identify her real motives and desires. Conversely, when she tries to define herself through the perception of others, she finds that most of them do not see her as Rosa but as Burger's daughter, that is, as part of a family, class, or political group: she becomes the object of various categories that do great injustice to her particular subjectivity. Thus she always remains in danger of losing herself either in a narcissistic or sociopolitical labyrinth: once more she oscillates between the poles of self-presence (-interest) and self-absence (-denial).

Although Rosa is critical of the bondage imposed by her parents' radicalism, she does not rush over to the apparent freedom of bourgeois society which she knows has its own forms of solipsism and ideological imprisonment. She is critical of Conrad's idea of freedom because she is aware of its essentially narcissistic nature; his preoccupation with his own desires and emotions precludes all consideration for others. She feels that consumer society imprisons the individual in his own desires—he can only escape the object of his desire by acquiring it, but desire then fastens itself on another object. However, Gordimer's main criticism of bourgeois society is reserved for Rosa's visit to France. In the meantime Rosa finds little to choose between communism and capitalism. Both are hoarding for the future in their different ways and both are equally cruel and violent; the domestic and colonial violence of European bourgeois society is no different for Rosa than the brutality of Stalinist communism.

Thus hemmed in by various unresolved dialectic oppositions, Rosa is strongly tempted to escape through the fundamental South African alterity: the blacks. But she knows that white South Africans use blackness as a way either "of perceiving sensual redemption, as romantics do, or of perceiving fears, as racialists do" (*BD*, 135), and she realizes that her communist colleagues often use blacks in the former manner: the overthrow of apartheid and the freedom of Africans is their sacred goal. Even though she knows that her parents' relationships with black individuals are based invariably on genuine personal bonds that transcend their redemptive usage, she distrusts her own motives and therefore avoids the temptation to continue working against apartheid under the leadership of Marisa, a dynamic and charismatic black woman. She is also afraid that by working with Marisa she would be choosing an acolyte destiny once more and putting herself in a different kind of bondage.

Unable to resolve the various contradictions in which she finds herself or unable to escape through an African alterity, Rosa finally decides that perhaps she can resolve her problems more easily if she left South Africa. Her hesitation in leaving is overcome by an epiphanic experience of cruelty, a merciless beating of a donkey, which uniquely brings the disjunct subjective and objective worlds together for a moment:

> I didn't see the whip. I saw the agony. Agony that came from some terrible centre seized within the group of donkey, cart, driver and people behind him. They made a single object that contracted against itself in the desperation of a hideous final energy. Not seeing the whip, I saw the infliction of pain broken away from the will that creates it; broken loose, a force existing of itself, ravishment without the ravisher, torture without the torturer, rampage, pure cruelty gone beyond control of the humans who have spent thousands of years devising it. (*BD*, 208)

Rosa is perfectly aware that she could easily stop this violence; the black man would easily succumb to her white authority. Yet she refuses to do so because she feels that this specific instance of pain is a product of a whole chain of torture, that the man's cruelty is a translation of his own suffering and frustration produced by the apartheid system of South Africa. Her dilemma is twofold: first, she does not know at what point it is appropriate to intercede in this ecology of suffering; second, she herself, as a product of that ecology, is responsible for the ordeal: "If somebody's going to be brought to account, I am accountable for him, to him, as he is for the donkey. Yet the suffering—while I saw it it was the sum of suffering to me" (*BD*, 210). This epiphany is produced by the only moment in the novel where the objective and subjective worlds coincide. Not only is all the personal anguish of Rosa reflected by the pain of the donkey, but also her awareness of the complex psychic, familial, and historical "ecology" that defines her own identity is mirrored by her similar knowledge of the complex racial, economic, and political ecology that produces this specific objective instance of agony. Through her assumption of responsibility for the donkey's pain the two worlds coalesce. South Africa becomes the embodiment of human grief, and Rosa cannot bear the burden of that responsibility. She decides to leave: "After the donkey I couldn't stop myself. I don't know how to live in Lionel's country" (*BD*, 210). Thus she leaves Lionel's country, that is, South Africa, as well as the world of moral responsibility for others.

In the south of France, where she stays with another apostate, her father's former wife Katya, Rosa is transformed. Away from the secretive, antagonistic, and precarious social environment of South Africa, Rosa becomes livelier, happier, and more carefree amongst people who have dedicated their lives to an honest, but nonpredatory enjoyment of their desires—people whose only imperatives are pleasure, loyalty to friends, and the avoidance of taxes. For Rosa the major merit of this life is tolerance: in Antibe no one expects her to be more than what she is or seems to be, whereas her comrades in South Africa expected her to be "equal to everything." If she were not, she would be a traitor to humanity. Her transformation is symbolized by the new name the French have imposed on her. Rosa, named after Rosa Luxemburg, becomes "La petite Rose": the moral heritage is abandoned for an existentialism that is exclusively aesthetic. Rosa's preoccupations with the Communist party, her father, and her own apostasy are supplanted by her passionate love for a married man, Bernard Chabalier. Her reaction against her father's other-oriented ethos reaches its logical conclusion in the pleasure she takes in being Bernard's *mistress*, which, unlike the position of the wife, has no *public* obligations.

Rosa's reluctant decision to stay in this bourgeois paradise is suddenly shattered by her meeting with Baasie, her black "brother."

Baasie, whose real given name, Zwelinzima, means "suffering land,"
is now a physical and emotional embodiment of the plight of his
race and country: his body and face show signs of physical torture
and all his emotions have coalesced into an overwhelming bitterness.
His vehement rejection of Rosa's attempt to revive their personal,
sibling intimacy is based on counter-racism. In this specific instance,
he resents what he considers to be the inordinate praise of Lionel
Burger's "heroism" in contrast to the neglect of innumerable Africans, including his own father, who take similar stands and suffer
similar fates. Rosa's repeated efforts to re-establish a subjective, personal bond between them is met by Baasie's insistence on severing
such ties because of the objective, racial difference between them. A
belligerent argument between them descends to insults that verge on
racism.

Rosa's immediate reaction to their quarrel and severance of relations is emotional; having learned to express her feelings through her
love for Bernard, Rosa now weeps for the apparent end of her personal ties with Africans. In trying to escape the moral burdens inherited from Lionel, she had not intended to abandon her personal
relations with her black friends, but she now realizes that in the increasing antagonism in South Africa, black-white relationships cannot remain apolitical. Further reflection reveals to Rosa facts that
become an important part of her decision to return to South Africa.
The fight with Baasie makes her realize in a personal manner the truth
of Lionel Burger's prediction that unless a substantial number of
whites support the African demand for majority rule the black reaction would transcend their political demands and become increasingly
and exclusively racist. The second reason for her return, she insists,
is not concerned with ideology or politics but only with suffering.
She had believed that by being an ordinary person, by shedding the
moral burden of her heritage, she could alleviate her anguish. But in
Antibe she sees that ordinary people are as tormented as she, or
Baasie, or Lionel. Because no one is immune from pain, she sees no
virtue in being an ordinary person: suffering for a particular cause
seems better to her than suffering for no reason. Thus her compassion for others is revived: soon after her return to South Africa she
begins practicing physiotherapy again—teaching crippled children
how to walk.

However, the most important reason for her return is one that
Rosa does not recognize consciously. While contemplating her quarrel with Baasie, Rosa sees that "[in] one night we succeeded in
manoeuvering ourselves into the position their history books back

home [i.e., in South Africa] have ready for us—him bitter; me guilty. What other meeting place could there have been for us?" (*BD*, 330). The last sentence recalls one of Nadine Gordimer's first short stories, "Is There Nowhere Else Where We Can Meet?" *Burger's Daughter*, then, circles or rather spirals around to the point of departure. Rosa does not possess the fear of the unnamed heroine of the short story, but the search for that other location where blacks can possess equality, dignity, and can control their own destiny and where the two races can meet as equals remains the same in both cases. Rosa, however, is politically and ideologically more sophisticated and committed than her earlier avatar. The main purpose and goal of Gordimer's fiction have remained the same while her style and technique have been refined. It is clear, then, that Rosa returns to South Africa in order to continue her search for that other location and that now both Rosa and Gordimer are perfectly aware that it is situated in the future, on the other side of a revolution that will overthrow apartheid.

Rosa's return to South Africa coincides with two significant radical events that signal the beginning of a cataclysmic revolt. The first is the treason trial of Orde Greer, a young Afrikaner journalist who is indicted for inciting violence and rebellion, for reading General Giap's theories of guerrilla warfare, and for attempting to procure information about South African defense installations and equipment. His involvement in radical activity is somewhat of a surprise for Rosa and the reader because earlier in the novel he is depicted, in contrast to Rosa, as a rather inept romantic desperately searching for a cause. The second even more surprising action is that of Marie Nel, Rosa's cousin. Marie, who has only been mentioned in the novel as a young spoiled brat and who has been working in Paris for the South African government, captures the newspaper headlines when she is arrested for harboring one of the leaders of NAPAP, an international terrorist organization connected with the Baader-Meinhof gang and the Japanese Red Army. A journalist's discovery of her family relation with the Burgers further fuels the right-wing outrage in South Africa. Gordimer provides us with no further information about Marie's character, motives, or drastic political transformation: this incident, along with many others toward the end of the novel, is deliberately shrouded in mystery.

These two events are closely followed by and symbolically linked with the actual series of riots by young African students that are collectively referred to as the Soweto riots. Gordimer depicts this rebellion, quite accurately on the whole, it seems to me, as a spon-

taneous uprising of black children who are frustrated with poor educational facilities and generally aroused by the rather vague Black
Consciousness Movement, which in turn is inspired by the Frilimo
and MPLA victories. She stresses the fact that the rebellion is by
children who, unconcerned with any elaborate communist theories of
proletarian revolution, burst forth in a popular movement that sur-
prises everyone. The initiative belongs entirely to the students.
Blacks who had avoided political parties "have begun to see themselves at last as they are; as their children see them. They have been
radicalized—as the faithful would say—by their children; they act
accordingly; they are being arrested and detained" (*BD*, 348). Those
who had already committed themselves to political action are in-
vigorated by their children's revolt.[40]

Rosa too becomes involved in what Gordimer implies is a general
unexpected revolt of the young against the apartheid regime in South
Africa as well as against the moribund bourgeois and communist cultures. However, the nature of Rosa's participation remains extremely
mysterious. BOSS suspects that part of her stay in London was devoted to activities that culminated in the Soweto riots, and the novel
is pointedly mute about various messages that Rosa receives prior to
her arrest. Rosa, now imprisoned with Marisa Kogosana, her old
friend Clare Terblance, and other comrades, immediately busies herself with establishing a system of communication within the prison
and with those on the outside. She is depicted as being livelier and
less reserved than before: she is, in fact, quite happily reconciled to
her destiny. She, too, along with the other rebels, is depicted as
being very young: her new short prison haircut makes her look fourteen—the age at which we see her at the beginning of the novel,
waiting outside the prison in order to visit her mother.

Rosa's renaissance traces a circle in Gordimer's work. Like Helen
Shaw at the end of *The Lying Days*, who imagines herself re-emerging
like a phoenix from the ashes of disillusionment, Rosa re-emerges
with renewed vitality from the despair that is caused by her predicament. She also traces another circle. Whereas at the beginning of the
novel she is angry and bitter toward her father, at the end she is
reconciled with him: her respect and acceptance are indicated by the
fact that her confessions in the last part of the novel are addressed
directly to him. She understands him now as a man who was motivated primarily by compassion and not by dogma: she feels that he
is more like Christ than Stalin. By the end of the novel Rosa, like
Lionel Burger, comes to accept a militant form of compassion as the
overruling priority of her life and faces the consequences with equa-

nimity. Rosa compares Lionel's sublime lucidity and elation to that of the black children marching arm-in-arm toward the rifles of the police.

Thus Gordimer ascribes the whole imminent revolution at the end of the novel to children. Rosa feels that the impending revolution is a vindication of the theories of her namesake, Rosa Luxemburg, who believed that the initiative for the revolution would come from the people, that theory would chase events. In this specific South African case revolt comes not from the people but from their children. (It is probably no coincidence that Gordimer published this novel in 1979—the Year of the Child.) What Gordimer is anxious to emphasize here is that the Soweto riots, or a later more cataclysmic revolution, are not or will not be a product of some diabolic plot masterminded in Moscow or Beijing, but that they are an indigenous rebellion by people who can no longer tolerate being treated as subhuman, evil slaves. The stress on children and spontaneity is designed to disarm the criticism of those liberals, inside South Africa and elsewhere, who would like to condemn the African recourse to violence as a communist plot. In this novel Gordimer is quite trenchant in her criticism of the liberal position. The motto of the second part of the novel, a quotation from Weng Yeng-Ming, "To know and not to act is not to know" and the fact that for the first time all her major white characters are Afrikaners, not Anglo-Saxon South Africans, clearly indict those who ritualistically grumble about apartheid but who are really quite acquiescent. By choosing her heroes from among the Afrikaners, perhaps Gordimer is also attempting to urge them to rebel against their own government. If so, one suspects that she may be indulging in a little wishful thinking.

If Gordimer's insistence on children and spontaneity seems somewhat sentimental, her depiction of Rosa's and Lionel's compassion, which is the substantial moral center around which the novel coalesces at the end, is anything but sentimental. Lionel's love for Rosa is impersonal, and she resents his failure to recognize her personal, individual needs. Yet the pattern of relationships in the novel consistently valorizes generalized and public compassion rather than private and egocentric love. Rosa's quasi-familial relations verify this pattern: her affair with Conrad, a pseudo-brother, is alienating and ultimately incestuous; her relation to her pseudo-mother, Katya, remains perfunctory; her love for Bernard is unable to compete with the demands of generalized compassion and political obligation; and her attempt to establish a personal relationship with Baasie, another pseudo-brother, is rejected by the latter. Rosa is equally compassionate toward all these people, but none of them are able to claim a personal, privileged position in her life, just as she is unable to do in Baasie's life. The bonds of the biological family are replaced in *Burger's Daughter* by the cohesiveness of the political "family." Throughout the novel members of the Communist party form an extended family that *does* look after its members, and at the end of the novel the same function is fulfilled by the "sisterhood" of Rosa, Marisa, Clare, and Leela Govinda in prison and Flora Donaldson who is their contact with the outside world. Thus in spite of criticizing some aspects of the Communist party praxis, Gordimer valorizes the power and efficacy of a compassionate political brotherhood. This form of deep sympathy is indirectly a product and a reflection of the apartheid system that attempts to prevent personal relationships across the color line and that therefore progressively forces those who resist apartheid to choose political alliances over personal friendships with people who may tacitly support apartheid.

Rosa's decision to choose impersonal compassion over the indulgence of personal desire is paralleled by the resolution of the dialectic of staying and leaving. *Burger's Daughter* contains the clearest and the most emphatic statement about that recurrent dialectic. Quite obviously, Rosa leaves South Africa in order to escape the burden of self-abnegating political obligations, and, even though in Europe she experiences the world of self-satisfaction, she returns because her acceptance of the universality of suffering enables her to bear the wretchedness of South Africa and thus once more to undertake her moral burden. However, in *Burger's Daughter* Gordimer compresses this dialectic into a shorter but morally more significant and powerful spatial movement. The novel begins with a fourteen-year-old Rosa waiting outside the prison walls and ends with Rosa, who looks fourteen, inside the prison walls. The dialectic has been reduced to a choice between staying out of prison or being willing to risk incarceration for one's beliefs and actions. The short spatial movement from one side of the wall to the other and the symbolic arrest of time signify a narrowing of Gordimer's black-and-white frontier society to the short spaces on either side of the moral dilemma. The choice is now entirely a *moral* one; neither time, that is, the belief that somehow "time" itself will provide a solution for the problems of apartheid, nor place, that is, being in South Africa or elsewhere, is a relevant criterion: either one acquiescently accepts apartheid by staying or leaving or one actively fights against it and accedes to the inevitable imprisonment. Just as Rosa willingly faces the consequences of her actions, so too Nadine Gordimer, by the very act of publishing

Burger's Daughter, shows her willingness to accept, in addition to the certain banning of her novel, her own banning or house arrest or even imprisonment.

Gordimer's novel is not only a *fictitious* resolution of a real moral problem, but the *publication* of *Burger's Daughter* constitutes an actual socio-political act which could have relatively harsh consequences for the author. The novel is also a political act to the extent that it is Gordimer's reply to the questions raised by the Black Consciousness Movement. The latter's rejection of white liberal-cum-radical sympathies and aid is rationally though not personally and emotionally acceptable for Gordimer because she feels that racial privilege has fundamentally altered the white South African psyche. The way forward for the white population lies through a radical self-examination:

> If we declare an intention to identify fully with the struggle for a single, common South African consciousness, if there is such a thing as white consciousness as a way to human justice and honest self-realisation, whites will have to take their attitudes apart and assemble afresh their ideas of themselves. We shall have to accept the black premise that the entire standpoint of *being white* will have to shift, whether it is under the feet of those who loathe racialism and have opposed it all their lives, or those to whom race discrimination is holy writ. . . . Could white consciousness—once you have decided what it is and how to put it into practice—provide a means for whites to participate in the legal and economic and spiritual liberation of blacks? Will it find a way in which whites themselves may at the same time be liberated from the image of the Janus Oppressor, the two archetypal stereofaces, grinning racialist or weeping liberal, of the same tyrant?[41]

Burger's Daughter can be seen as Gordimer's post-Soweto examination of white consciousness, as a reply to the Black Consciousness Movement and as the beginning of a dual attempt to arrive at the common South African postapartheid consciousness.

In her next novel, *July's People*,[42] set in the midst of a hypothetical, but really inevitable black rebellion which seems to have turned into a race war, Gordimer extends her explorations of the white South African consciousness. Her main purpose is to imagine and to examine the logical development of manichean relations in this apocalyptic setting. Yet with a sure instinct she avoids the actual military war, the bitter life-death struggle that ties the opponents in a bond of antagonistic reciprocity and that, by totally negating the other, retains and reveals nothing but the unqualified desire for absolute mastery. Instead she depicts, in a quiet pocket of the war, the struggle of consciousness between master and slave, between Maureen and Bamford Smales and their "servant" July who has helped them escape from the war in the cities by bringing them to his tiny village. By choosing "slavery," which is the cause and the latent form of the war (a postponement of the life-death struggle), Gordimer is able to depict the fundamental basis of South African society and to reveal the sublated aspects of the master-slave relationship. Early in the novel the narrator comments that "the circumstances are incalculable in the manner in which they come about, even if apocalyptically or politically foreseen, and the identity of the vital individuals and objects is hidden by their humble or frivolous role in an habitual set of circumstances" (*JP*, 6). Thus using the drastic change in apartheid society and an omniscient narrator (who has complete access to the minds of white characters and limited access to those of blacks) Gordimer reveals the hidden identities both of the masters, who are caught between the "blacks' rejection" of them and their own refusal to accept "white privileges," and of their loyal servant, July, whose inauthentic name, derived from a calendar, is reminiscent of Defoe's Friday.

The Smales are already endowed with an intellectual, social, and impersonal awareness of their dependency, particularly now that they are hiding from the war and July is mediating all their needs and desires. They even realize that July's decision to hide and protect them demonstrates the "logic" of a more profound reliance. However, the alien nature of the African village leads to a dislocation of Maureen's sensibility and facilitates a subjective realization of the deeper, existential quality of dependency, of the fact that the essence of the master's identity is predicated on the complete subservience and negation of the slave. The dual meaning of describing July as a "host" alerts one to this possibility early in the novel.

The parasitic nature of the master emerges through a series of confrontations between July and Maureen. She has traditionally controlled her house servant and still insists on doing so in spite of the changed circumstances and her own liberal inclinations. Each confrontation provokes a set of contradictory reactions from Maureen: as she becomes increasingly aware of the radical character of her dependency, she attempts to manipulate July in a progressively mean and desperate manner in order to retain her mastery. Each conflict is followed by a period of calmer reflection during which Maureen is able to contemplate her actions and attitudes. Gordimer represents this pattern of interaction through dense, concrete dialogues and descriptions of a totally alien village. The structure of the master-slave relationship is so deeply embedded in the mundane surface of life that the reader's gradual, hesitant comprehension of it produces a shock similar to that felt by Maureen. In the end the reader is as appalled as the heroine.

The initial conflict involves control of their automobile, which, because it is their only means of escape and because it symbolizes the technology that has allowed whites to control blacks in South Africa, becomes an important aspect of the Smales's definition of themselves. Conversely, African control of this technology, particularly military armaments that are later symbolized by Bam's shotgun, allows the blacks to overthrow the apartheid regime and win their independence. Thus, in struggling over the car, both master and slave are fighting to control the *means* of their independence. On a pretext Maureen demands and gets the car key from July, but in the process she provokes "an archetypal sensation," a mixture of contempt and humiliation that both master and servant experience. Recognition of these unspoken emotions makes Maureen realize that her own creed and world view, which she had previously assumed to be absolute, are in fact highly relative and ultimately predicated on economic as well as cultural factors. When she returns the keys to July the next day, his offended sensibility bursts forth in an accusation of her distrust, and by insistently using the language of master and servant, he exposes the hypocrisy of Maureen's position—of her desire to be the absolute master and her simultaneous refusal to recognize her compulsion. Even though the situation has changed and, as she later insists, master and servant are now on an equal footing, Maureen, neither willing to relinquish her authority nor to accept the nature of her dependence, attempts to master July by threatening to blackmail him.

The next confrontation, concerning Maureen's helplessness and superfluity in the village, eventually reveals to her that her attempt to cater to July's dignity as a man, while he is by definition a servant, had become the source of his humiliation and that this nexus of emotions between them is the only meaningful aspect of their relationship. This recognition produces a fear of herself in Maureen, and when July asserts himself by insisting that the Smales pay a visit to the local chief, thereby implying a reversal of the authority structure in South Africa, Maureen is deeply perturbed by the discovery that she could not possibly "enter into a relation of subservience with him" (*JP*, 101). Out of fear and frustration she accuses him of having stolen their car. After visiting the chief it gradually dawns on the

Smales that they are caught in a dramatic reversal of roles that is engulfing the country, that now they will need to know the intricacies of the African world just as the blacks had to understand and accommodate themselves to white laws and customs. Thus the Smales gradually recognize the *fact* of their servant's otherness, but they are still unable to understand the *nature* of this alterity.

In the process of contemplating July's alterity Maureen is appalled to discover that by not fighting along with other blacks and instead helping the Smales escape from the city chaos July runs the risk of being killed by the revolutionaries. Shocked by the recognition of July's loyalty, of their own unthinking imposition, and of the fact that the master-slave relation is predicated on the latent annihilation and sacrifice of the slave, Maureen feels that they must terminate this awful relationship by leaving. But they have nowhere to go and no means of transportation. Worse still, they find that various factors—the alien environment, the conflicts, their recognition of their parasitic dependence on July, and, most importantly, the latter's progressive reluctance to act as their slave—result in a disintegration of their own relationship and personalities. Bam and Maureen are entirely alienated from each other, and she even begins to lose a coherent sense of self (see, for example, *JP*, 139). While the dissolution of the master-slave relationship produces a corresponding disintegration of the master herself, ironically the resultant insecurity makes Maureen cling even more tenaciously to the servant.

When Bam's shotgun, the only means of self-protection and the emblem of mastership, is stolen, Maureen, once more interposing the slave between her desire and its object, insists that July is responsible for finding the gun. But the latter, finally tired of mediating the master's desires, refuses to do so. In order to maintain July's subservience, Maureen accuses him of petty theft. His angry reply makes her aware of the enormous burden put on July by the necessity of conforming to her image of him and of the falsity of her own pretense in making that image possible. With mounting panic she even realizes that "his measure as a man was taken elsewhere and by others" (*JP*, 152). She thus interprets his potential independence, which is on the verge of becoming actual, as a form of disloyalty to her, and in her anger decides to be disloyal to him. Her desire to "destroy everything between them" reveals the fundamental contradiction of the master-slave relation. By accusing him of being a traitor to the black cause, of profiting from the sacrifice of other blacks, and thus simultaneously denying his loyalty to his masters and their dependence on him, Maureen pretends to reject the very thing she ardently wants. A genuine acceptance of her desires would contradict her self-image as a liberal, while genuine rejection of them would contradict her fundamental nature as master. Gordimer stresses the convoluted complexity of this contradiction by ironically comparing Maureen and July to lovers surrounded by the "incredible tenderness of the evening." Like the previous confrontations, this final conflict is followed by Maureen's calmer recognition of the fact that the master's consciousness is absolutely preoccupied by July and that just as his existence had been abjectly dependent on Bam and Maureen in Johannesburg, so now theirs will be dependent on him.

Throughout the novel Gordimer contrasts the Maureen-July "affair" with the Bamford-July relationship. As yet uninitiated into the master-servant/white-black binary oppositions, Maureen's children easily mix with the blacks and are quite comfortable with their increasing dependence on July. Although Bam is a part of the overall master-slave dyad, he has rarely had to deal directly with July, and he is able to do useful work around the village. Thus he is less affected by the change than Maureen who does not have an independent working life and who has been the mundane master of July. Whereas Bam· gradually becomes despondent and abject, Maureen fights and attempts to manipulate July. Her deeper involvement thus reveals the sublated tension of the life-death struggle between master and slave. Unable to face the implications of this revelation, at the end of the novel when an unidentified helicopter lands near the village, Maureen succumbs to her animal instinct for survival and runs blindly toward it as her only possible means of escape, abandoning her husband, children, and "all claims of responsibility."

Thus once again Gordimer ends her novel with the desire to leave. But by being deliberately ambiguous about Maureen's fate—if the helicopter belongs to white South Africans, she will be safe; if it belongs to blacks she will probably be killed—Gordimer stresses the drastic and appalling nature of the master's self-recognition: Maureen is so horrified by her own perverse involvement with her servant and by her identity as master that she wishes to abandon it at any cost. Thus Gordimer brilliantly depicts the trauma of the master's coming-to-consciousness. However, *July's People* does not show the corresponding transformation of the slave-object into a fully independent subject. (For this process we have to turn to the fiction of Alex La Guma.)

The two novels that comprise the "revolutionary phase" of Gordimer's fiction have in common the obvious factor that they are both set in imagined revolutions within South Africa itself. Her characters' active or passive involvement in the intensity of the revolutions permits clearer definitions of their stands and consciousness. In *Burger's Daughter* Gordimer is able to clarify the values and priorities of a white consciousness that wants to move beyond liberal apology, whereas in *July's People* she is able to explore and delineate for the first time the fundamental underlying structure of South African society. However, a more important common denominator of the two novels is their attitude toward history, for both show that an attempt to leave South Africa is really a desire to escape from history. Rosa tries to avoid the burdens of apartheid and her responsibility by retreating into an idyllic, ahistorical setting in the south of France, whereas Maureen and Bamford wish to escape from the consequences of apartheid by withdrawing into a peaceful pocket of that war. But in both cases withdrawal leads to a further development of the protagonist's consciousness and to a realization that one cannot escape history. Rosa thus returns to accept her destiny by going to prison, and Maureen's "escape" from the village is in fact simultaneously a return to the war, a recognition of her own historical fate. Thus in the revolutionary phase of Gordimer's fiction, history is not merely an exploration of the roots of apartheid, as it was in the previous novels, but an acceptance of present responsibilities as they are defined by past segregation and injustice. Yet Gordimer's emphasis on history as an acceptance of present circumstances does not alter the fundamental thrust of her fiction, an imperative that she shares with Dinesen: a deliberate dissolution and reconstruction of white consciousness that will allow it to transcend the manichean bifurcations of the present and to work toward a more integrated and coherent future.

Of course this process of disintegration and reconstruction of self in Gordimer's fiction began much earlier in *The Lying Days* with Helen's recognition of herself as a "stranger" in South Africa and with her use of the phoenix metaphor. The strangeness, the social alienation produced by apartheid's ability to prevent Gordimer from bridging the gap between self and other, between the white and black African, has persisted and intensified throughout her writing career, and it has impeded her from thoroughly experiencing and depicting a multiracial, unified, and coherent cultural identity, which for her is "nothing more nor less than the mean between *selfhood and otherness,* between our respect for ourselves and our relationship with fellow men and women."[43] Thus the objective conditions of apartheid culture have forced Gordimer to write novels that, because they are repeatedly preoccupied with racial barriers and injustices of the colonial system, are, like the phoenix, avatars of themselves. All her novels repeat the same major pattern: her protagonists are confronted with obnoxious racial and/or political realities that force them to re-evaluate their attitudes to self and society and finally to take a stand that is more committed or radical than the one with which they commenced. The only exception to this pattern, *The Conservationist*, depicts, through a powerful subconscious attraction rather than a self-conscious reassessment, a far more radical, almost literal, disintegration of self than the other novels do.

The real measure of the alienation produced by apartheid is revealed through Gordimer's recurrent valorization of human relationships that are based on a generalized political compassion and through her corresponding devaluation of personal love or privileged egocentric relations. This pattern of relationships begins rather ominously with the shadow of the police, who are investigating violations of the Mixed Marriage Act, falling between Helen and Paul in *The Lying Days*. Their love is destroyed, directly and specifically, by the effects of apartheid's repressive laws. Gordimer replaces this affair with a deeper, though platonic and nonpossessive, intimacy between Helen and Joel. In *A World of Strangers* Toby's narcissistic bond with Steven is terminated by the latter's death, once more caused by the enforcement of apartheid laws, and his affair with Cecil is foredoomed to failure. Toby's purely personal ties are supplanted by the more political alliances with Sam and Anna. The disruption of the union between Gideon and Ann in *Occasion for Loving* is once again caused by racial segregation, and the resumption of the less personal but equally compassionate friendship between Gideon and Jessie depends upon the former's recognition of the political bond that could unite them. Although Elizabeth's marriage to Max, in *The Late Bourgeois World*, does have political overtones, it is destroyed by his egocentric demands and habits, and Gordimer substitutes for it and for Elizabeth's laconic affair with the liberal Graham the more dangerous and radical *political and personal* "love" between the heroine and Luke. In *A Guest of Honour* Bray's personal and yet clearly political commitment to Rebecca and Shinza supersedes his love and affection for his wife and Mweta. *The Conservationist* shows the complete disintegration of Mehring's personal relationships and a converse growth of an entirely *impersonal* union between him and the dead African. *Burger's Daughter*, as we have just seen, systematically devalues all personal intimacies and instead valorizes the political "family" of the Communist party and the "sisterhood" in prison, both of which are based on generalized political compassion. Finally, in *July's People* what Maureen had viewed as privileged personal compassion between her and July is shattered by the revelation of the underlying political and economic structure of the relationship.

This pattern of valorization reflects the debilitating alienation caused by apartheid's attempt to separate the whites from the blacks, the self from the other, but paradoxically it also demonstrates the only means of overcoming such alienation. Gordimer's valorization of the generalized, compassionate, socio-political relations is not designed to deny the possibility of viable personal intimacy, but rather to stress the importance of *social* relations, those between self and other, by devaluating various forms of individual and collective narcissism, including apartheid which, surely, is a major instance of systematized and institutionalized narcissism. As in *Occasion for Loving,* Gordimer is insisting that in the context of South African apartheid personal freedom cannot exist, for either the blacks or the whites, without the prior establishment of political liberty, and that, therefore, socio-political alliances must take precedence over the necessary and important but more luxurious freedoms of personal desires and relations. The latter must be subordinated to the former until the whole society is free. She implies that racial bifurcation and antagonism can be overcome only if white South Africans, like her protagonists, are willing to relinquish their personal preoccupations and accept their social and political responsibilities toward others who have been deliberately disfranchised. Quite simply, she is advocating the end of collective egotism. Thus the persistent chasm between self and other in South Africa and Gordimer's desire to bridge that gap lead her to a prolonged meditation (which spans eight novels) about the dissolution and rebirth of the self that is constantly seeking to unite with its other.

However, no alteration in the consciousness of Gordimer's protagonist seems to have the slightest effect on the objective existence of apartheid in South Africa. In fact, her constant attempt to fight racism through her fiction is an indirect recognition of the tenacity and power of the South African political system. In the face of such resistance her fiction understandably includes within it manifestations of a strong desire to turn away from the problems of apartheid. The dialectic of the desire to stay and leave that we have traced in all her novels provides one indication of her inclination. The other evidence is furnished by the contrast between the primary preoccupation with apartheid in her novels (*A Guest of Honour*, which is a projection of postapartheid South Africa, is a slight exception in this pattern) and the relative absence of those racial and political concerns from most of her short stories: the latter show that Gordimer can and wants to write about aspects of life that have nothing to do with race. However, because apartheid is such an obnoxious and predominant structural fact of South African life—it cannot be easily ignored—Gordimer is compelled to devote the major portion of her writing to it.

Unable or unwilling to turn away from apartheid, Gordimer makes a virtue of necessity by relentlessly examining the social and psychological effects of the manichean bifurcation. Faced by the wall of apartheid, she and her protagonists have only two choices: either they remain outside the wall or, according to their conscience, they choose to be imprisoned within the walls along with the black population. Gordimer's moral and political choice is clear and unquestionable; however, from an aesthetic viewpoint her political stand and concerns produce an interesting paradox. While she insists on writing about the objective, political conditions in South Africa, her fiction tends to become increasingly subjective, that is, her style becomes subjective, and she continues to be engrossed with the troubled consciousness of her liberal-cum-radical protagonists. The central space in her novels is never occupied either by blacks, who, like Baasie or Luke, function primarily as catalytic agents in the moral and political development of her white protagonists, or by white racists, who never make an appearance in her novels. Her fiction recognizes the traumatic presence of racism and graphically depicts the oppression of blacks, but her major preoccupation is always the personal and moral dilemma that her protagonists suffer due to their encounter with apartheid. This is a perfectly legitimate and, in Gordimer's hands, a very effective way of dismantling and examining the great South African lie, yet, as we shall see when we compare Gordimer's fiction to that of Alex La Guma, it is an approach that is fundamentally subjective.

The development of Gordimer's style clarifies the subjective nature of her fiction. Her first novel, written in a style that is essentially objective and realistic, is characterized by a more or less perfect equivalence between character and meaning. Helen Shaw and the other characters are nothing more than what they seem to be. From this point on, Gordimer's novels tend to become increasingly expressionistic and, at times, almost allegorical: her characters are prone to become representatives and embodiments of larger historical and ideological forces. This tendency culminates in her latest novel where Maureen is simultaneously an individual and an archetypal master. Although the characters in *A World of Strangers* and *Occasion for Loving* are leitmotifs, the objective conditions that surround them are still perfectly capable of explaining their beliefs, preoccupations, and actions. However, beginning with *The Late Bourgeois World* her novels show evidence of an increasing disjunction between representation of subjective experience and depiction of objective conditions: the former invariably overwhelms the latter. This pattern eventually culminates in the perfectly balanced, split narratives of *Burger's Daughter*.

However, the increasing predominance of subjectivity is accompanied by an obverse movement: a growing awareness of the fact that the nature and constitution of a specific individual or consciousness are determined by objective social conditions. Gordimer's gradual transference from the use of characters who are only themselves to those who represent larger cultural forces is attended by a transition from concern with personal freedom to an understanding of communal and historical determinism. For instance, Helen Shaw's moral growth proceeds through a series of more or less disconnected transformations, through "supplantings" of the self by other versions of the self, whereas Rosa is perfectly aware that her identity is perpetually transitional and indefinite and that it is a product of a complex and convoluted familial, social, and historical ecology. Thus while the stress on subjectivity increases and while the *representation* of social conditions continues to be attenuated in Gordimer's novels, there is a growing emphasis on the power of socio-historical determinacy and on the urgent need and potential efficacy of "impersonal" relations based on political compassion. Gordimer's most subjective novel provides the most dramatic example of this tendency. Although *The Conservationist* is dominated by the wild, uncontrolled subjectivity of Mehring's monologues and although the objective narrative is unable to clarify the ambiguities, the novel ends with an extremely impersonal union between self and other, between Mehring and the dead African. The urge to bridge the gap between self and alterity is elevated in this novel to a mystical union that transcends all socio-political relations. As the motto of *Burger's Daughter*, a quotation from Claude Levi-Strauss, "I am the place in which something has occurred," implies, Gordimer's increasing appreciation of the determining power and intricate complexity of objective-historical conditions—of the predicate in the above sentence—leads to a paradoxical and intense preoccupation with the subject of those conditions.

All these tensions and contradictions in Gordimer's fiction between the stylistic as well as structural aspects of subjectivity and objectivity, between self and society, between the desire to leave and the desire to stay are a direct product of the contradiction between her beliefs and the abrasive and restrictive conditions of apartheid society. The pervasive presence of this conflict between the largess, tolerance, and acuity of Gordimer's beliefs and feelings and the callousness, absurdity, and inhumanity of the apartheid system gives her fiction a powerful poignancy. The inclusion in the novels of the author's ambivalences about the necessity of fighting apartheid and her repugnance at having to contend with such an intolerant system echoes the reader's mixed feelings. On the one hand, we cannot help but admire Gordimer's persistence and courage in writing about the problems of apartheid, but on the other hand, we are compelled to feel a certain amount of regret that a writer of her talents is confined, by the abhorrence of political conditions in South Africa as well as by her own admirable choice, to portraying the effects of a fascist society on some of its inhabitants. Like the confessions of Rosa, all Nadine Gordimer's novels speak, with a gentle strength, an acute understanding and awareness, a finite patience, and a tolerant humanness, about the desire for liberation from social bondage, but, finally, with a clear recognition of the obnoxious reality, her fiction courageously and unhesitatingly advocates dismantling (violently, if necessary) the society that imprisons blacks as well as their white jailers. This combination of wistfulness and commitment makes Gordimer's fiction powerfully persuasive.

Chinua Achebe

The Generation of Realism

VERY LITTLE SIGNIFICANT *biographical* material is available about
Chinua Achebe because of his contemporaneity. Therefore, we cannot use the biographical mode in order to define the sociological
ground of his novels as we have done with the other authors studied
thus far. We may rely, however, on some of his own statements that
help us to locate his fiction in its social context and, more importantly, on a general understanding of the intellectual's predicament
under colonialism. Because virtually all these statements were made
after the publication of those of his novels that we will be examining,
they constitute a post facto realization by him of the influences and
imperatives that were produced by his exposure to colonial society.
We are not dealing with prior intentions of Achebe but rather with
his articulation of the sociological role and function of a writer in a
postcolonial society.

In the introductory chapter we have already examined the salient
features of colonial society that Balandier calls pathological.[1] At this
time we need to recall two specific aspects of the dilemma produced
by colonialist praxis: denigration and historical catalepsy. In order to
reinforce his sense of superiority the European insists that the native
is physically, psychologically, socially, and morally inferior to him,
and thereby he denigrates the colonized subject and inadvertently
creates a historical paradox for the latter. Because the moral validity
and the social momentum of the indigenous culture have been negated by European denigration and by the autocratic rule of the
colonial government, the African finds that if he adheres to the
values of his own culture, he chooses to belong to a petrified society.
However, if he accepts the Western culture, he finds himself engulfed
in a form of historical catalepsy, because by rejecting his own past

he belongs to a society that has no direction and no control over its own historical evolution.

Achebe's reaction to these aspects of colonial pathology provides us with the imperatives underlying his fiction. As an intellectual and a writer he is more sensitive to cultural denigration than to the actual material exploitation.[2] He is preoccupied with the "disaster brought upon the African psyche" during the period of colonization, and he defines quite clearly the kind of damage it can cause. For instance, Achebe encountered one of the major effects of imperialist denigration, the peripeteia of values, in his childhood; he amusingly recounts the shock felt by Christianized Africans and their resistance to the Igbo schoolgirls' performance of indigenous dances instead of the Maypole dance that customarily celebrated the coming of the Gospel to Nigeria. Similarly, he says, the Christianized African never used native pottery to draw water but rather preferred the foreign-made kerosene cans.[3] "In fact, to say that a product was Igbo-made was to brand it with the utmost inferiority."[4] Lack of confidence can become a disease for which there is no immunity, for it contaminates not only society and culture but even the indigenous *weather:* thus schoolboys prefer to speak of "winter" rather than of "harmattan" because of their fear of being considered provincial.[5] When a people have reached this stage in the rejection and perversion of their values, then their detractors need do no more, for inferiority has become a vicious circle; the racial arrogance of the colonialist then grows by what it feeds upon: "You begin by looking down on the person and then at the worst stage the person you are looking down on also begins to look down on himself. When you reach this situation you have made your point. You don't need to do any more, he will take over and continue to look down on himself, and this is in fact where we are in many ways, intellectuals as well as others. We are not really convinced yet that all is well with us."[6] This internalization of the imperialist idea of native inferiority is probably the worst form of psychic damage and for Achebe the internalization of such a negative self-image is a cardinal sin: "If I were God I would regard as the very worst our acceptance—for whatever reason—of racial inferiority."[7]

Achebe argues that by expressing the plight of their people and by showing how their sensibilities were traumatized by the colonial encounter, black writers have inevitably involved themselves in a dialectical polemic with Europeans: "They have found themselves drawn irresistibly to writing about the fate of black people in a world progressively recreated by white men in their own images, to their glory and for their profit. . . ."[8] Achebe identifies two authors whose depiction of Africa denigrates indigenous cultures and the existence of whose work draws him into the controversial situation. Joyce Cary, he says, perhaps "helped to inspire me, but not in the usual way. I was very angry with his book *Mister Johnson* which was set in Nigeria." Because he felt that Cary's depiction of Johnson was not only absurd but also insulting, he was inspired to write a novel based on his own version of the African experience.[9] Achebe is even more emphatic in his criticism of Conrad:

> *Heart of Darkness* is quite simply an objectionable racist book. What Africa stands for in Conrad's mind is very, very clear. Now if you are not an African you might read it differently—you might read it as the deterioration of the mind of a European. But that is for me only incidental. What is essential is why does it happen in Africa, you know, there is primordial evil there to which the evil in Kurtz responds, and it is that concept of Africa as evil which I am talking about. Now, Conrad may have craft as a novelist, though I think even that is overrated, but craft serving this kind of end is unacceptable to me.[10]

Whether or not one agrees with his interpretation of *Heart of Darkness*, the point remains that Achebe perceives the colonialist depiction of Africa as being decidedly derogatory and that this perception constitutes the essential thrust of the negative literary influence on him and other black writers.[11]

The indigenous writer, having become very sensitive to the ever-present denigration, reacts so strongly to the derogatory implication in Western literature that his response may push aside other values and pleasures of the literary text. In this sense the influence of English literature on the African writer is initially *negative:* his primary reaction, both chronologically and emotionally, is to reject the colonial depiction of Africa. Achebe's reaction against this kind of denigration, then, provides us with the *sociological* imperatives which influence him and other black writers. The targets of the negative reaction are not the formal and aesthetic aspects of colonialist literature, not the "craft" of Conrad for instance, but the social and moral attitude and perception of the writer which are ultimately grounded in the colonial sociology. Achebe has articulated very succinctly and emphatically what he considers to be the main obligations of the African writer who attempts to reject this denigrating perspective of the colonialist and to restore the self-esteem of the African.

The prime duty of the African writer, according to Achebe, is to reclaim the dignity of his past. It is his duty to show his own community that African people did not hear of culture for the first time from Europeans; that their societies were not mindless but frequently had a philosophy of great depth and value and beauty, that they had poetry and, above all, they had dignity. It is this dignity that many African people all but lost during the colonial period and it is this that they must now regain. The worst thing that can happen to any people is the loss of their dignity and self-respect. The writer's duty is to help them regain it by showing them in human terms what happened to them, what they lost.[12]

The seriousness and the weight of this imperative for Achebe cannot be overemphasized. Duty is perhaps too mild a word for it. At times he speaks of it as a "revolution" which he has to espouse in order "to help my society regain belief in itself and put away the complexes of the years of denigration and self-abasement."[13] At times, he speaks about this obligation in religious terms; the prolonged struggle to re-establish the lost dignity makes "one's work take on a missionary aspect which some people find offensive or rather disquieting. That does not bother me, because it can't be helped. It is almost a missionary effort to keep stressing that there was something here that was destroyed."[14] The desire to re-create the past and to re-establish its dignity through symbolic means, that is, through literature, constitutes one of the major imperatives behind Achebe's novels. However, it must be stressed once again that the metamorphosis of this desire into an articulated position took place after Achebe had written his major novels dealing with the past; prior to that the pressure was felt only as a vague need produced by the sociological and literary environment of colonialism.[15] The negative influence of the colonialist ideology and the need for restitution and vindication, then, constitute the sociological ground for Achebe's fiction.

However, before examining the manifestations of these social imperatives in Achebe's novels we need to consider an important qualification. Given the strength of Achebe's desire for restitution, one might reasonably expect the novels to show a marked tendency to romanticize the past. Achebe constantly seeks to avoid the temptation of such idealization because it would violate the integrity of the writer and defeat the attempt to restore the dignity and value of the past by depriving it of credibility.[16] His insistence on the realistic representation of the past is also grounded in what he considers to be the writer's responsibility to his society, which he equates to that of a teacher or a priest.[17] In addition to his desire to refurbish the past, Achebe is also motivated by the "conviction that the future direction of society is the concern of the artist."[18] Because the values of the traditional society have been destroyed by colonialism and the promises of independence have turned out to be hollow,[19] Achebe feels that in the resultant moral vacuum the writer must become the critic and guardian of social customs and institutions. In short, Achebe wishes the African writer to undertake the awesome task of alleviating the problems of historical petrification and catalepsy.

Achebe's perception of the writer's role as the mediator of values is reminiscent of the situation in which the French realists found themselves when their hopes in the future of the revolution were dashed by the enthronement of the bourgeoisie and when the glorious past of the republic had vanished. Just as the historical conditions in France led, according to Harry Levin, to the generation of realism as the prevalent mode of the novel,[20] so do similar conditions lead to realism in Achebe's fiction. We can best analyze and appreciate Achebe's fiction if we examine it through Georg Lukács's theory of realism, for both of these men are in essential agreement about the relationship between the writer and society. Lukács insists that man is an "ineluctably social animal" and that a writer's subjectivity is socially determined. "Talent and character [of a writer] may be innate; but the manner in which they develop, or fail to develop, depends on the writer's interaction with his environment, on his relationships with other human beings. His life is a part of his time; no matter whether he is conscious of this, approves of it or disapproves. He is part of a larger social and historical whole." His goals are socially determined and therefore his perspective and the form and details of his art are subsequently influenced: "The selection and subtraction he undertakes in response to the teleological pattern of his own life constitutes the most intimate link between a writer's subjectivity and the outside world."[21] Achebe too stresses the fact that the writer is a social being: "[he] lives in society, he lives with his fellows and he is really nothing except a member of society. What we regard as humanness is fostered by association with other people. The tool that we use, the basic tool which is language, is made by society and therefore you cannot really arrive at whatever it is you are looking for by gazing inwards."[22] Again, while discussing his role as a writer, Achebe emphasizes that his attempt to restore social dignity "is essentially a question of education, in the best sense of the word. Here, I think, my aims and the deepest aspirations of my society meet."[23] Given such proximity between Lukács's and Achebe's ideas about the social situation of the writer and about his responsibility to and role in society, it is important that Achebe's fiction be analyzed in terms of Lukács's notions of realism, for critics usually define his novels as realistic but seldom in a specific way.[24]

In applying Lukácsian theory to Achebe's fiction we shall focus on two specific criteria. Content, Lukács claims, determines form, and the focal point of all literary content will always be the question "What is Man?" If we put the question in abstract, philosophical terms then

> we arrive—for the realist school—at the traditional Aristotelian dictum . . . : Man is *zoon politikon*, a social animal. The Aristotelian dictum is applicable to all great realistic literature. Achilles and Werther, Oedipus and Tom Jones, Antigone and Anna Karenina: their individual existence . . . their "ontological being," . . . cannot be distinguished from their social and historical environment. Their human significance, their specific individuality cannot be separated from the context in which they were created.

Although Lukács's claim for the universality of this criterion is somewhat compromised by the polemical tone of his argument, it is a standard that, as we shall see, is particularly applicable to the novels under consideration. The second criterion, essentially a corollary of the first one, to be applied to Achebe's novels focuses on the question of narrative detail in realism and naturalism:

> Since human nature is not finally separable from social reality, each narrative detail will be significant to the extent that it expresses the dialectic between man-as-individual and man-as-social-being. It is these tensions and contradictions both within the individual, and underlying the individual's relation with his fellow human beings—all of which tensions increase with the evolution of capitalism—that must form the subject matter of contemporary realism.[25]

In examining Achebe's novels in terms of the above influences, imperatives, and criteria, we shall focus only on *Things Fall Apart*, *Arrow of God*, and *No Longer at Ease*,[26] because they deal with the colonial period, whereas *A Man of the People* does not. The consideration of his fiction will proceed by first analyzing the function of negative influence in the novels, then by briefly appraising the dignity restored to the Igbo culture, and finally by examining, according to the Lukácsian standards, the structure of these novels.

The negative influence of imperial ideology on Achebe is manifested in his novels through the juxtaposition of colonialist characters' and narrators' perspectives of indigenous cultures and through Achebe's allusions to the rhetoric of Conrad and Cary. Although the references to Cary and Conrad are sparse, the novels present a gamut of colonialist characters' views which, in *Things Fall Apart* and *No Longer at Ease*, condense and crystallize into succinct counterpoints to the narrators' perspectives. A systematic analysis of the colonial perspective will enable us to appreciate the need for restitution which underlies the novels.

Because the preliminary contact between the Igbos and the English in *Things Fall Apart* is made by the missionaries, the initial denigration is religious: in their attempt to convert some of the people, the Christians tell them that "they worship fake gods, gods of wood and stone: and that these deities . . . are not gods at all. They are gods of deceit who tell you to kill your fellows and destroy innocent children" (*TFA*, 134–36). In order to avoid a hasty generalization and to demonstrate that the European definition of all African religions as nothing but voodoo cults is prevalent but by no means universal in the colonial context, Achebe contrasts two missionaries, Mr. Brown and Mr. Smith. The former's genuine interest in Igbo beliefs leads him to debate the relative merits of Igbo and Christian theologies with the villagers in the hope of winning them over by reason. By using this approach, by showing some consideration for their faith, Brown wins their respect if not their conversion. However, he is soon replaced by the less tolerant and more simple-minded Mr. Smith, whose zeal and allegorical vision only allow him to see the world "as a battlefield in which the children of light were locked in mortal conflict with the sons of darkness" (*TFA*, 169). His strenuous attempt to convert the Igbos soon provokes a fight between the clan and the church which leads in turn to a battle between the colonial government and Umuofia.

The English government too acts on similar assumptions of native savagery, evil, and lawlessness. This administrative perspective is crystallized at the end of the novel when Achebe juxtaposes the district officer's hyperopic and superficial view of Okonkwo, the chief protagonist of the novel, to our perspective of him, which the novel has developed in all its psychological and cultural complexity and subtlety. The D.O. feels that "the story of this man who had killed a messenger and hanged himself would be interesting reading. One could almost write a whole chapter on him. Perhaps not a whole chapter but a reasonable paragraph, at any rate. There was so much else to include, and one must be firm in cutting out details. He had already chosen the title of the book, after much thought: *The Pacification of the Primitive Tribes of the Lower Niger*" (*TFA*, 191). Here we have a contrast not only between the complexity and intimacy of our knowledge of Okonkwo and the alterity implied in the D.O.'s perspective but also a contrast between the view of Igbo society as "primitive," with all its moral implication, and our view of the sophistication of that culture (which will be discussed later). In this juxtaposition of perspectives is contained the substance of the negative influence. Achebe includes in his novel the colonialist attitude to which he is responding and to which he owes, in a sense, the raison d'être of the novel itself.

Arrow of God also compares the shallow view of the colonialist with the narrator's intimate knowledge of Igbo reality. In fact, the contrast of perspectives in this novel is a direct continuation of that in *Things Fall Apart*, for the colonial administrators are now reading and discussing the merits of a book called *The Pacification of the Primitive Tribes of the Lower Niger*, which they intend to use as a manual of government. Although Achebe does not use the English attitude as a structural counterpoint in this novel, he does present some very cogent examples of colonialist ideology that he finds so offensive. Captain Winterbottom, the D.O., being unable to understand the specific reasons for the bribery and extortion that flourish under the colonial regime, can only ascribe them to the "elemental cruelty in the psychological make-up of the native" (*AG*, 65). Similarly, because he cannot see that the colonial government's imposition of native chiefs on a thoroughly republican Igbo political system will naturally lead to repression and abuse,[27] he attributes the chiefs' tyranny to an inherent "trait in the character of the negro" (*AG*, 121). These perspectives, which comprise the part of colonialist ideology that we have called the racial pathetic fallacy (i.e., the ascription of moral character to race and environment and, therefore, ultimately to nature), clearly demonstrate the nature of colonialist denigration against which Achebe reacts so strongly.

In *No Longer at Ease* the racial pathetic fallacy and other equally explicit racial generalizations are integrated in the novel so that they function in a structurally contrapuntal manner. Achebe opens the novel with the trial of Obi Okonkwo, charged with receiving bribes, and uses the English judge's inability to comprehend how a brilliant and promising young man like Obi can become corrupt as the question to which the rest of the novel furnishes an answer. Within this overall counterpoint Achebe includes another contrast between the "explanation" of Obi's crime offered by his superior in the civil service, Mr. Green, and the answer furnished by the rest of the narrative. Mr. Green explains Obi's immorality by claiming that the "African is corrupt through and through" because of the "fact that over countless centuries the African has been the victim of the worst climate in the world and of every imaginable disease. Hardly his fault, but he has been sapped mentally and physically. We have brought him Western education. But what use is it to him?" (*NLE*, 11). This, then, is the elaboration of the racial pathetic fallacy: climate and disease account for moral degeneration. Thus the judge's question and Green's explanation constitute the colonialist position to which the novel is, in a sense, the reply, for Achebe uses the rest of the narrative to show precisely how and why Obi succumbed to bribery.

The contrapuntal structure is strongest in this novel because Achebe makes Green repeat similar statements throughout the book in order to reinforce the structure, and because he allows Obi a limited comprehension of the negative influence. By indulging himself in a series of tirades comprised of pseudo-rationalizations, Green finally arrives at what seems to be the core of his attitude. While condemning the vacations and other privileges that black civil servants enjoy under a system developed by the British themselves, Green claims that "there is no single Nigerian who is prepared to forgo a little privilege in the interest of his country. From your ministers down to your most junior clerk. And you tell me you want to govern yourselves" (*NLE*, 144). The essential point behind these polemics is, of course, the issue of political independence. The novel is set in the period just prior to Nigerian independence when many English civil servants, afraid of being displaced by Africans, tenaciously argued that the natives were incapable of governing themselves.

Obi is well aware that such colonialist denigration has resulted in his sense of inferiority. While he is in London, studying for his B.A. in literature, he feels very self-conscious and inadequate when he has to speak to other Nigerian students in English:

> It was humiliating to have to speak to one's countrymen in a foreign language, especially in the presence of the proud owners of that language. They would naturally assume that one had no language of one's own. He wished they were here [Nigeria] today to see. Let them come to Umuofia now and listen to the talk of men who made a great art of conversation. Let them come and see men and women and children who knew how to live, whose joy of life had not yet been killed by those who claimed to teach other nations how to live. (*NLE*, 53)

him to free himself from it, for, as we shall see later, he does not Obi's understanding of the origins of his sense of inferiority permits succumb to the peripeteia of values. In spite of his emancipation, or perhaps because of it, Obi is not free from becoming involved in the colonial polemics. His training in literature enables him, and allows Achebe, to make a pointed comparison of Mr. Green and Mr. Kurtz (the protagonist of *Heart of Darkness*). Obi reflects that

> [Green] must have come [to Africa] originally with an ideal—to bring light to the heart of darkness, to tribal head hunters performing weird ceremonies and unspeakable rites. . . .
> . . . "By the simple exercise of our will we can exert a power for good practically unbounded." That was Kurtz before the heart of darkness got to him. Afterwards he had written: "Exterminate all the brutes." It was not a close analogy, of course. Kurtz had succumbed to the darkness, Green to the incipient dawn. But their beginning and their end were alike. (*NLE*, 103)[28]

These, then, are the literary manifestations of Achebe's preoccupation with the colonialist denigration of African cultures. The superficial views of the European "strangers" and the references to the attitudes of Cary and Conrad are included in Achebe's novels because they provide a stark contrast to the integrity, beauty, and cruelty of the Igbo culture that he depicts. These contrasts, then, constitute the literary embodiment of the dialectics of negative influence.

The moral condemnation and the superficial understanding of African cultures implied in the colonial ideology and perspective provoke Achebe to reproduce the *totality* of Igbo culture in his fiction. That he has succeeded in a judicious re-creation of his society is evident from a cursory reading of the novels and from the initial critical characterization of his fiction as anthropological literature. Although our task here is not to analyze or evaluate the Igbo culture itself in absolute or relative terms, such an appraisal may be useful in order to show the extent to which Achebe's fictive depiction of Igbo society is able to overcome the colonialist misrepresentation of it. It is instructive to contrast the appraisal of Achebe's fictive society by one English critic, William Walsh, with the usual colonialist claim that African societies are totally barbarous. Walsh describes the fictive society as one

> in which life is rounded and intricate and sensitively in correspondence with a range of human impulses. It admits both the aristocratic and the democratic principles. It is a life lived by a dignified clan of equals who meet together in an Athenian way . . . to make critical communal decisions. At the same time it allows for an exceptional man and for an organization based on achievement. Age is respected

but achievement revered. It is a universe which embodies a traditional and living morality and an order of reference by which the actual is comprehended and judged. Its religion is both mysterious and homely, answering to the instinct for the numinous and the need for practical good sense. Its vitality calls upon the sincerity of its followers and they support it with the conviction of living action. It produces impressive and beautiful artifacts in music, dance, and decoration and, above all, in conversation. "Proverbs are the palm oil with which the words are eaten." The limitation of its products, however, is their transience.

It is a society which is

> directly in touch with natural rhythms and processes. Not that this society, nor its most expressive art, its speech, gives any hint of primitive clumsiness. The sophisticated application of developed standards based on a wide scope of experience is a cultivated art, and this is what one is aware of in the speech, in the relationships of family life and even in the political management of men . . . as well as in the profounder religious experience. . . .[29]

This appraisal of Igbo society as re-created by Achebe is very telling when one compares it, for instance, to Cary's depiction of similar societies. That the changes in attitude from Cary to Walsh are partly caused by Achebe's fiction is not only a vindication of his crusade but also a tribute to his art. Walsh, however, overlooks one fundamental aspect of Igbo culture· its cruelty, which we shall examine later. Yet Achebe's unwillingness to shirk this aspect of his society only strengthens Walsh's characterization of the former's style: "Achebe's attitudes are quite uncoated with sentimentality, and uncontorted by anything neurotic or morbid or vengeful."[30]

Achebe's reproduction of a version of Igbo society in an objective rather than an idealist or subjective manner, though laudable in itself, does not constitute the essence of realism in his fiction. That lies, as we have said, in his intricate portrayal, in all his novels, of the struggles between various individuals and their societies, which are rendered more complex by the Igbos' attempts to realize simultaneously their aristocratic and democratic ideals. Achebe further complicates the dialectic between self and society by making his heroes the embodiments of the fundamental structures and values of their cultures. As Walsh puts it, Achebe's novels create an impression of massive cultural destruction "because of the fine balance drawn between a whole society and an impressive individual, and because of the way in which the fundamental predicament of the society is lived through in his life."[31] Achebe's heroes, then, are not only enmeshed in a struggle of the self-as-an-individual entity and the self-as-a-social-phenomenon but are also emblematic of the fundamental strengths and weaknesses, the beauties and cruelties of their societies.

If we take into consideration the emblematic function of Achebe's heroes along with the striking fact that *all* of them fall precisely at the point where they become alienated from society, then we can glimpse the intricacy of Achebe's portrayal of social alienation. As Raymond Williams says:

> What is impressive about *Things Fall Apart* is that as in some English literature of rural change, as late as Hardy, the internal tensions of the society are made clear, so that we can understand the modes of the penetration which would in any case, in its process of expansion, have come. . . . The strongest man, Okonkwo, is destroyed in a very complicated process of internal contradictions and external invasion.[32]

The most important internal contradiction, the social estrangement of Achebe's heroes due to their tenacious adherence to values cherished by society, depends for its success on the fact that from the beginning of the narratives the heroes are *potentially* alienated. Each narrative then gradually develops this potential until the protagonists experience the final calamities that result in their absolute alienation. We can best examine Achebe's representation of the inseparability of his protagonists' existence from their social and historical context and of the implication that the whole society collapses with their fall by first analyzing the process of alienation in each novel and then by comparing the progression of estrangement and social disintegration from novel to novel.

In *Things Fall Apart* the potential alienation of its chief protagonist, Okonkwo, is grounded in a conflict of social values that are embodied in the opposition of father and son. Okonkwo's father, Unoka, is lazy, improvident, perpetually indebted, and incapable of planning for the future. In a society proud of its martial prowess he is a coward who faints at the sight of blood; his only virtue is the ecstatic pleasure he derives from playing his flute. As a result, his village refers to him as *agabala*—a woman. Although his society is fairly tolerant of Unoka's "femininity," Okonkwo is mortified by shame, and his subsequent attempt to overcome his father's social failure becomes the major motive of his existence:

> his whole life was dominated by fear, the fear of failure and of weakness. It was deeper and more intimate than the fear of evil and capricious gods and of magic, the fear of the forest, and of the forces

of nature, malevolent, red in tooth and claw. Okonkwo's fear was greater than these. It was not external but lay deep within himself. It was the fear of himself, lest he should be found to resemble his father. (*TFA*, 16–17)

In order to transcend his fear of femininity, Okonkwo rejects the only virtues of Unoka—his gentleness and aestheticism. Through hard work and determination Okonkwo manages to become a successful farmer, but in the process his personality becomes harsh and his will inflexible.

At the very source of Okonkwo's success Achebe shows the potential for his alienation and fall—his exclusive reliance on tenacity and violence. Okonkwo's initial rise to fame through his victory in a difficult wrestling match at the age of eighteen prefigures his success and demise through the use of physical force. As he grows he becomes even more renowned as a warrior; at a relatively young age he is elected to the council of elders and made an *egwugwu*—a personification of one of the ancestral spirits at religious ceremonies. In spite of all this glory his personality remains rooted in violence: "He had a slight stammer and whenever he was angry and could not get his words out quickly enough, he would use his fists" (*TFA*, 8). In fact, anger is the primary mode of interaction between Okonkwo and his family. At the slightest provocation he will beat his wives and his eldest son, Nwoye.

Once more Achebe uses the dynamics of family relations, which mediate between self and society, to define more precisely the nature of his hero's flaw. Okonkwo dutifully fulfills the terms of his punishment for beating his youngest wife during the "Week of Peace," but he refuses to repent or show any outward signs of his contrition. Achebe's characterization of Okonkwo is insistently clear about the distortion of his psyche: "Okonkwo never showed any emotion openly, unless it be the emotion of anger. To show affection was a sign of weakness; the only thing worth demonstrating was strength" (*TFA*, 30). Even his neighbors demonstrate their understanding of and concern for his monomania by characterizing him as "the little bird *nza* who so far forgot himself after a heavy meal that he challenged his *chi*" (*TFA*, 32–33). In this opposition between Okonkwo and his *chi* (his personal god),[33] in his self-forgetfulness, and in his challenge to his *chi*, the novel clearly depicts the self-alienation, the self-distortion, and the hubris that precede his fall.

However, by placing the genesis of Okonkwo's character in the social and familial dialectic of the masculine and the feminine, Achebe also depicts the internal tension of the entire society. Okonkwo's character has been molded by the society's contempt for failure and laziness and its esteem for material and martial success. Achebe focuses and condenses this social desire for power by making Umuofia the most powerful village in the area and then by developing Okonkwo as one of the most successful warriors and farmers in this town. Okonkwo, then, becomes an emblem of the masculine values of Igbo culture. But, whereas the society balances its masculinity against a nexus of "feminine" values, such as its art, music, and folklore, and while it is capable of certain humane gentleness and flexibility, Okonkwo has become rigid, harsh, and unfeeling in his pursuit of virility.

Achebe brings this nexus of tensions within society and between Okonkwo and his society to a dramatic climax in the death of Ikemefuna, a teen-aged boy who has been singled out for execution in order to appease the spirit of a murdered woman. The delay of the sentence for three years allows Ikemefuna, who has been placed in the charge of Okonkwo, to develop strong emotional ties with the latter and his family and thus renders the eventual decapitation of the boy by Okonkwo himself even more horrifying than it would normally be. Achebe further heightens the cruelty of this situation by making Ezeudu, an elder of the clan, repeatedly admonish Okonkwo to dissociate himself from the ritual punishment: "That boy calls you father. Do not bear a hand in his death" (TFA, 55–56). He intends to follow Ezeudu's advice, but when the execution is botched and Ikemefuna runs to Okonkwo for protection the latter, dazed by fear, "[draws] his machete and [cuts] him down" because he is "afraid of being thought weak" (TFA, 59). Once more Okonkwo refuses to show compassion or contrition: he continues to insist to himself and to his friends that he ought not to be sentimental about the execution and that in any case he had no choice since the punishment had been ordained by the gods. His friend Obierika is unsympathetic: he does not question the actual sentence, but he also cannot condone Okonkwo's complicity in it. Thus Obierika and Ezeudu, both great warriors, demonstrate by their flexibility the increasing alienation of Okonkwo that is caused by his blind adherence to the limited image of virility.

Through an ironic supernatural coincidence, the accidental death of another teen-aged boy, Achebe sets the stage for Okonkwo's retreat into and possible modification by the feminine principle. Obierika has warned Okonkwo that his participation in the death of Ikemefuna is a sacrilege toward Ala, the earth goddess, for which he will be punished. The prophecy is fulfilled when, at Ezeudu's funeral,

Okonkwo's musket explodes and accidentally kills the dead warrior's teen-aged son. The revenge of Ala is thus manifested in Okonkwo's punishment for the manslaughter: "It was a crime against the *earth goddess* to kill a clansman, and a man who committed it must flee from the *land*. The crime was of two kinds, *male* and *female*. Okonkwo had committed the *female* because it had been inadvertent" (*TFA*, 117, italics mine). In this ironic twist of justice Okonkwo and his family are forced to flee to his *motherland* for seven years of exile. This dialectic shift allows Achebe to test the strength of his protagonist's fixation by providing him with the opportunity of restructuring his personality on a more balanced combination of masculine and feminine influences.

Okonkwo, however, is not predisposed to undergo any substantial change. Although exile does make him aware of his alienation ("He had been cast out of his clan like a fish onto a dry, sandy beach, panting" [*TFA*, 121]), neither this recognition nor the metaphoric but pointed lecture from his maternal uncle about the need to mollify his harsh masculine personality by repentance and by readmitting the gentler emotions has any substantial effect on Okonkwo. He listens politely to his uncle but refuses to be comforted (*TFA*, 123–24). Achebe emphasizes Okonkwo's continued fixation on virility through his hostility toward the missionaries who eventually come to the village of his exile. When the council of elders rejects Okonkwo's advice to wage a war against the Christians and their African converts, who have desecrated an Igbo deity in a zealous outburst, his reaction reveals his personal preoccupation: "This was a *womanly* clan, he thought. Such a thing would never happen in his *fatherland*, Umuofia" (*TFA*, 148, italics mine). But, as we shall see, Umuofia also succumbs easily to the colonial/Christian forces.

By recurrently basing the structure of motivation, values, and actions on the opposition of masculinity and femininity, Achebe exposes the underlying tensions of Igbo society that facilitate colonial penetration. Colonial/Christian forces infiltrate Umuofia while Okonkwo—the emblem of Umuofian masculinity and of their ability to resist European incursion—is in exile, that is, alienated from his society and from himself. The invading culture penetrates Igboland through the acquiescence of the feminine, flexible, and adaptable elements of Igbo society. Okonkwo's *maternal* village, against his counsel, welcomes the Christians and even provides them with free land. Similarly, Nwoye, who cherishes the feminine values of his culture, converts to Christianity because of his distaste for his father's harsh personality and insistence on virility.

Originally, Nwoye's personality encompasses masculine and feminine elements, with a preference for the latter; however, Okonkwo's constant naggings, beatings, and exhortations of masculine virtues progressively estrange Nwoye from his father and his martial values. The break between them becomes irrevocable for Nwoye when Ikemefuna, who had functioned as his elder brother for three years, is killed by Okonkwo: "Nwoye knew that Ikemefuna had been killed, and something seemed to give way inside him, like the snap of a tightened bow. He did not cry. He just hung limp. He had the same kind of feeling not long ago [when he had confronted for the first time the Igbo custom of leaving twins to die in the forest because they were considered evil]" (*TFA*, 59–60). Nwoye's distaste for the cruel rigidities of these traditions and the hardening of emotions necessitated by them is echoed by others in Umuofia: Obierika laments the severity of Okonkwo's exile and questions the abandonment of his own twins. The harsh inflexibilities of the masculine values leave Nwoye emotionally depleted, and consequently he is attracted by the apparent gentleness of Christianity:

> It was not the mad logic of the Trinity that captivated him. He did not understand it. It was the poetry of the new religion, something felt in the marrow. The hymn about the brothers who sat in darkness and in fear seemed to answer a vague and persistent question that haunted his young soul—the question of the twins crying in the bush and the question of Ikemefuna who was killed. He felt a relief within as the hymn poured into his parched soul. The words of the hymn were like the drops of frozen rain melting on the dry palate of the panting earth. (*TFA*, 137)

By describing the predicament of the father and the son through the imagery of heat and water Achebe links their alienation. Both of them are deficient; in order for them to become more balanced individuals they must assimilate some of the cultural elements against which they react so vehemently. Achebe establishes a structure of dialectic alienation between father and son and grounds it firmly in social causality: Okonkwo's reaction to his father is caused by society's relative intolerance of weakness and ineffectuality, just as Nwoye's rejection of his father is caused by society's tolerance of the sacrifices of twins and Ikemefuna. Okonkwo and Nwoye react to their society in opposite directions: there is no common ground between them, no synthesis seems achievable. This opposition and imbalance in society, embodied by father and son, cause it to fall apart under the impact of Western imperialism.

Under the influence of Christianity, Nwoye's alienation from his culture becomes absolute. When Okonkwo discovers his son's conversion to Christianity his masculinity is once more offended: "To abandon the gods of one's *father* and go about with a lot of *effeminate* men clucking like old hens was the very depth of abomination" (*TFA*, 142, italics mine). Okonkwo tries to kill his own son who is consequently forced to desert permanently his parents and his culture. Okonkwo's alienation too becomes absolute, but not before he makes a last heroic effort to assert his own values which have been reinforced by his exile; the humiliation of Nwoye's apostasy and of his own exile, which only reaffirms his resolution and faith in masculinity, thus becomes a functional parallel to the influence of his father: it increases his need for power over others and makes him blind to the virtues of flexibility and accommodation. After seven years he returns to Umuofia ready to resume his esteemed position in society and to reassert his virility.

Yet during his absence Umuofians have changed substantially. The people, who seem reluctantly enamoured with the residual presence of Western culture despite their fear of it, have permitted the erection of a church and have even accommodated themselves to the authority of a district officer representing the colonial government. In their preoccupation with the Europeans, Umuofians ignore Okonkwo's return and thus inadvertently sabotage his plans for a triumphal homecoming. Unable to understand this transformation, he can only appraise the situation in terms of his limited perspective of power and violence: "He mourned the fate of his clan, which was breaking up and falling apart, and he mourned for the warlike men of Umuofia, who had so unaccountably become soft like *women*" (*TFA*, 168, italics mine).

However, the continuous friction between the two cultures provides Okonkwo with the opportunity to counsel war against the intruders. When, after a series of misunderstandings and disagreements between the Christians and the villagers, the latter burn the church upon Okonkwo's advice, he regains some of his previous self-confidence and elation: "It was like the good old days again, when a warrior was a warrior. Although they had not agreed to kill the missionary or drive away the Christians, they had agreed to do something substantial. And they had done it. Okonkwo was almost happy again" (*TFA*, 176). But his exultation is short-lived. The elders of the clan, including Okonkwo, are soon deceived, imprisoned, humiliated, and punished by the district officer. At a subsequent gathering of the clan Okonkwo impulsively kills one of the government messengers who had come to disband the meeting, but the Umuofians, instead of following his lead, become confused and allow the other messengers to escape. Okonkwo finally realizes that this lack of support means that the people have changed while he has remained static and that he is now entirely alienated from the society which had praised his courage, skill, and strength. Rather than face further humiliation through arrest, imprisonment, and probable execution, Okonkwo quietly commits suicide.

In keeping with Achebe's irony, the complete alienation of father and son is quite ambivalent. The ambiguity of Okonkwo's social standing is revealed by the dilemma of his friends who cannot give him a decent burial because suicide is a major sin in Igbo ethics, but who still feel that he was "one of the greatest men in Umuofia." Similarly, Nwoye's alienation from his community is based on an elaboration of values that Okonkwo rejects but that the society accepts. The feminine values (the pride in linguistic and poetic skills, in refined ritual, in plastic arts, and in social manners), the sophisticated application of developed standards that William Walsh discusses, are cherished by the Igbos as much as material success and courage in battle. Father and son together represent the entire gamut of social values, and their different dilemmas reveal how the self is formed, and alienated, by a complex calculus of personal desires and social obligations and pressures. The absoluteness of their alienation through suicide and desertion of community represents the end of a specific—cohesive, totalized, yet contradictory—phase of Igbo culture rather than the complete annihilation of the society; characters like Obierika and Ezeudu, who are capable of flexibility, compromise, and adaptation, will ensure the survival of the culture in one form or another. Thus Okonkwo and Nwoye dramatically symbolize the contradictions and tensions between various facets of Igbo society that cause it to succumb easily to the invasion of a militarily and technologically superior civilization.

This basis of Achebe's realism, this grounding of individuals in society and their definition through struggles that are couched in terms of socially significant values, is even more emphatic in *Arrow of God*. In this novel he embodies in one socially and religiously powerful individual the contradiction between the aristocratic and democratic principles inherent in Igbo culture as well as the conflict caused by the desire for personal power and the demands of social obligation. By focusing these problems through Ezeulu, the chief priest of Umuaro, Achebe convincingly injects the conflict between individual and society into all the mundane details of his narrative.

Because an analysis of the manner in which all the details are impregnated with the conflict cannot be undertaken in the time and space available here, we shall focus on the basic structure of this conflict.

Ezeulu's power and position as chief priest of Umuaro, a confederacy of six villages, are themselves products of seemingly social democratic values: in the distant past the six villages, isolated and unprotected against slave raiders, had united by creating a new deity, Ulu, to guard them. Although Ezeulu feels that Ulu created and continues to protect Umuaro, the narrative keeps repeating the fact that in the past deities and their priests had been removed from their office because they had become redundant. Until the end of the novel, the narrator leaves this conflict between religious autocracy and republicanism in an ambiguous state in order to emphasize the socioreligious tensions that lead to an explosive disintegration of Umuaro.

If the religious basis of Ezeulu's power is somewhat ambiguous, his function in society leaves no doubt about his pivotal position. His obligations are clearly manifested in the ceremony of purification during which he assumes the sins of all the villagers and through his divine power absolves them and himself. Ezeulu's exhaustion and sickness after such a ceremony are seen as a "necessary conclusion to the festival," as a part of the general sacrifice. The office of the priest as well as Ezeulu's physical health is imbued with socioreligious significance: in his annual exhaustion lies the salvation of the community. His function as the spiritual mediator of his society is accompanied by his more practical, though equally religious, social functions such as calculating the time for and announcing the festivals for planting and harvesting. Because without his ritual permission and blessing these vital functions cannot be undertaken, Ezeulu has great power over his society as well as a great obligation toward it: next to Ulu, his priest becomes the central embodiment of society's desires, values, and organization.

Parallel to this presentation of Ezeulu's obligations as a social being, Achebe also establishes emphatically the priest's desire for personal power and, stemming from that, his tendency toward alienation. Although the specific origin of his thirst for power is left uncertain, it seems to be based on resentment that manifests itself in innumerable petty ways as well as in his substantial understanding of and desire for the efficacy of the colonizing culture. The pettiness is presented as an integral part of his personality from the very beginning of the narrative: "But for the present he was as good as any young man, or better because young men were no longer what they used to be. There was one game Ezeulu never tired of playing on them. Whenever they shook hands with him he tensed his arm and put all his power into the grip, and being unprepared for it they winced and recoiled with pain" (*AG*, 1). His desire for substantial power is represented by what he considers the sacrifice of his son, Oduche, who is commanded to become a Christian convert in order to master the secrets of Western culture and technology. He recognizes that European culture will determine the dominant mode of life, and he tries to impress it on his son:

> When I was in Okperi I saw a young white man who was able to write his book with the left hand. From his actions I could see that he had very little sense. But he had power; he could shout in any face; he could do what he liked. Why? Because he could write with his left hand. That is why I have called you. I want you to learn and master this man's knowledge so much that if you are suddenly woken up from sleep and asked what it is you will reply. You must learn it until you can write it with your left hand. (*AG*, 213)

His magical view of literacy, coupled with his accurate appraisal of European strength, only augments his desire to master the new culture. Yet Ezeulu is not a simple megalomaniac. He has a deep sense of obligation to the values and integrity of his culture: when the district officer offers to establish him as the *political* chief of Umuaro (in order to teach the natives how to rule), the priest contemptuously dismisses the office that is entirely alien to Igbo political practice. Thus his desire for authority is not based entirely on egotism; it also stems from his view of the importance of his *religious* office.

Nevertheless, Ezeulu's ultimate alienation from self and society lies in his rather complex search for power. His fall originates from the apparently contradictory desires to dominate others and to be isolated from them: he avoids the otherness of people either by subordinating them to his demands or by ignoring them through a retreat into priestly isolation: "Ezeulu's only fault was that he expected everyone—his wives, his kinsmen, his children, his friends and even his enemies—to think and act like himself. Anyone who dared to say no to him was an enemy. He forgot the saying of the elders that if a man sought for a companion who acted entirely like himself he would live in solitude" (*AG*, 105). Ezeulu's arrogance, isolation, and egotism all seem to stem somewhat naturally from his priestly function and position. By balancing his adamant faith in Ulu and in his own office with his desire for personal power, the novel creates a deliberate ambiguity: it becomes impossible to determine whether his desire to control others is an idiosyncratic product of his personality or whether it is a natural extension of the socio-religious power vested in the hereditary priesthood.

Ezeulu's social obligations and his desire for power, which are equally serious concerns for him, could coexist in a parallel state without any friction if personal and socio-political ambitions and rivalries did not bring them together. However, the existence of such competition entangles the obligation to society and to self in an inextricable manner from the very beginning of the narrative. The priest of another village within the federation of Umuaro is jealous of Ezeulu's precedence over him and is also accurately aware of Ezeulu's desire to dominate, whereas the latter recognizes the vindictive motives behind the objections of other priests but does not sense any impropriety in his own megalomania. The main concern of *Arrow of God* is the gradual and plausible development of the conflict caused by these rivalries, during the course of which the English colonial government intervenes in order to dominate the entire Igbo people.

Ezeulu's contemplation of his real power as chief priest prefigures the inevitable conflict between his social obligations and his attempts to dominate others, which finally causes his society to fall apart and irrevocably alienates him from it:

> Whenever Ezeulu considered the immensity of his power over the year and the crops and, therefore, over the people, he wondered if it was real. It was true he named the day for the feast of the Pumpkin Leaves and for the New Yam feast; but he did not choose the day. He was merely a watchman. His power was no more than the power of a child over a goat that was said to be his. . . . No! the Chief Priest of Ulu was more than that, must be more than that. If he should refuse to name the day there would be no festival—no planting and no reaping. But could he refuse? No Chief Priest had ever refused. So it could not be done. He would not dare. (*AG, 3*)

Ezeulu, however, does do precisely that in the final clash of the novel. When he is called to the district officer's headquarters, the elders of the clan refuse to send a delegation with him since he is considered to be a friend of the white men. But when the colonial government imprisons him for several months (because he arrogantly refuses to accept the appointment as political chief), he is unable to keep count on the lunar calendar by the traditional method. He only resumes the count after his release, and consequently he can theoretically announce the beginning of the harvest, the New Yam feast, several months later than it is due. This literal mindedness is, of course, a revenge on his people for not honoring him with a delegation and for allowing him to be imprisoned. Ezeulu thus turns his social responsibility into personal power disguised in religious garb. Just as his obligation and the power are great, so are the consequences drastic for both society and Ezeulu.

The immediate result is the destruction of the current structure of Igbo society. The religiosity of the people is sufficiently strong so that they will not harvest the yams without divine blessing through Ezeulu. Yet they are saved from potential starvation by the opportunistic intervention of the Christians who promise that their God will protect the people from the wrath of Ulu if they bring their thank offerings to the church. Out of desperation the villagers gradually convert to Christianity in order to harvest their crops. In fact the church improves on the traditional Igbo tribute which is one yam per family: the missionaries ask the people to bring "not only yams, [but] any crop whatsoever or livestock or money" (AG, 246). This introduction of monetary fluidity into the traditional socio-religious system is a certain mark of its disintegration. The displacement of Ulu by the Christian God and the replacement of the symbolic and usage values, implied in the socially codified offering of one specific species of yam imbued with religious meaning, by the metonymic exchange value of money, which is bereft of any intrinsic or symbolic value, define the end of the traditional culture.

While the society and culture of Umuaro are disintegrating, Ezeulu, tormented by guilt for his actions, gradually drifts toward madness. He interprets the natural death of his favorite son as a sign of Ulu's withdrawal of protection, and the shock of this desertion finally drives him mad, thus cutting him off from all coherent social discourse in a culture that has begun to lose its own traditional coherence. The people of Umuaro interpret his insanity as Ulu's judgment against his priest and thus as a vindication of the democratic principle of Igbo society: "no man however great was greater than his people . . . no man ever won judgment against his clan" (AG, 261). However, as the narrator reminds us, the colonialists are the final beneficiaries of this conflict.

By choosing an individual whose function is pivotal to his society and by developing his conflict of obligations to self and to society in such a way that the final result is extreme for both, Achebe has developed in Arrow of God the most dramatic yet plausible version of the dialectic between man-as-individual and man-as-social-being. Although this dialectic is less dramatic in Things Fall Apart, it is more tense because of Okonkwo's personality. If this dialectic approximates tragic stature in these two works, in *No Longer at Ease* it becomes farcical, but it never disappears: it is central to all Achebe's novels.

The farcical nature of the struggle in *No Longer at Ease* is due primarily to the devaluation of traditional life in a society that is now thoroughly colonial. The prime "value" of this new society is money, and the prime mode of obtaining such currency is extortion, a given, pre-existent fact that permeates all levels and modes of life. Although the genesis of corruption is not provided in this novel, it is shown in *Things Fall Apart* and *Arrow of God*, and we must examine it briefly because an understanding of its nature and origin is important to our appraisal of the conflict in *No Longer at Ease*.

The corruption in the previous novels is not generated deliberately by the colonial administration; nevertheless, it is an inevitable result of the nature of colonial authority. The English district officers are almost completely ignorant of indigenous culture and languages, whereas the Africans are equally ignorant of the English institutions and values that are being imposed upon them. In this gap of ignorance between the governors and governed, deception and bribery flourish in a healthy and vigorous manner. For instance, the district officer in *Things Fall Apart* levies a fine of 200 bags of cowries from the people of Umuofia, but his messengers increase the sum to 250 bags and keep the difference because they are confident that the absence of any substantial communications between the government and the people ensures that such corruption will go undetected. Corruption, then, is caused by the fact that there is no coherent cultural connection between the government and the public: the English have imposed on the Igbos a series of institutions that have been generated in a radically different culture.

In the fifty years or so between the setting of *Things Fall Apart* and the time of *No Longer at Ease*, around the 1950s, the corruption has permeated all aspects of life, and, consequently, respect for the new political and economic institutions is nonexistent: "In Nigeria the government was 'they.' It had nothing to do with you or me. It was an alien institution and people's business was to get as much from it as they could without getting into trouble" (*NLE*, 38). Not only political government but other cultural institutions and practices, such as labor (*NLE*, 79), the family (*NLE*, 128), and even sexual responsibility (*NLE*, 136), are in an advanced stage of disintegration. No social product or service has intrinsic merit any more, and the entire population seems to be motivated only by money—the medium of exchange has quickly become the goal of human activity and the measure of a man's social and moral worth.

In this corrupt and disintegrating society Achebe puts as his chief protagonist a rather quixotic idealist who has just returned from England with a B.A. in Literature. Obi Okonkwo, the grandson of the hero of *Things Fall Apart*, had gone straight from missionary school to England and consequently is ignorant of the realities of a Nigerian city. His naiveté in all walks of life is best symbolized by the contrast between a melodramatic and clichéd poem about Nigeria, which he had written in England, and the slums of Lagos where he is when he recalls that poem. The juxtaposition between the scene in the poem,

> How sweet it is to be beneath a tree
> At eventime and share the ecstasy
> Of jocund birds and flimsy butterflies;

and the scene in the slums, where from a wide-open storm drain next to a meat stall comes the "very strong smell of [a dog's] rotting flesh" (*NLE*, 22–23), typifies the idealism of Obi and the reality of Lagos. Characteristically, Obi takes himself very seriously and pontificates about how "our people have a long way to go" (*NLE*, 40).

The narrative foreshadows the substantial aspects of the collision between Obi and Nigerian society by an ironic presentation of his naive, moralistic attitude toward his countrymen's peripeteia of values, which causes the colonized person to abandon indigenous social traditions because they are considered inferior and then to emulate the colonizer's values because they are supposedly superior. Thus the educated Nigerian in *No Longer at Ease* wears "a black suit, bowler hat, and [carries] a rolled umbrella" in the middle of a hot October day; the semi-educated Nigerian uses pompous and malapropian English and refuses to eat indigenous food. Obi, on the other hand, insults all well-wishers by dressing in shirt sleeves, by using unimpressive English, and by asking for Igbo food (*NLE*, 35–39). These deliberate contrasts are, from the narrative viewpoint, rather ironic, but for the society of Lagos they are offensive.

However, the crucial aspect of Obi's idealism and naiveté is demonstrated in his approach to corruption: he believes that it could be easily cured either if a few men at the top would set good examples or if a benevolent dictator were to take over the government and eradicate bribery and extortion. In his typically moralistic and self-righteous manner, he considers himself one of those enlightened people who will set the correct example by never accepting a bribe. After he has refused the first one he is offered, he compares his elation to the "feeling he had some years ago in England after his first woman." She had complimented him by equating him to a tiger, and now, after the encounter with the briber, he has a similar sensation. The irony of this inappropriate analogy is that sexual consummation had initiated him from innocence into experience, whereas rejection of the bribe prevents him from experiencing the real world: he remains engulfed in his own moralism and vanity.

Obi's real initiation into knowledge of the world, and consequently into the conflict between allegiance to self and society, develops gradually through his social obligations and his own spendthrift habits. The tenacious ability of his naiveté to withstand the onslaught of social demands, which are made ultimately in terms of money, produces a slow and tense initiation which, ironically, is completed by the time he reaches the nadir of his alienation. Obi's prime obligation is to the Umuofia Progressive Union whose members had "taxed themselves mercilessly" in order to support his studies in England. In addition to repaying their loan, he soon discovers that he has to give a monthly allowance to his parents, who cannot live adequately on his father's pension, he has to pay his brother's school fees, and, every time he returns to his village, he has to entertain all the neighbors and relatives. These social obligations, translated into monetary terms, conflict with his own needs. Immediately after becoming a well-paid civil servant, he buys a car on time installments without even budgeting for it, and he follows this extravagance by hiring a chauffeur in order to keep up his image as a civil servant. These symbols of his position take their toll in the form of insurance payments, vehicle licenses, income tax, and so forth. Obi soon finds himself living beyond his means and decides to borrow, but no sooner has he done so than he is obliged to pay for his mother's two operations and for his girl friend's abortion.

Under these financial pressures Obi finally recognizes and examines the conflict between personal needs and social obligations:

> They had taxed themselves mercilessly to raise eight hundred pounds to send him to England. Some of them earned no more than five pounds a month. He earned nearly fifty. They had wives and school going children, he had none. After paying the twenty pounds he would have thirty left. And very soon he would have an increment which alone was as big as some people's salary.
>
> Obi admitted that his people had a sizeable point. What they did not know was that, having labored in sweat and tears to enroll their

kinsman among the shining elite, they had to keep him there. (NLE, 96)

Obi cannot satisfy all these demands for money with his own salary, yet he scornfully rejects his friends' advice that he accept bribes, and he continues to be shocked and offended by the various monetary and sexual offers he receives from the scholarship candidates whose applications he has to judge. Because his financial problems continue, he becomes trapped between his morality and the personal and social demands. He eventually attempts in vain to resolve his dilemma by choosing to be practical.

But the shallowness of Obi's morality and his general practical inefficacy in this, as in all matters, are best illustrated by the development of his affair with Clara, a nurse who belongs to the *Osu* caste (an Igbo version of the untouchables) and who can therefore only marry within her own group. Obi, emancipated by his Western education, considers this restriction primitive and attempts to shrug it off. However, since the prejudice against *Osus* is deeply ingrained, society views Obi's willful insistence on this marriage as the product of his "mission-house upbringing and European education [that] had made him a stranger in his country" (NLE, 72). When the president of the Umuofia Progressive Union attempts to counsel him against this engagement, Obi's westernized notions of distinctions between private and public life explosively manifest themselves: "don't you dare interfere in my affairs again" he yells (NLE, 82). This is the first instance of an exclusive notion of personal privacy in Achebe's novels, and it is a clear index of the complete disintegration of the old culture and the rise of new values.

Obi, however, is a naive idealist who has little conviction about his decision: "Perhaps it was not a *decision* really [to marry Clara]; for him there could only be one choice. It was scandalous that in the middle of the twentieth century a man could be barred from marrying a girl simply because [she was an Osu]" (NLE, 72, italics mine). Obi's desire to marry Clara is not based on a conscious decision and deliberate awareness of the consequent social disapprobation but rather on a vague moral notion of how things ought to be. In the face of mounting opposition—Obi's father, although a Christian catechist, is firmly against the marriage, and his mother simply promises to commit suicide if he marries Clara—Obi's vague moral outrage crumbles. After fighting with his parents, Obi realizes that his conviction is not strong enough to withstand their opposition, that his moral anger "[comes] from the periphery, and not the center" (*NLE*, 130). Clara, realizing Obi's indecision, breaks off the engagement in spite of her pregnancy while Obi flounders aimlessly, his insistence on marriage completely forgotten. With the evaporation of Obi's flimsy moralism, the opposition between Obi and society over Clara also dissolves into a monetary concern—expenses for her abortion and the ensuing medical complications.

Thus all oppositions between Obi and society reduce themselves into demands for money, into the metonymic confusion of bourgeois society. Obi proves to be completely ineffectual in managing his money which mediates between his personal needs and his social obligations. Unable to conserve his financial resources or to save his affair with Clara, Obi succumbs to the pressures of a corrupt and restricted society and easily abandons his moral scruples, for he decides to accept bribes. However, he is so ineffectual in doing this that he is soon trapped, tried, and convicted by the government.

In this seemingly simple novel, Achebe has constructed some complex ironies around the questions of social coherence and alienation. He has created a society that is estranged from itself, that is rendered powerless by its lack of control over its own organization, and that has no allegiance to its government. Corruption, predicated on the absence of social cohesion, loyalty, and integrity, is then an index of this alienation, but the people in this society have come to accept disorganization and bribery as normal, and in relation to that norm it is Obi, with his callow integrity and moralism, who is alienated. The friction caused by his attitudes increases as he comes into conflict with the demands to repay his obligations to society and to conform to its prejudices, and eventually it leads him to examine his motives and idealism. In doing so he discovers "a good deal that he could only regard as sheer humbug" (*NLE*, 146). When his mother dies, Obi feels a release from guilt and senses the end of his moralism: "Beyond death there are no ideals and humbug, only reality. The impatient idealist says: 'Give me a place to stand and I shall move the earth.' But such a place does not exist. We all have to stand on the earth itself and go with her at her pace" (*NLE*, 156). This progression from innocence to experience reaches its turning point in the trial and conviction of Obi. For by being convicted and being labeled a criminal, he becomes thoroughly alienated from the ideals of the colonizing regime, represented here by the English court system, and at the same time he becomes an initiate of the corrupt colonized society which, as the doctor who performs Clara's abortion says, is comprised entirely of criminals (*NLE*, 138). Adherence to his idealistic values, which are strongly influenced by his Christian and English education, alienates him from the Nigerian society and, conversely, his estrangement from the values represented by the English court reconciles and initiates him into the "criminal" colonial society.

This kind of irony can permeate the dialectics of man-as-individual and man-as-social-being only in a colonial society where confusion is caused by two incompatible value systems and where a moral vacuum is created by the absence of legitimate cultural authority. Whereas the societies in *Things Fall Apart* and *Arrow of God* have a sound and viable set of cultural values that are just beginning to crack under the pressure of European influence and whereas alienation in those novels is caused by the ossification of indigenous values, the society in *No Longer at Ease* has disintegrated and is characterized by incoherence, and the alienation is then caused by adherence to integrity which is foreign to that colonized society. In all the novels, however, alienation is caused essentially by the espousal of goals and ambitions that are incongruent with the changing social praxis.

Achebe's novels are thus constantly preoccupied with the relation of man to his society. They are essentially novels in the tradition of realism, that is, they recognize that "every action, thought and emotion of human beings is inseparably bound up with the life and struggle of the community, i.e., with politics; whether the humans themselves are conscious of this, unconscious of it or even trying to escape from it, objectively their actions, thoughts and emotions nevertheless spring from and run into politics."[34] We have seen in our analysis of the novels that Achebe refuses to divide the human personality into mutually exclusive private and public sectors; all the private dilemmas, ambitions and understandings of his heroes are firmly grounded in public interaction. In fact, the problems of his characters are only comprehensible in terms of the respective public values that surround the individuals. This insistence on representing the individual as a complex social being is the basis of a realism that is further strengthened by his deliberate depiction of the totality of the Igbo culture in response to the denigration inherent in the colonial perspectives: Achebe does not attempt to justify the moral soundness of Igbo culture by idealizing it. Realism, then, is his aesthetic as well as ethical response not only to colonialist views of African societies but also to the social dilemma of African cultures that are attempting to come to terms with the disorganization that is the legacy of colonialism.

Yet in spite of Achebe's realism his novels are unable to escape or transcend the social dilemma to which he is heir. His realism, based on his view of the symbiotic relation between the individual and society and augmented by the calm neutrality of his style (the absence of sentimentality, resentment, or a vengeful subjective bias, the judicious use of narrative distance, and an economy and simplicity of presentation), as well as the richness and complexity of the cultures and individuals that he depicts, makes Achebe the best contemporary African writer. Yet despite the objectivity which accounts for his successful writing, Achebe's fiction remains a complex and subtle reflection of his predicament as a writer in a culture that is still experiencing radical transformation. The subjective element does not distort or color the narrative details of each novel; it can only be seen through a comparison of the stature and alienation of his heroes which subsequently reveals the conflict between traditional and transitional values that pervade all his novels.

In *Things Fall Apart* there is no substantial disagreement between the values of Umuofia and Okonkwo even though he becomes alienated from his society. The Umuofian community is proud, martial, self-contained, and self-sufficient; it is characterized by the egocentricity of a healthy, self-perpetuating organism. Okonkwo, with his adamant will, his reliance on physical force and anger, and his pride and courage, manifested finally in his suicide, is quite compatible with his society up to a point. Umuofia and Okonkwo diverge in their ability to compromise: whereas the society, motivated by a healthy instinct for self-preservation, is willing to change and accommodate the new militarily superior culture, Okonkwo is an inflexible monomaniac who destroys himself through his compulsive preoccupation with martial values. Thus from the societal and narrative viewpoints Okonkwo's absolute alienation, his death, represents the tragic fall of a man admirable in every way except for his ossified "masculinity." In mourning his death, Umuofia grieves the end of its own ascendancy and its unique culture. There is thus a certain grandeur and poignancy in his fall; the only criticism that Achebe implies throughout the narrative is a mild regret of Okonkwo's rigidity and unwillingness to compromise.

In contrast to the heroic stature of Okonkwo, the position of Ezeulu at the end of *Arrow of God* (set in a somewhat later period than *Things Fall Apart*)[35] is neither as grand nor as tragic. Society now behaves in a less proud and self-sufficient manner than its counterpart in the previous novel. A more "feminine" society, with its stress on art and religion, Umuaro is already predisposed toward compromise: the very foundation of Umuaro, a complex union of six villages, constitutes an accommodation; so does its agreement to provide labor for the road-building projects of the colonial government; and the massive conversion to Christianity at the end of the novel is a radical concession. Ezeulu too believes in and urges compromise: he mediates the quarrel between Umuaro and Okperi, attempts to negotiate with the colonial government, and forces one of his sons to become a Christian. But as all these examples illustrate, he only accommodates external forces—within Umuaro itself he wishes to be the absolute master. When the delegation of elders requests that Ezeulu readjust the calendar in order to permit harvesting, the latter callously adheres to his own schedule. Thus a major rift, an irreconcilable opposition, develops between Ezeulu and his society. Ezeulu's madness, that is, his inability to communicate coherently with others, is symbolic of his social alienation, and his subsequent displacement and ultimately that of Ulu arouses neither pity nor awe. Umuaro views his madness as a vindication of the society's democratic principles and his fall as its salvation from starvation. The people have little time or inclination to sympathize with the mad, arrogant priest as they busy themselves with the changing situation. At the end of the novel, Achebe shifts the focus from the plight of Ezeulu to that of society, thereby depriving the priest of the stature enjoyed by Okonkwo in the previous novel.

The stature of the hero and the power and integrity of society are diminished drastically in *No Longer at Ease*. In this novel the community is completely compromised—it is thoroughly corrupt and alienated. Pride has become snobbery, personal interdependence has turned into bothersome obligation, and all other values are now mediated by and reduced to monetary considerations. Within this society of "criminals" Achebe places a quixotic character whose weaknesses—callow moralism, a flimsy sense of superiority, and a lack of conviction and will power—ironically parallel the social disintegration. In this highly ironic novel Obi's fall, his integration into the community through the initiation of criminal conviction, can hardly be called tragic. Society views his trial as the product of his own ineptitude in receiving bribes, and his moralism is for them no more than a curious anomaly. People neither mourn his plight nor do they see any significance in his conviction. In contrast to the fall of his grandfather, Okonkwo of *Things Fall Apart*, Obi's demise is a paltry farce.

Viewed in this historical progression from grandeur to farce, Achebe's novels demonstrate a nostalgia for the past. The society and individuals in the precolonial past of *Things Fall Apart* are clearly superior compared to the social chaos and moral vacuum of the preindependence Nigeria of *No Longer at Ease;* as social disruption, caused by the impact of colonialism and the novelty of European cultures, progresses rapidly from the setting in the first novel to that in the third, so conversely does the stature of the heroes and the integrity of the culture diminish. Achebe's fourth novel, *A Man of the People* (which we have not examined because, strictly speaking, it is not concerned with a colonized society) further continues this trend of degeneration from grandeur to farce.

Achebe's nostalgia must be distinguished from the romantic ethnology of the Negritude movement, for, unlike the latter, he neither portrays an idealized, monolithic, homogenized, and pasteurized "African" past, nor does he valorize indigenous cultures by reversing the old colonial manichean allegory as, for instance, Leopold Senghor does. Just as Achebe carefully limits his fiction to a specific culture (the Igbo society in *Things Fall Apart* and *Arrow of God* and the more mixed community of Lagos in *No Longer at Ease*), so he diligently avoids idealization by including in his fiction an implicit criticism of the less admirable aspects of social and individual life. Even though his fiction eschews a perfect utopia, a lost golden age, it does nevertheless manifest a powerful, but problematic nostalgia for the past.

The problematics of Achebe's nostalgia are produced by his ambivalent attitude toward his characters and their respective societies. All three of his major protagonists fall not only because they are alienated from their society but, more importantly, because their personalities and characters become ossified around certain traditional values: Okonkwo, as we have seen, falls because he is only capable of basing his actions on "masculine," martial values; Ezeulu becomes mad because he forgets the symbolic nature of his function as priest of Ulu and instead literally identifies his personal whims and desires with the god whom he represents; and Obi is apprehended and convicted for bribery because the tenacity of his naive idealism prevents him from adjusting himself to the practical considerations of a corrupt social praxis. All three characters are inflexible, calcified monomaniacs in their different ways. However, they all represent values that, from their own social as well as from more general viewpoints, are in themselves substantial and respectable. Okonkwo's pride, courage, and diligence are perfectly laudable, as are Ezeulu's desires to uphold the principles and rituals of his theology and religion and to augment the power of Ulu and eventually of Umuaro by appropriating some of the "magical" power from the

Christian-colonial culture. Obi's valorization of honesty, integrity, and fairness represents the common aspirations of all cultures. Thus while Achebe criticizes the petrification of his protagonists, he seems to be quite sympathetic to their values and their desire to adhere to them. The ironic fall of the characters despite their sound values is a fundamental characteristic of all Achebe's fiction.

The hero's alienation from society in the course of his demise, the development of the rift between individual and society, clarifies Achebe's ambivalence. While the characters perish due to their ossification, the societies to which they belong manage to survive because of their adaptability. Umuofians do not follow Okonkwo's aggressive lead because they understand perfectly well that such a course is suicidal—they know that colonial troops have annihilated another village, Abame, which attempted to resist the European invasion. Similarly, Umuaro chooses Christianity in order not to perish from starvation, while the society of Lagos is entirely preoccupied with the daily business of "survival," that is, with earning money and getting ahead. In the process of adapting and ensuring their continuity, these societies naturally undergo drastic modification and abandon their traditional values.

By changing, these societies become prey to the problems of historical catalepsy because assimilation of European values obviously does not mean that the entire Western culture, including its own coherence or direction will be transferred automatically or completely to the colonized country. The process of adaptation is necessarily a gradual and painful one during which various aspects of the indigenous and European cultures are combined and during which the colonized or "independent" society gropes its way toward a new synthesis; as Balandier has pointed out, this is a period and a process of great ambiguity.[36] Thus colonialism necessarily produces in its subject society a period of profound cultural and historical hiatus, a time of chaos during which, as Achebe says, old values no longer apply and new ones have not yet been found. No Longer at Ease portrays such a society paralyzed by corruption, cynicism toward the colonial government, confusion about old and new values, a lack of social coherence, and an absence of historical direction. Achebe points to the anxiety, frustration, and confusion of such a period by drawing the titles of two novels, Things Fall Apart and No Longer at Ease, from two modernist poems, W. B. Yeats's "The Second Coming" and T. S. Eliot's "The Journey of the Magi," that address themselves to moments of radical historical transformation.

Thus Achebe's novels can be seen as products of a conflict between the desire to retain traditional values, represented by the ossified characters, and the recognition, manifested in the adaptability of society, that change and assimilation are absolutely necessary for survival. The characterization of Okonkwo and Ezeulu as men who embody the best values in their culture and of Obi as a champion of basic universal morality represents Achebe's desire for the integrity and heroism of the past, for values other than the corrupt ones that flourish in the moral vacuum of preindependence Nigeria. But the fall of these heroes through their petrification and society's willingness to adapt represent Achebe's recognition that the desired values are calcified, that they are no longer viable. Yet the progressive degeneration of community from novel to novel demonstrates his awareness of the disorientation, incoherence, corruption, and lack of direction that characterizes all colonized and postcolonial societies. Thus assimilation leads to catalepsy while the retention of a traditional culture produces petrified people. The conflict between the need to change and the desire to conserve the past constitutes the ambivalent and problematic nature of Achebe's nostalgia. The conflict between man-as-social-being and man-as-individual is, of course, also attributable to the tension caused by the transition from a traditional, more communal culture to one that valorizes individualism.

Achebe's novels can be best understood as analyses *and* products of the historical problems created by colonization. The European control of African societies, the violent collision between different cultures, and the temporary deprivation of African independence inevitably created confusion and a subsequent lack of direction in the colonized culture. Achebe's fiction examines this period of cultural conflict in order to restore the pride of Africans in their own past by demonstrating that indigenous societies, contrary to colonial claims, did have their own morality and cultural sophistication. By doing so his novels hope to enhance the Africans' understanding of their present and thereby to provide a more definite direction to their future.

Yet it would seem that the problem of historical catalepsy is more obstinate and intricate than one might imagine, for in writing about that period Achebe seems to have been trapped by the ambivalent nostalgia that characterizes his vision of the past (and which is also manifested in the irony of his writing novels about Igbo culture in English). His writing seems as yet unable to proceed beyond this nostalgia and the problem of historical catalepsy: the worlds of his novels degenerate from the heroism of the distant past to the farce of the near past and the present. They do not proceed beyond the present to depict a positive vision of the future or to valorize some specific cultural attributes for potential cultivation. Despite his view that the writer is responsible for the future direction of society, he has not yet attempted to undertake that difficult task in his fiction. I do not wish to imply that the dilemma of historical catalepsy can be attributed to Achebe's short-comings as a *writer*, for what he has written is excellent. But I must stress that the question of historical direction is a pervasive cultural problem to which Achebe and all Third World writers and intellectuals are heir. Achebe must be credited with the most sustained exploration of this problem, for he has created the richest, the most realistic, and the most substantial vision of a problematic African past that spanned the period of colonization. One can only hope that he will continue to examine the present repercussions of this important dilemma.

Ngugi wa Thiong'o

The Problems of Communal Regeneration

LIKE CHINUA ACHEBE, Ngugi wa Thiong'o[1] is also caught up in the dialectics of the negative influence of colonialist literature. Unlike Achebe, however, Ngugi is neither insistently preoccupied with this influence nor concerned with analyzing the subtle but devastating effects of the colonial literary denigration of Africa. Nevertheless, he has pointed out the distasteful and inaccurate portrayal of Africa and its inhabitants in a gamut of literary, historical, and philosophical works ranging from Rider Haggard and Elspeth Huxley to Hugh Trevor-Roper and Hegel.[2] Of particular interest to this examination is the fact that he has singled out Isak Dinesen's claim that the "mental growth of the Kikuyu, Kavirondo and Wakamba" people is arrested "suddenly at a stage corresponding to that of a European child of nine," whereas the Somalis are arrested between the ages of thirteen and seventeen. Dinesen's use of the distorted evolutionary theory current at the turn of the century and her use of the Conradian metaphor of African darkness being illumined by European light are offensive as well as uninformative about Africans, but Ngugi's analysis of such portrayals reveals a misplaced emphasis. He argues that such denigration was practiced because the "colonizer instinctively knew and feared the threat posed by men with confidence in their own past and heritage. Why else should he devote his military might, his religious fervour, and his intellectual energy to denying that the African had true Gods, had a culture, had a significant past?"[3]

The subjugation of the Africans by the Europeans was surely not based on their fears of African cultural integrity per se but was necessitated by the economic drives that formed the basis of the imperial thrust. The initial decision to colonize is based on a desire for material profits; only subsequently do the imperial forces develop arguments about the moral and cultural backwardness of the colonized people and about the white man's burden in order to rationalize and mask their actions with a benevolent theory. Colonial subjugation and domination are established and maintained through actual military and technological superiority, not through ideological rationalizations. Thus Ngugi's attempt to attribute cultural destruction to the colonizer's *fear* of the Africans implies that the latter were indeed powerful. Contrary to European claims, colonized cultures did possess moral integrity and validity, but they were not powerful enough to resist colonization. The point is that Ngugi's interpretation tends to romanticize the relations between the two cultures. This kind of idealization implies an inability, or at least an unsuccessful effort, to extricate oneself from the affective aspects of negative influence, from the resentment caused by colonial denigration. It is ironic that Achebe, who deliberately and systematically examines the complexities of negative influence, has successfully disengaged himself from the affective quagmire of this dialectic, while Ngugi, who feels that African writers are too preoccupied with their past,[4] seems to have been initially unable to do so. As a result, his first two novels graphically depict his entanglement in the peripeteia of values, whereas his third novel, written after a study of Frantz Fanon's work, shows a sudden disengagement from the ambivalences, ambiguities, and contradictions of the colonial society.

The peripeteia of values, as we have seen, is a sudden change in the cultural orientation of the colonized subject. By choosing the apparently superior values of the European, the African implicitly rejects his own being, because it is a product of the culture he is abandoning, and therefore subjects himself to profound conflict and confusion. Because his initial understanding of the alien culture is bound to be superficial, the man who exposes himself to this peripeteia (as he is systematically encouraged to do by the colonizer) tends to be characterized by an abstract and vague view of the world and of his own predicament. As Frantz Fanon has shown, this syndrome and its various symptoms can only be cured by a thorough political understanding of the colonial situation and the real relative merits of the different cultural values. In order to understand fully Ngugi's entanglement in such a peripeteia and his sudden extrication from it before the publication of his third novel, we shall need to examine briefly his childhood experiences in the shrill and violent social atmosphere of the Mau Mau rebellion in Kenya in the 1950s. The available facts about Ngugi's life are rather scant and sometimes inaccurate; nevertheless, if we put them in the relevant sociological context we can draw adequate conclusions about the experiential imperatives that eventually become the dominant structures of his novels.

Ngugi was born in 1938 in Limuru, part of the Gikuyu area of Kenya. According to Jahn, Schild, and Nordmann, he was sent by his mother to a Christian mission school in 1946 and then in 1947 to a Gikuyu school at Karinga, where "he was educated until 1955, except for the period from 1948 to 1950 when there were no lessons because of Mau Mau." In 1955 he entered Alliance High School, another "missionary school," and then attended Makerere College from 1959 to 1964.[5] The information is accurate except for the crucial closing down of schools during the Mau Mau rebellion which began at the end of 1952. Thus Ngugi must have left his school in 1952 or 1953 and not in 1948 as Jahn claims.[6] In any case the information is skeletal and does not possess much significance unless we realize the extent of physical violence, the prevalence of fear and uncertainty, and the intensity of bitterness and despair on the one hand and of hope and expectation on the other that must have gripped the Gikuyu community during the Mau Mau rebellion and that probably had a profound effect on the mind of a fifteen-year-old boy like Ngugi.[7]

In order to gauge the impact of this social situation on Ngugi, we shall focus on three aspects of the socio-cultural ambiance in Kenya around 1953: the cultural effects of land alienation, the importance of education for the Gikuyu and, consequently, the impact of its deprivation, and finally the messianic fervor that characterized Gikuyu politics at that time. Ngugi's novels are all focused on various combinations of these three factors, and it is safe to speculate that his repeated concern with these issues is probably determined by their pervasive importance during the rebellion.

We have already discussed in detail, in the chapter on Isak Dinesen,[8] the extent of land alienation that took place in the Gikuyu area, and therefore we will only recapitulate here the essential features of that disinheritance. Given the aim of the British colonial policy, which was to settle the best agricultural land in Kenya with English and European farmers, there was an inevitable clash between the colonial government and the Gikuyu, who happened to be the owners of the best arable land. The piecemeal appropriation of Gikuyu land was finally systematized by the 1921 ruling of the colonial court that all land—even that which had previously been put aside for African "reserves"—was now Crown land and that all natives were to be considered tenants-at-will on land that they had owned for generations. The conflict based on the ownership of land was further accentuated by the oppositions inherent in the European and African modes of production. The European system was capital centered, whereas the African one was precapitalistic in the sense that it consisted of subsistence farming and that it did not offer the means of production, especially labor, for sale on the market. Independent peasant and capitalist settler production therefore existed as sharply antagonistic modes, and any effective development of the one precluded an equivalent development of the other in the same social universe. In order to obtain land the colonial government herded the Africans into overcrowded reserves, and to induce the natives to offer their labor on the wage market the colonialists coerced the Africans to work through the implementation of various taxes and through the prohibition of native cultivation of lucrative "cash" crops such as coffee and tea. Thus the African was systematically deprived of his land and induced to become a serf, known in Kenya as the "squatter."

The important aspect, from our point of view, of this disinheritance of the Gikuyu is the cultural upheaval it caused. Land is the central factor around which the Gikuyu socio-cultural system is organized. As Jomo Kenyatta has pointed out, land is

> the most important factor in the social, political, religious, and economic life of the tribe. As agriculturists, the Gikuyu people depend entirely on land. It supplies them with the material needs of life, through which spiritual and mental contentment is achieved. . . . Thus the earth is the most sacred thing above all that dwell in or on it. Among the Gikuyu the soil is especially honoured, and an everlasting oath is to swear by the earth (*Koirugo*).

After documenting in detail the importance of land to the cultural integrity and dignity of the Gikuyu, Kenyatta concludes that "a culture has no meaning apart from the social organization of life on which it is built. When the European comes to the Gikuyu country and robs the people of their lands, he is taking away not only their livelihood, but the material symbol that holds family and tribe together. In doing this he gives one blow which cuts away the foundations from the whole of Gikuyu life, social, moral and economic."[9] Thus the brunt of the colonial endeavor in Kenya fell on the Gikuyu who consequently not only lost their land but saw their society fall apart and felt their cultural identity threatened. From the very beginning of colonial encroachment the Gikuyu had responded with unsuccessful armed rebellions and ineffectual political protests which culminated in the 1940s with the increasing demands for African political representation in the government. The prolonged conflict was rapidly coming to a head; it was evident, as George Delf says, that "by the end of 1947, African nationalism was set on a course which must lead inexorably either to the end of white rule or to an explosion."[10] Instead of finding a progressive solution for the problem, the colonial government responded to the nationalist movement with its habitual answer: suppression. At the end of 1952 it arrested the leaders of the nationalist movements and consequently provoked its followers to wage a guerrilla war which came to be known as the Mau Mau rebellion.

The material plight of the Africans which fueled the nationalist movement is summed up by a United Nations survey of 1953 that showed that the average annual income of Africans was £27, that of Asians £280, and that of Europeans £660.[11] Yet ignoring the reality of the situation, both the colonial government and the white settlers became hysterical. They declared a state of emergency, imposed martial law on the Gikuyu area, and characterized the Mau Mau as a movement that showed the resurgence of "primeval forces" and that was controlled by "witchdoctors" and "atavistic barbarism."[12] The emergency further traumatized and disrupted the Gikuyu community: those who did not go into the forests to join the Mau Mau were "relocated," their original homes were burnt down, and they were forced to live in villages that were surrounded by barbed wires and ditches. Those pseudo-concentration camps were supplemented with real concentration camps where Mau Mau suspects were "detained" and tortured, while the so-called loyal Gikuyu were organized into a Home Guard unit to fight against the Mau Mau. All schools were closed in the Gikuyu area and general martial law, with curfews and other restrictions, was imposed, allowing the people only an hour or two a day for farming.

The elaboration of a specific aspect of this struggle between the English and the Gikuyu, the dispute over the substance and process of education, is essential to a thorough appreciation of Ngugi's novels. The history of colonial education in Kenya clearly reveals the contradiction between the theory of the white man's burden and the actual practice, which was exactly the opposite. Richard D. Heyman has shown that in spite of the avowed policy of the Colonial Office in England, from the 1840s onward, to educate its colonized subjects in the areas of "gardening, health and domestic sciences," and also in arithmetic, the English language, and Christian training, the policy was not systematically implemented in the colonies. The actual control of education in Kenya was in the hands of the missionaries and the local colonial government who systematically attempted to withhold it from the Africans. The administration was anxious to promote agricultural and vocational training (while simultaneously prohibiting Africans from growing "cash" crops), but it discouraged a liberal, humanistic education because the blacks supposedly lacked adequate intelligence to benefit from it. In fact, the government limited liberal education because a policy of tokenism only permitted them to accept a few natives into the civil service and because they feared that the limited number of jobs coupled with a rise in the Africans' expectations due to literacy would cause political problems.[13]

Similarly, the missionaries used education to induce Africans into their evangelist mission. Their school system was centered on a belief that manual labor was a panacea for African indolence, slovenliness, and moral degeneration. Such an "education" proved convenient for the missionaries because it provided them with free manual labor. Similarly, they would not teach English since they were more concerned with producing African missionaries who could preach in the vernacular.[14] The government would not allow English to be used as a medium of instruction before standard seven, and, because mission schools only went up to standard four, English was never taught. In addition to preventing the Africans from acquiring an English education, the missionaries also attempted to deprive them of their own cultural values by the moral condemnation of all practices that were "heathen and un-Christian."

The Africans, on the other hand, preferred a liberal and postprimary academic education rather than a token vocational one because it would allow them to obtain white-collar civil-service jobs which paid better than any other kind of work. Furthermore, they clearly perceived the value of academic education and particularly of the mastery of English language for their independence struggle. As Edward H. Berman puts it, "The Kikuyus perceived, quite accurately, that English, the medium of the ruling European elite, was the language of power. . . . They were fully cognizant that inability to communicate in English would be a crucial factor in the perpetuation of their subordinate status in the colony."[15] The importance attached to academic education by the Gikuyu can be seen in their sacrifices to obtain it: when in 1925 the government gave them limited power of taxation for education, the Gikuyu in three districts were able to raise £10,000 for a high school, £2,000 for an industrial school, and

£3,000 for a technical school.[16] These sacrifices are impressive when we consider that even in 1953 the average annual income of the African was £27.

The adamant desires of the Gikuyu for an English academic education and the equally strong colonial policy of preventing them from obtaining it led naturally to a prolonged conflict. A brief highlight of that struggle will clearly show that while the Gikuyu were trying to preserve aspects of their own society and to assimilate parts of the English culture, the colonialists were eager to perpetuate the subordinate status of the Gikuyu by preventing them from realizing either of their aims. Thus in 1928, when the Kikuyu Central Association (KCA) schools became the locus of growing political awareness, the government closed them down because they were "found to be permeated with false and seditious doctrines." When in the following year the Church of Scotland Mission (CSM) condemned female circumcision, an important part of Gikuyu religious rites, and refused to tolerate it among its converts and students, the Gikuyu sentiment coalesced around this issue until it became a symbol of their resistance to the European cultural manipulations and impositions. Eighty percent of the students and teachers resigned from the CSM schools and formed the Kikuyu Independent School Association (KISA) and the Kikuyu Karinga Education Association (KKEA), thus replacing the banned KCA schools. When the government did recognize the legitimacy of KISA schools it sought to control and hamper them, whereas KISA in open violation of government regulation began to use English as the medium of instruction throughout primary and secondary educational institutions. This form of struggle continued until the outbreak of the Mau Mau rebellion in 1952 when all the Gikuyu schools were closed.[17] It is a significant indication of colonial policy and intention that in 1953 the administration spent £50 per annum on the education of a white child whereas it allocated three shillings (or £0.15) for each African child.[18]

This was the atmosphere in which Ngugi was forced to leave school in 1953 at the age of fifteen. Thus for him the closing of schools was a major deprivation because at that time the anxious Gikuyu society, torn apart by high hopes of independence and simultaneous fears of repression, had invested a great deal of emotional and material energy in the future success of those who, like Ngugi, were lucky enough to receive a decent liberal education. Since the Gikuyu believed that mastery of the English language and culture would help their attempt to regain political control of their country, the young, educated people bore the burden of their hopes and expectations. The burden felt by those who attended KISA and KKEA schools was different in its political emphasis from that experienced by those, like Ngugi, who went to mission schools,[19] for the Gikuyu schools stressed the traditional history of their people and their right to repossess the land, thus implicitly advocating revolution, whereas the Christian institutions discouraged political awareness among their students. Nevertheless, children from both school systems equally felt the weight of the future on them:

> I was living in a colonial situation but I did not know it. Not even when I went to school. I went to missionary schools where we were told over and over again that we were potential leaders of our people. We were being trained to be good responsible leaders. Education was not aimed at a knowledge of self and the reality of the black man's place in the world. What we did not know was that we were being groomed to become a buffer state between the propertied white rulers and the harsh realities under which the African peasants and workers lived.[20]

The critical awareness of colonialist intentions is clearly a later development in Ngugi's consciousness. As a child or a young man he was probably very much preoccupied with himself as a potential leader. Yet preoccupation with self-importance is not an entirely isolated phenomenon; it is accompanied by an affective understanding, derived from personal, nonacademic experience, of the economic and political predicament of the peasants.

Such knowledge comes from his own family situation: "I grew up in a small village. My father and his four wives had no land. They lived as tenants-at-will on somebody else's land. Harvests were often poor. Sweetened tea with milk at any time of the day was a luxury. We had one meal a day—late in the evening." Then he witnesses the alienation of land and the relocation of his people: "One day I heard a song. I remember the scene so vividly: the women who sang it are now before me—their sad faces and their plaintive melody. I was then ten or eleven. They were being forcibly ejected from the land they occupied and sent to another part of the country so barren that people called it the land of black rocks." Ngugi then recapitulates the gist of the song which voices the women's hope of reclaiming their own land from white settlers and puts all this hope on the shoulders of the young children who might eventually be able to attain that goal. After the song Ngugi focuses on the effect of this scene on him: "They were in a convoy of lorries, caged, but they had one voice. They sang of a common loss and hope and I felt their voice rock the earth where I stood literally unable to move."[21] The central experience, in this affective understanding of the Gikuyu predicament, is a realization that the young have to bear the burden of leadership: they have to become the saviors of the culture.

Yet the understanding of this mandate is intellectually confused or imperfect. It is clear that one has to become a leader, but the nature of the leadership is as yet unformulated by the young, politically naive mind. On the one hand, the child comprehends that the Gikuyu are being oppressed and that he is being asked to relieve their misery, but on the other hand he is encouraged by the mission schools to become a mediator between the African peasants and the colonialists rather than a liberator of the former. Finally, to these conflicting demands and to the imperfect understanding of his own role is added the shock caused by the deprivation of the means (i.e., education) of becoming either a rebellious leader or a mediator. This, then, was the ambiance that surrounded Ngugi in 1953 when he was fifteen and when he could no longer go to school.

The burden of leadership that could have been felt by Ngugi at this time, however, cannot be fully appreciated unless we also examine the deep roots of the messianic tradition around the 1950s. James Olney has pointed out how *all* Gikuyu biographies trace the ancestry of the tribe back into the mythic past, which includes the ancient prophetic tradition centering on Mugo wa Kibiro's prediction that a savior would come to liberate them from English colonial occupation. "Few Gikuyus of the time [1940s and 1950s] doubted that Kenyatta represented the fulfillment of Mugo wa Kibiro's prophecy." Kenyatta systematically used this messianic tradition to further the political aims of the Gikuyu and consequently the atmosphere at the time was extremely charged with the religious expectations aroused by the coming of the savior. Both the tradition of the prophecies and its fulfillment in the person of Kenyatta are vast subjects which have been adequately documented elsewhere. The details need not be recapitulated here, but one cannot insist too strongly on the fervent feelings of loyalty, sacrifice, and expectation that were aroused by Kenyatta. The importance, from our point of view, of this messianic tradition and fervor is that once again it puts emphasis on leadership and salvation. Ngugi's attempt to come to terms with these forces provides the impetus behind his first two novels. These imperatives are reinforced by the fact that Ngugi wrote the two novels while he was an undergraduate student of literature at Makerere College, that is, while he was still preoccupied with the processes of education and presumably of leadership.

Weep Not, Child (1964) and *The River Between* (1965)[22] both have the structures of truncated *bildungsroman*, that is, both follow the development of a child into adolescence but both are anticlimactic; neither of the novels adequately resolves the question of what precisely has been learned by the central adolescent protagonist. The novels attempt to depict how the heroes come to terms with the ambiguities, conflicts, and anxieties of their societies which are in the process of being radically transformed by the impetus of the colonialist culture. Thus the novels are documents that record social change, as Raymond Williams has argued, as well as autobiographical statements, as James Olney's interpretation shows.[23] Yet both these interpretations fail to reveal the central experience of the novels that is available only through a combination of biographical and sociological approaches. An analysis of the novels within the context outlined above will show that these inadequately resolved novels are testaments of the conflict and confusion caused by the peripeteia of values in a colonial situation.

Weep Not, Child is set in the Kenya of the 1940s and 1950s, and it ends amidst the violence of the Mau Mau war. It is thus the most autobiographical of Ngugi's novels; Njoroge, its child protagonist, is about the same age as Ngugi would have been at that time. Through the family background of Njoroge we are furnished with the social ambiance very much like the one we have constructed above. We see that the farm of Ngotho, Njoroge's father, had been appropriated while he was conscripted in the support forces for the army and that he now lives as a "squatter" on his property which is "legally" owned by a white farmer. The effect of this is particularly drastic because Ngotho believes that land is a sacred gift to the Gikuyu from God and because he lives in a precapitalist world where value cannot be easily transferred, particularly from land to other commodities: "Any man who had land was considered rich. If a man had plenty of money, many motor cars, but no land, he could never be counted as rich" (*WNC*, 41). Land is invested with a spiritual value that transcends economic functions and the English property laws. Thus Ngotho carefully tends the farm on which he is "squatting" and which he does not own according to the British legal system: "Ngotho felt responsible for whatever happened to this land. He owed it to the dead, the living and the unborn of his time, to keep guard over his shamba [i.e., farm]" (WNC, 55). Ngotho's inability to either comprehend or resolve this contradiction between his own notions of legal and spiritual tenure and the alien system of ownership or to change the situation confuses and emasculates him.

As a consequence of this emasculation, the family structure begins to disintegrate, reflecting in a microcosm the general social fragmentation. Boro, Ngotho's eldest son, who has also been conscripted and has served in Asia in the Second World War and returns to a scarcity of land and absence of jobs, no longer respects his father's authority. He gradually drifts to the city and, having become involved in the Mau Mau movement, attempts to persuade his father to take the oath of allegiance to the rebellious group. This reversal of authority roles marks the passing of initiative to the younger generation, and eventually the impetus of this shift is felt by Njoroge.

Njoroge inherits the burdens of initiative due to his privileged status as the only member of the family to receive a formal education. The very decision to educate Njoroge is a recognition of the change in values precipitated by the arrival of the new culture. Initially, formal learning is seen mainly as a means of acquiring material prosperity, but soon it comes to represent the achievement of more intangible goals such as the exorcism of the shame that Ngotho feels for not having land and for being a squatter. The premium that is put on education by this disintegrating society can be measured by the fact that two brothers' entire wages are consumed by Njoroge's school fees. When Njoroge graduates into secondary school, the investment ceases to be the exclusive property of his family and is taken over by the whole village: "Whatever their differences, interest in knowledge and book learning was the one meeting point between people such as Boro, Jacobo and Ngotho. Somehow the Gikuyu people always saw their deliverance as embodied in education. When the time for Njoroge to leave came near, many people contributed money so that he could go. He was no longer the son of Ngotho but the son of the land" (WNC, 148).

Along with these direct and indirect pressures to excel in academic pursuits, Njoroge is also influenced by the fervor of the messianic prophecies that seem about to be fulfilled. People like Ngotho who have been spiritually crushed frequently voice their hope and faith in deliverance from colonial bondage by "the black Moses," Jomo Kenyatta. For Ngotho "Jomo stood for custom and tradition purified by grace of learning and much travel." But now that Kenyatta is arrested and seems to have been defeated, Ngotho wonders if he could "put his faith in his youngest son Njoroge" (*WNC*, 110). Although Ngotho never actually expresses this transference of faith, Njoroge has managed to intuit his father's hopes.

The manner in which Njoroge internalizes these influences, desires, hopes, and fears reveals the conflicts and confusion caused by the change of values in a transitory society. Njoroge is a naive and solitary child whose understanding of the explicit and implicit demands being made on him reflects from the very beginning a rather abstract conception of education and of his own role in society: "He knew that for him education would be the fulfillment of a wider and more significant vision—a vision that embraced the demand made on him, not only by his father, but also by his mother, his brother and even the village. He saw himself destined for something big, and this made his heart glow" (*WNC*, 64–65). The vagueness of the notion of academic education allows him to use that as a panacea—it "held the key to the future": "He always thought that schooling was the very best that a boy could have. It was the end of all living" (*WNC*, 63). As the political situation grows worse (the Emergency has been declared and Njoroge's stepmother and brother have been put in detention for violating the curfew), Njoroge adheres even more tenaciously to his vision of education: "Through all this, Njoroge was still sustained by his love for and belief in education and his own role when the time came. . . . Only education could make something out of this wreckage. He became more faithful to his studies. He would one day use all his learning to fight the white man, for he would continue the work his father had started" (*WNC*, 120). Njoroge loves *education;* he cares neither for particular subjects or ideas nor does his vision encompass specific goals or projects; his whole experience focuses on the emotional attitude to "education" and does not seem to be involved in the particular processes of learning or growing. His preoccupation with the affective pleasure derived from these abstract conceptions of education becomes progressively more intense as the political situation deteriorates. Njoroge reacts to the economic pressures on the Gikuyu, to their cultural humiliation, and to the confusion and anxiety of the days preceding the Mau Mau war by escaping into his dreams of "education." When the rebellion breaks out and Kenyatta is arrested and imprisoned, Njoroge's fantasies become even more grandiose: he now envisions himself not only as a potential educated leader but also as the new messiah.

His vision of himself as a leader gradually shades into the religious sphere until he loses himself in "speculations about his vital role in the country. He remembered David rescuing a whole country from the curse of Goliath." Yet he retains a modicum of humility and feels "a bit awed to imagine that God may have chosen him to be the instrument of His Divine Service" (*WNC*, 134–35). He soon begins his task of comforting his peers, who are afraid of the chaos during the rebellion, with platitudes such as "Peace shall come to this land." When he graduates into secondary school and is honored by the whole village, he becomes much more self-confident: "at last his way seemed clear. The land needed him and God had given him an opening so that he might come back and save his family and the whole country." When he is asked about his plans after graduation, he can only reply that "I have not thought out my plans" (*WNC*, 148). His messianic visions are as insubstantial as his love of education.

However, all these hollow, egocentric fantasies soon crumble when Njoroge is confronted with reality. When his father dies from severe torture and castration that is inflicted on him because he accepts responsibility for a political murder that has in fact been committed by one of his sons, and when Njoroge himself is tortured in spite of all his innocence and naiveté, all his illusions and grandiose fantasies are shattered: "For the first time Njoroge was face to face with the problem to which 'tomorrow' was no answer. It was this realization that made him feel weak and see the emergency [i.e., the Mau Mau rebellion] in a new light" (*WNC*, 167). Thus it would seem that Njoroge has lost faith in the efficacy of education and the benign justice of a Christian God, which has been the basis of his messianic fantasies. When his father dies and his brothers have been either imprisoned or killed and when the girl he loves refuses to escape with him to Uganda, Njoroge attempts suicide, although he is easily dissuaded by his mother. The novel ends with Njoroge's admission to himself that he is a coward.

This rapid descent from the height of self-importance to the nadir of self-negation is enacted against the backdrop of a society in violent turmoil, which Ngugi depicts in graphic and effective detail. The different political views and the conflict between generations within Ngotho's family, the enmity and the hatred between Ngotho and Jacobo, whose loyalty to the British is rewarded with wealth and political power, the mixture of respect, fear, and hatred that Mr. Howlands harbors for Ngotho because he has occupied the latter's land, the former's desire to torture and kill the latter (which leads to the retaliatory murder of Howlands by Ngotho's son), Howlands's contempt for Jacobo's collaboration, Njoroge's love for Mwihaki,

Jacobo's daughter, and his brief friendship with Howlands's son—
all these complex entanglements and contradictions as well as the
graphic descriptions of torture and summary execution by the British
and the Mau Mau create a powerful microcosmic picture of a whole
society being ripped apart by economic and political conflict. The
novel brilliantly depicts the trauma and the ambiguities of a revolution. Yet Njoroge's actual experience is not derived from active involvement in this social upheaval; rather, he functions as a passive,
reluctant witness. His experience is that of a highly suggestible and
solitary adolescent who easily internalizes the hopes, frustrations,
and anguish of his society and then soothes his own trauma with
fantasies of self-aggrandizement. Unlike his peers who become more
worldly and involved because of the social disruption, Njoroge only
desires to escape first through his dreams, then by attempting to run
away with Mwihaki to Uganda, and finally by trying to commit
suicide. The grandiose oscillations in Njoroge's self-perception, then,
can be accounted for only partly by the violence and trauma that
surround him. The rest of the explanation lies in the peripeteia of
values that engulfs him and in the narrator's attitude to his major
protagonist.

The peripeteia of values causes the confusion that is ultimately
responsible for the isolated fantasies that comprise the central experience of this novel. The change in values begins with the negation
of Gikuyu culture and is followed by an understanding of the colonial situation and a justification of the rebellion. The whole impetus
to abandon Gikuyu tradition is best characterized by the attitude of
the white headmaster of Njoroge's secondary school. He treats his
African students with due courtesy and respect but

> he believed that the best, the really excellent could only come from
> the white man. He brought up his boys to copy and cherish the white
> man's civilization as the only hope of mankind and especially of the
> black races. He was automatically against all black politicians who in
> any way made people to be discontented with the white man's rule
> and civilizing mission. (WNC, 158–59)

Such an exhortation involves the rejection of native society and a
simultaneous espousal of imperfectly understood English values as
well as the emasculation of the political will of indigenous people.
Njoroge exhibits the internalization of both tenets of this civilizing
program, but curiously he has succumbed to the peripeteia even before he comes under the influence of this headmaster. Thus, for instance, he prefers the name Lucia to any Gikuyu female names, and

he proudly associates with other Gikuyu who have abandoned indigenous values and have ardently but superficially imitated some aspects of European culture (*WNC*, 33–35). He also equates formal academic education, as well as the learning process in general, with the ability to speak and write English (*WNC*, 62). Similarly, whereas Ngotho considers land to be the prime value, Njoroge, who has never farmed, considers education, in his abstract conception of it, as the solution to all problems (*WNC*, 64–65). Thus, even before Njoroge is exposed to formal programs designed to change his values, he has already abandoned the ethnic and rural tradition and has begun to subscribe to the colonialist values which he does not really understand. Similarly, he has little interest in the intricacies of the political turmoil in the country, while his peers are thoroughly involved.

The exposure to various aspects of European values, of course, involves an intensive introduction to Christianity in the mission schools. Thus Njoroge, like other Africans, is able to find in the Bible a parallel to the plight of the Gikuyu and a divine justification for their rebellion: "the Gikuyu people, whose land had been taken by white men, were no other than the children of Israel about whom he read in the Bible. . . . the black people had a special mission to the world because they were the chosen people of God. This explained his brother's remark that Jomo was the Black Moses" (*WNC*, 78). However, whereas other Gikuyu use such analogies as a justification for their rebellion, Njoroge employs them as a balm to soothe the effects on him of the traumatic political situation: "Njoroge came to place faith in the Bible and with the vision of an educated life in the future was blended a belief in the righteousness of God. Equity and justice were there in the world. If you did well and remained faithful to your God, the Kingdom of Heaven would be yours. A good man would get a reward from God; a bad man would harvest bad fruits" (*WNC*, 77–78). We have already seen how he uses this influence of the Bible to fuel his messianic fantasies. The abandonment of indigenous values and the attraction and misunderstanding of foreign values leave Njoroge in a suspended state of mind; he is grounded in neither culture, and he is traumatized by the political chaos. Just as he soothes his own anxieties with his benign visions, so he feels he has to comfort other people. When he meets Howlands's son, Njoroge tries to calm his misgivings about the future of Kenya. To the boy's comment that things are "so dark now," Njoroge replies, "Yes . . . so dark, but things will be all right." Then the narrator comments, "Njoroge still believed in the future. Hope of a better day was the only comfort he could give to a *weeping child. He did*

*not know that his faith in the future could be a form of escape from
the reality of the present"* (WNC, 154, italics mine).

Here, then, we have the crux of the ambivalence, caused by the
peripeteia of values, that pervades the entire novel. There is a profound absurdity in Njoroge's self-evaluation which allows him pa-
tronizingly to comfort a boy his own age who seems to have a better
grasp of reality than Njoroge. Yet the narrator's comment, though
quite accurately appraising the psychological function of Njoroge's
messianism, does not reveal any sense of irony. In fact there is no
sign throughout the novel that the narrator ever recognizes the absurdity of his character's fantasies. If the final collapse of Njoroge's
grandiose vision of himself were presented in an ironic light, then
clearly *Weep Not, Child* would be a successful ironic *bildungsroman*
wherein the real education of the hero would lead to his realization
that "education" is not a panacea and that he is not a messiah. However, the narrator's attitude is never ironic; in fact it is entirely sympathetic. He is perfectly aware that Njoroge's vision is a form of
escape, but he neither criticizes it nor explains its psycho-social origins. His sympathy is clearly manifested in the lines from Walt
Whitman's poem, "On the Beach at Night," which are quoted at the
beginning of the novel and from which the title is derived:

> Weep not, child
> Weep not, my darling
> With these kisses let me remove your tears,
> The ravening clouds shall not be long victorious,
> They shall not long possess the sky. . . .

It is clear from these lines that the weeping child is Njoroge, whose
life is shadowed by the "ravening clouds" of the colonial occupation
and political turmoil. Yet the coincidence between the narrator's attitude toward Njoroge as the weeping child and Njoroge's view of the
English boy as the weeping child betrays the sympathetic rather than
the ironic nature of the narrator-protagonist relationship. The narrator insists that Njoroge, having finally abandoned his messianic fantasies, has come to terms with reality, but the actual portrayal of the
hero does not support this insistence. This contradiction is another
manifestation of the novel's ambivalent intention.

As we have seen, when Njoroge's messianic visions are shattered
by the harsh reality of physical torture, he attempts to find another
avenue of escape. After confessing to Mwihaki that the calamities
suffered by their families are his fault and that the guilt is entirely
his, Njoroge tries to persuade her to elope with him to Uganda. But

when Mwihaki, aware of the real demands of the social situation, refuses to do so in spite of her love for him, he accuses her of betraying him and then once more attempts to evade reality through suicide. Thus Njoroge has not really changed. He has neither come to
terms with the socio-political reality nor has he abandoned his
grandiose vision of himself. For by assuming all the guilt of his world
and by accusing Mwihaki of betraying him, Njoroge is still following
the model of Christ, of a messiah who assumed all human guilt, was
betrayed, and was then made a scapegoat. By voluntarily transform-
ing his self-image from that of a savior to that of a scapegoat Njoroge
still retains the egocentric attitude that is responsible for his isolation
from reality. This essential continuity in Njoroge's characterization
testifies to the powerful influence of Christianity on Ngugi himself,
for in spite of his intention of terminating Njoroge's messianic self-
image he has simply transferred the emotional investment of his
hero to a slightly different aspect of the same fantasy. And the fact
that Njoroge's "education" is presented only as a general disillusionment rather than as a subtle comprehension of a complex reality
further testifies to the truncated nature of this bildungsroman. The
inadequate change in Njoroge's character can thus be seen as a
result of the profound sympathy between narrator and character.
The absence of irony also implies the lack of critical distance between Ngugi and Njoroge.

If Njoroge's fantasies are products of the socio-religious factors
in the specific colonial situation, products, that is, of the effects of
land alienation, of the premium put on education by the Gikuyu, of
Christian and Gikuyu messianic influences, and of the peripeteia of
values, then the ambiguity in the narrative attitude to Njoroge can
be seen as a manifestation of the same forces. For, in the final analysis, it is Ngugi's inability to define adequately his stand toward
these factors, which, as we have seen, are a part of his own colonial
background, that must bear the responsibility for the textual ambivalence. The novel, then, can be seen simultaneously as a product and
a portrayal of the peripeteia of values in a colonial situation. The
persistent problems caused by the latter lead Ngugi to a reworking
of the same issues in his next novel, The River Between. The thematic
preoccupations of Weep Not, Child recur in a clearer and more dramatically vital manner in The River Between.[24]

Both the background and the foreground of The River Between
are directly concerned with an attempt to come to terms with the
peripeteia of values in a colonial situation. The plot of the novel, set
in the late 1920s and 1930s, is centered once more on a combination

of education and messianism, while the subplot examines the clash of values through the emotionally and culturally charged controversy over female circumcision. The geographical setting of the novel as well as the characterization of all the major protagonists are imbued with the dramatic and disruptive nature of cultural transition. The setting is allegorical: the events take place in the "heart and soul" of Gikuyu land and culture amongst the communities on two ridges that are ranged on either side of River Honia, which in Gikuyu means "Regeneration." Both ridges, Kameno and Makuyu, claim to be the sources of Gikuyu culture, but as the novel progresses the former, which is the home of the prophet Mugo wa Kibiro and his descendant, Waiyaki (the central protagonist), becomes the base for those who want to safeguard cultural purity, whereas the latter becomes the home of those who have converted to Christianity and have renounced various "evil" aspects of their original tradition. The ensuing conflict between the two ridges thus becomes emblematic of the problem of peripeteia experienced by the entire Gikuyu culture.

Characterization too is stylized to reflect this antagonism between the desire for cultural purity and the desire to abrogate the traditional society. Among the older generation, which provides the secondary characters, the opposition is embodied in Chege (Waiyaki's father) and Joshua. Chege, a minor prophet, embittered by the people's disregard for his claims, is realistically aware of the specific cultural and technological superiority of European society and thus, in spite of the inherent dangers, commands his son to attend the missionary school and master Western knowledge without absorbing its vices. He is simultaneously concerned with preserving Gikuyu purity and with ensuring its survival through the absorption of clearly efficacious aspects of Western culture. On the other hand, Joshua, a zealous convert who has become a self-righteous and puritanical minister, renounces Gikuyu culture, which he considers a dirty, heathen, and evil practice. He has entirely dedicated himself to his own and other people's salvation through Christianity. Ngugi balances the static and absolute cultural oppositions that are embodied in Chege and Joshua with the dynamic and relativistic attitudes of their children, Waiyaki and Joshua's two daughters, Muthoni and Nyambura, who attempt in their different ways to synthesize the two cultures.

The poignant and touching subplot depicts Muthoni's disastrous attempt to combine what she considers to be the best aspects of both cultures. Even though her parents will not permit her to undergo circumcision because the Christians have forbidden this ceremony, which for the Gikuyu is the most important rite of purification and rebirth, Muthoni decides that she must adhere to this custom. She still believes in the Gikuyu view that a girl can only become a woman through circumcision, and she is unable to comprehend how women in other cultures become women unless they undergo some such ceremony. She also believes, quite rightly, that there are no substantial contradictions between the tenets of Christianity and the rites of circumcision and thus tries to synthesize the two cultures by running away from home and going through the ritual under the tutelage of her aunt who lives in Kameno. Unfortunately, she soon dies from an infection contracted during the surgery. In addition to depicting the social consequences of the cultural clash in the form of the bitter dissensions and the subsequent disintegration of Joshua's family, Muthoni's apostasy reveals the more profound problems of cultural transition. The fact that her notion of womanhood is predicated on a specific physio-cultural ritual shows that peripeteia involves not only social but also metaphysical and cosmological changes; specific modifications in culture become meaningless unless the entire cultural gestalt is altered to accommodate the particular infusions. From the Gikuyu viewpoint the Christian interdiction of circumcision is profoundly meaningless. Thus both the Christian converts and the traditional Gikuyu interpret Muthoni's death as a vindication of their own righteous beliefs; for the Gikuyu it confirms the ancient prophecies that the new faith would divide "father and daughter, son and father," whereas for the Christians it confirms "the barbarity of Gikuyu customs" (*RB*, 62–63). The failure of communal compassion on both sides and the use of her death to justify their respective beliefs indicate the anxiety caused by the peripeteia. Adherence to either set of values at this stage is essentially an act of faith. Thus Waiyaki feels that Muthoni has died "on the high altar of [the] disruption" caused by the cultural clash. Muthoni's death radicalizes both factions and plays an important role in the novel's major consideration of peripeteia which centers on Waiyaki's role as messiah and educator.

Unlike *Weep Not, Child*, where the messianic possibility is entirely confined to Njoroge's fantasies, *The River Between* presents the prophetic tradition as an actual fact, though, as we shall see later, the narrative is once more characterized by a double intention. However, Waiyaki's messianic heritage is unambiguous. He is a direct descendant of Mugo wa Kibiro, and while he is still very young his father reveals to him Mugo's prophecy which is to become Waiyaki's mission:

"Salvation shall come from the hills. From the blood that flows in me,
I say from the same tree, a son shall rise, and his duty shall be to
lead and save the people! . . ."

Arise. Heed the prophecy. Go to the Mission place. Learn all the
wisdom and all the secrets of the white man. But do not follow his
vices. Be true to your people and the ancient rites. (RB, 24)

Waiyaki is shocked and bewildered by the inheritance of such a massive burden, and he momentarily entertains the possibility that his father is mad. However, throughout the novel, the narrator and some of the characters periodically reinforce the fact that he is a messiah, that he has some extraordinary power. In due time he is sent to the mission school, and we soon see the effects of peripeteia on him. Every time he returns to Kameno he seems to be increasingly uncomfortable with local customs and attitudes.

His messianic mission begins early in his life when Muthoni's controversial death leads the Siriana Mission School to dismiss all students whose parents are not Christian converts. Waiyaki, even though he has not completed his secondary education, starts his own school with the help of his fellow classmates (just as KISA and KKEA had done). His efficient administration and his success in persuading the people to invest time and money in the education of their children lead to a rapid proliferation of schools and to his fame. In fact he now does seem to have become the messiah:

They called him a saviour. His own father had talked of a Messiah
to come. Whom was the Messiah coming to save? From what? And
where would He lead the people? Although Waiyaki did not stop to
get clear answers to these questions, he increasingly saw himself as
the one who would lead the tribe to the light. Education was the light
of the country. That was what the people wanted. Education. Schools.
Education. (RB, 115)

His success catapults him into prominence at a young age. He becomes a member of the Kiama, that is, the council of elders, and later the people are made to take the oath to guard the purity of their culture in his name. In fact, he seems to be the perfect solution to the problems of peripeteia: "He was a man who, impregnated with the magic of the white man, would infuse the tribe with wisdom and strength, giving it new life" (RB, 104). By successfully mediating between the English and Gikuyu cultures and making the positive aspects of the former available to the latter, he seems to have fulfilled the prophecy. However, as the previous quotation suggests, Waiyaki's notion of "education" is just as abstract and vague as that of

Njoroge, and he has not the slightest idea about the nature of the ultimate goal toward which he is supposed to lead his people. Waiyaki repeatedly contemplates these goals and his own function and purpose, but his meditations are always confined to vague and general questions. He never makes an effort to think concretely or to resolve specific problems; he seems to have been paralyzed by the awesome nature of his mission. Similarly, Waiyaki keeps repeating to himself that he must reunite the tribe which has been bifurcated by Muthoni's death into the antagonistic camps of traditional Gikuyu and Chrisian converts, but again this remains a vague and empty dream. His political naiveté is amply demonstrated by his initial token participation in and eventual resignation from the Kiama because he wants to devote all his energies to "education." He is even unaware that his enemies control the Kiama and that they are using his name to win the loyalty of the people.

With the repeated warnings and admonitions from friends and enemies, Waiyaki finally comes to understand his own cultural predicament and the fact that his valorization of education has taken place in a political vacuum. He realizes that people do not desire education for its own sake, and that for them it is a means to prosperity and political independence; he sees that they are primarily concerned with regaining their land which has been appropriated by European settlers and that all other issues are secondary. Waiyaki thus subordinates education to unity, which in turn is seen as a means to achieve political freedom. In the process of this realization he also begins to understand himself as a product of the peripeteia of values. He feels that European traditions and values have much in them that would benefit Gikuyu culture, but that an attempt simply to replace the latter with the former would be unworkable and dangerous, for it would produce social disintegration. Unless the new culture could be adequately synthesized with and integrated into the cosmology of the old one, it would not satisfy human needs: "It would not be a living experience, a source of life and vitality. It would only maim a man's soul, making him fanatically cling to whatever promised security, otherwise he would be lost" (*RB,* 163). Waiyaki sees that Muthoni was a victim of this cultural clash and that he is in danger of becoming one too: "His father too had tried to reconcile the two ways, not in himself, but through his son. Waiyaki was a product of that attempt" (*RB,* 163).

However, Waiyaki's understanding resolves nothing. Soon after his realization, he is accused by the Kiama of violating his oath of purity and contaminating the tribe because he has fallen in love with

Muthoni's uncircumcised sister, Nyambura. At a village meeting they ask him to renounce her, and when he refuses the people deprive him of his authority and leave the fate of the lovers in the hands of Waiyaki's enemies in the Kiama. Thus in the final instance Waiyaki, by refusing to renounce Nyambura, chooses a personal form of cultural synthesis—between himself as a "pure" Gikuyu and Nyambura as a Christian convert. By so doing he renounces the substance of his political realization as well as his role as a potential messiah. Although Waiyaki's comprehension of his own predicament makes *The River Between* a much better resolved *bildungsroman* than *Weep Not, Child*, the final priority of personal over communal obligations reveals a series of narrative problems and limitations which show that the novel itself is a product of the confusion caused by the peripeteia of values.

It is quite clear that the narrator overtly intends to present Waiyaki as a man who is constantly concerned with communal welfare: "Waiyaki was made to serve the tribe, living day by day with no thoughts of self but always of others" (*RB*, 85). Yet the rhetoric of Waiyaki's contemplation and doubts demonstrates that he is entirely engrossed by his own potential as a messiah: all his dealings with other people always revert to the questions about his status and leadership. Waiyaki's preoccupation with his role wraps him in a kind of narcissism that isolates him from the political desires of his community. A tension between self and society is in fact an integral part of his messianic heritage. His father tells him that the prophecies of both Mugo and Chege were scorned by the people, and thus Waiyaki's anticipation of rejection may further isolate him from the community. In any case, the divine source of his authority, by providing him with *transcendent* knowledge, cuts him off from the Gikuyu to the extent that his vision of the future and his action based on it need not rely on a mundane familiarity with the people's social and political desires. Any time Waiyaki is at odds with the people he is able to use his faith in his role as a rationalization for his own decision. The isolation permitted by his position can be measured by the fact that he rarely consults anyone about decisions regarding education. This conflict between the covert and the overt intentions, between Waiyaki's narcissism and communal obligations, is accompanied by other problems in narrative intentions that reveal Ngugi's profound subconscious ambiguity about the nature of messianic calling.

The major problem of the novel is that Ngugi seems unable to decide whether to treat Waiyaki unreservedly as a real messiah or whether to portray him as a character whose prophetic calling is a self-delusion. Consequently, the authorial ambivalence manifests itself in the narrator's specific descriptions and indirect criticisms of Waiyaki, and in the portrayal of Waiyaki as a scapegoat. On the one hand, the narrator explains Waiyaki's exclusive concern with education as a product of colonial propaganda: "He wanted to concentrate on education. Perhaps the teaching of Livingstone [his English instructor at Siriana], that education was of value and his boys should not concern themselves with what the government was doing or politics, had found a place in Waiyaki's heart" (*RB*, 76). On the other hand, he presents Waiyaki's preoccupation as a part of his divine calling: "[The establishment of the Marioshoni school] had been Waiyaki's idea and even now he could not understand fully how his idea had borne fruit so quickly. He saw it as something beyond himself, something ordained by fate" (*RB*, 78). Thus Waiyaki is simultaneously subject to human fallibility and to divine surety. Similarly, the narrator indirectly criticizes his hero's ignorance of politics by endowing his colleague Kinuthia with a delicate understanding of the need to combine the long-range importance of education with the immediate desire of the peasants to regain control of their lands through some form of political action. Yet such criticisms of Waiyaki do not clarify the problem. While they imply that he may be a mere mortal with an imperfect understanding of events, the narrator and characters keep insisting that he is a messiah, and Waiyaki too assumes the same: he never questions the *fact* that he is an ordained prophet; he is just confused about the nature of his mission.

The end of the novel increases the ambiguity. It is fairly clear that Waiyaki has been turned into a scapegoat by the people who are concerned with repossessing their land and are anxious to preserve their own way of life. Thus they do not heed Waiyaki's pleas for unity with the Christian Gikuyu, and they will not condone his relationship with an uncircumcised woman. Ngugi seems to sympathize with Waiyaki's decision to choose a personal relationship over communal obligation as well as with the people's decision to protect their own culture while sacrificing a promising individual. But this does not resolve the ambiguity about Waiyaki—does his decision imply that he is not the messiah? What is one to make of his apparent failure, if indeed he has failed? None of these questions are answered by the final shift of the narrative to a description of the Honia River, the rhythm of which reaches into the heart of the people. The implication is that the process of regeneration, partly begun by Waiyaki, will continue, but we still do not know whether he is the messiah who, like Christ, has been turned into a scapegoat, nor do we have specific answers to the problems of peripeteia.

The persistent ambiguity about Waiyaki and the final recourse to scapegoating, which resembles so closely the pattern of grandiose self-delusion and vindication through persecution in *Weep Not, Child*, reveal once more the close sympathy between the narrator and his hero. This negation of the necessary critical distance between the two exposes *The River Between* as a product of subjective anxiety. If one considers Ngugi's predicament at the age of fifteen when, during the Mau Mau war, he internalized the social preoccupation with education, leadership, and messianism, then one can see that the ambiguity and the ambivalence of *The River Between* are a literary transformation of his traumatic experience. Waiyaki's insight into the anxiety caused by the peripeteia of values is quite applicable to the novel as a whole, for according to him this fear can make a man fanatically cling to whatever promises security. Ngugi's repeated preoccupation with messianism and education strongly implies that Ngugi looks to them for some sort of security, and the repeated absence of critical distance between narrators and characters demonstrates the strong subjective relevance of these themes for Ngugi. (As we will see the themes recur in a substantially altered form in *A Grain of Wheat*.) If *Weep Not, Child* and *The River Between* are products of peripeteia, they are also attempts to alleviate the anxiety caused by Ngugi's social inheritance: Njoroge's wish to escape from the chaos of war by eloping with Mwihaki to Uganda and Waiyaki's refusal to abandon Myambura (that is, the repeated decisions to choose personal fulfillment instead of communal obligations) are manifestations of the authorial desire to shed the burdens of messianic leadership.

It is a significant measure of Ngugi's emancipation from the messianic preoccupation that the only character in his next novel who is entirely lost in the vision of himself as savior is clearly portrayed as a pathological man. In addition to the decline of messianism, Ngugi's engrossment with education as a panacea is entirely absent in *A Grain of Wheat*. As a result, the substance, form, and style of this novel are markedly different from those of the previous ones. The dreamlike quality of the earlier novels, created by the powerful subjectivity of the protagonist's messianic fantasy which tends to isolate him from the community and excludes other viewpoints and criteria and by the sympathetic convergence of the narrator and character, is in *A Grain of Wheat* put in its proper perspective through a juxtaposition of the messianic and the very mundane concerns of various individuals.

This substantial change in Ngugi's style and vision is caused in part by his reading Frantz Fanon's *The Wretched of the Earth* just prior to writing *A Grain of Wheat*.[25] Fanon's influence need not be traced minutely in order to appreciate the major change that it has produced in Ngugi's views of the socio-political function of art, which in turn manifest themselves in the shape and substance of *A Grain of Wheat*. According to Fanon, if an intellectual in a colonial situation wishes to create an authentic work of art he must first understand the realities of his nation, and if he wishes to use the past, he should do so "with the intention of opening the future, as an invitation to action and a basis for hope. But to ensure that hope and to give it form, he must take part in action and throw himself body and soul into the national struggle." Furthermore, the writer must also remember that the colonial situation drives indigenous cultures underground and that it is "the fight for national existence which sets culture moving and opens to it the doors of creation."[26] Now although it seems that Ngugi has no direct participatory experience of the ·Mau Mau struggle, he was nevertheless a part of the society that was engulfed by the rebellion, and in this novel he has managed to re-create imaginatively the involvement of various types of individuals in such a struggle and to show how the fight does regenerate the culture.

In so doing, Ngugi has written a novel that allows the reader to experience the dynamics of a viable organic community. Ngugi creates a social organization that is based on sympathy derived from a communion of purpose which ensures that each individual will see the other as a complementary rather than an antagonistic being and will treat him as a concrete subject rather than as an object with specific use value. Ngugi portrays a community that, based on an inescapable interconnectedness of concrete individuals, is actively and consciously attempting to define and give meaning to itself. As Camus has pointed out, a rebel by virtue of saying no to oppression implicitly affirms a set of new values on the basis of which he will reorganize his life. The community in Ngugi's novel, having been caught up in the paradoxes of the peripeteia of values in a colonial society, is now in the process of rejecting some values and attempting to find new meaning for itself. The experience of community, predominantly manifested in the patterns of individual isolation and social interaction, is also strengthened by aspects of the novel's formal organization. The actual time encompassed by the action is only six days, but through the constant retrospections we experience the whole Mau Mau revolution and even the prerevolutionary childhood of the protagonists as well as the mythic past of the Gikuyu. These retrospections and the multiplicity of points of view through which we come to understand the characters create the experience of an organic community which can only be known through its historical and interpersonal interactions; in the novel there is no omniscient, privileged view of these interactions that constantly reshape the past, present, and future.

The patterns of isolation and interaction are so entangled that a critical analysis inevitably violates their organic nature. However, such a violation cannot be avoided because we can appreciate the community only if we understand the protagonists as individuals and then see their mutual involvements. In examining the permutations of isolation we shall confine ourselves only to the major protagonists in the novel, for it is essentially through them that we arrive at the experience of community. Ngugi uses five characters—Mugo, Karanja, Kihika, Gikonyo, and Mumbi—to contrast different kinds of personal isolation, love, and sympathy for others, and then he orchestrates a complex pattern wherein some characters move from isolation into community, some move in the opposite direction, while others remain relatively static. By contrasting and interweaving these movements Ngugi writes a polyphonic novel wherein the experience of social regeneration, communal coherence, and vitality lies not in the awareness of any single character but in the *interaction* between various individuals and in the reader's experience of this interaction. The nature and power of this polyphonic novel will become apparent as we examine each of the major characters.

The genesis of Mugo's isolation lies in his childhood. Because he is an orphan who is severely ill-treated by his aunt and consequently grows up without experiencing family warmth or mutual dependence, Mugo develops a defensive philosophy of self-isolation: "all his life he had avoided conflicts: at home, or at school, he rarely joined the company of other boys for fear of being involved in brawls that might ruin his chances of a better future. His argument went like this: if you don't traffic with evil, then evil ought not to touch you; if you leave people alone, then they ought to leave you alone" (*GW*, 221). Mugo becomes a hermit and avoids all involvement because it implies conflict for him. The subsequent emotional paralysis results in a monotonous life, and thus Mugo's need for recognition channels itself into messianic fantasies about himself which are further fueled by resentment.

The first substantial breach in Mugo's isolation is made by Kihika, a Mau Mau leader seeking shelter from the police. The latter, not realizing Mugo's pathological fear of involvement, asks him to organize a support group for the Mau Mau in Thabai, but Mugo resents the violation of his isolation and later betrays Kihika in the hope of achieving power and fame: "He would flash his victory before the eyes of his aunt's ghost. His place in society would be established. He would be halfway on the road to power. And what is greatness but power? . . . Yes—to be great you must stand in such a place that you can dispense pain and death to others without anyone asking questions. Like a headmaster, a judge, a Governor" (*GW*, 224). Mugo's betrayal of Kihika, however, is unknown to Thabai, and it earns him not power but contempt from the colonialists. Consequently, when Mugo, in a sudden and isolated act of involvement prompted by his guilt, defends Kihika's pregnant lover from a beating by the colonial police, he becomes a village hero, for the people are also aware that Kihika had obtained shelter from Mugo. His fame grows because he is sent to a concentration camp for defending the woman and because he refuses, in spite of severe torture, to admit that he took the Mau Mau oath. The irony, of course, is that Mugo does not confess to oath-taking because he never did participate in the Mau Mau ceremonies. Nevertheless, he becomes one of the heroes of the rebellion, and his name is always linked with Kihika's. During the four days prior to the independence of Kenya, when the actual action of the novel commences, Mugo's isolation is repeatedly broken by requests from the village that he be the chief speaker honoring Kihika at the independence celebration, by the request from Kihika's comrades that he help them to identify Kihika's betrayer, and by Kihika's sister and her husband, Mumbi and Gikonyo, who separately confide their personal problems to him because he seems strong and self-sufficient in his isolation.

Mugo fluctuates back and forth in his decision to accept the offer. At first, he resents the repeated violation of his isolation and again is afraid of involvement. Later he decides to use this opportunity to his own advantage, for he has also been asked to become the village chief. After repeatedly refusing the invitation to address the celebration, he decides to speak at the last moment and confesses his betrayal of Kihika because he can no longer live with his conscience. The significant point of these ironies of misunderstandings, however, is that they slowly draw Mugo out of his isolation and into the community by making him feel needed. For instance, the confidences of Mumbi and her request that Mugo mediate between her and her husband in order to resolve their marital difficulties begin to rehabilitate his emotional paralysis: "How was it that Mumbi's story had cracked open his dull insides and released imprisoned thoughts and feelings? . . . previously he liked to see events in his life as isolated" (GW, 196). He begins to reorganize his past life in some sort of moral or causal order, but the inspiration fades, and he relapses into his fragmented world. Mugo's awareness of himself as part of the community is never more than momentary but, as we shall see, his confession has important consequences for the regeneration of the community which has been torn apart by the Mau Mau war.

While Mugo is initially isolated and gradually, if momentarily, becomes a part of the community, Karanja is very much a part of that community in his youth but becomes progressively isolated from it. However, his alienation is similar to Mugo's in that it verges on the pathological. Karanja and Gikonyo are both in love with Mumbi, and, when the latter's suit is successful, Karanja has a fit and a vision that reveals his sense of isolation: "Everybody was running away as if each person feared the ground beneath his feet would collapse. They ran in every direction; men trampled on women; mothers forgot their children; the lame and the weak were abandoned on the platform. Each man was alone, with God" (GW, 109). When the Mau Mau rebellion breaks out and Gikonyo is sent to a concentration camp, Karanja, in order to remain with Mumbi, stays behind by confessing his oath and joining the colonial police. Thus, ironically, in order to maintain contact with Mumbi he further isolates himself, for his initial duty as an ex-Mau Mau is to put on a white hood and identify Mau Mau rebels that he has known personally. This device of identifying the rebel community without being recognized cuts him off completely from his society.

Through this deliberate isolation Karanja too develops a thirst for power. Whereas Mugo's desire for power expands itself in messianic fantasies because of the pathological nature of his alienation, Karanja's similar desires are actually gratified by action because his isolation is systematically antisocial. Yet his desire is essentially the same as Mugo's: to wield power over life and death without having to be responsible to any authority: "When he shot [the Mau Mau rebels], they seemed less like human beings and more like animals. At first this had merely thrilled Karanja and made him feel a new man, a part of an invisible might whose symbol was the white man.

Later, this consciousness of power, this ability to dispose of human life by merely pulling a trigger, so obsessed him that it became a need" (*GW*, 260). Isolation for Karanja pays dividends in the "invisible might" that it proffers him, and therefore he develops it into a creed. He tells Mumbi that "a time will come when you too will know that every man in the world is alone, and fights alone, to live."

Mugo desires isolation, but his inability to force people to keep their distance results in the communal pull that finally integrates him into society. On the other hand, Karanja, because of his very real antisocial power, is able to alienate all Thabai and eventually achieve the complete isolation that he had envisioned. After the war Karanja remains in the employment of the English colonialists because the Africans will not have him, but, given the nature of colonial racial relations, he is not accepted in any substantial way by the whites either—he only remains their servant. Ngugi depicts with great subtlety the combinations of awe and hatred, pride and subservience that characterize Karanja's attitude to his white masters, but the author betrays his dislike of Karanja through the conjunction of both the narrator's and the Africans' view of Karanja as the pet dog of his white masters. When the day of political independence arrives, Karanja's masters leave, and he is now entirely isolated. He has been singled out for assassination because it is thought that he betrayed Kihika, but when Mugo confesses he is released. In the end he is haunted by visions of his hooded self and, after having been rejected even by his mother, he leaves the village for an unknown destination. Of all the characters who experience some form of isolation Karanja is the only one who is not reintegrated into the community.

Yet the very desire to unify the community, to safeguard it against colonial domination and violation, can be a source of isolation, albeit a very different form. This is Kihika's version, which is characterized by a sincere concern for the generalized, transcendent welfare of the community as an abstract entity but which is callous to the personal needs and demands of and obligations to concrete individuals. Kihika's preoccupation has origins similar to those of the messianism in *Weep Not, Child* and *The River Between*. As a young boy he is exposed to the burden of communal defeat and consequently his heart becomes set on fighting the colonialist. Exposure to the stories of Gandhi's saintlike fight against the British and of Moses' liberation of the Jews from Egyptian domination leads Kihika to feed on "visions of himself, a saint, leading the Gikuyu people to freedom and power" (*GW*, 49). However, unlike the heroes

of the earlier novels, Kihika does not lose himself in self-aggrandizing
fantasies, but rather he finds them inspirational and uses them to
convince his followers. He has great admiration for Christ's and
Gandhi's abilities to unite people, and he is convinced that individuals should be sacrificed for the good of the people if necessary:
"Do you know why Gandhi succeeded? Because he made his people
give up their fathers and mothers and serve their one mother—India.
With us, Kenya is our mother" (*GW*, 103). For Kihika this is not
mere rhetoric; he does take the greatest risks and does finally sacrifice himself. However, sympathy for the abstract notion of the "people" is acompanied by a blindness toward the needs of the individual.
The romantic relationship between Kihika and his lover amply
illustrates that his preoccupation with visions of sainthood and revolution renders him incapable of treating her as an individual. His
disregard for the motives and desires of individuals is also responsible for his misreading Mugo's personality, and the mistake proves
fatal for Kihika. This sublime form of egotism, then, is responsible
for his isolation from the community that is composed of concrete
and particular individuals.

Gikonyo, on the other hand, is ruled in his social and personal
life by specific relationships. His mother had come to Thabai when
Gikonyo was a baby. Her life had been centered around the boy,
and in turn the adolescent Gikonyo's concern was to make his
mother happy. When Gikonyo marries Mumbi the family is enlarged, but the relationships remain the same; they are characterized
by concern for individual needs of specific people and are based on
personal, concrete sympathy. But the model family is broken up
when Gikonyo is sent to a concentration camp for having taken the
oath. At the camp he experiences the most "normal" form of isolation in the novel: the absence of community based on concrete and
specific relationships. His sense of alienation begins with the fear
that his death in the camp, away from his family, would result in
his spiritual nullification because he would not have a proper burial
and therefore would not be remembered by his descendants. He,
along with another prisoner, breaks the unwritten rule among the
rebels that forbids them to discuss their families or other matters relating to their homes. Soon after violating the rule he begins to yearn
for the family, and his sense of isolation becomes progressively
acute. The severe monotony of his existence in the desert camp begins to attenuate his personality: "Barbed-wire, barbed-wire everywhere. So it was today, so it would be tomorrow. The barbed-wire
blurred his vision. There was nothing beyond it. Human voices had

stopped. The world, outside, was dead" (*GW*, 128). The absence of community gradually obscures his sense of self so that coherence begins to fade as well:

> In his cell, Gikonyo found that everything—the barbed-wire, Yala Camp, Thabai—was dissolved into a colourless mist. He struggled to recall the outline of Mumbi's face without success; there was only a succession of images each one canceling out the one immediately preceding it. . . . He was both in and outside himself—in a trance, considering everything calmly, and only mildly puzzled by the failure of his memory. Maybe I'm weary, the thought crossed his mind. If I stand up everything that makes me what I am will rush back into activity. (*GW*, 128–29)

This experience of isolation is the most complete and radical one in the novel because here the absence of community ultimately implies the negation of the individual self. Unable to withstand such isolation, Gikonyo confesses the oath in order to return to his family.

Gikonyo only arrives in Thabai to find that his wife has had a child fathered by Karanja, who is now "Chief" of the village and to whom he has to report as a paroled detainee. In his bitterness he too retreats behind a defensive philosophy of isolation: "perhaps there had never been any communion between them, nothing could grow between any two people. One lived alone, and like Gatu, went to the grave alone. Gikonyo greedily sucked sour pleasure from this reflection which he saw as a terrible revelation. To live and die alone was the ultimate truth" (*GW*, 134–35). Thus, clutching his isolationist creed, Gikonyo channels his desire for power into his carpenter's trade and later into other business ventures. His sense of betrayal makes him unsympathetic and frigid, which in turn allows him to become a prosperous businessman and eventually a model of thrift and success. His alienation, however, continues almost to the end of the narrative, when Mugo's confession of betraying Kihika begins the regenerative process that allows Gikonyo to re-enter the community.

These various forms of isolation are supported by a more pervasive underlying social disintegration that is characteristic of colonial society. The relationships between the colonialists and the Africans are not those between the concrete, specific, and complex individuals, but between people who only see each other as role occupants, as servants and laborers on the one hand and as masters and usurpers on the other. The colonialist relationship is, of course, distilled by the pressure of the Mau Mau war. The absence of communication between whites and blacks is symbolized by the death of the deaf and mute Gitogo who, when the British soldiers order him to halt, continues to run and is therefore shot and counted as another Mau Mau terrorist who has been eliminated. The lack of understanding between the colonizer and the colonized is accompanied by the disintegration of the indigenous community under the colonial pressure. Karanja's hooded self, which allows him to identify the secret Mau Mau community without being recognized, symbolizes this disintegration. His job is not to identify the Mau Mau as specific individuals but only as political rebels, as "terrorists." The wider repercussions of the social distintegration caused by the colonialist relationship can be seen in the resultant isolation experienced by Karanja, Gikonyo, and Kihika, and in the community's view of Mugo as a hero, which is caused essentially by miscommunication.

It was against this disruption of community, which encompassed everything from the negation of the material base of society (land alienation and disruption of the mode of production) to the suppression of its symbolic and religious form (the capital punishment for those who administered the Mau Mau oath), that the Gikuyu rebelled. The goals of this war, then, furnish all the major protagonists of the novel, except Karanja, with a communion of purpose which is one of the basic necessities of a viable community. In order to seal this communion the Gikuyu take the oath to support the Mau Mau rebellion at all costs and to keep their pledge a secret. Conversely, in order to destroy this secret community, the colonialists are anxious to break the covenant by getting the rebels to confess their oaths. Thus the pledge becomes the formal bond that defines the community and serves as its symbol. Gikonyo's betrayal of this oath causes him a great deal of anguish, while Mugo's apparent determination not to betray it leads to his being adopted as the communal hero. Ngugi, however, does not present the communion of purpose at the overt, abstract level. Rather he portrays society concretely; the rebels rarely speak in abstract terms like "colonialism" or "freedom," but rather they are only concerned with alleviating specific material problems, and it is this pursuit of material goals that in fact unites them.

However, a community achieves vitality not only through personal solidarity but also through the positive presence of coherent meaning. If the latter is absent, the community, in order to maintain its viability, will invent meaning as best it can. Thus Ngugi is portraying a community that, because it is gripped by revolution, has not clearly articulated the meaning of its actions or goals. The society has defined itself negatively by saying no to colonial domination, but it is still in the process of redefining itself positively; it is a community in which meaning is transitional and not yet absolutely clear. Some of the characters are themselves aware of the vagueness of social semantics. For instance, General R. says, by way of explaining a minor character's fantasies about himself as a revolutionary hero, "He invents meaning for his life, you see. Don't we all do that?" The private creation of significance is the microcosm that reflects the macrocosmic need. Thus, the village invents and invests Mugo's life and actions with a meaning that is precisely the opposite of actual reality. Because the real heroes of the community, like Kihika, have been destroyed, the collective desire for heroes who can represent the total significance of the Mau Mau struggle forces the village to invent a hero, to invent, that is, embodied meaning.

However, while Thabai is attempting in its own way to reunite, redefine, and revitalize itself, the narrative has defined the meaning of community through the interaction of the characters. It must be re-emphasized that the viability and meaning of this community are not available to the self-perception of the villagers, who are still deeply involved in the transitional and tentative details of social reconstruction. But the significance of the embryonic structure of community is clearly visible in the narrator's organization of social interaction and in the reader's experience of it. Ngugi defines the meaning of a community through the interdependence of individuals and through the fundamental complementarity that underlies the divergence of their personalities and desires: their sense of separateness from one another varies in direct rather than inverse proportion to their sense of social union. *A Grain of Wheat* reveals the specificity of its characters not so much through their recognition of each other as self-contained subjects but rather through the narrator's presentation based on the understanding that the concrete individuality of each character will only manifest itself through the complexity of his interdependence on others. The narrative shows the characters' interaction in such a way that the organic unity of their personalities is manifested for the reader. Ngugi demonstrates that despite all jealousies, divisions, and betrayals, people still cannot escape each other, that in spite of all alienation and isolation their lives are inextricably intertwined.

As we have already seen, Gikonyo's feeling of isolation, which is the most "normal" in the novel, is dependent directly on his sense of social union. Separation from the specific persons he loves causes the attenuation of his own self; the sense of individuality is in this case directly dependent on his need for social union. At the opposite end from Gikonyo, Mugo's notion of individuality, predicated not on union but on the desire for isolation, is clearly shown to have pathological repercussions. However, it is more interesting that Mugo's desire for separation turns out to be untenable; from the moment that Kihika enters Mugo's hut, the more Mugo tries to isolate himself, the more he becomes involved in the community, until finally even his refusal to speak at the celebration is interpreted as modesty and leads to greater fame and an increased demand for his speech. This inability of an individual to separate himself from a society that sees him as an integral part of itself is the supreme affirmation in the novel of the binding power of a community based on sympathy.

Yet Mugo's absorption into the community is not purely gratuitous—he does perform a very vital function in the society. His final action, his confession, fits into the pattern of complementarity of wills which is essential for the cohesion of a community. Thus, where Kihika's callousness toward individuals may be undesirable in itself, its reverse, his concern for abstract humanity, is vital because it enables the Gikuyu to free themselves from colonial domination. Where Kihika's self-sacrifice, in spite of its eventual usefulness, cause a great deal of pain to the community (because of his assassination of a district officer Thabai is burnt down), Mugo's self-sacrifice, through his confession, is ultimately soothing; it becomes symbolic of the regeneration of open communication and has notable effects on Gikonyo and Mumbi. In a different manner Kihika and Gikonyo form a complementary unit that is essential for the community. Kihika's disregard for the individual and concern for the people in general are balanced by Gikonyo's lack of concern for the abstract conception of community, his betrayal of the Mau Mau covenant, and his powerful desire for concrete individual relationships with Mumbi and his mother. Whereas Kihika's attitude is necessary for the community's struggle to free itself, Gikonyo's attitude is necessary for the survival of that society. Similarly, even Karanja's defection to the colonialists can be seen as a complementary necessity because he is responsible for keeping Mumbi alive while the rest of the men are either guerrillas hiding in the forest or prisoners in the camps.

In this manner, Ngugi is able to reflect strength in one character as weakness in another, or to show that what at one time is a strength is at another moment a weakness. The community then becomes an ecological unit. People are tied to each other in ways that

they themselves fail to understand; the action of one man has repercussions on everybody. Through this focus what ultimately becomes
important is not the character of a given person but the relationships
between individuals. However, the attempt to represent the entire
complexity of relationships in an ecosystem through the literary devices of realism would be an infinite task. In order to surmount this
impossibility and in order to point out emphatically that the community which is reorganizing itself here is not just Thabai but the
entire Gikuyu society, Ngugi finally resorts to a figurative method.
The regeneration of the whole Gikuyu culture is implied in the symbolic references of two characters, Gikonyo and Mumbi, to the
mythic ancestors of their society, Gikuyu and Mumbi. The slight
variations between Gikonyo and Gikuyu is reduced further by Kenyatta's claim that in the correct Gikuyu phonetics "Gikuyu" should
be pronounced "Gekoyo."[27] This analogy is strengthened by Mumbi's
joking references to this parallel (*GW*, 92) and by Gikonyo's feelings, while he is in a concentration camp, that his "reunion with
Mumbi would see the birth of a new Kenya" (*GW*, 121). It is in the
light of this analogue that Karanja's protection of Mumbi and the
effect of Mugo's confession on Gikonyo and Mumbi become significant contributions to their society.

Mumbi and Gikonyo, who had been alienated from each other
because she was forced to have a son by Karanja, have constantly
been confessing their problems to Mugo, whom Mumbi even asks to
act as a mediator. When Mugo finally confesses his betrayal of
Kihika, Gikonyo is shocked with the realization of the possible depth
of misunderstanding and therefore resolves to reopen communication
between Mumbi and himself. This commencement of communal
regeneration is emphasized by the title of the last chapter, "Haram-
bee," implying a coming together, a communal effort. It is further
stressed by Mumbi's restating the need for cooperation between her
and Gikonyo: "We need to talk, to open our hearts to one another,
examine them, and then together plan for the future we want" (*GW*,
250). The desire for communal cohesion and regeneration is finally
symbolized by the stool that Gikonyo plans to carve for Mumbi:

> He would now carve a thin man, with hard lines on the face, shoul-
> ders bent, supporting the weight. His right hand would stretch to
> link with that of a woman, also with hard lines on the face. The third
> figure would be that of a child on whose head or shoulders the other
> two hands of the man and woman would meet. Into what image
> would he work the beads on the seat? A field needing clearance and
> cultivation? A jembe? A bean flower? (*GW*, 279)

Later, as the relationship between them mellows, Gikonyo alters the image of the woman on the stool leg: "I shall carve a woman big with child" (*GW*, 281). The stool thus symbolizes the rebirth of Kenya. However, it is a renaissance that does not stress freedom and independence, rather it emphasizes dependence and the need for communal effort, for clearance and cultivation. This, then, is the final vision of the symbolism that is subordinated to the realism used in the portrayal of the community. Both Mugo and Kihika are the grains of wheat that have been sacrificed so that the wheat may grow again, and Gikonyo and Mumbi, that is the Gikuyu people, and their descendants are the beneficiaries of those sacrifices.

The emotional and intellectual thrust of this novel, then, is utopian, that is, Ngugi depicts a model of social relations that could lead to a more integrated community, but his vision is neither naive nor entirely idealistic. Throughout the novel and particularly toward its end, Ngugi clearly shows that while the peasants have been sacrificing themselves for national independence, a group of educated "leaders" are waiting in the wings to take over the spoils of the struggle. The novel contains an implicit warning that unless the peasants are vigilant, the politicians, who simply wish to replace the colonialist bureaucrats, will be the real beneficiaries of the sacrifices. Ngugi accurately perceives that the racial conflict that characterizes colonial societies will be replaced in the neocolonial nations by the emerging class struggle between an indigenous elite and the vast bulk of the people, who will be exploited once more for the ultimate benefit of the excolonial powers. In his next novel, *Petals of Blood*, Ngugi systematically explores this struggle.

A Grain of Wheat is a novel that portrays in a substantial way the regeneration of a community that has disintegrated in the process of freeing itself from direct colonial domination. The substantiality of this novel, manifested in its concreteness and specificity, is clearly evident when we compare it to the problematic nature of the desire for freedom in Ngugi's two previous novels. In extricating itself from that ethereal preoccupation with messianic salvation, *A Grain of Wheat* sheds further light on the genesis and nature of that preoccupation. When Mumbi is young she is inspired by Kihika's talk of Moses, Christ, and Gandhi to "visions of a heroic past in other lands marked by acts of *sacrificial martyrdom; a ritual mist* surrounded those *far-away lands and years,* a vague richness that excited and appealed to her" (*GW*, 102, italics mine). This is precisely the attitude that characterizes the messianism of *Weep Not, Child* and *The River Between*. These novels are preoccupied with the vague richness and the ritual mist that surround a rather romantic conception of sacrificial martyrdom; they are lost in the abstract possibilities, in the dreams of sainthood, rather than being concerned with the attempt to realize concrete possibilities. If we view these novels in isolation, then their abstraction and various shortcomings can be explained away as the products of a failure of imagination. But if they are placed in their appropriate socio-biographic context they can be seen as the products of a sensibility that, traumatized at a young age, attempts to seek refuge in messianic and educational panaceas. Thus these novels also testify to the cultural effects of colonial domination. As Georges Balandier has pointed out, the political energy and frustration of a colonized people will manifest themselves in messianic and revivalist religions because all normal *political* channels for these energies are blocked by colonial repression.[28] As Ngugi's novels and his autobiographical statements show, the kind of Christian missionary schools that he attended strongly discouraged the expression and even the conception of political grievances and encouraged the channeling of all energies into the religious sphere.

His first two novels, then, can be seen as products of the acceptance of that education, and *A Grain of Wheat* can be seen as his emancipation from that influence. It is significant that Kihika, its chief messianic hero, abandons his schooling in order to avoid a severe beating which is his reward for objecting, quite rightly, to the Christian ban on female circumcision on the grounds that there is nothing in the Bible that forbids it. The paradox of the peripeteia of values that is posed in Kihika's use of the Bible remains unresolved in the previous novels and is only resolved in *A Grain of Wheat* by abandoning formal education, that is, education dominated by the colonialists. Such abandonment, then, testifies to the distance that Ngugi has achieved between his earlier preoccupations and his later concerns expressed in *A Grain of Wheat*. The results of that distance are the freedom from the problems of peripeteia and the consequent ability to portray the dynamics of communal coherence without being overtaken by the messianic urge.

Thus Ngugi's novels clearly depict the effects of colonialist education and the necessity of an adequate political understanding of colonialism in order to overcome these effects. Colonialist education, by attempting to divert the African person from a political understanding of his situation, is responsible for the problems of peripeteia of values. When the colonized person is unable to understand the political aspects of his situation, the result is a confusion that permeates the rest of his activity. Thus the major characters of both *Weep Not, Child* and *The River Between* as well as the very conception of these novels are confused by the author's inability to evaluate the political aspects of society. However, after reading Fanon's analysis, Ngugi is able to subordinate the egotistic messianic fantasies of his characters to the more substantial economic and political concerns that naturally dominate a colonized society which is fighting to regain control of itself.

Ngugi's liberation from the quagmire of the peripeteia of values is best indicated by the very different nature of subjectivity that pervades the three novels. His first two novels tend to be characterized by a subjectivity that subsumes all reality. The dominance of both novels by messianic characters, with their divine, privileged viewpoints, creates an egocentricity that is further buttressed by the narrator's profound sympathy with their election. The result is an attenuation of reality which, in the final analysis, can be defined only through a multiplicity of viewpoints. Consequently, both novels manifest a strong contradiction between the predominant subjectivity and the objective reality within the novel, which graphically embodies itself in the ontological and epistemological gap between the messiah, whose being, knowledge, and purpose have a divine origin, and the community, which is condemned to the imperfect knowledge and the vicissitudes of the historic realm. The hypnotic power of the privileged subjectivity can be seen in the fact that despite Ngugi's realization that Waiyaki is a product of peripeteia, he is unable to rescue *The River Between* from its effects. However, in *A Grain of Wheat* subjectivity manifests itself in the various forms of isolation, in the desire of a character to withdraw from others, but this tendency is balanced by a strong pull from society. This dialectic of isolation and communality, or subjectivity and objectivity, is best exemplified by the struggles of Mugo, which culminate in the touching and courageous confession that objectifies his personal guilt and thereby begins a process of communal regeneration. We can see the complexity and subtlety of this dialectic in Gikonyo's confession of the Mau Mau oath, whereby he sacrifices an abstract, symbolic communal bond for a more concrete and specific form of communality. Instead of the privileged subjectivity and the independence of the messiah, *A Grain of Wheat* is pervaded by a diffused interconnectedness and interdependence of imperfect individuals. The absence of egocentricity is manifested in the representation of each character and in the narrative structure of the novel. The meaning of the novel is available only through a juxtaposition of the different characters' versions of reality and through an understanding of the temporal/ historical development of their attitudes to various events. Thus, for instance, reality is drastically changed for Gikonyo and others by Mugo's confession toward the end of the novel. The implication is that similar revelations would constantly keep changing the reality, which therefore is only available through a retrospective, historical understanding. Thus with the exception of the analogical center of the novel, which is primarily a condensing device, the interdependence of individuals, and the revelation of meaning through multiplicity of viewpoints and through historical retrospection give *A Grain of Wheat* a formal structure that accurately represents the actual composition of a viable and coherent community. Ngugi's definition of community and the implications it has for present and future African societies makes *A Grain of Wheat* a unique novel in African fiction.

Alex La Guma

The Generation of Marginal Fiction

THE LIFE AND the fiction of Alex La Guma perfectly illustrate the predicament of nonwhites in South Africa and the effects of apartheid on their lives. His participation in antiapartheid politics and his subsequent imprisonment and exile provide him with a first-hand knowledge of the aspirations, frustrations, and deprivations of the disfranchised and enslaved segment of the South African population. Due to the *racial* basis of all South African social organization, his political and social experience can be considered generic to the extent that *all* nonwhites are treated as interchangeable objects by the Afrikaner regime. Thus La Guma is able to articulate this generic experience of the disfranchised South African in two ways. The substance of his novels depicts the poverty, squalor, arbitrary justice, imprisonment, and political oppression of the blacks and "Coloureds" as well as their attempt to fight apartheid, while the structure and style of his writing reflect the spiritual attenuation of life that results from socio-political disfranchisement.

Born in Cape Town in 1925, Alex La Guma has been surrounded and formed by the acrimonious, antagonistic political atmosphere of the South African society.[1] Unlike Nadine Gordimer, he became aware of politics not through literature but through the fact of his political exclusion on racial grounds and through a radical family tradition. Jimmy La Guma, Alex's father, was a noted leader of the nonwhite struggle against apartheid and a member of the central committee of the South African Communist party. His entire life was dedicated to the formation of various trade unions and political organizations that attempted to overcome white supremacy. Alex himself joined the Communist party when he was quite young and became a member of its Cape Town district committee until it was banned in 1950. Thereafter, he participated in the preparations for the Congress of the People, a nonracial political convention held in Johannesburg in 1955, which drew up the freedom charter, but for his dedication to democratic rights, he was arrested, along with 155 other men and women, and charged with attempting a violent overthrow of the government. The ensuing Treason Trials lasted five years before the defendants were acquitted and allowed to return to their normal lives. However, even before the trials were over the government arrested 20,000 people of various races throughout South Africa during the state of emergency that followed the Sharpeville and Langa massacres of those protesting against the Pass system. La Guma, who was jailed along with the others during the Emergency, was once again arrested in 1961 for planning a strike to protest the inauguration of the Verwoerd Republic.

The government responded to Alex La Guma's increasing prominence in antiapartheid politics by systematically harassing and isolating him. To counter the growing violence against apartheid, the government passed the Sabotage Act which permitted the minister of justice to place anyone under house arrest by a simple decree. Amongst the first casualties of this act, La Guma was confined from December 1962 onwards to his own house for twenty-four hours a day for five years. The Sabotage Act also allowed the government to isolate him further by prohibiting the reproduction of his statements in any form. Following the passage of the thirty-day no-trial act, La Guma was taken from house arrest and put into solitary confinement, although he was eventually released. Thereafter, he continued to live in isolation in South Africa until he managed to escape to London in September 1966, where he lived for some time before moving to Cuba.

La Guma's writing career began in 1956 when he joined the staff of a progressive newspaper, *New Age*, for which he wrote striking vignettes about life in Cape Town. However, when he was forced to abandon journalism in 1962 because a shortage of funds forced the newspaper to reduce drastically its staff, La Guma became completely isolated from his community; his house arrest precluded any re-employment and participation in the social and political life of his country, and because he was a banned person, all his novels were published outside South Africa. *A Walk in the Night* (1962) was published in Nigeria, *And a Threefold Cord* (1964) and *The Stone Country* (1967), in Berlin, *In the Fog of the Seasons' End* (1973), in New York, and *Time of the Butcherbird* (1981), in London.

His novels graphically depict various facets of South Africa's disfranchised population: his first novel draws a portrait of the precarious and alienated life in the "Coloured" slums of Cape Town; his second book records the dignified attempt of shantytown dwellers to survive against hunger, apartheid, and the winter; his third depicts life in a South African jail; his fourth describes a few days in the life of a man working in the political underground; and his latest novel depicts a man revenging ten years of unjust imprisonment. In spite of their diversity, all these novels have one fundamental factor in common: they all treat the marginality of life for nonwhites in South Africa. Although not all his novels take up the latter as their theme, they inevitably end up commenting on and indirectly depicting the material, social, political, and spiritual poverty to which apartheid relegates the darker, "inferior" people. Thus La Guma's novels constitute a transformed, fictive version of his own marginality, which initially consists in his social and political disfranchisement and then is followed by enforced internal isolation and later "voluntary" exile. His personal experience of exclusion from a full and free life is only a more dramatic version of the *generic* exclusion experienced by all nonwhite South Africans. His novels, then, are chronicles of the effects of the manichean bifurcation imposed by apartheid.

The predicament of nonwhite South Africans manifests itself in La Guma's fiction primarily and most forcefully in the dialectic opposition between his assumption that each individual has the right to live a decent life and his depiction of the actual deprivation of that right. The first term of the dialectic is usually tacit, whereas the elaboration of the second term constitutes the bulk of La Guma's fiction. The individual's right to self-fulfillment—the right to elect his own government, to live where he wants, to receive adequate compensation for his labor, to shape his children's education, to marry whomever he wants—is not generally articulated in the novels because La Guma, assuming its universal theoretical acceptance, chooses to focus on its absence by describing in detail the abject deprivation of the black people's lives. The absence of the first term and the ineluctable presence of the second in La Guma's novels also accurately reflect the actual conditions in South Africa: the vast majority of nonwhites in that country, though perfectly aware of their disfranchisement and their aspirations, are not in the habit of articulating the demand for their rights. Only when a character is actively and systematically engaged in pursuing his rights, as in *The Fog of the Seasons' End*, does the author allow him to elaborate the first term of the dialectic.

The second major contradiction of South African life that underlies all La Guma's fiction is the nature of the nonwhite individual's racial experience. While each black, "Coloured," or Indian person in South Africa is intuitively aware of himself as a unique being, the white society that controls him recognizes and treats him only as a generic being, as a "kaffir" (devil), as an interchangeable unit of a homogeneous group, and, in moments of extreme hostility and deliberate rejection, as a "thing." Thus his experience of self as an individual is constantly accompanied and negated by experience of self as a *generic* being who, in spite of his individual qualities, is inevitably condemned to poverty, pseudohumanity, and an absence of dignity and pride. His life is constantly characterized by a sense of oppression and inferiority because, even if he does not believe himself to be deficient, he is politically and socially unable to reject the inferiority that is imposed on him. This feeling is also accompanied by a pervasive sense of guilt caused by his enforced acceptance of a subjugated status and by his awareness that from the white viewpoint he is culpable of various crimes and attributes simply because of his race. Thus in a practical sense the South African nonwhite, like the Indian untouchable, experiences his generic condemnation as a hereditary quasi-ontological fact.

The opposition and tension between the experience of self as a significant individual and as an insignificant unit of a condemned caste, as well as the dialectic opposition between the assumption of self-fulfillment and the actual deprivation, lead to a profound alienation of the individual that La Guma's fiction tries to remedy by defining various communities within which his characters can find a healthier balance of personal freedom and communal obligations. The societies that he creates range from those that are held together by arbitrary circumstances to those that are shaped by the pursuit of definite political goals, but in comparison to normal communities the ones in La Guma's fiction remain politically, socially, economically, emotionally, and legally marginal. Furthermore, the life of each person in these societies is rendered even more precarious by internal conflicts and contradictions between individual freedom and communal demands and between the sacrifice of viable but limited present communities for those of the political underground or the potentially more comprehensive ones of the future. La Guma's fiction explores these experiences of deprivation, alienation, and marginality, and its major imperative is the search for viable communities that do not exploit its constituents.

La Guma's style is also a product of these social tensions and contradictions. His novels verge on naturalism similar to that of Norris and Dreiser: often his heroes are entirely at the mercy of an authoritarian society and an oppressive environment. The politically unaware characters of his early novels are condemned to suffer the fate of people without initiative or resources, whereas his later heroes, involved in organizations attempting to overthrow apartheid, seem capable of changing their environment. However, whether the protagonists are victims or rebels, La Guma makes their experiences available to us through a careful and detailed description of the specific and concrete immediacy; rarely does he discuss poverty or lack of freedom in abstract terms, nor does he spend much time in articulating the consciousness of his characters as, for instance, Gordimer does. He confines himself to placid and factual accounts of concrete human behavior and the material surface of society. Yet these calm descriptions are deceptive because the concrete objectivity masks a powerful and explosive hostility of the characters as well as the narrators. This aspect of La Guma's style is best illustrated by an example from *A Walk in the Night,* his most violent novel.

Michael Adonis, the protagonist of the novel, has just been stopped for no particular reason by two white policemen who proceed to search him. In spite of his anger and humiliation, Michael knows that instead of looking into their eyes, which would be construed as a challenge to their authority, he should focus his attention on "some other spot on their uniforms." This realization is immediately followed by a detailed, qualified description of one of the policemen's hands: "The backs of his hands where they dropped over the leather of the belt were broad and white, and the outlines of the veins were pale blue under the skin, the skin covered with a field of tiny, slanting ginger-colored hair. His fingers were thick and the knuckles big and creased and pink, the nails shiny and healthy and carefully kept."[2] Just as Michael avoids the recognition of his humiliation and represses and controls his rage by focusing on the minute details of the policeman's exterior, so the quasi-naturalistic style of La Guma masks the seething rage and frustration of the nonwhite experience in South Africa. The strategy that Michael uses to repress the emotions involved in the confrontation with the police is also employed by the narrator to avoid the elaboration of Michael's emotions. Just after Michael has been fired from his job, the narrator describes him as follows:

> Around him the buzz and hum of voices and the growl of traffic blended into one solid mutter of sound which he only half-heard, his

thoughts concentrated upon the pustule of rage and humiliation that was continuing to ripen deep down within him.

The young man wore jeans that had been washed several times. . . . (*AWTN*, 1)

The mention of rage is followed by a minute description of Michael's jeans and other clothes. Thus the concrete and detailed surface of the novels is a deliberate mode of controlling the feelings of the characters and the narrators: rage and violence are violently suppressed by the calm, naturalistic objectivity of the prose.

The characters in *A Walk in the Night*, set in the slums of Cape Town's district six, are so deprived and degraded that they are virtually unaware of the possibilities of self-fulfillment. All of them, with the exception of Michael Adonis, are street urchins, petty gangsters, and alcoholics whose aspirations are extremely limited. Only Michael, who has just been fired at the beginning of the novel from his menial job in a factory, has been involved in the normal world of economic production and consumption, yet even his aspirations are limited to a modest wish for economic and civil liberty. However, La Guma incorporates the dialectic of the desire for self-fulfillment and apartheid's negation of that desire in the symbolism of Michael's surname and in his transformation during the narrative. By the end of the novel (a span of about six or seven hours—from five in the evening to midnight), Michael has joined a gang of thieves and is about to embark on his first "job." Like the promise inherent in the beauty and youth of Adonis, Michael also embodies the potential for a decent life. And like the mythic hero, who spends half his life above ground, in the light, and half in the underworld, in darkness, Michael is a mixture of light and dark: he is a "Coloured" South African who symbolizes the desire for self-fulfillment, which the whites enjoy, and the actual deprivation, which the blacks suffer. Finally, his transition from a legitimate job to his membership in the "underworld" of gangsters, which coincides with the diurnal shift from light to darkness, further consolidates this symbolism.

On the whole, however, the novel emphasizes the absence of a decent life by graphically portraying poverty, police tyranny, arbitrary justice, and the people's despair. The squalor of the slums is typified by the following description:

Once, long ago, it had had a certain kind of dignity, almost beauty, but now the decorative Victorian plaster around the wide doorway was chipped and broken and blackened with generations of grime.

. . . the tramp of untold feet and the accumulation of dust and grease and ash had blurred the squares so that now it had taken on the appearance of a kind of loathsome skin disease. A row of dustbins lined one side of the entrance and exhaled the smell of rotten fruit, stale food, stagnant water and general decay. (*AWTN*, 20)

The poverty of the people is represented by the street urchins fighting for cigarette butts and by a family of seven living in a one-room apartment. The tyranny of the police is characterized by Raalt who extorts money from a "Coloured" club owner and then beats him for over-familiarity. The injustice reaches its climax at the end of the novel with Raalt killing the wrong man simply because he is wearing a yellow shirt. Repetitions of such squalor, poverty, violence, and terror pervade the entire novel.

Within this ambiance of tensions and contradictions La Guma weaves a plot that is profoundly ironic because it relies entirely on coincidence and arbitrariness for its development: the degree of arbitrariness almost negates the very idea of plot. Michael, having just been fired from his job, happens to meet Willieboy, a young thug, and later Foxy, a petty gangster, in a dingy cafe. On his way from the cafe to a bar Michael is unnecessarily harassed by white policemen, and he again meets Foxy in the bar. He sees the latter once again on his way home, where he meets and has a drink with Doughty, a senile alcoholic Irish actor. Because Michael is offended by an apparently innocuous remark made by Doughty, he kills him and retires to his own apartment. Meanwhile, Willieboy comes to borrow money from Michael, but when he finds that the latter does not answer, he decides to try Doughty. While he is in Doughty's room another tenant sees him and assumes that he has killed the old man. Alarm is raised, the police come and proceed to search for Willieboy. They finally find and kill him. While he is bleeding to death Michael is embarking on his first "job" with Foxy who has blackmailed him into joining the gang because he has seen Michael sneaking from the side of the building while the police are investigating Doughty's death. Such an arbitrary plot, politely ignored by most critics, has a definite purpose other than confirming the naturalistic attitude that pervades the whole novel. On the surface the plot demonstrates the characters' inability to control their lives and shape their destinies: they are victims of chance and circumstance. However, a more subtle, though still arbitrary causality underlies the circumstantiality of the plot: these characters and events are linked by the transference of repressed hate and violence that is facilitated by the *racism* of apartheid South Africa. In a society where the individual is treated and distinguished *generically*, as a "black," a "white," or a "Coloured," it becomes much easier for a man to transfer hatred from one individual to another of the same race. The following analysis will clarify the prevalence of generic perception and the system of transference in the novel.

Michael Adonis is dismissed from his work because of a minor dispute with his white foreman which soon descends into racial insults: Michael resents being called a "cheeky *black* bastard" and retaliates by calling the foreman a "no-good *poor-white*" (*AWTN*, 4, italics mine). In Michael's description of this incident to Willieboy we see that his anger and resentment shift fairly swiftly from the foreman to the "whites." Given the South African caste system, it is quite probable that Michael was dismissed because he was not adequately humble before his white master, but what is important from the fictional viewpoint is that the shift of Michael's emotions from the specific (foreman) to the generic ("whites") has already generalized his resentment and made it easily transferable to another white man. His resentment is augmented by the police search which too is motivated by generic rather than specific reasons: as an individual Michael has done nothing to warrant a search, but unable to challenge the police he once more represses his anger and indignation. In the bar Michael nurses his growing hatred as he drinks and listens to a taxi driver's gruesome, vividly detailed tale of transferred emotion and violence which exacerbates Michael's feelings and functions as an unsatisfactory fictional outlet for his anger. By the time he reaches home, Michael is "nursing the foetus of hatred inside his belly" and is ready to give birth to some form of violence (*AWTN*, 21). While drinking with Doughty, Michael becomes increasingly angry at the latter and begins to blame him for his dismissal from the factory. Doughty, whose vulnerability makes him a perfect recipient of the transferred hatred, attempts to entertain and pacify Michael by inaccurately quoting the following lines from *Hamlet:*

> I am thy father's spirit;
> Doom'd for a certain term to walk the night,
> And for the day confined to fast in fires,
> Till the foul crimes done in my days of nature
> Are burnt and purged away.

He then equates himself and Michael to the ghost ("That's us, us, Michael, my boy. Just ghosts, doomed to walk the night" [*AWTN*,

26]). Michael, however, resents this characterization and without premeditation or a specific intent, hits Doughty on the head with a bottle of port and kills him.

This murder, which is surprising, even shocking, because in contrast to the gruesome violence of the taxi driver's tale it is so understated and unexpected, is clearly caused by Michael's transference of his hatred of the white apartheid regime onto a defenseless white man who happens to live in a "Coloured" district. Michael's objection to being called a ghost clarifies the underlying motive. The equation of Michael and Doughty to the ghost is neither innocuous nor, as Michael Wade argues, a symbolic gesture of equality between two racial groups, a sudden transformation of relationships, which the subjected group is unequipped to accept.[3] Rather, it seems to me, Michael resents the telling, though unintended accuracy of this analogy: Michael and the other "Coloureds" and Africans *are* ghosts in the sense that they are constantly treated as subhumans consigned to the darkness of a moral, political, social, and economic purgatory. The narrator has already made this equation prior to Doughty's remark: "In some of the doorways people sat or stood, murmuring idly in fast-fading light like wasted ghosts in a plague-ridden city" (*AWTN*, 19). The novel equates the "foul crimes" of apartheid to those suffered by Hamlet's father. Up to this point the narrative has focused on Michael's movement from the cafe to the murder of Doughty. Now, however, it swiftly juxtaposes different scenes, describing the actions of Raalt and Andries (the policemen), Willieboy, and Michael, in order to set in motion a series of transferences that culminate in the murder of Willieboy.

The next sequence of transferences begins with Raalt nursing an unstated grievance against his wife while he is on patrol in the sixth district. Like Michael's anger, Raalt's is already generalized and repressed. However, now the narrator presents the motives and the potential transference very explicitly. Raalt is bored: " 'I wish something would happen. I'd like to lay my hands on one of those bushman bastards and wring his bloody neck.' He found little relief in transferring his rage to some other unknown victim, but took pleasure in the vindictiveness and his manner increased the discomfort of the driver who did not know what it was all about, but only sensed the rage that was consuming his companion" (*AWTN*, 36–37). When Raalt is extorting money from a night-club owner, what he takes to be the latter's familiarity, a violation of the caste distance, gives him an excuse to beat the owner. However, his rage remains unappeased, and therefore when he is given a description of Willieboy (kinky hair and yellow shirt), he refuses to call the detectives, as he should, and decides to take matters into his own hands.

Meanwhile Willieboy has begun to develop his own anxieties which soon turn into anger, for although he keeps insisting to himself that he is innocent of Doughty's murder, he knows that given the summary justice of the apartheid system his circumstantial incrimination is quite sufficient for his arrest and conviction. He proceeds to drown his self-pity in drink at a brothel and then suddenly transforms his anger into an unwelcome chauvinistic defense of "Coloured" prostitutes against some white American sailors. Having been repeatedly victimized, he finds and beats his own victim, an old alcoholic who has no money.

After this point La Guma breaks the pattern of sudden, uncalculated violence that results from repressed and transferred emotions. Instead, he systematically builds up the suspense and tension before depicting the deliberate, brutal, and callous act of violence that climaxes the series of transferences, and, by using Willieboy as a scapegoat, purges the violence that permeates the novel. Just after Willieboy has assaulted the drunk, La Guma leaves him like a frightened animal, paralyzed in the headlights of Raalt's patrol car while the narrator turns his attention for a whole chapter to Michael's hesitation and eventual ritualistic initiation into Foxy's gang.

When he returns to the confrontation between Raalt and Willieboy, La Guma augments the suspense and tension by delaying the moment of death. Andries's internal monologue, which provides the initial distraction, is followed by Raalt's recognition of Willieboy—anonymous face, kinky hair, and yellow shirt—and the subsequent chase of the latter, through the alleys and streets, over walls and roofs of the slums, described in graphic detail through the imagery of the hunter and the victim. The intense concentration of both the predator and the prey, the silences and noises of the hide-and-seek, the cunning, rapid, intuitive movements of both men, and the gathering crowd's antipathy toward the police, all heighten the tension until Willieboy is finally cornered and shot by Raalt, much to the consternation of Andries. Raalt, refusing to call an ambulance, bundles Willieboy into the police van and allows him to bleed to death while he buys cigarettes and chats with the owner of the restaurant.

Thus the series of violent transferences culminate in the deliberate, unnecessary, and callous murder of Willieboy, who is portrayed as a scapegoat, an innocent victim of a series of synchronic as well as diachronic transferences. La Guma emphasizes the synchronic series by compressing the entire novel into six hours, a walk during just *one* night in the purgatory of a South African slum, and by rapidly juxtaposing different scenes he stresses the simultaneity of the action. The diachronic series, revealed through Willieboy's delirious and shocked recollection of his past as he bleeds to death, show him as a victim of the violence that filters down from apartheid society through his father to his mother and then finally to himself, whose innocence La Guma indicates by reducing him to a whimpering child just before his death.

These series of transferences are just as arbitrary as the plot is coincidental. Michael, who is unable to retaliate against the white foreman and the police, and Willieboy, who also realizes that he can do nothing to prevent the summary justice of apartheid society from blaming him for the murder, are both forced to vent their hostility and frustration on the most readily available and helpless individual whose guilt or offense is entirely irrelevant to them. Similarly, for Raalt any black or "Coloured" individual will serve as a recipient of his anger and hostility. Thus in apartheid society personal relations are characterized by racial projection; the individual is judged and treated solely in terms of his color. La Guma stresses this fact by making Raalt's recognition of Willieboy depend *entirely* on the color of the latter's shirt: anyone wearing a yellow shirt would have served as a scapegoat. The interchangeability of individuals is further emphasized by the continued absence of Sockies. This man, who is supposed to be the "lookout" in Foxy's gang and who is never present in the novel, is the constant object of Foxy's search. He thus designates an empty space that can be filled by anyone; Sockies is not important as an individual; only his function in the gang is of consequence.

The individual in *A Walk in the Night* is forever caught between his own sense of unique individuality and his feeling, derived from his racial treatment, that he is merely a functional, generic being. The latter view of the self predominates in the novel. Willieboy, for instance, is painfully aware of his own insignificance and anonymity which he attempts to overcome by dressing flamboyantly and behaving like a tough young hoodlum. However, in spite of these measures, he continues to remain "something less than nondescript, part of a blurred face of the crowd, inconspicuous as a smudge on a grimy wall" (*AWTN*, 69). Michael too is oppressed by a similar feeling of insignificance which is momentarily alleviated by a sense of uniqueness derived from murdering Doughty. However, his sense of individuality quickly fades when he realizes that he can never publicly acknowledge his deed. Like the right to self-fulfillment, individuality is made conspicuous by its absence in the novel. For the nonwhite South African the only escape from the real deprivation and generic perception lies in forming or belonging to a new community which, though demanding certain sacrifices and self-imposed limitations, will nevertheless recognize his individuality and treat him as a complete rather than a marginal being. *A Walk in the Night* simultaneously depicts the absence of and the need for such a community; the characters are only subconsciously aware of their need for such a society, while the novel itself only provides unworkable alternatives.

The problem of a viable community is focused through Michael's desires. Other than the policeman he is the only major character in the novel who has belonged to the normal, productive economic society until he is ejected from it and thus made completely redundant. His hostility toward apartheid society and his need to belong are manifested in his conflicting desires immediately after Doughty's murder. When Willieboy knocks on his door, Michael only wishes to be left alone, but as soon as the knocking stops, he tells himself that he should get married and live a normal family life: thus Michael desires isolation when others demand some form of interaction, but as soon as communal demands cease he wishes to become involved in a community. Between his expulsion from the economic community and his confused, contradictory desires the novel interposes two transient "communities": the cafe where Michael eats and the bar where he and other customers find Dutch courage "against the crushing burdens of insignificant lives" (*AWTN*, 12). La Guma contrasts these two instances of "communities" that are in fact random collections of individuals without mutual obligations with two alternative societies that are based on mutual support and dependence. The first of these exists as a powerful potential bond between Michael and Joe, a young, innocent, almost saintly street urchin who lives a hermitic existence by the sea. Michael's occasional fraternal gestures of buying meals for Joe are repaid by the latter's offer of a genuine Christian moral fraternity: when Michael is about to join Foxy's gang, Joe attempts to prevent him by preaching against the immorality of the gang and by asserting his right "to look after" Michael.[4] Yet such an offer is far too saintly and self-abnegating in the violent and unjust world that constitutes the novel. Joe's offer is a utopian vision that Michael rejects without hesitation.

Instead he joins the only group left, Foxy's gang, which does constitute a genuine, though legally marginal, community. It has its own system of obligations and supports: Michael's role as the look-out for the gang is crucial to their success even though it has a rather limited function; reciprocally, Foxy supports Michael by soothing his wounded pride and generally praising him out of his depression. When Michael decides to join the gang he is obliged to go through an initiation ceremony by smoking marijuana and later by tacitly acknowledging the gang members' mutual dependence and fear prior to the crime.

Yet membership in the gang is only a partial and rather dubious liberation for Michael from isolation and loneliness. Like his former participation in the "legitimate" apartheid economy, his involvement in the gang is not an act of free choice. When he is first asked to join, Michael, feeling rather elated and courageous because of the murder, withholds his decision in order to savor his freedom of choice. However, his autonomy and elation are soon curtailed by the gang's blackmail—having seen him sneak out of the building after Doughty's murder they threaten to reveal his complicity unless he takes the place of Sockies. Thus like the oppressiveness of apartheid which pervades the novel, the gang is an alternate fate that awaits Michael; at every turn of the scene Foxy, the gang leader, is waiting to ask Michael or Willieboy if they have seen the ever-absent Sockies. The gang is as ubiquitous a presence as apartheid. Thus Alex La Guma provides Michael with two communities that are dialectically opposed in certain aspects and leaves him with no choice but to accept one or the other. The white, economically productive, "legitimate" society is diametrically opposed to the black, parasitic, illegitimate underworld of the gang. Either Michael can belong to the former by swallowing his pride and repressing his emotions or he can share the general quasi-ontological guilt of his caste by rejecting white society, actually committing a murder, and becoming a criminal. However, another theoretically viable communuity, the nonwhite organization that dedicates itself to the political overthrow of apartheid, is not yet an alternative in La Guma's fiction.

In *A Walk in the Night* La Guma's answer to the oppression of the white authoritarian government is emotional and apolitical. For the deprivation and degradation that apartheid society imposes on his characters, La Guma can only provide a reaction in the same terms. To the arbitrary persecution of apartheid, the characters reply with equally arbitrary and emotional violence; to the exclusionist legal and economic monopoly of apartheid, the characters can only

respond with crime and theft. La Guma does not allow his characters or narrator to transcend the terms imposed by apartheid. Thus
the plot as well as the emotional and political structures of the novel
is metonymic; all relations and developments are based on contiguity. The plot, as we have seen, proceeds through coincidence.
The generic nature of race relations allows one individual to be
substituted for another without any significant alteration in the
original intention or function of an act or event. Because the whites
see all blacks as alike, and because the blacks see all whites as oppressors, the relations in this novel are characterized by seriality,
that is, by the systematic denial of the subjectivity of each individual
and his subsequent treatment as a substitutable unit in a series of
people conceived as objects. The novel is a testament to the oppressive restrictions of a quasi-ontological caste system imposed by
apartheid on the South African society as well as on the imagination
of its writers. The generic nature of race relations in society is reflected by the metonymic structure of the novel. The profoundly
pessimistic attitude of La Guma's first novel is gradually replaced
by more optimistic *political* solutions in his succeeding books.

La Guma's next novel, *And a Threefold Cord,* is far more subdued
in tone than its predecessor. Whereas the latter is characterized by
actual violence and a narrative tone that is constantly attempting
to suppress a violent outrage, *And a Threefold Cord,* though depicting a fight, a murder, a police raid, and the incineration of two children in a shanty house, is pervaded by a calm, neutral narrative tone
that is used to describe the stoic fortitude and resolve of the characters struggling against abject poverty and degradation. The novel,
which depicts terrible social and economic conditions, is saved from
cloying sentimentality by the lack of self-pity or even a persistent
sense of outrage. A tone of stoic resignation dominates the novel.
Although the major protagonist is aware of the need for solidarity
and formation of a new community, *And a Threefold Cord* is pervaded by as much fatalism as *A Walk in the Night.*

The novel is brief and simple: it focuses on the struggle for survival of the "Coloured" Pauls family who live in a crumbling house
constructed from pieces of metal and cardboard packing cases in a
shantytown outside a large city in the Cape Province. The bulk of
the narrative is dedicated to Charlie Pauls's anxiety about and attempts to patch the leaking roof of the house before the rainy season
begins in earnest. The plot consists of a few events that take place
arbitrarily and coincidentally while Charlie fusses with the roof for
about a week. In the course of acquiring a piece of metal from a

lonely and isolated Afrikaner garage owner, George Mostert, Charlie attempts in vain to bridge the interracial gulf by inviting the latter to their house. In the meantime, Charlie's old, sick father dies, and on the day of his funeral there is a police raid during which the hero's brother is arrested for murder, and his sister gives birth to a baby. The next day his mistress's house burns down, killing her two children who are locked in it. The novel ends with Charlie realizing that he has not quite managed to fix the leak, and that in the face of family and communal disasters the surviving individuals will remain strong only if they unite. Thus Charlie's recognition marks the epogee of the novel's didacticism indicated by its title drawn from Ecclesiastes 4:9–12.

Judged purely by this plot, the novel is a weak and paltry affair. It is saved, however, from such a fate by the strength of its descriptive passages which are clearly more important than the narrative. The novella is best appreciated if it is seen as a prose painting: La Guma's deliberate, at times precise, at times evocative and almost fond descriptions of the atmosphere, the shantytown, and the Pauls' house better depict the conditions of existence than do the actions of the characters. For instance, the following sketch of the road that runs by the shantytown evokes more powerfully the gulf between the white and the black worlds than the brief relationship between Charlie and Mostert:

> On the concrete road, night-traffic swept by, rubber skimming over stippled surface, sounding like sprayed water; headlamps cut cones of yellow light out of the blackness and did not touch the smell of fermenting rubbish that mingled with the live smell of boiled six-penny meat bones, or the dead smell of rusty metal and rotten wood. The lights of high-powered headlamps, surging away in the darkness, did not touch the lights in the shanties, the glow of paraffin lamps or coals embering in a pierced drum. The rich automobile beams swept above the tiny chinks of malnourished light that tried to escape from the sagging shanties, like restless hope scratching at a door. Along the highway the night-traffic spun past and did not notice the tumbledown latrines that circled the listing shacks and shipwrecked people like sharks in a muddy sea.[5]

The repeated juxtapositions emphasize the physical and, by extension, moral discontinuities between the two worlds, while the speed and technology of the white society are contrasted with the primitiveness and stagnation of the shantytown.

Another example of La Guma's terse descriptive style is the following extended metaphor describing a man who sells water from one of the few taps in the whole shantytown, which, ironically, is inundated and destroyed by rain. The ironies of absence and abundance, of the need and the fear of water are entwined within the scathing criticism of a man who profits by selling drinking water to the majority of residents who have no access to it. "Water is profit. In order to make this profit, the one who sells the water must also use it to wash his soul clean of compassion. He must rinse his heart of pity, and with the bristles of enterprise, scrub his being sterile of sympathy. He must have the heart of a stop-cock and the brain of a cistern, intestines of lead pipes" (*AATC*, 114). The merging of the man and the product does perfect justice to the moral transformation necessitated by the economic exploitation of others.

The bulk of the description, however, focuses upon the threat of rain, upon the actual drizzles and downpours, and upon the consequences of precipitation. The weather, often personified, functions as the major oppressive element. The novel opens with the approaching rains:

> Then it was July and the laden clouds marched in from the ocean, commanded by the high wind, to limp, footsore, across the sky and against the ramparts of the mountains. For a while the mountains held them at bay, so that the rain harried only the coastline, and a veil of rain hung over the barbed peaks. The flanks of the rain fell into the sea. The high, grey-uniformed fog closed the mountains from the sky and the rest of the world, and hung like an omen over the land. (*AATC*, 17–18)

This malevolent rain permeates the novel, washing away the foundations of shanties, soaking through them, tearing away their roofs and sides, and killing old people who can no longer withstand the cold and dampness. Almost every scene and chapter begins and concludes with a description of the rain. It is an elemental force that brackets the lives of shantytown residents.

Like the repressiveness of apartheid society that permeates the atmosphere of *A Walk in the Night*, the rain in *And a Threefold Cord* becomes the elemental force that oppresses the people who have been rendered economically redundant by apartheid. It becomes the objective correlative of their fate under the manichean regime, for their poverty, which leaves them at the mercy of the weather, is a product of apartheid. Thus the clouds and the sky become, in a sense, the active agents of oppression: Charlie views the rain as a deliberate trap, and the narrator describes it as a hungry monster. Mostert's weak decision to reach across the race barrier for companionship is melted away by the rain, and when Freda's two children are being burnt to death the sky is described as sneering at their human plight. Charlie Pauls's fight to preserve the house against this malevolent force becomes a symbolic struggle against apartheid: survival of the house means the survival of a community.

The house also becomes the measure of the deprivation suffered by the nonwhites in South Africa as well as of their aspiration toward a "decent" life. Charlie's father had hoped to build a better house for his family, but circumstances forced him to construct the house with flattened fuel cans, sheet metal, rusty nails, packing cases, strands of wire, pieces of cardboard, a pair of railway sleepers, and other junk that they have begged, scavenged, and stolen. The preservation of this house, with its crooked floors caused by the sagging of its crude foundation, with its rusted and constantly leaking roof, and with its cracked stove and furniture made of crates, becomes the chief occupation of Charlie who is otherwise unemployed. The family's poverty can be measured by the dilapidated shack as well as by the fact that Charlie's sister lives in a "motor-car crate," where she gives birth to her baby, and by the death of his father due to the inability to afford a doctor. Poverty also causes the death of Freda's children because, while she is out, she attempts to keep them warm with a faulty primus stove which explodes and immediately turns the cardboard house into a furnace. The shantytown dwellers are condemned to an entirely marginal existence: their income is so low that even if they can obtain regular employment they cannot afford government subsidized housing; their political rights have been eroded to the point where police can break into their bedrooms at will in order to check their passes; and their social and cultural life is so deprived that their children are forced to play on garbage dumps instead of obtaining an education.

Yet in spite of the poverty and marginality, they tenaciously adhere to the assumption that they are entitled to live a materially and culturally decent and respectable life. In fact, respectability is not only a distant vision or fantasy for the Pauls family, but a very prominent part of their actual daily life. Their proper manners, their sense of sexual and moral propriety, and their values and goals—the disapproval of drinking, the heavy investment in a decent funeral in spite of their poverty, and the consuming importance of a substantial and respectable house—are indistinguishable from European bourgeois ethos and practice. In their imitation of middle-class life they even try to fence off yards and gardens around their shacks.

La Guma emphasizes the incongruities between their behavior and their predicament in an ironic exchange between Charlie and an Afrikaner police sergeant when the latter breaks into Freda's shack where Charlie has been sleeping. To the sergeant's questions about drugs, Charlie answers that they are "respectable" people who do not use drugs. However, when the policeman discovers that Charlie and Freda are sleeping together without being married, he amuses himself by sneering at their respectability and by calling Freda a "black whore." Given her sense of rectitude Freda is devastated by such an insult, and Charlie decides that he must marry her in order to alleviate the shame. La Guma uses the contrast between the natural dignity and respectability of the Pauls family and the degradation and poverty deliberately imposed on it to stress dramatically the opposition between the assumption of rights and their actual absence. The assumption, more overt and clearer than in the previous novel, creates the more subdued tone of *And a Threefold Cord* because the dignity and stoicism allow the characters and the narrator to control their moral outrage, the free expression of which is responsible for the pattern of transference and the metonymic organization of the previous novel.

The Pauls family functions in this novel as the embryo of a community, and La Guma tests its viability by subjecting it to various coincidental disasters and concludes that although it is resilient it could benefit from further unity and coherence. The solidarity of the family is conveyed primarily through Charlie's attempts within the family as well as outside (where he involves himself in fights) to protect Ronald, his angry and alienated younger brother. Charlie is as unsuccessful in defending his brother, who is arrested for murder, as he is in befriending Mostert, who is susceptible to flattery but fearful of the genuine companionship offered by Charlie. All deliberate attempts to protect or expand the community prove to be fruitless in this novel. Thus apart from the traditional occasions of communal unity such as births and deaths which draw friends and neighbors together, the characters are only able to experience and express rather inarticulately a simple and fundamental notion of community. Several times Charlie speculates briefly about communism, "poor people's union," redistribution of wealth and so on, but neither he nor the narrator ever explores the complexities and the viability of these notions: the inarticulate ideas remain mere slogans. Similarly, the symbolic end of the novel, where Charlie watches a bird dart suddenly straight into the stormy sky, remains flamboyant but vague: there is no indication of *how* Charlie, like the defiant bird, will overcome the quasi-ontological problems of his social situation.

And a Threefold Cord thus divides itself into two unequal segments. On the one hand, we have the excellent descriptions of the physical environment (the malevolent rains, the slum, the Pauls house), of the impoverished conditions, and of the stoicism and dignity of the characters; on the other hand, we have the simplicity and poverty of the theme which is essentially expressed as a slogan— "we should unite" or simply "unite." These differences are reducible to an unusual opposition and tension between the richness and precision of the indicative segment (or mood) of the story—the description of physical environment and human dignity—and the vagueness and simplicity of the imperative segment (or mood) which has neither an articulated subject nor a well-defined complement or object—it exists simply as an exclamation.

This bifurcation, which unbalances the novel, is an important stage in the development of La Guma's fiction. The sense of moral outrage, victimization, and the absence of viable communities that are the preoccupations of *A Walk in the Night* give way in *And a Threefold Cord* to individuals who, because they belong to a minimal community, are not constantly aware of their own victimization and therefore not characterized by self-pity. The absence of outrage permits the characters and the narrator of the latter novel a certain measure of calm and stoicism while the absence of victimization and self-pity allow a sense of "respectability" and dignity. The excellence of the indicative segment of the novella is a product of these emotions, while the relative simplicity of the imperative components is a result of uncertainty about the future direction of the individual, the community, and the whole South African political process. The imperative uncertainty as well as the preoccupation with the house and the family are most probably a reflection of, or are certainly influenced by, the fact that the novel was written during La Guma's confinement under constant house arrest, which must have rendered his own future quite uncertain and indefinite. However, his succeeding novels define in a clearer and sharper manner the nature of the political imperative for nonwhite South Africans who are imprisoned by apartheid.

In fact, La Guma's next novel, *The Stone Country*, is an allegory set in a prison in the Cape Province. The prison, immaculate and attractive from the outside, barren, emasculating, repressive, and rigid from the inside, is, of course, South Africa. The allegorical condensation allows La Guma to present a succinct portrait of the kinds of changes that take place in the nonwhite society when some of its members begin to consider the efficacy of various responses to political oppression and to challenge the rule of the apartheid government. The setting also affords La Guma a bold irony: by presenting the bulk of the story, which covers about four days, through the main protagonist's recollections that take place on a single Sunday, and by thus contrasting the narrative with the hymns continuously sung by some prisoners, La Guma implicitly comments on the incongruities of the repressive inhumanity of a society that is proud of its Christian heritage and its divine election.

The prison also becomes the symbol of the deprivation suffered by the nonwhites and particularly of the restriction of their political freedom. Within the general terms of this allegory the brutality of the prison guards and the savagery of Butcherboy, a gigantic prisoner whose terrorization of the other prisoners is tacitly approved and sometimes commissioned by the prison administration, represent the South African government's use of violent physical force as the primary means of coercing the nonwhite population. Like South Africa, the prison is a racially segregated society where the white prisoners receive decent food and amenities while the "Coloureds" and Africans are separated into overcrowded cells. The guards (representing the white population), who are themselves imprisoned by their fear and vigilance of the prisoners, manipulate and coerce the nonwhites to fight each other. The prison, like a "diseased harlot," has a seductive exterior but its interior is physically, psychologically, and morally corrupt.

Within this general allegory of deprivation La Guma includes two characters, George Adams and the Casbah Kid, who represent specific instances of oppression in South Africa. George's imprisonment for distributing political pamphlets reflects the complete absence of political freedom for nonwhites in South Africa. Once inside the prison, George soon discovers that he is entirely at the mercy of the guards who refuse to recognize any of his "rights": the fulfillment of his needs seems dependent on their whims and desires. He finds that if he is not absolutely acquiescent, that if he does not emasculate himself completely, the guards consider him a rebel.

In contrast to this fairly straightforward depiction of political control, La Guma has the Casbah Kid tell a rather gory tale about his parents that becomes a representation of the disintegration experienced by black families in South Africa. As a young boy, habitually starved and brutalized by his father, he witnesses his mother's suicide, which she disguises as a murder by her husband. Instead of using his knowledge of the father's innocence to free him, the Kid tortures him with it before the father is hanged. Thus traumatized in early childhood, the Kid matures into a surly, sullen, and mean thug who is imprisoned for murder and commits another one while in jail. This silent and profoundly alienated youth embodies the effects of the general poverty enforced by the apartheid economy and of the deliberate and callous separation of families imposed by the Pass laws. Through the Kid's trial La Guma further indicts the vicious circle of violence used by the South African government. The judge, in his efforts to aid the government's attempt to improve the social conditions in South Africa, decides to punish brutal murders, which cause terror and confusion among the people, by violently eradicating the perpetrators. The irony, of course, is that violence originates in the repressiveness of apartheid. The Kid is condemned to death not only for the murder of his victim but by his entire life. His condition in life inexorably leads to his actions and eventually to his death. Not only does La Guma present the Kid as an inevitable victim of his circumstances, but he also imbues the character with a profound resignation and fatalism: the opportunities in his life are determined by his race and are thus limited in a quasi-ontological manner. When the little boy who later becomes the Casbah Kid is found in the apartment where his mother is lying dead and his father is unconscious from drinking, he is suffering from contusions, a black eye, a broken arm, malnutrition, and tuberculosis. La Guma emphasizes the marginality of the Kid's life, and of other black South Africans, by swiftly cutting from the boy's precarious existence to the equally impoverished life of the condemned prisoner.

Whereas the portrayal of the Kid reverts to the fatalism and naturalism of La Guma's first novel, George's imprisonment for political activism represents a qualitative change in the author's treatment of the dialectic opposition between deprivation and the assumption that the individual is entitled to certain basic political and material rights. Whereas *A Walk in the Night* and *And a Three-fold Cord* emphasize the deprivation in contrast to the *implied* rights, this novel endows George with a clear awareness of individual rights and depicts a specifically organized and directed attempt to fight for them. La Guma defines the goals and means of this political struggle through George's predicament and behavior in prison. George's political agitation in jail centers around his demands for respectful treatment and the minimum material comfort to which he is entitled. On his second day in prison he arouses the wrath of a guard by calling him "Sir," which implies respect but also a certain kind of equality, rather than addressing him as "Boss," which clearly connotes the acceptance of subservience. He repeats this subtle challenge to authority in a bolder manner the next day by insisting that the prison be managed according to the rules rather than according to the guards' whims. The prison official's attempt to punish him indirectly (through a beating by Butcherboy) for his insubordination and for assuming the respect only entitled to a white man is fortunately foiled by another prisoner's intervention. However, when George once more addresses the guard as an equal he is sent to solitary confinement.

George's rebelliousness, though determined, is rather mild mannered. Neither a zealot nor an intellectual, he is an ordinary man who has simply become tired of apartheid: "He had gone to meetings and had listened to the speeches, had read a little, and had come to the conclusion that what had been said was right. He thought, falling into dreamless sleep, there's a limit to being kicked in the backside. . . ."[6] In contrast to other prisoners who romanticize the political struggle, George is perfectly aware of his modest role and of the slow, uncertain prospects for change. He is motivated neither by indignation nor by hate: his rebellion naturally springs from his personal, rather idiosyncratic sense of compassion and dignity. The morning after Butcherboy has been killed, when everyone is anxious to dissociate himself from the murder, George naively manifests his compassion by insisting that he would like to stay with the body. Similarly, he wishes to tell the truth about that death in the inquiry. His willingness to share his food and cigarettes with other prisoners and his rejection of their hierarchic organization based on brute strength constantly astound his fellow inmates and eventually earn him their respect. Just as he treats other prisoners (and the guards) with respect and dignity so he naturally expects others, including the guards, to treat him.

La Guma deliberately chooses this mild-mannered rebel as a representative of the nonwhite South Africans' political aspirations in order to negate the shrill, outraged, "ideologically" motivated, communist-inspired intellectual or demagogue who fills the traditional image of the agitator. George's honest demands for respect and equality more accurately represent the sentiments of most nonwhite South Africans than the articulate and complex political demands of an intellectual would. Furthermore, the former's natural compassion is far more seductive than would be the logical argument or exhortations of self-sacrifice, common struggle, and so forth of the latter.

George's political work and "agitation" in prison, then, constitute the political imperative of this novel. La Guma clarifies the nature of this imperative by contrasting the Casbah Kid's fatalism with George's belief in the possibility of change and by thus identifying fatalism as an attitude produced by brutality and deprivation, whereas the will to change, embodied by George, is defined as a product of self-respect, dignity, and a sense of equality. Similarly, La Guma depicts the pleasures and sacrifices of political work by contrasting the prisoners' and administration's attitudes to George: whereas the former respect, admire, and protect him, the guards attempt to crush him by brutal force and to isolate him from the other prisoners.

The dramatic though rather evanescent effect of the new political imperative on the prison/South Africa is depicted through the transformation caused by George's presence and behavior. The criminal inmates' general respect and deference toward political prisoners change to elation and pride as they begin to identify with George's successful challenge to the administration. They view him as their representative and begin to entertain thoughts of a general rebellion. The gradual transformation of the morose and taciturn Casbah Kid into a more humane and warmer person symbolizes the general change wrought by George's dignity, generosity, and compassion. However, the most significant political change is mediated through the attitude and actions of a "gentleman gangster," Yusef Ebrahim (alias the Turk) who, being more sophisticated and knowledgeable than other prisoners, immediately romanticizes George's political work without distorting its real significance. When George refuses to accept the Turk's warning that prison is a jungle where every man must only be concerned with his own survival, Turk decides that he has to protect this rather innocent political partisan. Thus George's "naive" concern for equality and communal responsibility has already begun to transform the Turk by making his intentions contradict his warning. Turk's metamorphosis is completed when he intervenes in George's imminent, potentially fatal beating by Butcherboy. He rationalizes his interference by adopting the exact rhetoric of George's argument about one's responsibility for others. George's "naive" assumptions are ultimately responsible for these changes.

Thus, within the allegorical scheme of the novel, the carefully staged, ritualistic, and exquisitely described fight between Butcherboy and the Turk represents a struggle between the South African government's use of brute force to dominate and control the nonwhite population and the latter's desire to resist the rule based on violence. The will to fight is derived from a communal concern, from a sense of responsibility for others, but the successful overthrow of a primitive, violent government is not entirely due to the communal concern; Butcherboy is stunned and hurt by the Turk, but he is killed by the Casbah Kid, who unobtrusively drives a thin spike into the thug's heart. The Kid is simply motivated by revenge against Butcherboy's earlier brutalization of him, which epitomizes the treatment he has received throughout his life and which has left him with a single dominating desire for vengeance. Thus La Guma demonstrates how the demand for equality, the respect for oneself and others, the sense of responsibility for others, and the desire for vengeance can coalesce to overthrow the rule of apartheid and to form an alternative community.

Yet La Guma does not allow himself to romanticize dramatic changes by building a utopian view of revolution on them, for he clearly shows that the new community and purpose can be quite evanescent. The day after Butcherboy's death George is sent off to the isolation block for his insubordination; the Casbah Kid, in order to avoid the inquest of Butcherboy's death, deliberately provokes the guards so that he too has to join George in isolation; and the Turk is removed to the hospital for treatment of injuries received during the fight. With the dispersal of the men responsible for the changes, the prison society, now under the influence of Butcherboy's henchmen, soon reverts to its former organization. La Guma thus implies that neither can one easily overturn apartheid's entrenchment in violence nor can a new enduring community be established by sudden and dramatic changes: freedom from apartheid government can only be achieved by steady, incremental efforts of the whole community. He emphasizes this point by comparing two modes of obtaining freedom. George's slow transformation of the prison society, with its inherent problems of maintaining the continuity of changes that are, at times, almost imperceptible, is contrasted to three prisoners' dramatic and sudden bid to gain personal freedom. Their complex and carefully planned escape is only partly successful. La Guma once more ironically uses coincidence and arbitrariness to show the futility of such attempts. Only one of the three prisoners, the cowardly and effeminate Koppe, who has no prior knowledge of the plan, no desire whatsoever to escape, and who is forced by the others to leave with them, is able to jump over the prison wall without any deliberate effort. The other two prisoners are caught in spite of their elaborate plans and precautions; *individual* attempts to escape from the prison of South Africa seem to fail because of the individual's lack of control over his plans and environment, and success thus seems to depend on chance. La Guma, by contrasting the alternative approaches to freedom, stresses the greater viability and efficacy of the efforts to obtain political liberty for the community, only through which method can any individual gain his personal freedom. The novel ends with George's return to the main part of the prison where presumably he will start agitating again.

Thus for La Guma, freedom seems to depend on the recognition of political and communal necessity. Because the prison represents the absence of liberty, the imperative and indicative aspects of this novel are inextricably intertwined. A description of the prison, a definition of the restriction it imposes on the inmates, is a necessary first condition for a description of the prisoners' goals and their struggle against bondage. The imperative to regain control over one's destiny is the obverse side of the necessity for describing and defining the oppressive conditions of society. Imprisonment and rebellion, deprivation and the struggle for a decent life are in perfect opposition in this novel: each one can be defined only in terms of its opposite. The dialectic tension between oppression and the desire for freedom as well as the coalescence of the indicative and imperative aspects of this novel, which together define the basis of its excellence, are accompanied by another major change. The life of George Adams is even more marginal than that of Michael Adonis or Charlie Pauls, but it is a life of *voluntary* marginality: George chooses to be involved in antiapartheid politics, for which he is imprisoned, and he chooses to be insubordinate, for which he is put in isolation. His control over his own destiny marks the end of the naturalistic tendency in La Guma's fiction, and his deliberate choice of a particular form of marginality, his subordination and sacrifice of personal freedom and self-concern for a larger communal interest, mark the beginning of a new phase.

La Guma's next novel, *In the Fog of the Seasons' End*, extends and clarifies the different preoccupations of his earlier novels. What had before been an opposition between the *assumption* that individuals have a right of access to certain basic forms of self-fulfillment and the *deprivation* of this right, with the major stress falling on the latter, now becomes an overt and explicit struggle between the colonized nonwhite and the colonizing white sections of the South African population: the initial overt statement of the issues involved in this fight, in the form of a brief debate between a political prisoner, Elias, and a major in the secret police, is followed by the story of a sustained struggle between the police and one cell of an underground revolutionary movement which is attempting to depose the South African government. Yet because the depiction of this struggle nec-

essarily involves some cloak-and-dagger scenes, La Guma cautiously
avoids sensationalism by understating the drama, by making his
characters weary rather than elated, and by ironically equating the
precarious conditions of the fight to the unreality of "gangster" and
"Western" films that will restore one to the normal world of complex
reality at the end. He is perfectly able to eschew a romantic view of
revolution, for by the end of the novel one is left with a feeling of an
arduous and precarious struggle that will probably kill all the protagonists and continue into the next generation.

The debate between the major and Elias, the latter a relatively important leader of the underground, states the classic arguments of
the proponents and opponents of apartheid. The major claims that
because blacks are inherently incapable of governing themselves the
benevolent white government is providing them with jobs, houses,
and education, but that Africans like Elias, forever dissatisfied and
ungrateful, are being misled by clever priests, lawyers, communists,
and Jews, and that in turn they are corrupting other blacks. The
major finds African demands for better education an absurd imper-
tinence: "I have heard that some of your young people even want to
learn mathematics. What good is mathematics to you? You see, you
people are not the same as we are. We can understand these things
which are best for you. We have gone far to help you, do things for
you. Yet you want to be like the Whites. It's impossible."[7] The African presumption to equality arouses the major's wrath, which he
expresses in the description of his duty: "It is my duty to destroy
your organization. Already you people are on your knees; soon you
will be on your bellies. Soon we will stomp you out altogether"
(FSE, 5). The major's antipathy and adamant beliefs collide with
Elias's equally strong sense of bitterness and desperate pride. For
Elias the South African government is nothing but a source of injustice and exploitation: "You have shot my people when they have
protested against unjust treatment; you have torn our people from
their homes, imprisoned them, not for stealing or murder, but for not
having your permission to live. Our children live in rags and die of
hunger. And you want me to cooperate with you? It is impossible"
(FSE, 5–6). These equally uncompromising positions are in fact only
the intellectual manifestations of a complex political and military
struggle that has been underway in South Africa since the middle
sixties and a small segment of which is depicted in this novel. La
Guma's narrative, a complex series of retrospections and juxtapositions that depict the lives of people involved in various underground
operations, simultaneously presents the different forms of depriva-

tions, the political and paramilitary fight to depose the government, the price paid by the individuals involved in this struggle, and the new kinds of communities that are formed in the process. A separate consideration of each of these areas will inevitably distort the series of juxtapositions and retrospections that create a formal pattern perfectly consonant with the secretive, discontinuous, anxious, and uncertain experiences of the underground protagonists.

In the process of furnishing details about the background of various characters, in this novel La Guma builds up the most thorough portrait of deprivation thus far. He presents the economic exploitation of the nonwhites as the pervasive and fundamental fact of South African society. According to the apartheid doctrine, whites always have preference over other races: "Coloured" workers are displaced from their jobs in order to make room for whites; residents of "Coloured" and black sections of towns are moved en masse whenever whites desire to appropriate those areas; widows of black miners are awarded a total of £40 in compensation whereas white widows receive £15 per month for the rest of their lives. The life of the rural African is plagued by starvation and disease. If he is lucky enough to immigrate to the city, like Elias, he finds himself condemned to live in racially and sexually segregated workers' quarters that are combinations of prisons and slums. He then has to work at underpaid menial jobs that sap all his strength and leave him a broken penniless man.

Although the antiapartheid movement seeks to alleviate this material lack, the characters in the novel seem more aroused by the social and political injustices they suffer, for these are the avenues through which they are controlled. Through a deliberately stylized, hypothetical ritual in which an African everyman is interrogated and given his pass, La Guma shows the nature of bondage that this system imposes. The pass completely controls a person's movements and employment—he even needs permission to *leave* a job. La Guma characterizes this modern form of slavery as follows:

> When African people turn sixteen they are born again or, even worse, they are accepted into the mysteries of the Devil's mass, confirmed into the blood rites of a servitude as cruel as Caligula, as merciless as Nero. Its bonds are the entangled chains of infinite regulations, its rivets are driven in with rubber stamps, and the scratchy pens in the offices of the Native Commissioners are the branding irons which leave scars for life. (*FSE*, 80)

Elias's initial acquisition of the pass provides a specific instance of the humiliation caused by this ritual and bondage: because the officials do not believe that he is seventeen, they force him to take off his trousers and, judging by his genitals, they peg his age at twenty. This degradation seems to haunt Elias for the rest of his life.

This kind of debasement is a generally effective means of controlling the black psyche—it is a part of the strategy of dehumanizing the African: in this novel the worst insult that whites hurl at a native is to call him a "thing." However, the apartheid regime tries to control the Africans in a more thorough and doctrinal manner through their education: a "Coloured" teacher complains to Beukes, the major protagonist, about being forced to teach his students that the present order in South Africa is preordained, that it is useless, even sinful, to struggle against it, that the Boer War was a holy crusade, that the theory of evolution is a heresy, and that modern psychology is a cardinal sin (*FSE*, 86). However, instead of reading such propaganda, the students are surreptitiously studying theories of guerrilla warfare. Caught between manichean oppositions, the students receive a paltry education.

As the introduction to the Gordimer chapter indicated, the South African government's political control over the nonwhite population became absolute during the sixties. Because all the overt parliamentary and civil channels for black political aspirations were systematically blocked, the African had no choice but to develop a clandestine opposition that would attempt to depose the government by force. This shift to covert political and military activity is echoed in this novel by Elias's gradual involvement in the underground after he is dismissed from his job for participating in a strike, and by Isaac's similar change in allegiance after he witnesses the indiscriminate whipping of blacks during the course of a national strike. An important landmark in this shift was the Sharpeville massacre, which La Guma depicts, once again in a stylized manner, as a confrontation between rather festive Africans who have gathered simply to return their passbooks and the highly suspicious and nervous police who see the gathering as part of a diabolical plot and consequently kill indiscriminately. The absence of political rights for nonwhites culminates in the ability of the police to imprison a man indefinitely on mere suspicion of crime or political activity. La Guma represents this epitome of political deprivation through Elias's arrest and torture, which begins with a security agent urinating on his face, progresses through severe beatings, and culminates in the application of electric shock to his legs and genitals.

La Guma thus presents a highly antagonistic manichean political situation: the exploitation and humiliation suffered by the Africans arouse in them a violent hatred which the narrator depicts through Elias's repeated fantasies of killing his oppressors and through Isaac's constant doodling of guns on scraps of paper. Yet once more La Guma eschews a romantic view of black rebellion by showing that Beukes's political motives are mixed and his commitment somewhat uncertain: Beukes perseveres because "sometimes . . . [he] understood why, often because there was nothing else to do" (FSE, 49). Beukes's rebellion due to the lack of an alternative not only stresses the realism of a reluctant uprising but also represents a political transformation of the fatalism that characterized *A Walk in the Night*. Whereas Michael Adonis has no alternative but the acceptance of his socio-political predicament, Beukes has no choice but to rebel against apartheid society: what was earlier viewed as a quasi-ontological situation is here understood as a political necessity to fight. Thus the goal of the underground movement is now clearly stated in the pamphlets that Beukes is distributing.

The vast bulk of the novel is dedicated to the depiction of how Beukes as well as Elias and Isaac play their parts in this embryonic revolution. Beukes's function, distributing pamphlets to subagents, recruiting new members for the movement, and smuggling some volunteers out of the country for guerrilla training, provides the plot and the drama of the novel. In order to avoid the vigilance of the security police, he is constantly on the move—changing his name, shunning his own home, traveling only at night whenever possible, and sleeping at different people's houses. When we first see Beukes, he has just spent two nights in a gully because he has been unable to use the house of a fearful friend. He then continues, with the help of a sympathetic taxi driver, to his next resting place and, because he is exhausted, sends his friend to pick up the pamphlets. The next day he begins to distribute the leaflets, first visiting a schoolteacher, then an Indian garment worker, and finally arriving at his last contact, Isaac, only to find that the latter is absent because the security police are chasing him. The day after the pamphlets have been distributed to the public, Beukes meets Elias in the house of an unknown person to discuss the transportation of some guerrilla volunteers. In the police raid that ensues Elias is captured and subsequently tortured to death, while Beukes manages to escape with a flesh wound. He successfully takes a chance in being treated by a "Coloured" doctor, who turns out to be sympathetic to the underground, and then proceeds to his next rendezvous, with the driver who will smuggle the recruits to the north, and discovers to his delight that one of the volunteers is his good friend Isaac. The novel ends with

Isaac leaving the country and Beukes returning to his precarious work.

The narrative of these seven or eight days is so discontinuous that it matches perfectly the abnormality, marginality, and precariousness of the protagonists' experiences. The abnormality of Beukes's life can be measured by his systematic avoidance of his home: during the course of the narrative he can only think with a mixture of anxiety and pleasure about his wife and child, but he can never see them because he is afraid that the security police might be waiting outside his house or that he might lead them to his family, which exists in the narrative only as a poignant absence. His constant fear is another index of his marginality. He is almost paranoid about footsteps in corridors and people whom he mistakes for security police; he makes elaborate detours to avoid any policeman and always attempts to become anonymous by mixing with crowds; and he moves about at night and hugs the shadows of buildings in the daytime whenever possible. The nature of Beukes's work prevents him from enjoying most of the normal aspects of his life and distorts his personality: it leads to an emptiness, a "hollowness of abandonment" (*FSE*, 147), that renders him as marginal as Michael Adonis. He is sustained by the belief in his struggle, but the uncertainty and remoteness of the goal are disheartening. La Guma reveals the oppressive weight of this marginality through the reaction of Isaac, who, after successfully evading the security police who have come to arrest him, realizes that he can no longer function effectively in the underground since his identity is known. His choices are now simple: he must fight openly, within or from outside the country, or he must succumb to arrest, torture, and death. Thus the freedom from the secretiveness and marginality of the underground produces a feeling of elation and liberty in him.

Yet La Guma's portrayal of the burdens of marginality is profoundly ironic. Isaac, like all of La Guma's other nonwhite characters, resents being regarded as an object, a "thing": he wishes to be treated as a subject. But like Beukes, once he joins the underground he avoids recognition because anonymity is so important to his work. Thus the desire to be recognized as a subject will never be fulfilled so long as the manichean doctrine of apartheid is not entirely discarded. The irony of his position is that he can only overcome involuntary marginality, to which he is consigned by the political system, by choosing another form necessitated by the clandestine nature of his struggle. By opting for voluntary marginality the oppressed South African finds a form of liberation in the recognition of his own imprisonment.

In this novel the South African (colonialist) society and the underground movement become locked in a fatal manichean struggle. The apartheid regime, by destroying the old African communities, by forcefully dissolving any new groups that black individuals attempt to form (trade unions, political parties, and the like), by prohibiting integration into white society, and by preaching a doctrine of superiority, completely atomizes black society and renders the individual radically marginal. Beukes and his friends attempt to counter this destructive control by forming a community the sole purpose of which is the violent overthrow of its oppressor and the survival of which is entirely dependent on its success in doing so. *In the Fog of the Seasons' End* marks the apogee of the manichean struggle in colonial society. However, in the process of depicting this struggle, La Guma poignantly portrays the painful growth of a precarious community.

As we have already seen, the characters pay a high price in personal marginality and the sacrifice of a normal family life for the generation of this new community. Elias has no family, Isaac leaves his parents and siblings behind when he goes off for guerrilla training, and Beukes pines for his wife and child whom he dares not contact. Thus a new organization can be formed only at the expense of human warmth and companionship. In addition to these sacrifices, membership in the underground community confers its own rewards and exacts its own price. The mutual care, concern, and respect within the group are a marked departure from the sense of victimization and abandonment experienced by La Guma's previous characters. Within this ambiance the individual is perceived by others as a dignified subject for the first time: Isaac breaks his initial appointment with Beukes in order not to lead the police to his friend; at the end of the novel Beukes is overjoyed to see that Isaac has avoided arrest; and during the police raid Elias makes sure that Beukes escapes even if he himself is captured. Thus the individual begins to sacrifice himself for other members of the community. When Elias is being tortured, Beukes's fate depends entirely on the former's courage and perseverance. This burden of responsibility for others weighs heavily on both men, for many lives depend on them, and they often wonder about their ability to withhold information under torture. As Beukes clearly realizes, his work obliges him to trust his life to those above and below him in the underground hierarchy, yet he can never be sure that one of them is not an agent of the security police. Thus the burden of responsibility for others is balanced by an absolute, radical dependence on others. This extreme form of respon-

sibility and dependence creates a community that is an understandably distorted version of the obligations and supports of a normal
society and that lifts the individual out of his status as a helpless
object of apartheid society.

The liberation of the individual-as-subject, his acceptance of the
full responsibility for his and the community's destiny, results in a
more constructive awareness and more deliberate use of his past and
a more definite projection of values and goals into the future. Elias's
personal past, like that of most of La Guma's characters, is full of
poverty, degradation, sickness, and bitterness. Yet because he has
grown up in the countryside he has been exposed through folklore
and myth to the oral history of his ancestors who fought with the
initial Afrikaner and British invaders. He deliberately uses his image
of their dignified and heroic challenge to the colonizers in order to
sustain his moral strength while being tortured by the security police.
Thus for the first time La Guma uses the African past, which is more
powerful because it is a mythic past, to sustain a character's dignity
and beliefs in his present task and in the future community. La Guma
similarly uses children to create a sense of posterity that will inherit
the real benefits of the present sacrifice and struggle. In spite of his
and his family's dangerous predicament, Beukes is happy that he
has had a child, for the latter sustains his beliefs and supports his
endeavors in the present. The schoolchildren who are reading man-
uals of guerrilla warfare provide a more definite link to future continuation of the struggle. The novel ends as Beukes, after waving to
Isaac and two younger men leaving for guerrilla training, turns to
"the children [who] had gathered in the sunlit yard" (*FSE*, 181).
Thus in this novel the desire to overthrow the South African government, to create a new community, and to accept the responsibility
for one's life leads to a new consciousness of and participation in
one's own history. Political awareness and strugggle allow the characters to become agents of their history. Past, present, and future are
understood and defined in terms of the single most important imperative—the African control of African destiny and culture.

In the Fog of the Seasons' End is a very tense novel finely balanced
on the equilibrium of its contradictions and tensions produced by the
opposition of social and personal forces. The novel juxtaposes different scenes from the lives of the three main protagonists, contrasting
past happiness with present anxiety, past humiliation with present
hatred, scenes of torture with reminiscences of love, the lives of
frivolous people with those of the dedicated. It balances captivity
and torture against freedom and elation, hate against love, and fear

against hope; it sacrifices one form of community for another, the family for the underground, one desire for another; it pits the continued Afrikaner domination, subjugation, and enslavement of the Africans against the latter's attempt to depose the apartheid government; it locks the whites and blacks in a fatal manichean struggle without room for compromise; and it mythologizes the African past for present consumption and then sacrifices the present for a future freedom. The presentation of these tensions and contradictions through swift juxtapositions and flashbacks is perfectly consonant with the discontinuous experience of the characters, which, as Beukes says, is like "being on a ferris wheel" (*FSE*, 174).

From a purely formal viewpoint the novel initially appears to be circular. It opens with a prologue describing Elias's torture by the secret police, and it ends with two chapters that are temporally coterminous with the prologue—the penultimate one depicting the continued torture of Elias and the final one showing Beukes dispatching volunteers for guerrilla training. Thus the "real" present of the beginning and end brackets the immediate past that consists of the activities that lead to the real present. Both these temporal planes are in turn irregularly punctuated by retrospections of varied lengths that take us into the distant past of the major characters. The discontinuity created by these temporal juxtapositions is enhanced by the shocking contrasts between deliberately incongruous scenes, for example, Elias's torture on the one hand and the depiction of a black nanny worrying about the possible diaper rash of her white charge, on the other. Finally, the disjunctive quality of the novel is intensified by the manner in which various minor characters connected with the guerrilla cell are rendered: in the present they are portrayed with striking specificity and concreteness, but in keeping with the secrecy of clandestine guerrilla contacts their pasts are allowed to remain completely unknown and their futures are left as intriguing loose ends. All these formal devices produce not a circular but a helical novel, the apparent circularity of which is, on another plane, a perfectly straight line. The formal characteristics of the novel accurately reflect the lives of the guerrillas, who deliberately espouse marginality, discontinuity, and indirectness in order singularly and coherently to pursue and reach their goal in the shortest possible time under the given circumstances.

These formal characteristics not only reflect the mundane, tactical experiences of the guerrillas but also reveal the development of a more profound ontological understanding. When Elias is being tortured he is aware that because of the nature of his clandestine activity he is, and always has been, poised on the edge of extinction. This clear perception of death, of one's radical finitude, leads the guerrilla to a certain anxiety about his being and potentiality. While he firmly dedicates himself to a definite goal in life (the violent over-throw of the apartheid system), he is aware that the concrete poten-tiality of the self will only manifest itself through praxis. Thus, for instance, Elias and Beukes often wonder how they will behave under torture, whether or not they will betray the cell. While characteriza-tion reveals these insights, the temporal structure of the novel, that is, the present concerns, shows that for them history, the scrutiny of their past, is also a product of personal political praxis. Whereas in the first two novels accidents (historical contingencies) are oppres-sive because they lead not to the actualization of potentialities but to an attenuation of control, in the next two novels the characters arrive at moments for political action by understanding past oppres-sions and contingencies, and in turn they later incorporate these moments into an articulate awareness of history. It is because of this comprehension of the unending, cyclical nature of political struggle and their own history that the guerrillas now project themselves with anxiety and care into the future.

This projection, accompanied by a transformation of the individual from seriality to group consciousness, is entirely free from egocentric motives. Instead of the oppressor-victim-oppressor transferences that characterize serial relations, we have in this novel a liberation of the individual through the group: because the freedom of the in-dividual is now dependent on and bound up with the freedom of other cell members, each person gives through the group the power, recognition, respect, and freedom that he receives through the same group. Through this form of rebounding reciprocity the self recog-nizes its freedom in the communal political action in which it has become involved. Thus freedom is defined as responsibility and de-pendence, while authentic being emerges as being-for-the-other.

This specification of self defines the essential nature of La Guma's realism. For Georg Lukács a realistic novel is one that manifests in its detail and structure an ontological, dialectical conflict between self-as-an-individual and self-as-a-social-being. *In the Fog of the Seasons' End* allows us to extend this definition because it transcends the dialectical conflict: in this novel the self-as-an-individual dis-covers his being in his existence for others, in his existence as a social being. Thus the realism of this novel is simultaneously manifested in its mimetic accuracy, in its representation of the dialectical con-flict, and, most significantly, in its revelation of authentic being through a transcendence of the dialectical conflict. And the transcendence is the product of a meditation, an exercise in phenomenological reduction, that also determines the form of the novel. The pain, torture, and imminent presence of death at the beginning and end of the novel bracket out the possibilities of the mundane, manichean world and permit a consideration of the significance of the immediate and distant past and of the authentic self and its concrete possibilities. In direct opposition to his naturalism, which reflects the shrinking of human potentiality and the stance of the impotent, alienated spectator, La Guma's realism represents the expansion of potentiality and the effects of action. Just as the guerrilla, taking his destiny into his own hands, manipulates his socio-political environment, so does the author reveal meaning in this novel through the manipulation of *narrative* events rather than a complete reliance on description. It is significant that the only vestiges of naturalism in *In the Fog of the Seasons' End* are the two stylized passages describing the ritual of obtaining the pass card and the Sharpeville massacre of Africans protesting against the pass; that is, both passages deal with the system that is used to impose a serialized, quasi-ontological racial status upon the African. Both these descriptions represent the viewpoint of the hypothetical African, of the serialized, oppressed everyman. The fact that the rest of the novel consists of the narrator manipulating specific characters implies that La Guma now sees seriality and its representation, naturalism, as realms from which the individual has emerged. In contrast to the predominantly indicative mood of his naturalistic fiction this novel gives evidence of the ascendance of a modified imperative mood, which, although still consisting of commitment to political action, is modulated by a constant interrogative meditation about the nature of freedom, community, and the self. Politicization, then, results in an increasing awareness and transcendence of the original quasi-ontological status.

This ability of La Guma's protagonist to take control of his own destiny represents a dramatic coming-to-consciousness not only of the social conditions in South Africa but also of the only way out of those oppressive circumstances. Initially deprived of all socio-political control over his own life, the black South African is confined to the extremely narrow existence of an "object" to be used for the benefit of the apartheid regime: he is relegated to the realm of abject marginality. Within these narrow limits he has only one choice: either he can acquiesce in his treatment as a marginal object or he can deliberately choose to become a marginal subject as Beukes does. His choice of the latter implies that freedom for the oppressed man lies in his recognition of his own marginality, in his awareness of his social condition. *In the Fog of the Seasons' End* thus brings to consciousness that absolutely necessary condition for the liberation of the black South African—his coming-to-consciousness.

However, La Guma's next work, *Time of the Butcherbird*,[8] overly intent upon advocating armed rebellion, ignores the subtle and complex insights of the previous novel. It is quite similar to *And a Three-fold Cord* in that it is dominated by exquisite descriptions, although they are not systematic or consistent emblems of apartheid, and in that the central imperative is once again relatively simple. Instead of a desire for unity, this novella is structured around the pursuit of revenge. Like the previous novel, this one also consists of juxta-positions and retrospections, but the contrasting scenes from the lives of three major characters (and minor ones that surround them) tend to remain isolated until the end, and the flashbacks neither re-veal a complex, intertwined past nor do they illuminate the necessity of present conditions and events. Most of the juxtapositions and retrospections seem almost gratuitous.

The three major characters are clearly emblems of larger social forces: Shilling Murile, just freed from prison and determined to kill Hannes Meulen, represents the exploited black's desire to avenge past and present injustices; Meulen, a farmer about to be elected to the Parliament, symbolizes the Afrikaner tradition and its almost casual, careless cruelty toward the blacks; and Edward Stopes, a de-jected, unsuccessful salesman, typifies the English-speaking South African liberal. Murile and Meulen are causally connected: ten years prior to the beginning of the action the latter had been responsible, not through premeditation but rather through casual cruelty, for the death of Murile's brother. As a result of Murile's subsequent impul-sive retaliation he had been sentenced to jail for ten years for at-tempted murder. In the two days that span the novella, Murile, just released from jail, kills his old enemy as well as Stopes who happens to be talking to Meulen in the local hotel. Thus the novel implies that the bystanders who have profited from apartheid will also feel the effects of the struggle between the Africans and the Afrikaners.

The novel also attempts to assert a kind of inevitability through the final conjunction of these three separate narratives that, by tracing the histories of these men and their families, imply that the deep roots of these communities will lead to a bitter struggle. How-ever, the implied inevitability is strongly undermined by the preva-lence of coincidences. The random element in the novel is best typi-fied by the death of Jaap Opperman, Meulen's foreman, who was also responsible for the death of Murile's brother. Opperman is shown to have inherited and internalized a deep fear of snakes supposedly used in African witchcraft. In order to free himself from this fear Opperman deliberately walks into a gorge protected by African magic, and, of course, he is killed by a snake's bite. The narrative significance of this incident remains extremely vague. Such reliance on coincidences is accompanied by a weak definition of history, for although Murile insists that earlier injustices must be remembered, indeed treasured and savored, the past is only used to fuel the desire for revenge: Murile has no plans beyond killing Meulen. The past does not lead to better understanding of the present or future: the complex interrogative meditation of the previous novel is entirely absent in *Time of the Butcherbird*. Similarly, the definition of self as being-for-other is negated here. Murile refuses to subordinate his desire for personal vengeance to a communal political struggle. After having killed Meulen, Murile unknowingly shifts from his habitual use of the first-person singular to the first-person plural, thus revealing the subconscious beginning of a communal commitment. The weakness of such a transformation is underscored by the coincidence between Murile's execution of Meulen and the simultaneous strikes of Africans in the country and the city.

The final description of a desert landscape, using imagery of artillery and war, refers rather vaguely to the "wind of change." However, change comes not through coincidences but through deliberate and complex awareness, planning, and action. These, it would seem, are overwhelmed by the urgency of the desire for revenge. Even though this imperative is much stronger here than the one in *And a Threefold Cord*, this novella too is divided into the indicative and the imperative moods that do not coalesce. The disjunction between the objective and subjective desire as well as the reliance on coincidences implies a frustration, an inability to act, which finds an outlet in wish fulfillment. La Guma's exile and his inability to participate *directly* in the attempt to overthrow apartheid could result in such a novelistic structure. Frustration can lead to impatience, which in turn can translate itself into an urgent desire for hasty action that is perfectly understandable and may have important political and military functions but tends to displace entirely the complex meditations and insights of the previous novel. As a consequence, *Time of the Butcherbird* straightforwardly advocates and valorizes heroic participation in an armed war.

That political awareness should play such a significant role in the content and direction of La Guma's fiction is not at all surprising. In a society founded on massive political disfranchisement, *political* liberation will inevitably become the primary preoccupation of practical life and of literary endeavor. In a state where the police can break into one's bedroom, at will and without the slightest concern for one's "feelings," in order to check the skin color of a lover, it is probably impossible to write novels about the passionate power of love or about the delicacies of refined human sensibilities. It is clear that for La Guma and his intended audience the political novel is more relevant and important. Yet the irony of his fiction-as-social-praxis is that the South African people, who would find his novels most useful and pertinent, cannot read them because all his works and utterances are banned by the government.

This political excommunication renders La Guma's novels completely marginal. In the first place this is true because, as we have seen, his fiction is preoccupied with depicting the political, social, personal, and emotional marginality of the disfranchised South Africans. Second, his fiction is marginal in its style and substance: his style is simple and succinct, and his novels are short and terse—they lack the digressions and embellishments born of luxury and plenitude. Third, his novels are marginal in the sense that they limit themselves to a naturalistic and realistic depiction of the political facts of life in South Africa and contain a minimal amount of "fictional" elaboration: they are lean and sparse novels that constantly speak of lack and fortitude. Finally, his fiction is marginal because it is banned in South Africa, and thus not available to those of his countrymen best able to benefit from and appreciate it, and because in West Europe and the United States there is little demand for political fiction. Those who are inclined to read political novels tend not to be interested in La Guma or Nadine Gordimer, preferring instead the fiction of Alexander Solzhenitsyn, which revives the legacy of the Cold War by once more valorizing the freedom of Western institutions against the restrictive practices of the Russian "other," or the fiction of V. S. Naipaul, which revives the legacy of colonialism by further valorizing the goodness and civilization of the West against the unredeemable evil and barbarity of the Third World "other." That is, they prefer to read those writers who cater to different versions of the original Western manichean presuppositions that have subsequently been elaborated and refined so systematically by the apartheid regime of South Africa.

Conclusion

THIS STUDY HAS been concerned with two major factors: the relations between literature and its social context and the negative aspects of the relationship between colonial and African literature. In the first case I have not focused on the idiosyncratic background of literary texts but rather on their generic social and historic preconditions. Thus I have implicitly treated the texts as expressions of the nexus of economic, political, and social factors that define their colonial context, which, in spite of local variations, displays a fundamental structural uniformity consisting of the manichean opposition between subject and object, self and other, white and black. In the second case, the relationship between colonial and African fiction, I have focused on the African reaction to colonial images of Africa and its inhabitants and consequently on the antagonistic relation between these two groups of literature. In this final chapter I shall analyze these and several other issues, thereby coalescing the textual-contextual relations examined in the preceding chapters. In so doing, I shall be drawing some generally valid conclusions, but I will also be forced to leave some paradoxes and tangents unresolved and unexplored. Because I have chosen the six authors on the basis of their paradigmatic value and dialectical opposition to each other the following generalizations about colonial and African literature will be valid in their potential inclusiveness, but undoubtedly many critics will rightly feel that the consideration of other colonial and African writers would lead to specific modifications of these generalizations; the process of triangulation begun here can (and should) be extended considerably.

This entire study, from its initial definition of ideology as a sub-text embedded within the text to the last of the six specific studies of contextual-textual relations, is implicitly in agreement with Fredric Jameson's view that all literature is informed by the political unconscious, that it "must be read as a symbolic meditation on the destiny of community," and that the primary function of literary analysis is the "unmasking of cultural artifacts as socially symbolic acts."[1] This mode of interpretation is best characterized as a "rewriting of the literary text in such a way that the latter may itself be seen as the rewriting or restructuration of a prior historical or ideological *subtext*," it being understood that the subtext, never self-evidently present, must itself be (re)constructed after the fact. The text always maintains an active relationship with its historical subtext by drawing the latter up into itself in order to submit it to the transformation of form, which in fact constitutes the "symbolic action" of the text. This relation is paradoxical in that the text "as though for the first time, brings into being that very situation to which it is also, at one and the same time, a reaction. It articulates its own situation and textualizes it, thereby encouraging and perpetuating the illusion that the situation itself did not exist before it, that there is nothing but a text. . . ."[2] In undertaking such an analysis this study has proceeded by first "grounding" the author in his/her class and society through an examination of the generic rather than the idiosyncratic aspects of the relationship. Within the colonial context this process begins with an identification of the major social contradictions, then examines their effect on and internalization by the author, and finally analyzes the manner in which these contradictions, now transformed into different avatars of the originals, define and determine the shape and substance of the texts.[3] Thus within what Jameson calls the first, or political, horizon of the text, this study analyzes the relation of each novel or autobiography to its specific, dense historical, economic, and political ambiance as well as to the fundamental manichean structure of all colonial societies, that is, to the prevailing allegory of white and black, good and evil (in all its socio-political permutations), and self and other.

Analysis of the relations between any colonial society and its literature must begin with the fact that the manichean structure of such a society is an economic, social, political, racial, and moral elaboration and distortion of a fundamental ontological opposition between self and other. In general, the self becomes clearly and fully itself, it returns to itself and recognizes its truth and the objective certainty of its own existence only through negation and mediation of the other: "It is in and through the revelation of my being-as-object for the Other that I must be able to apprehend the presence of his being-as-subject."[4] Thus rebounding reciprocity is made possible by the mutual relations between self and other as subjects who occasionally and often voluntarily function as objects for each other. Yet this ideal dialectical relation between self and other is in practice petrified in a colonial situation by the assumed moral superiority of the European which is reinforced at every turn by his actual military supremacy. The relation between self and other, subject and object, is also important because each novel is a combination, no matter how skewed, of subjectivity and objectivity: no work of art is entirely subjective or objective. Because each novel records and codifies *lived* experience, through the elaborative mediation of imagination, and thus constitutes an objectification of human subjectivity, the specific configuration in the combination of these two elements in a given novel will reveal the emotive intentionality of each author. Hence a careful analysis of subjectivity and objectivity in each writer's literary project, and the social practice implied therein, will permit us to comprehend the complex and delicate relation between fiction and its ground. The author's project, in the course of which he considers again and again the same or similar problems but at different levels of integration and complexity, reveals the repetitions, variations, and modifications of his emotive intentionality which constitutes the ideological structure that underlies his work. And in turn an examination of the ideological structure, which provides the common denominator between socio-economic and literary structures, finally allows us to define the modes of relation between society and its literature.

That the manichean organization of colonial society has a powerful limiting effect on its literature is a fact that has been recognized and succinctly articulated by Nadine Gordimer. Quoting Harry Levin, she defines "cultural identity as 'nothing more or less than the mean between selfhood and otherness, between our respect for ourselves and our relationship with our fellow men and women.' The dilemma of a literature in a multiracial society, where the law effectively prevents any real identification of the writer with his society as a whole, so that ultimately he can identify only with his colour, distorts this mean irreparably. And cultural identity is the ground on which the exploration of self in the imaginative writer makes a national literature."[5] What Gordimer implies here is that the manichean society is incapable of generating a *national* literature; it can produce African national and European colonial literatures, but the two cannot be combined. Such literatures will tend to retain and reflect in sublimated or overt forms the manichean polarization and valorization of the bifurcated society. However, an attempt to transcend the manichean dichotomy can produce, as it does in Gordimer's work, fiction that is neither colonial nor national, but that defines the end of colonialism and points toward the development of a national consciousness and literature.

The relations between self and other and between literature and society, as well as the development of a "national" culture and literature, are mediated by ideology, which, we must insist once more, is not false consciousness but rather a distillation of *lived* relationships. It is an attempt to valorize one's position in the face of a threatening and multifarious alterity: its main purpose is self-validation. Ideology, as Jameson defines it, consists of "strategies of containment, whether intellectual or (in the case of narratives) formal."[6] That is, the writer, by unconsciously attempting to valorize the position of self and his group in the face of an antagonistic alterity, is most often unable to proceed beyond the limited (and limiting) *real* economic- and socio-political interests of his class or group. However, this relation between the Real and ideology, in which the latter seeks to mold and confine the former to suit individual and class desires, is profoundly symbiotic and treacherous: no matter how ardently and cunningly ideology may try to conceal reality and deny the existence of all social contradictions, reality invariably infiltrates ideology. Otherwise, of course, the latter could never be "demystified." Its unmasking is facilitated not only by the fact that a text takes up the world (and its contradictions) into itself, but also because in doing so ideology constructs, as Pierre Macherey argues, a "determinate image," a finalized codification of itself.[7] But we must disagree with him when he claims that the text reveals ideology "as an object rather than living it from within as though it were an inner conscience." To the extent that a text valorizes any aspect of a class ideology it *lives*—it actively engages in a *political*, albeit a symbolic *act*. As Macherey himself argues, if an ideology is incomplete, a text can complete it. We must thus agree with Jameson that "the aesthetic act is itself ideological, and the production of an aesthetic or narrative form is to be seen as an ideological act in its own right, with the function of inventing imaginary or formal 'solutions' to unresolvable social contradictions."[8] However, it is possible to argue that ideological "functions," as well as "solutions," of literature are many and varied, and that these functions ought to be distinguished from the "ideological intentions" that are embedded in the text: ideological intentions and functions are often identical but not necessarily synonymous. In fact this whole area needs to be charted through a psycho-political rhetoric of ideology. Following Terry Eagleton's suggestive essay,[9] we can begin by making provisional distinctions between the overt or cognitive structure of an ideological discourse or text and its covert, emotive, or "ideological" structure. The former can be defined simply as the conscious textual "intention" to represent or depict a certain kind of world or a particular theme, while the latter can be defined as the unconscious selectivity and closure according to which the "depicted" world is organized—that is, the emotive structure can be seen as the product of a *will* or *desire* to secure the relative coherence or position of the individual and the group to which he belongs. Thus we must agree with Eagleton that paradoxically the overt, cognitive structure of an ideological discourse is in fact subordinated to its covert, emotive structure and that the former is "on the whole articulated according to the demands, the field of discursive play, of the emotive 'intentionality' it embodies." Where repression, or the distance between the cognitive and emotive intentionalities, is greater, the differences between their textual manifestation will be more dramatic; where the distance is lesser, the two will tend to converge. Finally, we must distinguish between these two intentionalities and the ideological function of a text; if a work of literature is defined as a symbolic *act* or a rhetorical *practice*, then it is clearly legitimate to examine its possible "objective effects" or its "functions" (as opposed to its motivating impulses) in the world where various classes are attempting to valorize their positions. At this stage we can distinguish two major types of functions. In the case of hegemonic literature that is justifying an established ascendancy, the ideological function of the text, in its existence as a symbolic *act*, is to "solve" contradictions in order to secure a coherent world, but in its existence as a determinate *object* the ideological function of the same text is to *preserve* the contradictions it wishes to solve. Although the nonhegemonic text as *act* and *object* often parallels these functions, its more important ideological function is somewhat different. Because a nonhegemonic group is still coming to terms with its relatively insecure position, because it is as concerned with defining and clarifying its values and priorities as with "subverting" the ascendancy of the dominating group, the primary ideological function of its texts as *acts* and *objects* is to bring to consciousness the deep contradictions afflicting the subjugated group and thereby to "solve" these contradictions by making them available to conscious, discursive analysis. Compared to hegemonic texts, nonhegemonic ones tend to be less preoccupied with maintaining the stability and coherence of the individual and the community: they are more tolerant of heterogeneous definitions of self and society.

As we have seen, the cognitive intentionality of Joyce Cary's romances is simply to present "universal" themes such as the "wars of beliefs" in an African setting, which supposedly permits greater transparency than the more "complex" European environments. However, the organization of these romances is in fact determined by a powerful emotive intentionality—a desire to maintain the dominance and coherence of the colonizing self and group in the face of an alterity considered hostile and evil. Enmeshed in a complex series of colonial contradictions and overtaken with paranoia, Cary is threatened with a potentially disastrous disintegration of self. Therefore, the incongruity of the colonial system and the incoherence of the self become linked: if Cary can demonstrate that the system is coherent, then his own dilemma would be mitigated; justification of colonialism implies the self-validation of Cary. Thus he "resolves" the contradictions by displacing and projecting them onto others. His own insight into the colonialists' reluctance to implement their avowed policy of "civilizing" the natives is first transformed into a criticism of governmental *inefficiency* and then transferred to characters like Marie and Mrs. Vowles, who are subsequently dismissed as *incoherent* anarchists. Similarly, after subjecting the major contradiction (between overt and covert colonial policies) to a series of permutations, Cary projects it onto the "accultured" Africans who are portrayed as being incapable of combining the two worlds. The contradictions of his situation become the incoherence of their schizophrenia.

Thus the ideological function of Cary's romances is to legitimate and reinforce colonialist ideology. Because all blacks who attempt seriously to emulate European values are allowed neither to become "civilized" nor, indeed, to live, the colonial officers in Cary's romances return once more to governing the other savages who are content to be themselves. The universe of his fiction is bereft of any historical progress: the colonialist desire to maintain the status quo is accurately represented by the fact that all the romances, with the exception of *An American Visitor*, depict a disturbance that ends with the elimination of "agitators," and the coherence of the colonial world is saved once more from the monstrous demands of an evil other. The success of Cary's romances in reinforcing colonialist ideology is verified by the criticism, quoted at the beginning of the second chapter, of Harry Barba and Golden L. Larsen, both of whom implicitly support the perpetuation of colonialism by amplifying Cary's assumption that the Africans are irrevocably savage. This "effect" of the racial romances and Cary's compulsive attraction to this form demonstrate that as political *acts* these texts do *live* the ideology from within—they are rather like religious mantras designed to induce belief. However, as determinate *objects* they codify the fundamental principles of that ideological world: the perception that organizes this universe is simultaneously allegorical and metonymic. It is allegorical in that it explains and orders external, accidental physical differences in terms of internal, moral differences, in terms of the binary opposites of good and evil; it is metonymic to the extent that it conflates parts and wholes. Once black skin is categorized as a sign of moral inferiority, black individuals become interchangeable units of an evil group.

The cognitive intentionality of Isak Dinesen's autobiographies is to recapture her life on the Kenyan coffee farm. However, the emotive intentionality of her writing, like Cary's, is defined by a will to coherence, a desire to recapture the putative unity of a preindustrial, feudal life. This intention, deriving its impetus from a Rousseauesque nostalgia for the "natural man" and a Coleridgean desire to establish a pantisocracy, takes the social form of the utopian community that she established on her farm. Dinesen overcomes the contradictions of the manichean bifurcation by positing a binary opposition of black and white, men and women, and so on, such that by complementing each other the opposites form a transcendent synthesis. Unlike Cary, Dinesen treats the Africans as subjects and, in spite of the prevailing manicheanism, mediates their transition from an oral to a literate culture and in turn allows them to mediate her movement into mythic consciousness, which eventually affects the structure of her autobiographies and the form of her "tales." However, utilizing the inequality of the colonial society, Dinesen unequivocally subordinates and internalizes the native-other-as-subject—through a powerful introjection she remains the firm subjective center around which the world is organized. But this coherence of self and the universe is achieved through a complete repression of all unpleasant biographical events.

In Dinesen's texts, the ideological function of which is to outflank both the increasingly powerful bourgeois society and colonial manicheanism, the codification of social relations on the farm is manifested as an affective metonymic organization. Her desire for unity and coherence, for the "secret that connected the phenomena of existence," is presented in the texts as phenomenological and aesthetic structures based on the pattern of mythic thought: at the social and aesthetic levels mythic consciousness allows her to unite various aspects of African life and landscape under the metaphor of prelapsarian paradise, while at the epistemological and ontological levels it permits her an organization based on an essentialist and atomistic metonymy. A corollary of this ideological function is the negation of history. In contrast to industrial society's emphasis on linear progress, both the synchronic nature of mythic consciousness that stems from the fundamentally ahistorical oral culture and the atemporal organization of Dinesen's autobiographies imply a rejection of history, which signifies for Dinesen the decay of utopia, of the prelapsarian paradise. Her negation of history even influences her subsequent choice of literary form: the tale, a vehicle for collective rather than individual experience, and its emphasis on destiny once more reject the historicity implied in the efficacy of genuinely lived human experience which never apprehends itself as fate.[10]

Dinesen's world, like Cary's, is atemporal and ahistorical. But whereas his is full of conflict and violence, suppressing a desperate desire for coherence and peace, hers is characterized by edenic bliss, perfection, and congruity; whereas Cary's fear and rejection of the blacks lead to the dualistic structure of racial romances, with their manichean tensions and polarities, Dinesen's genuine fondness and respect for the natives lead to the strong, inclusive, monistic structure of her autobiographies. Northrop Frye has classified such a world as one "in which everything is potentially identical with everything else, as though it were inside a single infinite body." Thus Dinesen's universe of "displaced myth," with its "romantic tendency to suggest implicit mythic patterns in a world more closely associated with human experience," is essentially aligned to Cary's racial romances, with their propensity "to displace myth in a human direction and yet, in contrast to realism, to conventionalize content in an idealized direction."[11] This formal proximity of Cary's and Dinesen's texts attests to the powerful influence of the colonial context on the literature it generates: the manichean bifurcation and the enforced subservience of the natives encourage and feed the different forms of colonialist subjectivity which provide the bases of both Cary's and Dinesen's texts.

Unlike Cary and Dinesen, Nadine Gordimer was born in Africa. Yet the colonial manichean bifurcation is so deep and complete that Gordimer's relation to Africans is also mediated by the experience of the "stranger"; that is, through her "second birth" she realizes that the enormous economic and political distance between blacks and whites can only be bridged if the Europeans are willing "to take their attitude apart and assemble afresh their ideas of themselves." Thus, like Dinesen, she discards her colonial, manichean heritage and embarks on a lengthy examination of colonial government and consciousness. This cognitive intention, however, is quite close to the emotive intentionality of her work: because she is consistently aware of psychic repression and of the crucial role of rebounding reciprocity in the formation of communities, she attempts to unmask the unconscious aspects of colonialist mentality—particularly its attachment to the privileges that prevent an honest self-examination. The emotive intentionality of her fiction, a will to discover a "decent" basis for a subjective and communal stand, leads to the repetitive pattern of her novels: appalled by various aspects of racism, apartheid, and colonialism, her characters are forced to examine the complex relation between self and society. Such a speleology of unconscious desire reaches its climax in Maureen's recognition of herself as master in *July's People*. By deliberately situating her fiction within the gap between apartheid theory and actual practice, between liberal pretense and actual callowness, and by repeatedly examining the conflict between the desire to leave and to stay, Gordimer's fiction simultaneously reveals the absence of and the desire for a viable, humane, and just interracial community which would free the individual from the debilitating contradictions of a manichean society.

The ideological function of Gordimer's (nonhegemonic) fiction as *act* and *object*, then, is to bring to consciousness the major contradictions between the whites' patronizing or abhorrent attitude to blacks and the former's actual parasitic dependency on the latter. Her novels also reveal the tenacious hold of liberalism on individuals in spite of its ideological bankruptcy. However, on a more positive note, Gordimer's novels also indicate several necessary conditions for a better society. The first of these is the recognition of a more productive relation between self and other. The role of Africans gradually changes from her early novels, where black individuals are mirror images of white protagonists, to the later novels, where they are distinctly different and even dramatically opposed to the heroes and heroines. This progressively stronger recognition of the alterity of blacks represents a coming-to-consciousness of rebounding reciprocity, and it leads Gordimer to redefine self and community. The conflict between the desire to leave and to stay is in fact a local version of the struggle between self-as-individual and self-as-social-being: the wish to abandon the demanding collective problems of apartheid and to gratify *personal* desires motivates the protagonist to leave, but the sense of obligation toward others forces him/her to stay. Thus all Gordimer's novels are concerned in one way or another with the formation of communities, which are defined increasingly in terms of *political* rather than *personal* efficacy. The meaning and value of personal freedom depend for Gordimer on the prior achievement of political freedom, which is usually a product of prolonged historical struggle. Thus, unlike Cary's romances and Dinesen's autobiographies, Gordimer's novels are historical in the sense that their plots unfold against the backdrop of specific events in the political history of South Africa. However, her novels also tackle the crucial problem of historical amnesia, which, according to *A Guest of Honour*, is responsible for the bankruptcy of European liberalism. If liberalism cannot secure the emancipation of black South Africans, then the goal must be pursued through a radical change in historical direction: the prison community to which Rosa belongs at the end of the novel is achieved through a deliberate rejection of European society.

Gordimer's confrontation with the manichean society—the exposure of its contradictions and the indication of alternate relations between self and society—leaves its mark on the form of her novels. The conflict between subjective desires and objective conditions manifests itself initially in the stylization of the politically opposed characters and situations in *A World of Strangers, Occasion for Loving, The Late Bourgeois World*, and *A Guest of Honour*: this codification of opposition between subjective desire and communal obligation implies an alienation that is further augmented by the fact that the representation of subjective feelings tends to overpower the depiction of objective conditions in the last two of these novels. This tendency resurfaces most emphatically in the split narrative of *The Conservationist* where the overwhelming subjectivity tends to invent its own universe and then projects it onto the "objective" world, thereby expressionistically distorting it. The subjective/expressionistic bias can be interpreted as a sign of the anguish produced in the author/narrator by the onerous objective social conditions that tenaciously resist change and thereby encourage a retreat into the self. This effect of manichean society on Gordimer's fiction is temporarily rectified by *Burger's Daughter:* the absorption of the opposition between social conditions and personal predicament into the substance of the novel results in a more appropriate balance between the subjective and objective narratives. The recognition of the effects of the social circumstances allows the novel to transcend and correct the influence of those situations on its style. However, *July's People* returns once more to an exploration of subjective experience. But, unlike the subjectivity in the works of Cary and Dinesen, which derives its intensity from the desire to maintain a coherent self, in Gordimer's fiction it is a product of her willingness to embrace incoherence in order to root out unconscious biases and desires.

In some respects the cognitive intentionality of Achebe's fiction is also relatively close to its emotive intentionality because Achebe is so thoroughly conscious of the fact that a major ideological function of his novels is the refutation of authors like Joyce Cary. The cognitive intention, an attempt to provide an alternate, more just picture of European colonization and African cultures, is closely paralleled by the emotive intention that stems from the relation between self and other in the colonial context. As we have noted, the colonizer tends to regard the native as an "object," and sooner or later the latter, through a dialectic of shame and pride, becomes aware of the other's "look" and of himself as the terminus of that gaze. Consequently, he becomes ashamed because by allowing himself to be treated as an object he allows his freedom to escape him. Conversely, he recognizes the greater freedom of the other-as-subject. Based on an awareness that this is an important ontological relation, Achebe's fiction is designed to transform the African's status from that of an object to that of a subject whose complexity the colonialist is unable to comprehend. Achebe's major narrative strategy for redefining the African as subject is, of course, the contrapuntal structure of his novels. A second strategy is his careful, unidealized presentation of the concrete *totality* of Igbo culture. However, Achebe is so deeply influenced by the subject-object dialectic that even the most fundamental decisions that form the bases of his fiction are determined by it. Thus the treatment of others as objects becomes one of the major causes of his heroes' demise: Okonkwo's use of Ikemefuna as an object leads to his decline; Ezeulu's treatment of the whole community as an object results in the final catastrophe; and Obi's callow preoccupation with corruption renders him insensitive to others' subjective needs. Finally, the emotions that almost exclusively form the character of Okonkwo—and, in more complex and modified forms, those of Ezeulu and Obi—are shame and pride.

Thus the ideological function of Achebe's novels is to bring to consciousness various aspects of the colonial experience. The major function of his novels as symbolic *acts* is the refutation of Cary's romances through his own realism. A secondary function is to preserve, through a judicious use of language, imagery, and plot, a permanent image of the concrete totality of a vanishing oral culture. However, as determinate *objects,* his novels bring to consciousness the conflict between historical catalepsy and cultural petrification that engulfs the colonized man.

Because the most traumatic experience of Ngugi's life is the disintegration of Gikuyu society during the Mau Mau war, the cognitive
level of his novels is preoccupied with a portrayal of various stages
of Gikuyu struggle against colonization. The emotive intentionality
of the first two novels correspondingly manifests itself as a desire to
alleviate suffering and reunite the community. However, the former
emotive intention is so strong that it overwhelms the will to coherence and results in novels dominated by subjectivity and abstract
idealism. The ideological function of these novels as *acts* is to avoid
the pain of colonial subjugation by retreating into a mythic universe,
into a fantasy world where problems can be solved by divine intervention. But Ngugi's recourse to divine knowledge, which tends to
insulate his messiahs from human reality, is contradicted by the historical origins of the Gikuyu dilemma, which demands concrete political and historical knowledge. The resultant confusion manifests
itself most poignantly in the contradictory portrayal of Njoroge as a
traumatized victim, who needs to be calmed, and as a messiah, who
will soothe the pain of others. This confusion itself reveals the
ideological function of these novels as determinate *objects*. The above
contradiction and the vague awareness of the dangers of the
catalepsy-petrification problem—Waiyaki, for instance, is urged to
master European knowledge *and* remain faithful to the values of his
own culture—bring to consciousness the confusion of the colonized
man who has no control over his destiny: the novels are symptomatic
products of the peripeteia of values and of the catalepsy-petrification
problem.

The emotive intentionality of *A Grain of Wheat* lacks the urgent
need to soothe a traumatic experience, and consequently the will to
communal coherence is carefully mediated through considerations of
communal organization, obligation to self and society, and historical
development. As we have seen, by juxtaposing different scenes and
characters, by using flashbacks, by developing a complex web of relations between characters, and by demonstrating that the strengths
and weaknesses of various personality traits are determined by the
demands of circumstances, Ngugi defines community in a dramatically different manner: the ideological function of *A Grain of Wheat*
as *act* and *object* is to provide a *viable* symbolic resolution to real
social contradictions. In this novel Ngugi clearly demonstrates that
the self is only definable through the mediation of the other and that
isolation from others leads to the complete attenuation of the self.
While he admits the efficacy of abstract relations to others, he valorizes concrete relations as the only lasting basis of communal organi-

zation. Thus he defines the community as a mediated totality that is available to each member only through a thorough and incessant awareness of concrete interdependence, which makes available to the individual an infinite number of possibilities and thus allows him to become a perpetual center of infinite concrete potentiality. Conversely, it becomes evident that each character, through his oath to support the Mau Mau movement and through his particular and different sacrifice, betrayal, and guilt, is equally responsible for the concrete configuration of the community at any given stage. Thus in his or her own way each character is the center of the community—each character is a grain of wheat with a concrete potentiality for germination and fruition. Paradoxically, then, the will to coherence in this novel produces an extremely heterogeneous and delicately balanced "unity"; the "coherent" self, defined as being dependent on the community, is in fact radically dispersed among others.

A Grain of Wheat also demonstrates a profound understanding of the function and importance of history: in fact the novel is an exercise in historical investigation. Because each succeeding revelation about the heroism, betrayal, or culpability of a given character alters the entire configuration of the past, the novel implies that history is never a finished product but a constantly changing dialectical awareness, that both self and community are constant projects that will never achieve absolute completion or plenitude. Ngugi's view of history is also appropriately ironic: he shows that accidents and circumstances bring out people's potentiality and that the subsequent actualization of the latter leads to the movement of history—that history is meaningful in spite of its accidental nature. (This, of course, is directly opposed to the notion of history in a universe dominated by messiahs.) Finally, in the figure of the stool and the child, A Grain of Wheat ends by symbolically projecting its definition of community into the future. Unlike Achebe's fiction, where accidents lead not to the potential plenitude of future meaning but rather to the flight of all past significance and coherence, and unlike Ngugi's previous novels, where coincidences compound current suffering and confusion, A Grain of Wheat is a unique utopian novel in the African canon.

The social and political dilemmas faced by Alex La Guma are generally the same but are specifically different from those that Achebe and Ngugi encounter. Although the formative experiences of Achebe and Ngugi took place in colonial societies, they were both writing during the imminent or actual dissolution of the British Empire in Africa. Even the alienation of these writers by colonialism was mitigated to some extent by their constant contact with their communities. However, the South African colonial society is quasi-permanent and far more oppressive than the British rule in Nigeria or Kenya: La Guma has to contend with a situation that is categorically and absolutely manichean. As a consequence of these differences, La Guma's fiction depicts the quintessential predicament of the colonized man. At the level of cognitive intentionality his novels best represent the nature and effects of colonial oppression as well as the structure and dynamics of the gradual rebellion against apartheid.

As we have seen, all La Guma's fiction represents the tension between the black individual's *lived*, quasi-ontological experience of "objectness" and his sense of individual self-worth. His first novels concentrate on the experience of the object while the last three tend to focus on that of the subject and community. The emotive intentionality of all five novels, a desire to alleviate the suffering caused by apartheid, is identical, but the strategies vary drastically. In the first two novels the only avenue of escape lies through the transference of violence and the eventual scapegoating which temporarily purges the oppression. The ideological function of these brief naturalistic novels in their capacity as symbolic *acts* is merely to point to the marginality of black life under apartheid. However, as determinate *objects* these novels, with their metonymic/contiguous organizations and their drastic subordination of the imperative mood to the indicative mood, bring to consciousness the structure of political seriality which imprisons the colonized man in South Africa. The next two novels demonstrate that the only viable route to freedom lies through the formation of groups that can wage a prolonged political and military struggle against apartheid. As symbolic *acts* their ideological function is to valorize the emergence of the individual as a dignified subject and of the group that facilitates that development. As determinate *objects*, these texts bring to consciousness the values of authentic being as being-for-the-other, of community as constituted by rebounding reciprocity, and of the absolute and primary necessity of coming-to-consciousness about one's social and historical condition. *Time of the Butcherbird* is ideologically regressive: its ideological function is to valorize individual vengeance rather than collective action and to reveal that the frustrations of exile are most easily qualified by fantasies of revenge. La Guma's project thus demonstrates the systematic, if painful, emergence of the subject, the transformation of the slave into an individual who is the master of his personal destiny (though not yet of his world).

The fundamental fact that becomes evident from the preceding studies of the six authors is that the colonial society, with its highly charged, allegorical manicheanism and its peculiarly inhumane drama, generates such a powerful socio-political-ideological force field that neither colonial nor African literature is able to escape or transcend it. All six writers are obliged to come to terms with the manichean structure in their own ways: they may decry or simply depict its existence and effects, they may try to subvert it or overcome its consequences, or they may valorize it; but regardless of the overt thematic content of their writing, they cannot ignore it. The *personal* preoccupations, prejudices, and experiences of these writers, combined with local differences in colonial practice, produce the formal and thematic variety of their literature, but the significant similarities in the ideological structure of their works are determined by the nature of colonial society. Thus the manichean world accounts for the structural similarity of Cary's racial romances and Dinesen's mythic autobiographies in spite of the diametrical opposition of the two writers' attitudes toward Africans, and even Gordimer's fiction, like Cary's and Dinesen's work, tends to be dominated by an intense and problematic subjectivity despite her adamant opposition to manichean apartheid. Similarly, the struggle against various facets of colonial society explains the fundamental convergence in the ideological preoccupation of Achebe, Ngugi, and La Guma in spite of all the geographic, cultural, and thematic differences. A general consequence of the manichean social structure is that colonial literature tends to be more interesting for its subjective, noetic qualities, that is, for the *nature* of its perception rather than for the complexity of what it perceives. Conversely, the noematic aspects of African literature, that is, the complexity of the world it reveals, make it more fascinating than do its perceptual processes.

A major factor that cuts across all variations and similarities is what we have termed the "negative influence" of colonialist practice, ideology, and literature on African fiction, which in many ways is a response to colonialist literature. This antagonist relationship between colonial and African literature can be subsumed under what Jameson has termed the *dialogic* structure of class discourse. Within this second horizon, constituted by the tension and struggle between classes, the individual text (or the entire work of an author) can be refocused "as a *parole*, or individual utterance, of the vaster system, or *langue*, of class discourse." And we must insist, along with Jameson, that the study and affirmation of nonhegemonic literature "remains ineffective if it is limited to the merely 'sociological' perspective of the pluralistic rediscovery of . . . isolated social groups;

only an ultimate rewriting of these utterances in terms of their essentially polemic and subversive strategies restores them to their proper place in the dialogical system of social classes."[12] This is particularly true of the relation between colonial and African literature.

As Dinesen points out (SG, 90–91), the colonialist dismisses African cultures and their pasts as being utterly useless, barbaric, and evil. What we need to stress at this stage is the manner in which the native internalizes these negations. The colonized man's initial acceptance of being treated as an object leads to a solidification and alienation of his possibilities, to the utter absence of the world he has previously perceived and organized. Sartre's phenomenological description of the effect on the self produced by the presence of the other is very appropriate for the colonial encounter: "The appearance of the Other in the world corresponds therefore to a fixed sliding of the whole universe, to a decentralization of the world which undermines the centralization which I am simultaneously effecting."[13] This is not only phenomenologically but also sociologically and politically the case in the colonial situation: because of his military superiority the colonizer is able to impose his will and his entire world—his social, political, legal, and moral system—on the colonized. Through the disintegration of the Igbo world and the final switch to the district officer's view of Okonkwo as an interesting object, Achebe's *Things Fall Apart* clearly depicts such an imposition and the subsequent sliding of the African universe. However, we must insist that African societies do not disintegrate because of the mere *presence*, in some abstract sense, of the colonizer or even because of colonialist ideology. The real destruction is achieved through military superiority, which ensures an effective dismantling of native socio-political-cultural institutions, and through the imposition of new economic order. Both the colonizers and the colonized are perfectly aware that in the final analysis military power and not ideology is responsible for defeat or victory. Thus a colonized writer like Achebe is angered by the ideology embedded in Cary's racial romances because it attempts to justify real domination and destruction: ideology by itself is unable to sustain hegemony of one group over another.

Thus when the African writer reacts to the denigration of his past and present culture by embarking on a redefinition of self and society through a negation of the prior European negation, his literary "polemics" must be read as the ideological component of a more concrete socio-economic struggle. Negation of the negation in the African colonial situation can take many forms. Achebe aims to replace the European view of Africans with a more authentic and specific, though unidealized, version that is free from the manichean allegory: he attempts to replace Cary's racial romances (and by implication Dinesen's mythic autobiographies) with African realism. In contrast to Achebe's engagement in a more properly *literary* dialogue, Ngugi chooses to redefine the African self by attempting to negate colonial *political practice* (which seriously disrupted the Gikuyu community) through a literary effort to reintegrate the community: his success in doing so would show one way in which *actual* disintegration could be partly overcome. Finally, La Guma responds to the absolute manicheanism of apartheid with absolute negation. The black guerrilla fighter in South Africa can only have the freedom to define self and society if he first destroys the supremacy of the white other. To the extent that this implies a total dismantling of the apartheid system, La Guma's fiction advocates a negation on all fronts. These aspects of a "dialogue," echoed in many African novels, constitute a fundamental component of contemporary African literature.

On the colonialist side of the "dialogue," the works of Cary and Dinesen define two of the most fundamental ideologemes of colonialist ideology. An ideologeme, the minimal "unit" around which class discourses are organized, is simultaneously a pseudo-idea, susceptible to conceptual description, and a proto-narrative, a kind of ultimate class fantasy about "collective characters."[14] The two colonialist ideologemes coalesce around the classification of the native as a degraded savage and as a noble savage. According to O. Mannoni, the genesis of this fantasy lies in the complexity of the desire to flee the other-as-subject, which can lead to "a serious rupture of the image of these others or to a failure in the process of synthesis whereby the image is formed. The image falls into two parts which recede farther and farther from one another instead of coalescing; on the one hand there are pictures of monsters and terrifying creatures, and on the other versions of gracious beings bereft of will and purpose—Caliban and the cannibals at one extreme, and Ariel and Friday at the other."[15] The transformation of these ideologemes into narratives is clearly embodied in the works of Cary and Dinesen respectively. Judged in terms of existent colonialist ideologemes, Gordimer is clearly not a colonial writer. For her the African fits neither of these categories; he is simply an other whom she wishes to know as a subject and an equal, although she is prevented from doing so by the apartheid regime.

The other fundamental factor involved in the development of

African literature is, of course, literacy. It is important not only in the obvious mechanical sense but also because it leads to the development of a historical consciousness and consequently, once again, to the prevalence of realism. According to Ian Watt and Jack Goody,[16] the primary effect of literacy is to disrupt the process of "structural amnesia." That is, literacy, by permitting the recording of particular facts and thus making available in time a dense and specific past, will not allow memory, the major mode of temporal mediation in oral cultures, to eliminate facts that are not consonant with or useful for contemporary needs. Literacy also destroys the immediacy of personal experience and the deeper socialization of the world and consequently the totalizing nature of oral cultures. Hints of the destruction of such a world are, once again, evident in Achebe's *Things Fall Apart*. Literacy then leads to the development of historic consciousness by allowing any (literate) individual to scrutinize the fixed past, to distinguish between truth and error, and consequently to cultivate a more conscious, critical, and comparative attitude to the accepted world picture. Such an attitude eventually produces a sense of change, of the human past as an objective reality available to causal analysis, and of history as a broad attempt to determine reality in every (diachronic) area of human concern. This in turn permits a distinction between "history" and "myth."[17] For Ernst Cassirer the development of literacy in Greece produced the evolution of both the historical and the "scientific-empiric" culture from a "mythic" one. A similar transition was obviously taking place in Africa during the colonial period, and it provided Achebe the opportunity to depict the end of a "totalized" oral culture and Dinesen the occasion to slip back into the oral "mythic" culture.

The development of historical consciousness creates an ambiance that provides preconditions similar to those that Ian Watt feels were conducive to the rise of the novel in England. As we have just seen, literacy tends to valorize individual experience over the efficacy of a traditional, collective view of the world; it obviously encourages specificity and particularism; and by sharpening the historical sense, it allows personality to be defined through its past and present self-awareness, and it permits greater individualization through the definition of a particular time and place. Similarly, it encourages the production of authentic accounts of individual experiences—a tendency that is further strengthened by the dialectics of negative influence. At the more obvious formal level Achebe's realism consists of his implicit commitment not to idealize the society that he depicts but to bring his fictive world to us in all its concrete particularity by ensuring an accuracy and precision in the correspondence of words and things. Through a judicious use of Igbo terms and transliteration of proverbs, Achebe is brilliantly successful in evoking the tonality and flavor of the Igbo culture. His ability to present an Igbo reality through the English language without compromising either the reality or the language is an indication of his artistic skills and the success of his realism.

However, because colonialism politicizes its world, African novels, unlike the early English novels, tend to be concerned with public and political issues. Therefore, they not only satisfy the formal criteria of Ian Watt but also the structural requirements of Georg Lukács. As we have already seen, the conflict between man-as-social-being and man-as-individual that permeates all Achebe's plots is a product of his own experience of the transition from a communal to an individualistic society. His realism is also a reflection of the transition from a society that is a concrete totality to one that has disintegrated. Oral cultures, which allow their members to experience the totality of symbol-referent relationships in an immediate and personal manner and thus permit them to socialize the world more deeply than literate cultures do, create a society that is a concrete totality to the extent that all its phenomena are understood and immediately grasped in terms of their relations to and situation in the total cultural process. Achebe reflects such concrete totality in the conception and organization of his novels. At the level of detail the nature of this realism is best illustrated by the substitution, encouraged by the Christian Church at the end of *Arrow of God*, of money for yams as spiritual offerings. The yam represents both the economic *and* moral orders of life in that it is simultaneously a mere commodity, produced and consumed mundanely, and an object endowed with specific moral and spiritual significance, whereas money introduces a secularization and commodification of the world that is so essential to capitalistic societies. At the narrative level Achebe's use of the folktale within his novel represents the embedding of a form appropriate to collective life within a form that is the product of a highly individualistic experience. More significantly, however, this complex tension between oral and literate cultures informs the very structure of *Things Fall Apart*, which embodies all the tensions, contradictions, and values of the society in the desires and circumstances of Okonkwo. Thus what Charles R. Larson calls the "situational plot" of this novel,[18] that is, Achebe's use of the first twelve chapters to describe the Igbo culture in detail rather than to develop a plot, is really designed to allow us to understand Okonkwo as an integral part of the concrete totality. Once we have recognized his function as the emblem of his society, we can better appreciate that his demise at the end represents not just the death of an individual but the falling apart of "things," that is, of concrete totality.

Another cause of the realism of African fiction lies in its reaction to the universalism and romanticization of Africa inherent not only in colonial literature but also in the Negritude movement. The anglophone novelists and the Negritude poets share a common concern with the reclamation of culture, the resurgence of African dignity, the viability of communal ethics, and so forth. However, the latter group attempts to achieve its goals through systematic reversal of the colonialist manichean valorization and through the effort to define the "African personality" *as a continental phenomenon.* This manner of negation, however, still retains the colonialist's *allegorical* view of the world and his metonymic reduction of all "Negroes" to a common denominator. In contrast to these predominantly francophone poets, who have all become alienated expatriates because of their submission to the French colonial policy of assimilation, the anglophone novelists have spent their formative years in close contact with their own cultures and have thus developed an intimate knowledge of their worlds and a sense of security about the dignity and moral efficacy of their heritage. As a consequence of this background, these novelists are more concerned with representing their societies as specifically as possible. The difference between these two groups of writers is partly due to the differences between French and English colonial policies, but it is also a product of historical development that Fanon has articulated succinctly. According to him, once independence has been achieved the focus of colonized literature changes: "From being a reply on a minor scale to the dominating power, the literature produced by natives becomes differentiated and makes itself into a will to particularism."[19] This desire for specificity is evident, once more, in the kind of realism typified by Achebe's fiction. The implied belief behind this will to particularism is that the dignity of African cultures will be restored more efficaciously through specific and concrete representation than through the insistence of an abstract proclamation. This attitude is, of course, perfectly summed up by Soyinka's famous remark that a tiger does not have to go around proclaiming its "tigritude."

Yet there is a profound paradox in this will to particularism which leads Achebe to represent the specificity of Igbo culture through the alien medium of the English language which was formulated and has been consistently modified by a significantly different experience of reality. There are two closely aligned facets in this paradox: the political and the literary. From the political viewpoint what is significant is that the introduction of the English language, and consequently of the whole English culture, opens up a new world for the colonized man. But once he has learned to command that language he finds himself condemned to participate in the physically and culturally different worlds of the colonizer and the colonized, which are both engaged in a manichean conflict. Simply by using the alien medium the colonized writer is involved in an antagonistic dialogue. This facet of the paradox is parallel to the achievement of political independence by the African countries: just as the African nationalistic movements overcame the autocracy of colonial government by appealing to the principle of universal suffrage prevalent in the metropolitan countries, so do African writers negate the colonialist depiction of them as savages by using metropolitan language and literary forms; they overcome the colonialist "romance" of Africa by using metropolitan "realism."

From a more literary viewpoint, the colonized intellectual finds that he is absolutely obliged to learn the alien language because, even if the indigenous language were to be translated with the aid of a European alphabet, the majority of the colonized people would not be able to read whatever he wrote. Even if there were a certain amount of indigenous literacy, the writer would find the colonized world anxious to use the alien language rather than the vernacular. The ensuing alienation from his own community forces the colonized intellectual to use the European language in order to avoid complete isolation. Thus the only avenue of escape for the indigenous writer lies in the use of the alien language. William Walsh, in his appreciation of the Igbo culture re-created in Achebe's fiction, laments the fact that this society, in spite of its artistic achievements and the cultivated subtleties of its language, is transient because it cannot record itself for the future. The irony, then, is that while literacy and the English language contribute to the destruction of this transient society they also allow writers like Achebe to fix and preserve the vanishing culture by creating an image of it in their novels. Northrop Frye has argued that it is the link with history and temporal context that has confined the novel as a predominant form to the Western world. But now literacy, by destroying the oral cultures in Africa and rendering possible the development of historical consciousness, has made the novel an integral part of the new syncretic African societies.

Notes

1 Introduction

1 Sunday O. Anozie's *Sociologie du Roman Africain* (Paris: Aubier-Montaigne, 1970), a rather abstract structuralist typology, and Jeffrey Meyers's *Fiction and the Colonial Experience* (Totowa, N.J.: Rowman and Littlefield, 1968) both ignore the economic conflicts, political repressions, social tensions, and ideological contradictions that characterize colonial history. Dorothy Hammond and Alta Jablow's *The Africa That Never Was: Four Centuries of British Writing About Africa* (New York: Twayne Publishers, 1970) is an excellent study that does take into account economic, political, and ideological factors. It is, however, a vast survey that is more anthropological than literary.

2 M. M. Mahood, *The Colonial Encounter: A Reading of Six Novels* (Totowa, N.J.: Rowman and Littlefield, 1977), pp. 3, 170, 171.

3 Georges Balandier, "The Colonial Situation: A Theoretical Approach," in *Social Change: The Colonial Situation*, ed. Immanuel Wallerstein (New York: John Wiley, 1966), p. 37.

4 C. K. Meek, W. M. Macmillan, and E. R. J. Hussey, *Europe and West Africa: Some Problems and Adjustments* (London: Oxford University Press, 1940), p. 40.

5 Balandier, "Colonial Situation," p. 37.

6 Joel Kovel, *White Racism: A Psychohistory* (New York: Random House, 1970), p. 65. For a detailed discussion of racism as a projection of libidinal forces see chap. 4, "The Fantasies of Race," in Kovel's study, and chap. 1 of O. Mannoni's *Prospero and Caliban: The Psychology of Colonization* (New York: Frederick A. Praeger, 1964).

7 Frantz Fanon, *The Wretched of the Earth* (New York: Grove Press, 1968), p. 41. Fanon provides a detailed psychological study of this manicheanism in his *Black Skin, White Masks* (New York: Grove Press, 1967).

8 Fanon, *The Wretched of the Earth*, p. 93.

9 For a detailed discussion of the dependence of the colonizer's identity upon his sense of superiority and his racism see Mannoni, *Prospero and Caliban*, chap. 2.

10 See the preface by Jean-Paul Sartre to Albert Memmi's *The Colonizer and the Colonized* (Boston: Beacon Press, 1969), p. xxvii. For a slightly different but essentially complementary explanation, see Kovel, *White Racism*, p. 19.

286 Notes

11 Balandier, "Colonial Situation," p. 47. The systematic hindering of the Africans' attempt to obtain Western education is discussed for the Nigerian region by R. Cliguet and P. J. Foster, "French and British Colonial Education in Africa," in *Perspectives on the African Past*, ed. Martin A. Klein and G. Wesley Johnson (Boston: Little, Brown and Co., 1972), pp. 429–40, and for Kenya by Richard Heyman, "Assimilation and Accommodation in African Education: The Kikuyu Independent School Association," African Studies Association Paper, 1972.

12 For the development of these methods I am specifically indebted to two people. The idea of grounding literary texts in social reality through a scrutiny of the author's biography is derived from Jean-Paul Sartre's "progressive-regressive" method outlined in his *Search for a Method* (New York: Alfred A. Knopf, 1963). For the definition of the relations of cognitive and emotive structures of the text I am indebted to Terry Eagleton's "Ideology, Fiction, Narrative," *Social Text*, no. 2 (Summer 1979): 62–80. More generally, I have relied on many other theoreticians of the sociology of literature. I would like to acknowledge here a particular indebtedness to Fredric Jameson's work, particularly his *Marxism and Form: Twentieth-Century Dialectical Theories of Literature* (Princeton: Princeton University Press, 1971) which I have found invaluable.

13 Hammond and Jablow, *Africa That Never Was*, pp. 20, 23.

14 Raymond Williams has tangentially examined this issue in *The Country and the City* (London: Oxford University Press, 1973). In the last chapter of his study he extends his analysis to the fiction of authors like Joyce Cary, who represents the metropolis, and Chinua Achebe, who represents the country. Williams's suggestive comparison is, in fact, responsible for the commencement of the present study which in the end differs considerably from that of Williams.

15 Some critics have already begun an analysis of this area, but more rigorous work still remains to be done. Charles R. Larson, *The Emergence of African Fiction* (Bloomington: Indiana University Press, 1971), makes interesting and useful observations about the differences between English and African plots.

16 Jack Goody and Ian Watt, "The Consequences of Literacy," in *Literacy in Traditional Societies*, ed. Jack Goody (London: Cambridge University Press, 1968), pp. 27–68.

17 See chap. 3, pp. 131–39, of Basil Davidson's *Let Freedom Come: Africa in Modern History* (Boston: Little, Brown and Co., 1978).

18 I have chosen not to analyze Achebe's *A Man of the People* and Ngugi's *Petals of Blood* because they are set in neo-colonial rather than colonial societies. Although this does not make them radically disjunct from the authors' other novels, the wide scope of my study necessitates fairly strict boundaries. Besides, the representation of neo-colonial cultures in African literature deserves a separate full-length study.

19 Davidson, *Let Freedom Come*, see esp. chap. 5.

20 Ibid., p. 227.

2 Joyce Cary

1 See, for example, M. M. Mahood, *Joyce Cary's Africa* (Boston: Houghton Mifflin, 1964), or M. J. C. Echeruo, *Joyce Cary and the Novel of Africa*

(New York: Africana Publishing Co., 1973). Jonah Raskin, *The Mythology of Imperialism* (New York: Random House, 1971), pp. 194–309, unequivocally denounces Cary's imperialist bias. However, since Raskin is primarily concerned with the denunciation of political immorality, his analysis does not do justice to the relation between the form of Cary's fiction and the politics of the colonial situation.

2 Harry Barba, "Cary's Image of Africa in Transition," *University of Kansas City Review* 29 (1963): 293.

3 Ibid., pp. 294, 293.

4 Golden L. Larsen, *The Dark Descent: Social Change and Moral Responsibility in the Novels of Joyce Cary* (New York: Roy Publishers, n. d.), pp. 25, 59.

5 See, for instance, Andrew Wright, *Joyce Cary: A Preface to His Novels* (London: Harper, 1958), and Robert Bloom, *The Indeterminate World: A Study of the Novels of Joyce Cary* (Philadelphia: University of Pennsylvania Press, 1962).

6 Christopher Fyfe, "The Colonial Situation in *Mister Johnson*," *Modern Fiction Studies* 9, no. 3 (1963): 226–30; Arnold Kettle, *An Introduction to the English Novel* (London: Hutchinson and Co., 1953), 2: 174–84.

7 Mahood, *Joyce Cary's Africa*, pp. 3–85 deals with the biographical material and the rest of the book with Cary's African novels.

8 Ibid., pp. 106, 188, 189 (italics mine).

9 Dorothy Hammond and Alta Jablow show in the third chapter of their excellent survey of imperial literature on Africa, *The Africa That Never Was: Four Centuries of British Writing about Africa* (New York: Twayne Publications, 1970), pp. 74–113, that there is a remarkable similarity in the colonialists' attitude to their task and toward Africa. Their argument that Cary was more idealistic about the imperial mission than most of the other colonial officers is substantially correct.

10 Malcolm Foster, *Joyce Cary: A Biography* (Boston: Houghton Mifflin, 1968), p. 83. Although most of my information about Cary's life in Nigeria is derived from Foster's biography (the only substantial source in print) my interpretation of the material is quite different from Foster's because mine stresses the dynamics of political and racial relations in a colonial society.

11 Ibid., pp. 82–83, 84.

12 From Lord Lugard's *The Dual Mandate*, quoted by Mahood, *Joyce Cary's Africa*, p. 12.

13 Foster, *Joyce Cary*, p. 142.

14 Ibid., p. 92.

15 Ibid., pp. 153, 138, 153.

16 Ibid., p. 152. For Cary's elation at the formation of the Civil Service Association, see p. 212.

17 Mahood, *Joyce Cary's Africa*, p. 73. Mahood also gives supporting evidence: when Cary was leaving for Lagos, he was informed in a booklet that education was being promoted in Nigeria. In fact, however, out of a population of 10 million Nigerians, there were only 250 children in school.

18 Alfred Schutz, "The Stranger: An Essay in Social Psychology," *American Journal of Sociology* 49, no. 6 (1944): 503.

19 Hammond and Jablow, *Africa That Never Was*, p. 82.

20 Joyce Cary, "Africa Yesterday: One Ruler's Burden," in *The Case for Afri-*

can *Freedom and Other Writings on Africa by Joyce Cary*, ed. Christopher Fyfe (Austin: University of Texas Press, 1962), pp. 203–9.

21 Foster, *Joyce Cary*, p. 154.

22 Cary, *The Case for African Freedom*, p. 24. The imagery of this nightmare is clearly reminiscent of Conrad's *Heart of Darkness* and in a sense even validates Conrad's view that the conjunction of ideology of superiority, unlimited power over "inferior" natives, and social isolation can lead to a breakdown of the "civilized" mind. The result of such breakdown in both Kurtz and Cary are similar: Cary's attitude toward the natives is quite close in sentiment to Kurtz's "Exterminate the brutes"—with the major difference that Cary never actually acted on these sentiments. Though, as the rest of the chapter shows, he did vent these sentiments in his novels.

23 Foster, *Joyce Cary*, p. 148.

24 Ibid., p. 160.

25 For a discussion of the traditional colonialist preference of the "pagan" and the dislike for the educated African see Hammond and Jablow, *Africa That Never Was*, pp. 74–113, and Fyfe, "The Colonial Situation in *Mister Johnson*," pp. 227–28.

26 Foster, *Joyce Cary*, p. 211.

27 Albert Memmi, *The Colonizer and the Colonized* (Boston: Beacon Press, 1969), pp. 20–51, presents a strong case for the virtual impossibility of a white man in the colonies remaining uncontaminated by the colonial dichotomies. A European who may not be a racist and may be a fervent egalitarian will most probably be lulled by the privileged status that he is offered in the colonies into supporting the colonial system. Hammond and Jablow's discussion of the prevalent colonialist attitude toward natives at the turn of the century shows that Cary's view was essentially the same as those of his peers (*Africa That Never Was*, pp. 74–113).

28 *An American Visitor* (1933; reprint Carfax Edition, London: Michael Joseph, 1949), p. 79. All further references to Cary's novels will be included in the text of this chapter. The page numbers will refer to the Carfax edition abbreviated as follows: *Aissa Saved* (*AS*); *An American Visitor* (*AV*); *The African Witch* (*AW*); and *Mister Johnson* (*MJ*).

29 For an account of the African demands for Western education and the reluctance of the colonial government to provide it, see R. Cliguet and P. J. Foster, "French and British Colonial Education in Africa," in *Perspectives on the African Past*, ed. Martin A. Klein and G. Wesley Johnson (Boston: Little, Brown, 1972), p. 429.

30 This device is too pervasive to be catalogued. Suffice it to note some occurrences in *Aissa Saved*, pp. 17, 19, 21, 50, 90, 144, 151, and 153.

31 For similar descriptions of the hysterical crowd see *AS*, pp. 54, 88–90, 160, and *AW*, p. 231.

32 For a charitable interpretation of this state of mind see Echeruo, *Joyce Cary and the Novel of Africa*.

33 See Hammond and Jablow, *Africa That Never Was*, p. 119.

34 See ibid., and Echeruo, *Joyce Cary and the Novel of Africa*, pp. 92–94.

35 Jack Wolkenfeld, *Joyce Cary: The Developing Style* (New York: New York University Press, 1968), p. 47.

36 Joseph Conrad, *Heart of Darkness* (New York: Norton and Co., 1963), p. 20.

37 See Hammond and Jablow, *Africa That Never Was*, p. 100, for a description of this pervasive belief.

38 Northrop Frye, *The Secular Scripture: A Study of the Structure of Romance* (Cambridge, Mass.: Harvard University Press, 1976), p. 50.

39 For the importance of a multiplicity of viewpoints for the style of realism, see J. M. Lotman, "Points of View in a Text," *New Literary History* 6, no. 2 (1975): 339–52. Lotman argues that

the crucial point for the style of realism in particular, which aims to escape from the subjectivity of semantic-stylistic points of view and recreate an objective reality, is the precise relationship between these multiple centers [of points of view] and the various (contiguous or mutually superimposed) structures: *they do not replace each other, but form relationships. . . . Because of all this, the literary model* [of realist writing] *recreates the most important aspect of reality—the impossibility of any one definitive and exhaustive interpretation.* (Italics mine)

40 Northrop Frye, *Anatomy of Criticism: Four Essays* (Princeton: Princeton University Press, 1957), pp. 304–5.

41 Hammond and Jablow, *Africa That Never Was*, p. 183.

42 Cary, *The Case for African Freedom*, p. 13.

43 *The Case for African Freedom* would furnish a good text for a study in the simultaneity and multiplicity of contradictions. Compare, for instance, the statement on p. 34, "We need not argue with the racialist. If there is difference in race it is not so great as the difference between individuals," with the statement on p. 36, "But I think there is substance in the charge that the small clerk in the post office or the railway does often show his boredom in rudeness, and this is the natural defect of a racial temperament which prefers friendly to formal relation."

44 Frye, *Anatomy*, pp. 304–5.

45 Ibid., p. 137. "The central principle of displacement [from myth to romance] is that what can be metaphorically identified in myth can only be linked in romance by some form of simile: analogy, significant association, incidental accompanying imagery, and the like."

46 Ibid., p. 306.

47 Fredric Jameson, "Magical Narratives: Romance as Genre," *New Literary History* 7, no. 1 (1975): 135–63.

48 Frye, *Secular Scripture*, p. 57.

49 For an elaboration of the relation between religion and politics in colonial society, see Georges Balandier, "Messianism and Nationalism in Black Africa," in *Perspectives on the African Past*, ed. Klein and Johnson, pp. 465–82.

3 *Isak Dinesen*

1 Dorothy Hammond and Alta Jablow, *The Africa That Never Was* (New York: Twayne Publishers, 1970), p. 157.

2 Parmenia Migel, *Titania: A Biography of Isak Dinesen* (New York: Random House, 1970), p. 10.

3 Isak Dinesen, *Out of Africa* (New York: Random House, 1972), p. 135. All further references to *Out of Africa* and *Shadows on the Grass* (New York:

Random House, 1974) will be included in the text of this paper. *Out of Africa* will be abbreviated as *OA* and *Shadows on the Grass* as *SG*.

4 Donald Hannah, *Isak Dinesen and Karen Blixen: The Mask and the Reality* (New York: Random House, 1971), p. 29.

5 O. Mannoni, *Prospero and Caliban: The Psychology of Colonization* (New York: Praeger, 1964). For definitions of dependence and inferiority see chap. 1.

6 Ernst Cassirer, *The Philosophy of Symbolic Form* Vol. 2 *Mythical Thought* (New Haven: Yale University Press, 1955). See chap. 1 for the definitions of empiric and mythical consciousness.

7 Quoted in Hannah, *Isak Dinesen and Karen Blixen*, p. 50.

8 E. A. Brett, *Colonialism and Underdevelopment in East Africa: The Politics of Economic Change, 1919–1939* (New York: NOK Publishers, 1973), p. 169.

9 Richard D. Wolff, *The Economics of Colonialism: Britain and Kenya, 1870–1930* (New Haven: Yale University Press, 1974), pp. 53–66.

10 Wolff, *Economics of Colonialism*, p. 139, Brett, *Colonialism and Underdevelopment*, p. 176 respectively.

11 Wolff, *Economics of Colonialism*, p. 86.

12 Ibid., pp. 96, 98–99, 138.

13 Ibid., pp. 104, 127.

14 Ibid., pp. 105–7. As Wolff comments, this decline in population was far greater than any decline that could have been caused by tribal warfare. The figures thus expose the hollowness of the traditional colonialist excuse that they were bringing peace to Africa so that the natives could thrive.

15 Mannoni, *Prospero and Caliban*, p. 127.

16 Jomo Kenyatta, while he was a student in England, sent Dinesen a copy of his paper on Gikuyu religion as a token of his appreciation of her interest in native culture. See Frans Lasson and Clara Svendsen, *The Life and Destiny of Isak Dinesen* (New York: Random House, 1970), p. 137.

17 Hannah, *Isak Dinesen and Karen Blixen*, p. 33.

18 Peter Beard, ed., *Longing for Darkness: Kamante's Tales from Out of Africa* (New York: Harcourt Brace Jovanovich, 1975), unpaginated. Because the book is unpaginated, I have numbered it myself. The count begins with the contents page as the first page.

Although one ought to be grateful to Beard for recording Kamante's reminiscences, it is difficult not to be frustrated by the manner of his presentation. The conversations with Kamante are conducted in English and, given his very limited knowledge of English, the result is that he sounds like a childish idiot. Furthermore, the conversations are transcribed by a child and the book consists of photocopies of the transcription.

One result of this is the perpetuation of the image of the African as a child (witness the letter from Jacqueline Bouvier Onassis to Kamante, included in this book, where she seems to praise the quality of Kamante's reminiscences by stressing the fact that her *children* really enjoyed the book).

However, the more important shortcoming of the presentation is that because of the language problem the reminiscences become relatively uninformative. They are like the letters from the servants to Dinesen which, she says, have depth and a desire to communicate something important but which, having "traveled many thousand miles, seem to speak and speak, even to scream at you, but which tell you nothing at all" (*OA*, 80).

19 Ibid., pp. 49, 54–55, 162.

20 Mannoni, *Prospero and Caliban*, p. 108.

21 Cassirer, *The Philosophy of Symbolic Form*. This and the following excerpts are an attempt to condense a complex and involved extended definition which can be found between pp. 29 and 47. For a complete definition see the first chapter of the book.

22 Cassirer, *The Philosophy of Symbolic Form*, pp. 40–41.

23 Ibid., p. 77.

24 Ibid., p. 175.

25 Hannah, *Isak Dinesen and Karen Blixen*, p. 34.

26 Cassirer, *The Philosophy of Symbolic Form*, p. 7.

27 Judith Thurman's recent biography of Dinesen, *Isak Dinesen: The Life of a Storyteller* (New York: St. Martin's Press, 1982), which appeared too late to be incorporated in this study, provides further concrete evidence that corroborates my interpretations. However, it does not examine the specific nature of African influence on Dinesen's attitudes or on her preferred aesthetic form, the tale.

28 Hannah, *Isak Dinesen and Karen Blixen*, p. 102. For a complete discussion of the role of imagination in Dinesen's fiction see chap. 4 of his book.

29 David Daiches, *Literary Essays* (London: Oliver and Boyd, 1966), p. 207.

30 Cassirer, *The Philosophy of Symbolic Form*, p. 36.

31 Apparently the chameleon is most often used to bring God's gift of immortality to man. Dathorne concludes that in African mythology "the chameleon plays its sacred roles as an arbitrator in the creation of life and as a grim messenger in the fortuitous occurrence of death." See O. R. Dathorne, *The Black Mind: A History of African Literature* (Minneapolis: University of Minnesota Press, 1974), pp. 18–19. Dinesen's use of the chameleon is very much in keeping with the traditional usage.

32 Cassirer, *The Philosophy of Symbolic Form*, p. 64. Cassirer does not identify these operations of mythical thinking as metonymic, but they are clearly that.

33 Ibid., pp. 62–65.

34 The radical nature of this mythical concrescence is illustrated by the power of name magic and object magic. Thus, for instance, in the realm of object magic, a man can be tortured to the same degree that some of his hair or a piece of his toenail are tortured even when these are no longer attached to his body. For a discussion of this aspect of the "law of Concrescence" see ibid., pp. 37–43.

35 Ibid., p. 36.

4 *Nadine Gordimer*

1 Frederick A. Johnstone, *Class, Race and Gold: A Study of Class Relation and Discrimination in South Africa* (London: Routledge and Kegan Paul, 1976), pp. 35, 37.

2 E. Hellman, "The Crux of the Race Problem in South Africa," in *South African Dialogue: Contrasts in South African Thinking on Basic Issues*, ed. N. J. Rhoodie (Philadelphia: The Westminster Press, 1972), p. 59.

T. R. H. Davenport, *South Africa: A Modern History* (London: Macmillan Press, 1977), p. 292.

4 Brian P. Bunting, *The Rise of the South African Reich* (Harmondsworth, England: Penguin, 1964), pp. 124–29.

5 Basil Davidson, Joe Slovo, and Anthony R. Wilkinson, *Southern Africa: The New Politics of Revolution* (Harmondsworth, England: Penguin, 1976), p. 105.

6 John Dugard, "The Legal Framework of Apartheid," in Rhoodie, *South African Dialogue*, p. 96.

7 Bunting, *Rise of the South African Reich*, pp. 205–6.

8 Ibid., pp. 208–13.

9 Frederick A. Johnstone, "White Prosperity and White Supremacy in South Africa Today," *African Affairs* 69, no. 275 (1970): 134.

10 Davidson, Slovo, and Wilkinson, *Southern Africa*, p. 105. According to the authors these gaps would be considerably larger if agricultural, domestic, and railway worker's wages were to be included.

11 For instance, regulations based on a 1970 act attempted to prohibit Africans from working as assistants in shops, cafes, as receptionists, telephone operators, and so on (see Davenport, *South Africa*, p. 298).

12 See Johnstone, "White Prosperity," pp. 129–30.

13 George M. Fredrickson, *White Supremacy: A Comparative Study in American and South African History* (New York: Oxford University Press, 1981), see particularly chaps. 5 and 6.

14 Ibid., p. 239.

15 The following account of apartheid ideology is based on D. T. Moodie's analysis in *The Rise of Afrikanerdom: Power, Apartheid, and the Afrikaner Civil Religion* (Berkeley: University of California Press, 1975).

16 Quoted in ibid., p. 248.

17 This relation is thoroughly explored by Bunting, *Rise of the South African Reich.*

18 Quoted in ibid., p. 216.

19 Nadine Gordimer, "What Being a South African Means to Me," *South African Outlook*, no. 107 (July 1977), p. 88.

20 Nadine Gordimer, "Leaving School—II," *London Magazine* 3, no. 2 (1963): 59, 63.

21 Unless otherwise noted most of the above information is derived from "What Being a South African Means to Me."

22 In addition to the sources cited in these notes, see the articles by Nadine Gordimer listed in the bibliography.

23 "Nadine Gordimer Talks to Andrew Salkey," *Listener* 82, no. 2106 (1969): 184–85.

24 Nadine Gordimer, "Where Do Whites Fit In?" *Twentieth Century*, no. 165 (April 1959): 328, 326, 328.

25 Nadine Gordimer, "Is There Nowhere Else Where We Can Meet?" in *Some Monday For Sure* (London: Heinemann, 1976), pp. 3–5.

26 Nadine Gordimer, *The Lying Days* (New York: Simon and Schuster, 1953). All further references to this novel will be abbreviated as *TLD* and incorporated in the text.

27 For a more extensive analysis of this association see Michael Wade, *Nadine Gordimer* (London: Evans Brothers, 1978), pp. 27–30.

28 Nadine Gordimer, *A World of Strangers* (London: Jonathan Cape, 1958). All further references to this novel will be abbreviated as *AWOS* and incorporated in the text.

29 See chap. six of Haugh's *Nadine Gordimer* (New York: Twayne Publishers, 1974), pp. 106–15. Haugh is generally hostile to Gordimer's political preoccupation, which he feels is detrimental to the quality of her writing. He values her short stories far above her political novels because they "have universal appeal, *even though* they arise from the African scene. They are not 'about' Africa . . ." (p. 161, italics mine). However, he views the novels as "becalmed in the arid wastes of sociology" (p. 106).

30 Nadine Gordimer, *Occasion for Loving* (New York: Viking Press, 1960). All further references to this novel will be abbreviated as *OFL* and incorporated in the text.

31 Rose Moss argues that the unsuccessful affair between Gideon and Ann implies a corresponding failure in Gordimer's imagination—"her imagination sometimes seems blocked at the point where the road leads out of the territory she shares with the authorities she detests." See her article "Hand in Glove/Nadine Gordimer: South African Writer: a Case Study in Censorship," *Pacific Quarterly Moana* 6, nos. 3/4 (1981): 106–22. However, it seems to me that this approach ascribes an intention to Gordimer and then criticizes her for not fully realizing it. Gordimer firmly subordinates her imagination to the realities of apartheid and racism; she is less concerned with portraying ideal possibilities (the hypothetical transcendence of racial barriers) and more with depicting the debilitating effects of those barriers. As I argue later in this chapter, Gordimer deliberately confines herself to the "territory" of apartheid in order to chart it as thoroughly as possible.

32 Nadine Gordimer, *The Late Bourgeois World* (New York: Viking Press, 1966). All further references to this novel will be abbreviated as *TLBW* and incorporated in the text.

33 Nadine Gordimer, *A Guest of Honour* (New York: Viking Press, 1970). All further references to this novel will be abbreviated as *AGOH* and incorporated in the text.

34 For a different interpretation of this novel, see Peter Nazareth, *The Third World Writer: His Social Responsibility* (Nairobi: Kenya Literature Bureau, 1978). In his chapter entitled "The White Stranger in a Modest Place of Honour," Nazareth argues that Gordimer uses Bray to examine the problems of an African nation that has recently become independent. However, it seems to me that Gordimer is exploring and defining the scope of liberal ideology and its efficacy in a revolutionary situation.

35 The novel is replete with examples of Bray's myopia. See for instance pp. 120–21, 161, 220, 244–45, 291, 325–26, 399, 431, and 433.

36 Examples of summaries and debates are too numerous to be discussed in detail. Suffice it to indicate their recurrence: *AGOH*, pp. 52, 256, 279, 316, 323, 335, 367, 372, 379, 414, 415, and 421.

37 Nadine Gordimer, *The Conservationist* (New York: Viking Press, 1974). All further references to this novel will be abbreviated as *TC* and incorporated in the text.

38 Nadine Gordimer, *Burger's Daughter* (New York: Viking Press, 1979). All

further references to this novel will be abbreviated as *BD* and incorporated in the text.

39 The ratio of pages devoted to objective and subjective narratives gives a rough indication of the shifting emphasis: part one, 8 : 11; part two, 8 : 2; part three, 8 : 4.

40 Nadine Gordimer's stress on the spontaneity of the children causes her to overlook the implication of the major reason that led to the Soweto riots. The efficient cause of the rebellion was the attempt by the South African government to substitute Afrikaans for English as the medium of instruction in African primary and secondary schools. Because Afrikaans is an entirely local language, it would effectively cut off future generations of blacks from the rest of the world, and thus make them entirely dependent on the white South Africans. The students' recognition of this ingeniously diabolical move demonstrates that sophistication rather than naiveté underlies their spontaneity.

41 These quotations are parts of a speech that Nadine Gordimer delivered to the University of Cape Town students after the Soweto riots. See "What Being a South African Means to Me," pp. 89, 92.

42 Nadine Gordimer, *July's People* (New York: Viking Press, 1981). All further references to this novel will be abbreviated as *JP* and incorporated in the text.

43 Nadine Gordimer, "Literature and Politics in South Africa," *Southern Review: An Australian Journal of Literary Studies*, no. 7 (1974), p. 226.

5   Chinua Achebe

1 Georges Balandier, "The Colonial Situation: A Theoretical Approach," in *Social Change: The Colonial Situation*, ed. Immanuel Wallerstein (New York: John Wiley, 1966), p. 37.

2 My own unpublished interview of Chinua Achebe, November 1975.

3 Achebe, "The Novelist as Teacher," in *African Writers on African Writing*, ed. G. D. Killam (Evanston, Ill.: Northwestern University Press, 1973), p. 3.

4 Achebe, "The Role of the Writer in a New Nation," in ibid., p. 9.

5 Achebe, "The Novelist as Teacher," p. 3.

6 From my own interview; see also "The Role of the Writer in a New Nation," p. 9.

7 Achebe, "The Novelist as Teacher," p. 3.

8 Achebe, "The Black Writer's Burden," *Presence Africaine* 31, no. 59 (1966): 135.

9 Lewis Nkosi, "Conversation with Chinua Achebe," *Africa Report* 9, no. 7 (July 1964): 20.

10 From my own interview. Achebe provides a more thorough, though equally impassioned analysis of *Heart of Darkness* in his "An Image of Africa," *Massachusetts Review* 18, no. 4 (1977): 782–94.

11 Conrad's influence on Third World writers will continue to be a problematic and debated issue. For an excellent article analyzing different Third World reactions to Conrad, see Peter Nazareth, "Out of Darkness: Conrad and Other Third World Writers," *Conradiana* 14, no. 3 (1982): 173–87.

12 Achebe, "The Role of the Writer in a New Nation," p. 8.

13 Achebe, "The Novelist as Teacher," p. 3.
14 From my own interview.
15 Ibid.
16 See "The Role of the Writer in a New Nation," pp. 9–10.
17 See Achebe's "The Novelist as Teacher," and his interview with Ernest and Pat Emenyonu, "Achebe: Accountable to Our Society," *Africa Report* 17, no. 5 (1972): 27.
18 From my own interview.
19 The writer "found that the independence his country was supposed to have won was totally without content. The old white master was still in power. He had got himself a bunch of black stooges to do his dirty work for a commission." See Achebe's "The African Writer and the Biafran Cause," in his *Morning Yet on Creation Day: Essays* (New York: Anchor Press, 1975), p. 145, and his "The Role of the Writer in a New Nation," p. 12.
20 Harry Levin, *Gates of Horn: A Study of Five French Realist Writers* (New York: Oxford University Press, 1963), p. 79. See particularly the chapter on "The Dynasty of Realism."
21 Georg Lukács, *Realism in Our Time: Literature and the Class Struggle* (New York: Harper and Row, 1964), pp. 54–55.
22 From my own interview.
23 Achebe, "The Novelist as Teacher," p. 3.
24 See, for instance, Gerald Moore's analysis of Achebe's novels in his *Seven African Writers* (London: Oxford University Press, 1962), pp. 58–72. The notion of realism which is used in this chapter is not concerned with the attempt to "verify" Achebe's representation of Igbo society in his novels by referring to the "actual" Igbo sociology. Such an approach, which is undertaken with sociological rigor in Sunday O. Anozie's *Sociologie du Roman Africain* (Paris: Aubier-Montaigne, 1970) and which is implied in the autobiographical methodology of James Olney's *Tell Me Africa: An Approach to African Literature* (Princeton: Princeton University Press, 1973), seems to subordinate literature by using it as documents to verify anthropological and sociological studies.
25 Lukács, *Realism in Our Time*, pp. 19, 75.
26 Chinua Achebe, *Things Fall Apart* (Greenwich, Conn.: Fawcett, 1969), *Arrow of God* (New York: Doubleday, 1969), and *No Longer at Ease* (Greenwich, Conn.: Fawcett, 1969). All references to these books will be incorporated in the text of the chapter and will be abbreviated as *TFA*, *AG*, and *NLE*.
27 See Victor C. Uchendu, *The Igbo of Southeast Nigeria* (New York: Holt, Rinehart and Winston, 1965), pp. 19–20 on "Egalitarianism" and pp. 39–48 on "The Igbo Ways in Government." For a more detailed study of the Igbo political system see Mazi Elechukwu Nnadibuagha Njaka's *Igbo Political Culture* (Evanston: Northwestern University Press, 1974).
28 In *Arrow of God* too, Achebe refers to Cary and Conrad: The D.O., habitually unable to sleep, would toss about "until he was caught in the distant throb of drums. He would wonder what unspeakable rites went on in the forest at night, or was it the heart-beat of African darkness? Then one night he was terrified when it suddenly occurred to him that no matter where he lay awake at night in Nigeria the beating of the drums came with the same constancy and from the same elusive distance. Could it be

that the throbbing came from his own heat-stricken brain?" (*AG*, 32–33). The language in this quotation clearly refers to Conrad but the situation is also reminiscent of Cary's *The African Witch*.

29   William Walsh, *A Manifold Voice: Studies in Commonwealth Literature* (New York: Barnes and Noble, 1970), pp. 49, 58.

30   Ibid., p. 52.

31   Ibid.

32   Raymond Williams, *The Country and the City* (New York: Oxford University Press, 1973), p. 286.

33   The *chi* is an extremely complex and fluid concept which is difficult to define succinctly. Njaka summarizes it as follows: "A personal spiritual being; the manifestation of the Supreme Being in man. The Chi is man's other self, his spiritual double, and the essence of the Supreme Deity in beings and things . . ." (*Igbo Political Culture*, p. 154). Each man has a unique *chi* functioning as his alter ego. For a more thorough definition of it, see Chinua Achebe's "Chi in Igbo Cosmology," in his *Morning Yet on Creation Day*, pp. 159–75.

34   Georg Lukács, *Studies in European Realism* (New York: Grosset and Dunlap, 1964), p. 9.

35   I have analyzed Achebe's novels in an order determined by the historical period that they examine rather than in the order of their publication. I have done so to clarify his attitude to the past as it progresses from the initial encounter between the English and Igbo cultures to the problems of preindependence Nigeria.

36   Georges Balandier, *Ambiguous Africa: Cultures in Collision* (New York: Pantheon Books, Inc., 1966).

6   Ngugi wa Thiong'o

1   Around 1970 James Ngugi changes his name to Ngugi wa Thiong'o. (For the circumstances surrounding the change of name see Ime Ikkideh's introduction to Ngugi's *Homecoming: Essays on African and Caribbean Literature, Culture and Politics* [New York: Lawrence Hill, 1972], p. xi). This change in name is clearly symbolic of Ngugi's rejection of Western, particularly Christian influence which he now considers undesirable.

2   See his essay "The Writer and His Past," in *Homecoming*, pp. 39–46, especially pp. 41–44.

3   Ngugi, "Towards a National Culture," *Homecoming*, p. 9.

4   See his essay "The Writer and His Past," *Homecoming*.

5   Janheinz Jahn, Ulla Schild, and Almut Nordmann, *Who's Who in African Literature: Biographies, Works, Commentaries* (Tubingen, West Germany: Horst Erdmann Verlag, 1972), pp. 255–58.

6   Donald E. Herdeck, *African Authors: A Companion to Black African Writing, 1300–1973* (Washington, D.C.: Black Orpheus Press, 1973) also provides cursory information about Ngugi's biography but makes no mention of the closing down of school. However, Richard D. Heyman does confirm that the schools were closed toward the end of 1952. See his paper, "Assimilation and Accommodation in African Education: The Kikuyu Independent School Association," delivered at the 1972 African Studies Association convention.

7 The effect of the events on Ngugi's mind is conjectural; there is no available biographical information to confirm or deny the following analysis. The only aspect of the interpretation that can be confirmed relates to Ngugi's education.

8 See the chapter on Dinesen and particularly the works of E. A. Brett and Richard D. Wolff cited there.

9 Jomo Kenyatta, *Facing Mount Kenya: The Tribal Life of the Gikuyu* (New York: Random House, 1962), pp. 22, 305.

10 George Delf, *Jomo Kenyatta: Towards the Truth about the Light of Kenya* (London: Victor Gollancz, 1961), p. 145.

11 Fred G. Burke, "Political Evolution in Kenya," in *The Transformation of East Africa: Studies in Political Anthropology,* ed. Stanley Diamond and Fred G. Burke (New York: Basic Books, 1966), p. 210.

12 Fred Majdalany, *State of Emergency: The Full Story of Mau Mau* (London: Longmans, Green and Co., 1962), p. 72. Majdalany's account is very sympathetic to the settlers and is thus a good sample of the colonialist version of the events in Kenya. That the declaration of the "Emergency" was a hysterical reaction is clearly illustrated by the casualty figures: during the seven years of the Emergency, from 1952 to 1959, 32 white civilians and 63 members of the security forces were killed, whereas 11,500 supposed Mau Mau and 2,000 other Africans were killed in the same period. Furthermore the Emergency produced an interesting vindication of Kenyatta's contention that to deprive the Gikuyu of their lands was to deprive them of their culture. The Mau Mau, essentially a Gikuyu movement, maintained its solidarity by making its members take a series of loyalty oaths—a custom deriving its power from the role of oaths in Gikuyu religion. In order to weaken the Mau Mau the colonial government made the administration of such oaths a capital offense, thus proving that in order to retain control of land they would have to destroy the very heart of Gikuyu culture.

13 Richard D. Heyman, "Assimilation and Accommodation in African Education," pp. 3, 6–8.

14 Edward H. Berman, "African Reactions to Missionary Education," African Studies Association Paper, 1972, pp. 1–7.

15 Ibid., p. 5.

16 Heyman, "Assimilation and Accommodation," p. 9.

17 Ibid., pp. 8–16.

18 Burke, "Political Evolution in Kenya," p. 210.

19 See James Olney, *Tell Me Africa: An Approach to African Literature* (Princeton: Princeton University Press, 1973), p. 102. Olney also discusses the conscious and deliberate pursuit of European education by the Gikuyu as their chief "weapon" in the fight for independence, pp. 116–18.

20 Ngugi, "The Writer in a Changing Society," *Homecoming,* p. 49.

21 Ibid., p. 48.

22 All three of Ngugi's novels, *Weep Not, Child* (New York: Macmillan, 1969), *The River Between* (London: Heinemann, 1965) and *A Grain of Wheat* (London: Heinemann, 1967), are published under his discarded name, James Ngugi. The novels will be abbreviated respectively as *WNC, RB,* and *GW* and all references to these novels will be included in the text of the essay.

23 See chap. 24 of Raymond Williams, *The Country and the City* (New York: Oxford University Press, 1973) pp. 277–88, and chap. 2 of Olney, *Tell Me Africa*, pp. 79–123.

24 Peter Nazareth, *An African View of Literature* (Evanston, Ill: Northwestern University Press, 1974), p. 153, n. 7. Nazareth insists that because *The River Between* was actually written before *Weep Not, Child*, although published after the latter, any interpretation of the two novels that argues or assumes a development of some sort from *WNC* to *RB* is invalid. However, it seems to me that the greater stylistic maturity of *RB* and the more satisfactory reworking of the paradoxes of peripeteia of values justifies an analysis of the two novels in the order of their publication.

25 Nazareth, *An African View of Literature*, p. 128. Fanon's influence on Ngugi is also clearly evident in his collection of essays, *Homecoming*. See especially the essay "Towards a National Culture." According to Nazareth the original title of *A Grain of Wheat* was *Wrestling with God*. This further confirms Ngugi's religious and messianic preoccupation. Recently Ngugi has reconfirmed Fanon's influence on his writing; he read *The Wretched of the Earth* while writing *A Grain of Wheat*. See the interview of Ngugi in *Index on Censorship*, 9, no. 3 (1980): 22.

26 Frantz Fanon, *The Wretched of the Earth* (New York: Grove Press, 1968), pp. 232, 244.

27 Kenyatta, *Facing Mount Kenya*, p. xv, n. 1.

28 Georges Balandier, "Messianism and Nationalism in Black Africa," in *Perspectives on the African Past*, ed. Martin A. Klein and G. Wesley Johnson (Boston: Little, Brown and Co., 1972), pp. 465–82.

7 *Alex La Guma*

1 The following biographical information about Alex La Guma is derived from Brian Bunting's introduction to *And a Threefold Cord* (Berlin: Seven Seas Publishers, 1964).

2 Alex La Guma, *A Walk in the Night* (Evanston, Ill.: Northwestern University Press, 1967), pp. 10–11. All further references to this novel will be abbreviated as *AWTN* and included in the text.

3 Michael Wade, "Art and Morality in Alex La Guma's *A Walk in the Night*," in *The South African Novel in English*, ed. Kenneth Parker (New York: Africana Publishing Co., 1978), pp. 187–88.

4 Michael Wade provides a thorough and interesting analysis of Joe's Christian offer. However, his interpretation seems rather unnecessarily influenced by his reading of Graham Greene. See ibid., pp. 164–91.

5 Alex La Guma, *And a Threefold Cord* (Berlin: Seven Seas Publisher, 1964), p. 87. All further references to this novel will be abbreviated as *AATC* and included in the text.

6 Alex La Guma, *The Stone Country* (Berlin: Seven Seas Publishers, 1967), p. 74. All further references to this novel will be abbreviated as *TSC* and included in the text.

7 Alex La Guma, *In the Fog of the Seasons' End* (New York: The Third Press, 1973), p. 4. All further references to this novel will be abbreviated as *FSE* and included in the text.

8 Alex La Guma, *Time of the Butcherbird* (London: Heinemann, 1979).

8 Conclusion

1 Frederic Jameson, *The Political Unconscious: Narrative as a Socially Symbolic Act* (Ithaca: Cornell University Press, 1981), pp. 70, 20. Most of the conclusions about the relations between literature and society toward which I have been working in these six studies have recently been articulated cogently by the theoretical program of the above study. This conjunction is useful because Jameson's program provides a theoretical ground for my specific analyses, which in turn illustrate aspects of his theory. I shall assume the reader's familiarity with Jameson's theory and will therefore not explicate thoroughly the terms and concepts that I borrow from his work.

2 Ibid., pp. 81–82.

3 Jameson distinguishes real social contradictions from their ideological avatars, aporia and antinomy, which inform and animate literary texts: "What can in the former [social contradictions] be resolved only through the interventions of praxis here [in the realm of ideology] comes before the purely contemplative mind as logical scandal or double bind, the unthinkable and the logically paradoxical, that which cannot be knotted by the operation of pure thought, and which must therefore generate a whole more properly narrative apparatus—the text itself—to square its circle and dispel, through narrative movement, its intolerable closure" (ibid., pp. 82–83). Because I have not begun my study with this useful distinction, I shall use "contradiction" for both contextual and textual avatars.

4 Jean-Paul Sartre, *Being and Nothingness* (New York: Philosophical Library, 1956), p. 256.

5 Nadine Gordimer, "Literature and Politics in South Africa," *Southern Review: An Australian Journal of Literary Studies,* no. 7 (1974), p. 226.

6 Jameson, *The Political Unconscious,* pp. 52–53.

7 Pierre Macherey, *A Theory of Literary Production* (London: Routledge and Kegan Paul, 1978), p. 132.

8 Jameson, *The Political Unconscious,* p. 79.

9 Terry Eagleton, "Ideology, Fiction, Narrative," *Social Text,* no. 2 (Summer 1979), pp. 62–80.

10 For a more systematic and pointed development of Dinesen's notion of destiny and its central importance in her tales see the marionette play "Revenge of Truth" which Dinesen wrote at a very young age and later incorporated in her tale "The Roads Around Pisa," in *Seven Gothic Tales* (New York: Random House, 1934), pp. 165–216.

11 Northrop Frye, *Anatomy of Criticism* (Princeton: Princeton University Press, 1957), pp. 136, 139–40, 136–37.

12 Jameson, *The Political Unconscious,* see pp. 83–88.

13 Sartre, *Being and Nothingness,* p. 255.

14 Jameson, *The Political Unconscious,* see pp. 87–88.

15 O. Mannoni, *Prospero and Caliban: The Psychology of Colonization* (New York: Praeger, 1964), p. 5.

16 All the following appraisal of the effects of literacy is based on their article "The Consequences of Literacy," in *Literacy in Traditional Societies* ed. Jack Goody (London: Cambridge University Press, 1968), pp. 27–68.

17 I do not mean to imply here that Africa did not have a history during the period when oral cultures prevailed. Obviously it did. But the historical consciousness clearly cannot function adequately without literacy. Similarly, I do not wish to imply here or elsewhere that what Cassirer calls "mythic" cultures are unable to reason logically or causally—Levi-Strauss has demonstrated in *The Savage Mind* that they can. However, it seems to me that Cassirer is right in implying that the logic and causality of "primitive" cultures are more "magical" than those of "empirical" cultures.

18 Charles R. Larson, *The Emergence of African Fiction* (Bloomington: Indiana University Press, 1971), p. 42.

19 Frantz Fanon, *The Wretched of the Earth* (New York: Grove Press, 1968), p. 239.

A Selected Bibliography

Achebe, Chinua. *Arrow of God.* New York: Doubleday, 1969.
———. "The Black Writer's Burden." *Presence Africaine* 31, no. 59 (1966): 135–40.
———. "The English Language and the African Writer." *Transition* 4, no. 18 (1965): 27–30.
———. "An Image of Africa." *Massachusetts Review* 18, no. 4 (1977): 782–94.
———. *Morning Yet on Creation Day: Essays.* New York: Doubleday, Anchor Press, 1975.
———. *No Longer at Ease.* Greenwich, Conn.: Fawcett, 1969.
———. *Things Fall Apart.* Greenwich, Conn.: Fawcett, 1969.
Ackley, Donald G. "The Male-Female Motif in *Things Fall Apart.*" *Studies in Black Literature* 4, no. 4 (1974): 1–7.
Anozie, Sunday O. *Sociologie du Roman Africain.* Paris: Aubier-Montaigne, 1970.
———. *Structural Models and African Poetics: Towards a Pragmatic View of Literature.* London: Routledge and Kegan Paul, 1981.
Barba, Harry. "Cary's Image of Africa in Transition." *University of Kansas City Review* 29 (1963): 291–96.
Beard, Peter, ed. *Longing for Darkness: Kamante's Tales from Out of Africa.* New York: Harcourt Brace Jovanovich, 1975.
Bennett, George. *Kenya: A Political History: The Colonial Period.* London: Oxford University Press, 1963.
Berman, Edward H. "African Reactions to Missionary Education." African Studies Association Paper, 1973. (The African Studies Association Papers listed in this bibliography are available from The Research Liaison Committee, African Studies Association, 218 Shiffman Center, Brandeis University, Waltham, Massachusetts.)
Bishop, Rand. "On Identifying a Standard of African Literary Criticism: Characterization in the Novel." *Journal of New African Literature and Arts,* 11/12 (Summer/Fall 1971): 1–18.
Bloom, Robert. *The Indeterminate World: A Study of the Novels of Joyce Cary.* Philadelphia: University of Pennsylvania Press, 1962.
Brett, E. A. *Colonialism and Underdevelopment in East Africa: The Politics of Economic Change: 1919–1939.* New York: NOK Publishers, 1973.
Brown, Lloyd W. "Cultural Norms and Modes of Perception in Achebe's Fiction." *Research in African Literature* 3, no. 1 (1972): 21–35.

Bunting, Brian. *The Rise of the South African Reich*. Harmondsworth, England: Penguin Books, 1964.

Cary, Joyce. *The African Witch*. Carfax Ed. London: Michael Joseph, 1949.

——. *Aissa Saved*. Carfax Ed. London: Michael Joseph, 1949.

——. *An American Visitor*. Carfax Ed. London: Michael Joseph, 1949.

——. *Art and Reality: Ways of the Creative Process*. New York: Harper, 1958.

——. *The Case for African Freedom and Other Writings on Africa*. ed. Christopher Fyfe. Austin: University of Texas Press, 1962.

——. *Mister Johnson*. Carfax Ed. London: Michael Joseph, 1949.

Carroll, David. *Chinua Achebe*. New York: Twayne Publishers, 1970.

Cassirer, Ernst. *The Philosophy of Symbolic Form* Vol. 2 *Mythical Thought*. New Haven: Yale University Press, 1955.

Clarke, Leon E., comp. *Through African Eyes: Cultures in Change*. New York: Praeger, 1972.

Collins, Harold R. "Joyce Cary's Troublesome Africans." *Antioch Review* 13, no. 3 (1953): 397–406.

Cook, David. *African Literature: A Critical View*. London: Longmans, 1977.

Curtin, Philip D., ed. *Africa and the West: Intellectual Responses to European Culture*. Madison: University of Wisconsin Press, 1972.

——. *The Image of Africa: British Ideas and Actions*. Madison: University of Wisconsin Press, 1964.

Dathorne, O. R. *The Black Mind: A History of African Literature*. Minneapolis: University of Minnesota Press, 1974.

Davenport, T. R. H. *South Africa: A Modern History*. London: Macmillan Press, 1977.

Davidson, Basil. *Africa in History*. New York: Doubleday, 1969.

——. *Let Freedom Come: Africa in Modern History*. Boston: Little, Brown and Co., 1978.

——, Joe Slovo, and Anthony R. Wilkinson. *Southern Africa: The New Politics of Revolution*. Harmondsworth, England: Penguin Books, 1976.

Delf, George. *Jomo Kenyatta: Towards the Truth about the Light of Kenya*. London: Victor Gollancz, 1961.

Diamond, Stanley, and Fred G. Burke, eds. *The Transformation of East Africa: Studies in Political Anthropology*. New York: Basic Books, 1966.

Dinesen, Isak. *Out of Africa*. New York: Random House, 1972.

——. *Shadows on the Grass*. New York: Random House, 1974.

Eagleton, Terry. "Ideology, Fiction, Narrative." *Social Text*, no. 2 (Summer 1979): 62–80.

Echeruo, M. J. C. *The Conditioned Imagination from Shakespeare to Conrad*. New York: Holms and Meier, 1978.

——. *Joyce Cary and the Novel of Africa*. New York: Africana Publishing Co., 1973.

Emenyonu, Ernest. "Ezeulu: The Night Mask Caught Abroad by Day." *Pan-African Journal* 4, no. 4 (1971): 407–19.

——, and Pat Emenyonu. "Achebe: Accountable to Our Society." *Africa Report* 17, no. 5 (1972): 21–27.

Fanon, Frantz. *Black Skin, White Masks*. New York: Grove Press, 1967.

——. *The Wretched of the Earth*. New York: Grove Press, 1968.

February, V. A. *Mind Your Colour: The "Coloured" Stereotype in South African Literature*. London: Routledge and Kegan Paul, 1981.

Felger, Robert. "Black Content, White Form." *Studies in Black Literature* 5, no. 1 (1974): 28–30.

Foster, Malcolm. *Joyce Cary: A Biography*. Boston: Houghton Mifflin, 1968.

Fredrickson, George M. *White Supremacy: A Comparative Study in American and South African History*. New York: Oxford University Press, 1981.

French, Warren G. "Joyce Cary's American Rover Girl." *Texas Studies in English Literature and Language* 2 (1960): 281–91.

Frye, Northrop. *Anatomy of Criticism: Four Essays*. Princeton: Princeton University Press, 1957.

————. *The Secular Scripture: A Study of the Structure of Romance*. Cambridge, Mass.: Harvard University Press, 1976.

Fyfe, Christopher. "The Colonial Situation in *Mister Johnson*." *Modern Fiction Studies* 9, no. 3 (1963): 226–30.

Gann, L. H., and P. Duignan, eds. *Colonialism in Africa: 1870–1960*. 5 vols. London: Cambridge University Press, 1969.

Goody, Jack, ed. *Literacy in Traditional Societies*. London: Cambridge University Press, 1968.

Goonetilleke, D. C. R. A. *Developing Countries in British Fiction*. London: Macmillan Press, 1978.

Gordimer, Nadine. "Apartheid." *Holiday* 25 (April 1959): 94–95.

————. *Burger's Daughter*. New York: Viking Press, 1979.

————. "Censored, Banned, Gagged." *Encounter* 20, no. 6 (1963): 59–63.

————. "Chief Luthuli." *Atlantic* 203 (April 1959): 34–39.

————. *The Conservationist*. New York: Viking Press, 1974.

————. *A Guest of Honour*. New York: Viking Press, 1970.

————. *July's People*. New York: Viking Press, 1981.

————. *The Late Bourgeois World*. New York: Viking Press, 1966.

————. "Leaving School—II." *London Magazine* 3, no. 2 (1963): 58–65.

————. "Literature and Politics in South Africa." *Southern Review: An Australian Journal of Literary Studies*, no. 7 (1974): 220–36.

————. *The Lying Days*. New York: Simon and Schuster, 1953.

————. "Modern African Writing." *Michigan Quarterly Review* 9, no. 3 (1970): 221–31.

————. "Nadine Gordimer Talks to Andrew Salkey." *Listener* 82, no. 2106 (1969): 184–85.

————. "The Novel and the Nation in South Africa." *Times Literary Supplement*, August 11, 1961, pp. 520–23.

————. *Occasion for Loving*. New York: Viking Press, 1960.

————. *Some Monday for Sure*. London: Heinemann, 1976.

————. "A South African Childhood: Allusions in a Landscape." *New Yorker*, October 16, 1954, pp. 121–43.

————. "What Being A South African Means to Me." *South African Outlook*, no. 107 (July 1977), pp. 87–89.

————. "Where Do Whites Fit In?" *Twentieth Century*, no. 165 (April 1959), 326–31.

————. *A World of Strangers*. London: Jonathan Cape, 1958.

————. "A Writer's Freedom." *English in Africa*, 2, no. 2 (1975): 45–49.

————. "Writing Belongs to All of Us." *Forum* 3, no. 6 (1954): 18–23.

Gurr, Andrew, and Angus Calder, eds. *Writers in East Africa*. Nairobi: East African Literature Bureau, 1974.

Hammond, Dorothy, and Alta Jablow. *The Africa That Never Was: Four Centuries of British Writing about Africa*. New York: Twayne Publishers, 1970.

Hannah, Donald. "In Memoriam Karen Blixen." *Sewanee Review* 71, no. 4 (1963): 585–604.

————. *Isak Dinesen and Karen Blixen: The Mask and the Reality*. New York: Random House, 1971.

Haugh, Robert F. *Nadine Gordimer*. New York: Twayne Publishers, 1974.

Heyman, Richard. "Assimilation and Accommodation in African Education: The Kikuyu Independent School Association." African Studies Association Paper, 1972.

Hoffman, Charles G. "Joyce Cary's African Novels: There's a War On." *South Atlantic Quarterly* 62 (1963): 229–43.

Howe, Irving. *Politics and the Novel*. Freeport, New York: Books for Libraries Press, 1970.

Howe, Sussane. *Novels of Empire*. New York: Columbia University Press, 1949.

Irele, Abiola. "The Tragic Conflict in Achebe's Novels." *Black Orpheus* 17 (June 1965): 24–32.

Iyasere, S. O. "Art, a Simulacrum of Reality: Problems in the Criticism of African Literature." *Journal of Modern African Studies* 11, no. 3 (1973), 447–55.

Jameson, Fredric. "Magical Narratives: Romance as Genre." *New Literary History* 7, no. 1 (1975): 135–63.

————. *Marxism and Form: Twentieth-Century Dialectical Theories of Literature*. Princeton: Princeton University Press, 1971.

————. *The Political Unconscious: Narrative as a Socially Symbolic Act*. Ithaca: Cornell University Press, 1981.

Johannessen, Eric O. *The World of Isak Dinesen*. Seattle: University of Washington Press, 1961.

Johnstone, Frederick A. *Class, Race and Gold: A Study of Class Relation and Discrimination in South Africa*. London: Routledge and Kegan Paul, 1976.

————. "White Prosperity and White Supremacy in South Africa Today." *African Affairs* 69, no. 275 (1970): 134–43.

Jordan, John O. "Cultural Conflict and Social Change in Achebe's *Arrow of God*." *Critique* 13, no. 2 (1971): 66–82.

Kenyatta, Jomo. *Facing Mount Kenya: The Tribal Life of the Gikuyu*. New York: Random House, 1962.

Kettle, Arnold. *An Introduction to the English Novel*. 2 vols. London: Hutchinson and Co., 1953.

Kibera, Leonard. "A Critical Appreciation of Alex La Guma's *In the Fog of the Season's End*." *Busara* 8, no. 1 (1976): 59–66.

Killam, G. D. *Africa in English Fiction: 1874–1939*. Ibadan, Nigeria: Ibadan University Press, 1968.

————. *African Writers on African Writing*. Evanston: Northwestern University Press, 1973.

————. *The Novels of Chinua Achebe*. New York: Africana Publishing Co., 1969.

Klein, Martin A., and G. Wesley Johnson, eds. *Perspectives on the African Past*. Boston: Little, Brown and Co., 1972.

Kovel, Joel. *White Racism: A Psychohistory*. New York: Random House, 1971.

Lagneau-Kesteloot, Lilyan. *Negritude et la Situation Coloniale*. Yaounde, Cameroon: Editions Cle, 1968.

La Guma, Alex. *And a Threefold Cord*. Berlin: Seven Seas Publisher, 1964.

————. *In the Fog of the Seasons' End*. New York: The Third Press, 1973.

————. *The Stone Country*. Berlin: Seven Seas Publisher, 1967.

————. *Time of the Butcherbird*. London: Heinemann, 1979.

————. *A Walk in the Night*. Evanston, Ill.: Northwestern University Press, 1967.

————, ed. *Apartheid*. New York: International Publishers, 1971.

Langbaum, Robert. *The Gayety of Vision: Isak Dinesen's Art*. New York: Random House, 1964.

Larsen, Golden L. *The Dark Descent: Social Change and Moral Responsibility in the Novels of Joyce Cary*. New York: Roy Publishers, n.d.

Larson, Charles R. *The Emergence of African Fiction*. Bloomington, Ind.: Indiana University Press, 1971.

Lasson, Frans, and Clara Svendsen. *The Life and Destiny of Isak Dinesen*. New York: Random House, 1970.

Laurenson, Diana T., and Alan Swingwood. *The Sociology of Literature*. New York: Schocken Books, 1972.

Lawrence, Margret. *Long Drums and Cannons: Nigerian Dramatists and Novelists, 1952–1966*. London: Macmillan, 1968.

Levin, Harry. *Gates of Horn: A Study of Five French Realist Writers*. New York: Oxford University Press, 1963.

Lindfors, Bernth. *Critical Perspectives on Nigerian Literature*. Washington, D.C.: Three Continents Press, 1976.

————. *Folklore in Nigerian Literature*. New York: Africana Publishing Co., 1973.

————. "Form and Technique in the Novels of Richard Rive and Alex La Guma." *Journal of the New Literatures and the Arts* 2 (1966): 10–15.

————. "New Trends in West and East African Fiction." *Review of National Literatures* 2, no. 2 (1971): 15–37.

————. "The Palm Oil with Which Achebe's Words Are Eaten." *African Literature Today* 1, no. 1 (1968): 1–10.

————. "Post-War Literature in English by African Writers from South Africa: A Study of the Effects of Environment upon Literature." *Phylon* 27 (1966): 50–62.

————. "Robin Hood Realism in South African Fiction." *Africa Today* 15, no. 4 (1968) 16–18.

Lloyd, P. C. *Africa in Social Change: Changing Traditional Societies in the Modern World*. Baltimore: Penguin Books, 1967.

Lotman, J. M. "Point of View in a Text." *New Literary History* 6, no. 2 (1975): 339–52.

Lukács, Georg. *Realism in Our Time: Literature and the Class Struggle*. New York: Harper and Row, 1964.

————. *Studies in European Realism*. New York: Grosset and Dunlap, 1964.

Macherey, Pierre. *A Theory of Literary Production*. London: Routledge and Kegan Paul, 1978.

Mahood, M. M. *The Colonial Encounter: A Reading of Six Novels*. Totowa, N.J.: Rowman and Littlefield, 1977.

———. *Joyce Cary's Africa*. Boston: Houghton Mifflin, 1964.

Mair, Lucy P. *Anthropology and Social Change*. New York: Humanities Press, 1969.

———. *Native Policies in Africa*. London: G. Routledge, 1936.

———. *The New Africa*. London: Watts, 1967.

———. *New Nations*. Chicago: University of Chicago Press, 1963.

Majdalany, Fred. *State of Emergency: The Full Story of Mau Mau*. London: Longmans, Green and Co., 1962.

Mannoni, O. *Prospero and Caliban: The Psychology of Colonization*. New York: Praeger, 1964.

Mazrui, Ali Al'Amin. *The Anglo-African Commonwealth: Political Friction and Cultural Fusion*. New York: Pergamon Press, 1967.

———. *On Heroes and Uhuru-Worship: Essays on Independent Africa*. London: Longmans, 1967.

———. *World Culture and the Black Experience*. Seattle: University of Washington Press, 1975.

Mbiti, John S. *African Religions and Philosophy*. London: Heinemann, 1969.

Meek, C. K., W. M. Macmillan, and E. R. J. Hussey. *Europe and West Africa: Some Problems and Adjustments*. London: Oxford University Press, 1940.

Memmi, Albert. *The Colonizer and the Colonized*. Boston: Beacon Press, 1969.

———. *Dominated Man: Notes Toward a Portrait*. New York: Orion Press, 1968.

Meyers, Jeffrey. "Culture and History in *Things Fall Apart*." *Critique* 11, no. 1 (1968): 25–32.

———. *Fiction and the Colonial Experience*. Totowa, N.J.: Rowman and Littlefield, 1968.

Migel, Parmenia. *Titania: A Biography of Isak Dinesen*. New York: Random House, 1970.

Moodie, D. T. *The Rise of Afrikanerdom: Power, Apartheid and the Afrikaner Civil Religion*. Berkeley: University of California Press, 1975.

Moore, Gerald. *The Chosen Tongue: English Writing in the Tropical World*. New York: Harper and Row, 1969.

———. *Seven African Writers*. London: Oxford University Press, 1962.

———. "Towards Realism in French African Writing." *Journal of Modern African Studies* 1, no. 1 (1963): 61–73.

Moss, Rose. "Hand in Glove/Nadine Gordimer: South African Writer: a Case Study in Censorship." *Pacific Quarterly Moana* 6, nos. 3/4 (1981): 106–22.

Mphahlele, Ezekiel. *The African Image*. New York: Praeger, 1962.

Nazareth, Peter. *An African View of Literature*. Evanston, Ill.: Northwestern University Press, 1974.

———. "Out of Darkness: Conrad and Other Third World Writers." *Conradiana* 14, no. 3 (1982): 173–87.

———. *The Third World Writer: His Social Responsibility*. Nairobi: Kenya Literature Bureau, 1978.

Ngugi, James. See Thiong'o, Ngugi wa.

Njaka, Mazi Elechukwu Nnadibuagha. *Igbo Political Culture.* Evanston, Ill.: Northwestern University Press, 1974.

Nkosi, Lewis. "Conversation with Chinua Achebe." *Africa Report* 9, no. 5 (1964): 19–21.

Nwoga, Donatus I. "Shadows of Christian Civilization: The Image of the Educated African in African Literature." *Presence Africaine* 79 (1971): 34–50.

Olney, James. *Tell Me Africa: An Approach to African Literature.* Princeton: Princeton University Press, 1973.

Parker, Kenneth, ed. *The South African Novel in English.* New York: Africana Publishing Co., 1978.

Parkinson, G. H. R., ed. *Georg Lukacs: The Man, His Work and His Ideas.* New York: Random House, 1970.

Povey, John. "The English Language of the Contemporary African Novel." *Critique* 11, no. 3 (1968–69): 79–96.

Ranger, T. O. "Connections Between Primary Resistance Movements and Modern Mass Nationalism in East and Central Africa." *Journal of African History,* part 1: 9, no. 3, 437–53; part 2: 9, no. 4 (1968): 631–41.

Raskin, Jonah. *The Mythology of Imperialism.* New York: Random House, 1971.

Ravenscroft, Arthur. *Chinua Achebe.* London: Longmans, 1969.

Rhoodie, N. J., ed. *South African Dialogue: Contrasts in South African Thinking on Basic Issues.* Philadelphia: The Westminster Press, 1972.

Rotberg, R. I., and Mazrui, Ali A. *Protest and Power in Black Africa.* New York: Oxford University Press, 1970.

Sartre, Jean-Paul. *Being and Nothingness: An Essay on Phenomenological Ontology.* New York: Philosophical Library, 1956.

———. *Critique of Dialectical Reason.* London: NLB, 1976.

———. *Search for a Method.* New York: Alfred A. Knopf, 1963.

Schutz, Alfred. "The Stranger: An Essay in Social Psychology." *American Journal of Sociology* 49, no. 6 (1944): 449–507.

Shelton, Austin J. "The Offended Chi in Achebe's Novels." *Transition* 3, no. 13 (1964): 36–37.

———. "The 'Palm Oil' of Language: Proverbs in Chinua Achebe's Novels." *Modern Language Quarterly* 30, no. 1 (1969): 86–111.

Stevick, Philip, ed. *The Theory of the Novel.* New York: The Free Press, 1967.

Stock, A. G. "Yeats and Achebe." *Journal of Commonwealth Literature* 5 (1968): 105–11.

Svendsen, Clara. *Isak Dinesen: A Memorial.* New York: Random House, 1965.

Thiong'o, Ngugi wa. *Detained: A Writer's Prison Diary.* London: Heinemann, 1981.

———. *A Grain of Wheat.* London: Heinemann, 1967.

———. *Homecoming: Essays on African and Caribbean Literature, Culture and Politics.* New York: Lawrence Hill, 1972.

———. *The River Between.* London: Heinemann, 1965.

———. *Weep Not, Child.* New York: Macmillan, 1969.

———. *Writers and Politics: Essays.* London: Heinemann, 1981.

Thurman, Judith. *Isak Dinesen: The Life of a Storyteller.* New York: St. Martin's Press, 1982.

Uchendu, Victor C. *The Igbo of Southeast Nigeria.* New York: Rinehart and Winston, 1965.

Unger, Roberto Mangaberia. *Knowledge and Politics.* New York: The Free Press, 1975.

Wade, Michael. *Nadine Gordimer.* London: Evans Brothers, 1978.

Walsh, William. *A Manifold Voice: Studies in Commonwealth Literature.* New York: Barnes and Noble, 1970.

Wallerstein, Immanuel. *Africa: The Politics of Independence.* New York: Vintage, 1961.

————, ed. *Social Change: The Colonial Situation.* New York: John Wiley, 1966.

————, and E. J. Rich. *Africa: Tradition and Change.* New York: Random House, 1971.

Watt, Ian. *The Rise of the Novel.* Berkeley: University of California Press, 1964.

Weinstock, Donald, and Cathy Ramadan. "Symbolic Structure in *Things Fall Apart.*" *Critique* 11, no. 3 (1968–69): 33–41.

Williams, Raymond. *The Country and the City.* New York: Oxford University Press, 1973.

Wilson, Monica. *Religion and the Transformation of Society: A Study in Social Change in Africa.* Cambridge: Cambridge University Press, 1971.

Wolff, Richard D. *The Economics of Colonialism: Britain and Kenya, 1870–1930.* New Haven: Yale University Press, 1974.

Wolkenfeld, Jack. *Joyce Cary: The Developing Style.* New York: New York University Press, 1968.

Wright, Andrew. *Joyce Cary: A Preface to His Novels.* London: Harper, 1958.

Wright, Edgar, ed. *A Critical Evaluation of African Literature.* Washington, D.C.: Inscape Publishers, 1973.

Index

Library of Congress Cataloging in Publication Data
JanMohamed, Abdul R., 1945–
  Manichean aesthetics.
  Bibliography: p.
  Includes index.
  1. African fiction (English)—History and criticism.
  2. Cary, Joyce, 1888–1957—Political and social views.
  3. Dinesen, Isak, 1885–1962—Political and social views.
  4. Colonies in literature.   5. Imperialism in
  literature.   6. Politics and literature—Africa.
  I. Title.
  PR9344.J36   1983   823'.91'09326   83–5808
  ISBN 0–87023–395–5